Praise for Student Voice Revolution

"In this troubling era in schools, Adam Fletcher offers a counter narrative towards empowerment of a successful school through Meaningful Student Involvement. Adam espouses engaging students to meaningfully elicit changes that create a powerful learning community and school where students want to be. Adam's work and this book are powerful tools to build an effective school from the ground up. I encourage every educator to read and re-read it. It should become a working tool that is referenced often and readily available for use."
—*Donnan Stoicovy, Lead Learner/Principal, Park Forest Elementary School, State College, Pennsylvania; President Elect, National Association for Professional Development Schools*

Praise for Adam Fletcher

"Adam Fletcher's work is especially relevant in getting young people to participate in the realms of politics and critical education."
—*Henry Giroux, McMaster University; author, Youth in Revolt: Reclaiming a Democratic Future*

"Adam is one of the most knowledgeable people in the world regarding student voice and youth rights... I highly recommend him as a presenter and a writer in our field."
—*Dana Mitra, Penn State University; author, Student Voice in School Reform*

"Adam's student-adult partnership frameworks have served as a foundation for the Youth and Adults Transforming Schools Together initiative. He stands alone in publishing user-friendly materials which can be used to explore this key concept. Adam is passionate about this work and inspires others with his commitment."
—*Helen Beattie, Executive Director, UP for Learning*

"Adam works tirelessly to create environments and cultures where youth develop and wield the knowledge and power to positively impact not only their lives but also society. He is one of the most knowledgeable, innovative, and effective facilitators, writers, educators, and thinkers in the field. Adam brings theory and reality together in praxis that reveals how utopic visions can become a reality."
—*Cristine Chopra, Executive Director, Santa Cruz Community College Commitment*

"Adam's work in student engagement, meaningful student involvement, youth-adult partnerships, and client-focused services have made him the 'go to' person on these issues nationally. Adam 'gets it' on a fundamental level about how to work 'with' not 'for' young people, how to create effective youth-adult partnerships, and about how adults, by changing their perception of youth, can redefine the change process itself."
—*Greg Williamson, Assistant Director for Partnerships & Collaboration Washington State Department of Early Learning*

"Adam is, quite simply, "The Guy," the one who gets things done, and the guy whom you can always count on. His passion for youth rights and voice knows no bounds, and he is relentless in his efforts to help shape the world into a better place for young people. If you want to help kick start a giant culture change in your youth program or school, Adam is your guy — because he is, quite simply, The Guy; there's not much more that needs to be said."
—*Daniel Bigler, Lecturer in Children's Studies, Eastern Washington University*

"Adam is a great facilitator and leader of youth and adults! Easy to work with, focused on a clear message and adaptable in every situation. It was a pleasure to work with Adam. He is committed to youth development and knows how to navigate change while remaining edgy enough to appeal to young people. Adam will do excellent work for your next event or any long-term development work."
— *Helena Stephens, Youth Manager at the City of Bellevue, Washington*

 "Adam is one of the most gifted, principled visionaries who empowers people of all ages and backgrounds to pursue authentic youth engagement in all sectors of society."
— *Wendy Schaetzel Lesko, President, Youth Activism Project*

"Adam is a high-energy professional with a true passion for youth development. Through our work together, Adam provided ongoing support to my team and I so that we could provide excellent service. Adam has endless commitment to the student experience, and does not limit the population to just young learners. To call Adam a champion of redefining positive youth experiences is an understatement. When it comes to providing growth, training and support opportunities for young people in our community, Adam has an unparalleled commitment to making great, positive and progressive change."
— *Sarah Lloyd, Youth Coordinator, Pacific Mountain Workforce Development Council*

About the Author

Adam F. C. Fletcher

Author, *Student Voice Revolution: The Meaningful Student Involvement Handbook*

Adam Fletcher is an internationally recognized leader in the student voice movement. The founder of SoundOut.org, Adam was a community educator for a decade before becoming Washington State's first student engagement specialist. Since founding SoundOut in 2002, he has worked with more than 500 K–12 schools across the United States, Canada, and around the world. He is a prolific writer who has published more than 50 books related to schools, youth and social change, as well as local history and more. Today, he is the president and owner of CommonAction Consulting, and lives in Olympia, Washington, with his daughter Hannah and their cat named Colette.

Learn more about Adam at adamfletcher.net

Also By Adam Fletcher

The Guide to Student Voice (2015)

A Short Guide to Holistic Youth Development (2015)

Facing Adultism (2015)

A Short Intro to Youth Engagement in the Economy (2015)

The Practice of Youth Engagement (2014)

A Unique Guide to Youth Engagement (2013)

The Freechild Project Youth-Driven Programming Guide (2013)

SoundOut Student Voice Curriculum (2012)

The Freechild Project Youth Voice Toolkit (2011)

The Freechild Project Youth Engagement Workshop Guide (2010)

The Freechild Project Guide to Social Change Led By and With Young People (2007)

Meaningful Student Involvement: Students as Partners in School Change (2005)

Stories of Meaningful Student Involvement (2005)

Meaningful Student Involvement Research Guide (2005)

Resources for Meaningful Student Involvement (2005)

The Freechild Project Guide to Cooperative Games for Social Change (2004)

Meaningful Student Involvement Idea Guide for Schools (2002)

Firestarter Youth Empowerment Curriculum (2001)

Other books by Fletcher include...

Guide to Fort Omaha (2017)

North Omaha History Timeline (2017)

North Omaha History, Volumes 1, 2 and 3 (2016)

Suffering Love, Laughing at Myself (2013)

Student Voice Revolution: The Meaningful Student Involvement Handbook

ADAM F. C. FLETCHER

FIRST COMMONACTION BOOKS EDITION, AUGUST 2017

Student Voice Revolution: The Meaningful Student Involvement Handbook
Copyright © 2017 by Adam F. C. Fletcher

All rights reserved. Published by CommonAction Publishing.

ISBN-13: 978-0-692-95444-7

For information on how to request permissions to reproduce information from this publication, please contact the author by visiting adamfletcher.net

For bulk orders contact CommonAction Publishing by visiting commonaction.org

Author photograph © Bruce McGregor
Book cover by Victoria Bawn
Interior design by Lucy Otis
Interior artwork by Victoria Bawn, Doug Smith and Lucy Otis
Some icons made by freepik at flaticon.com

Printed in the United States of America
10 9 8 7 6 5 4 3 2 1

Hands from above and a hand below
Hearts that care and time to sow
Were my life shortened this I'd know
This love in life is always ours to grow.

To my first teachers, my parents Charlette and Robert, and
for my best teacher, my daughter Hannah.

Table of Contents

Table of Figures

Table of Tables

Acknowledgments

This work owes its existence to my family, friends, colleagues, students, mentors and collaborators throughout the years. These people gave me the privileges of becoming a more effective researcher, committed practitioner and powerful advocate, and I stand eternally grateful. Re-envisioning the roles of young people throughout society has been my soul's calling, and these acknowledgments call out some people who have helped me answer it.

My family has been immensely supportive. I owe a special thanks to my daughter, Hannah, for being patient while I travel. She has taught me in so many ways. My mother and father, Charlette Harris and Robert Sasse, were my first teachers, and I'm grateful to them for my life and continued lessons. For their contributions to my professional and personal life, I also thank Jessica Vavrus and Robert Butts, both of whom are dedicated advocates for students and schools.

While I take full responsibility for developing the theory behind Meaningful Student Involvement, I am forever indebted to several collaborators throughout the years who have helped me hone my understanding, expand my thinking, and challenge my assumptions. The late Dr. Linda Gire-Vavrus was a critical ally, guide and writing mentor who I continually and sincerely appreciate. I am thankful for the support of my former colleagues at the Washington State Office of Superintendent of Public Instruction who started me on this path. Greg Williamson, Nasue Nishida and Sasha Rabkin were strong collaborators. I am appreciative of Gayle Pauley, Brenda Merritt, Julie Chace, Barbara Quick, Bill Mason, Denny Hurtado, Gilda Wheeler and many past collaborators including Rob MacGregor, Beth Kelly and others.

My colleagues at CommonAction taught me a lot, and have included Kari Kunst, Joseph Vavrus, Chelsea Nehler, Teddy Wright, Mike Beebe, Emma Margraf, Sekai Senwosret and Scott Le Duc. Rob Richards is a great collaborator and partner in this work today. Sue Paro's support of Meaningful Student Involvement was unflinching and without parallel. The HumanLinks Foundation provided essential funding to seed my work in this field, and I am appreciative of their contributions. Mishaela Duran and Heather Manchester were always been kind allies in their work throughout the field of education, and as close friends.

Others include Karen Young and Jenny Sazama of Youth on Board; Kate McPherson of Project Service Leadership; Wendy Lesko of the Youth Activism Project; Dr. Chris Unger of Northeastern University; Helen Beattie of Up for Learning! (formerly YATST); Donnan Stoicovy of Park Forest Elementary School; and Dr. Dana Mitra of Penn State University. Henry Giroux of McMaster University has been a comrade through my study and application of critical pedagogy. I also owe a special thanks to Roger Holdsworth of *Connect* magazine in Australia and Hazel Owen of Ethos Consulting in New Zealand, both of whom have published chapters of this book.

This work was written from my learning experiences in the education system and in my communities. Special thanks to all of my past clients and collaborators in the United States, Canada, Brazil, and other places, specifically the teams at Catalyst Miami; Alberta Education; University of Washington's GearUP Program; the New York State Center for Student Support Services; Action for Healthy Kids; Service Learning Seattle and Seattle Public Schools; as well as Educational Service District 123 and Educational Service District 113 in Washington; and many others. Thanks specifically to Dr. Dennis Harper of Generation YES; Dr. Giselle Martin-Kniep of

Communities for Learning; and Dr. Todd Johnson of ESD 113, as well as Lee Bucsko and Theresa Kimball. Lois Brewer of Service Learning Seattle in the Seattle Public Schools has been a wonderful supporter and ally for more than a decade. Her support for infusing Meaningful Student Involvement in service learning is unparalleled.

Special thanks to each of the people who read all or parts of the manuscript of this book for me, including Donnan Stoicovy, Cristine Chopra, Dana Bennis, Ellen Ebert, Mark Schulze, Jessica Werner, David Loitz, Dana Bennis and Paul Roc. Thank you each for your contributions, suggestions, criticism, and advice. My editor, Karen Hall, was a tremendous ally to whom I am very thankful. Thanks also to Beth Oppliger.

To the students who I have worked with over these years: I am very proud of you, no matter who you are or what you have done with what we learned together. Throughout the course of our work, you showed me something new, gave me different perspectives and helped me understand what I share in the following pages. You are the ones most responsible for this work, and the ones to whom I owe every part of it. Thank you for what you do and what we have done together.

Finally, I want to acknowledge some of the various schools, education agencies and nonprofit organizations I have worked with related to Meaningful Student Involvement. These are schools I partnered with, provided professional development to, ran programs for, or that have facilitated my *SoundOut Student Voice Curriculum*. They include:

Caroline High School (Caroline, Alberta, Canada); Colfax High School (Colfax, WA); Community Academy of Science and Health (Boston, MA); Cypress Creek Elementary School (Ruskin, FL); Engineering School (Boston, MA); Evergreen High School (Vancouver, WA); Dayton High School (Dayton, WA); Franklin High School (Seattle, WA); Friday Harbor High School (Friday Harbor, WA); Harbor High School (Aberdeen, WA); Harwood High School (Moretown, VT); Langley Middle School (Langley, WA); Lewis and Clark Middle School (Yakima, WA); Lewis and Clark High School (Spokane, WA); Monument High School (Boston, MA); Patchwork School (Boulder, CO); Ridgeview Elementary School (Yakima, WA); Pinnacle Charter School (Denver, CO); Roosevelt High School (Seattle, WA); Secondary Academy for Success (Bothell, WA); Schenectady Public Schools (Schenectady, NY); Social Justice Academy (Boston, MA); Spanaway Elementary School (Bethel, WA); Sumner School District (Sumner, WA); Vashon Island Student Link Alternative School (Vashon, WA); White River High School (Buckley, WA); Wishkah Valley High School (Aberdeen, WA); Yakima Public Schools (Yakima, WA).

Several district, regional and state education agencies have partnered with me to provide many programs and activities, and include:

Albany-Schoharie-Schenectady-Saratoga BOCES (Albany, NY); Alberta Ministry of Education (Edmonton, AB); Boston Public Schools Student Engagement Advisory Council (Boston, MA); Evergreen Public Schools (Vancouver, WA); Genesee Valley BOCES (LeRoy, NY); New York State Student Support Services Center (LeRoy, NY); Oneida-Herkimer-Madison BOCES (Utica, NY); Onondaga-Cortland-Madison Counties BOCES (Syracuse, NY); Oswego County BOCES (Mexico, NY); Seattle Public Schools Office of Equity and Race Relations (Seattle, WA); Seattle Public Schools Small Learning Environments Conference (Seattle, WA); University of Washington College of Education (Seattle, WA); University of Washington GEAR UP Program (Seattle, WA); Vermont State Department of Education HIV/AIDs Program (Montpelier, VT); Vermont Principals Association (Montpelier, WA); Washington State Office of Superintendent of Public

Instruction School Improvement Program (Olympia, WA); Washington State Office of Superintendent of Public Instruction Learn and Serve America Program (Olympia, WA); Washington State Office of Superintendent of Public Instruction Title V and Innovative Programs (Olympia, WA); Hillsborough Public School District (Tampa, FL); Educational Service District 113 (Tumwater, WA); Educational Service District 123 (Pasco, WA); Booker T. Washington High School (Miami, FL); Miami Beach Senior (Miami, FL); iTech@Thomas A. Edison Educational Center (Miami, FL)

The following nonprofit education organizations and businesses have also partnered with me and SoundOut focused on student voice and Meaningful Student Involvement:

HumanLinks Foundation (Bothell, WA); Vermont Principals Association (Montpelier, VT); National PTA (Arlington, VA); Charlotte Martin Foundation (Seattle, WA); Communities for Learning (Floral Park, NY); Youth On Board (Boston, MA); Generation YES (Olympia, WA); Cloud Institute for Sustainability Education (New York, NY); Washington State University Center for Bridging the Digital Divide (Pullman, WA); Youth Activism Project (Kennsington, MD); National Youth Rights Association (Washington, DC); Service Learning Northwest (Vancouver, WA); Institute for Community Leadership (Kent, WA); New Horizons for Learning (Seattle, WA); Project Service Leadership (Vancouver, WA); Youth Policy Action Center (Washington, DC); Wild Cow Studios (Olympia, WA); Institute for Democratic Education in America (Tarrytown, NY); Catalyst Miami (Miami, FL)

Much of the thinking in this book was information by these schools, agencies and organizations, and I'm deeply indebted for their support and encouragement.

Introduction

I wrote this book after more than a decade of work promoting Meaningful Student Involvement. It has been my privilege to work with more than 100,000 students, teachers, administrators, school support staff, community partners, parents, and others focused on student voice, student engagement, and Student/Adult Partnerships. I have worked with more than 100 projects in across all grade levels; higher education; local, state, and federal government education agencies in several countries; and with many nonprofit organizations in the United States and abroad. My work is far from original, and I stand on the shoulders of dozens of researchers and advocates who have been working for various components of Meaningful Student Involvement for more than 50 years. I have gathered these hypotheses into a unified theory of student voice, and it is my privilege to share Meaningful Student Involvement with the world.

I became the first-ever student engagement specialist at the Washington State Office of Superintendent (OSPI) in 2001. After a decade of youth work in community settings, I wanted to learn as much as I could from students and educators; unfortunately, I found no convenient avenue or willing audience that would teach me. My response came from the adage, "speak by listening." Meeting with dozens of schools across the state, I learned what student engagement meant in diverse educational settings across Washington. Many of these schools used service learning to promote academic achievement; others participated in OSPI's school improvement program. I quickly learned the difference between *talking* about Meaningful Student Involvement and *doing* it.

When funding for my work ended in 2003, the HumanLinks Foundation partnered with me to bring together the historical and modern lessons I had learned about Meaningful Student Involvement. Within a few years, I had written several publications, developed an online database, and began sharing what I had learned with schools across the United States and Canada. I launched projects with collaborators in 25 schools, learning and growing Meaningful Student Involvement by directly facilitating, partnering with educators and students, and examining on-the-ground action. This action research helped me identify a series of patterns emerging.

One of the patterns I saw was that when students talked about activities being meaningful, they specifically identified either the type of activity they were involved in or the issue they were addressing. Students were consistently identified education-focused issues as important, even as their interests in community-based issues waxed and waned. Instead of simply blaming adults or shouldering blame themselves for the conditions in their schools, much of the time students identified myriad factors responsible for student disengagement in learning. I summarize some of these factors in Tables 3 and 5 of this book.

However, all of this also showed me that a larger movement was emerging. Fifteen years later, it is increasingly easy to see a steady and growing global student voice movement. In the early 2000s that wasn't nearly as obvious. So, I brought these lessons together as the basis for my frameworks, which I called *Meaningful Student Involvement*. Adopting the lessons I learned from pedagogues such as John Dewey, Myles Horton, and Paulo Freire, I defined Meaningful Student Involvement as engaging all students in every school as partners in every facet of education for the purpose of strengthening their commitment to learning, community, and democracy.

I formed the Campaign for Meaningful Student Involvement in 2001. After researching hundreds of examples and dozens of studies related to engaging students as partners in schools, I decided what was needed was a unified theory of student voice. This theory was meant to bring together the divergent practice and research related to the roles of students in education, including student voice and student engagement. Working with partners across the country, I renamed the Campaign to SoundOut in 2002, and since then I have led the program as an online resource center and international training and consultation provider.

Since 2002, I have worked with more than 300 K-12 schools across the United States and Canada. I have piloted a variety of projects based on Meaningful Student Involvement in dozens of districts; consulted several national and international initiatives focused on student voice; and provided training and professional development to thousands of students and educators internationally. In 2008, I published the *SoundOut Student Voice Curriculum*, a classroom-based program designed to educate students about many of the lessons in this book. Since then the curriculum has been used with more than 2,500 middle and high school students across the United States, in the United Kingdom, Canada, and Australia. I have also spoke at dozens of education conferences on the topic of Meaningful Student Involvement, encouraging thousands of educators and school leaders to transform the roles of students throughout schools. This book will share several of my experiences in detail; lessons I have learned; the experiences of dozens of schools, districts, states and provincial education agencies; and education organizations across the US and around the world.

Chapter 1: Outline of Parts

I wrote this book to serve as a complete guide for potential practitioners, advocates, students and others who want to learn about Meaningful Student Involvement. Meaningful Student Involvement is my unified theory of student voice, and is fully examined throughout this book.

Part Two introduces the theory of Meaningful Student Involvement. It proposes that all students of all ages are full humans and introduces them as active partners in learning, teaching and leadership throughout education, instead of passive recipients. This part then highlights a short history of educational circumstances that have treated students as partners, and proposes there is a crisis of purpose in schools today that is solvable through shared responsibility. Part Two ends by summarizing how schools can change.

Part Three focuses on the related notions of student voice and student empowerment. Reviewing two distinct literature fields, it summarizes a wide swath of student voice literature related to curriculum, teaching, classroom management and school reform. It then introduces student engagement as a psychological, emotional and social factor in schools that intersects with student voice. Juxtaposing Meaningful Student Involvement against both, this Part positions the theory as a distinct, yet related, phenomenon with implications throughout the entirety of the education system.

Part Four examines my distinct "frameworks of Meaningful Student Involvement," which are formed by a series of mental models. Forming the practical basis of Meaningful Student Involvement, these models can guide practitioners and researchers alike. There are seven featured here, including Student/Adult Partnerships; the Cycle of Engagement; key characteristics; the Ladder of Student Involvement; adult perspectives of students; Spheres of Meaning; and a learning process. Based in my experience and studies, these models can be vital tools for planning, implementation and assessment of different practices.

In Part Five, I examine the benefits of this theory. Beginning by explicitly delineating the aims of Meaningful Student Involvement, the chapter then summarizes the research-based outcomes, in addition to identifying a wide variety of research that supports the theory. The impacts on learning and child and youth development are expanded on, and the chapter closes by exploring how this research impacts practice and is incorporated into practice.

Part Six explores planning for Meaningful Student Involvement. The book elaborates on different roles throughout the education system to consider, as well as different kinds of students that can become meaningfully involved. I then identify the different people and locations throughout education that can engage students as partners, including individual schools, local districts, state and provincial agencies, and federal agencies. There is a long list of issues that can be addressed through Meaningful Student Involvement, and strategies that can be considered to transform the theory into action. The book then expands on different ways to prepare individuals to become meaningfully involved, including students and adults. Places are considered to, with chapters on preparing schools and the education system at large. The final chapter in Part Six encourages the reader to consider the ethical implications of Meaningful Student Involvement.

Envisioning Meaningful Student Involvement in Action can be challenging for adults who are used to today's education system. In Part Seven, I expand on the idea, exploring different types of action in-depth. A comprehensive picture is painted as readers look at examples of students as school researchers, educational planners, classroom teachers, learning evaluators, systemic decision-makers and education advocates. Part Seven also addresses engaging disengaged students and gives examples of school wide and large scale programs. He also shares the need for healthy, safe and supportive learning environments that engender Meaningful Student Involvement for all learners.

Part Eight explores what is learned through Meaningful Student Involvement. It discusses grade-specific approaches to learning, sharing what happens in elementary, middle and high schools, as well as what adults can learn. This part identifies different roles for teachers specifically, and summarizes several learning strategies and classroom structures that can be used to catalyze learning with students as partners. I then examine how to acknowledge Meaningful Student Involvement, and shows how educators can build ownership in action.

Teaching students about school is a key to Meaningful Student Involvement. In Part Nine, I share a variety of ideas about this activity, from identifying the purpose of learning to understanding our own understanding of education. The constructivist nature of the theory is made plain as the educators are shown how to validate students' existing knowledge about schools and how they might expand their own and their students' understanding about the education system. I then identify how Meaningful Student Involvement can be taught through curriculum and instruction, school leadership, building design, student assessment, building climate and culture, student support services, education governance, school/community partnerships, and parent involvement. Stories of action highlight each item.

The Part Nine of the book proposes barriers and practical considerations affecting Meaningful Student Involvement. I show how the structure of education can be both a barrier and a solution to action. Other barriers examined in-depth include school culture, students themselves, and adults throughout the education system. The book shares a case examination for overcoming obstacles, and then details ways discrimination against students affects the meaningfulness of learning, teaching and leadership. It proposes a "student involvement gap" in addition to exploring convenient and inconvenient student voice.

Part Ten addresses assessing Meaningful Student Involvement. It thoughtfully examines different issues to be measured throughout activities, as well as ways to measure the effect of action on people, activities, and outcomes. This part also discusses how to sustain Meaningful Student Involvement.

Proposing there is an essential role for learners in democratic society, Part Ten also details what I call "The Public Student." This student is "any learner whose position is explicitly vital to the future of education, community and democracy." This part details what their positions in society are, why they are important and what they look like in practice.

Chapter 2: My Assumptions

Rising from my early work were my personal reflections on why I thought this work was important. The following are several of my assumptions about Meaningful Student Involvement.

1) Effective Learning For Every Student Can Only Happen Through Meaningful Involvement

In the beginning of their academic careers, students do not choose to attend schools. It is through compulsory attendance that many learners discover the pleasure of attendance and the joy of engagement. If and when they establish that pleasure and joy, they develop self-motivation through a sense of purpose. If they do not establish that pleasure and joy, they wrestle with self-motivation and seek external validation. If they do not receive that validation, they do not become effective learners in school. However, school attendance laws mandate they still be involved in schools. They may not be engaged and they may not share their voice in ways adults want to hear them, but they are still involved. Making student involvement meaningful can re-engage these students, as well as re-invigorate other students' self-motivation and sense of purpose. Indeed, meaningful involvement is the only way every student can experience effective learning.

2) All Students Belong At The Table

On average, students comprise 92% of the population of any school building. Yet most significant decisions about learning, teaching, and leading in schools are consistently made by the other eight percent. It is not enough to simply listen to student voice, either. Educators have an ethical imperative to do something with students, and that is why Meaningful Student Involvement is vital to school improvement. Students should be nothing less than full partners with equitable authority and responsibility as that of adults throughout the education system. This book examines this assumption in depth, identifying the pitfalls and possibilities of engaging all students as partners.

3) Every Student Counts

Traditional models of student leadership have centered on students who meet a specific mold. Consequently, the traditional student leader is now a typology in schools. Every student's voice counts, giving educators the responsibility to engage all students as partners throughout their classrooms, and leaving school leaders with the responsibility of engaging students in education policy-making, planning, research, and more. The experiences I detail throughout this Handbook will provide pragmatic examples of what this looks like.

4) Student Voice Is Not Enough

Student voice is present throughout schools all the time. It is the sound of students sharing their life experiences during class and the passion of students speaking at school board meetings. It is the friendships in the school lunchroom and the noise of the playground. It is also the bullies bullying and students texting answers back-and-forth illicitly during a test. All of this is student voice because these are forms of student expressions about education. Much like the pet fish in a fishbowl do not know they're surrounded by glass, the clear majority of students and educators have no idea they're surrounded by student voice.

Deep student engagement happens when students are actively engaged in identifying challenges, analyzing situations, creating responses, learning through action, and examining outcomes. Moving beyond student voice means engaging students as partners throughout their learning by providing space for students to become engaged, enthusiastic, and adamant advocates for themselves and their peers, as well as for education as a whole. Meaningful Student Involvement positions students as active partners throughout education, rather than merely as recipients or informants.

5) Involvement Matters

Involvement must matter to students. Simply assigning students a job is not enough; it can work against student engagement. Without the authority and responsibility required to make significant decisions throughout education, students often see their involvement is tokenistic or manipulative. This disengages them from schools. Involvement must matter to them, too, and not simply reinforce adults' beliefs. Connecting student involvement with grade-level expectations and acknowledging their contributions with classroom credit can create constructivist learning experiences that can enhance student outcomes in many areas. This Handbook features research supporting that, and much more.

6) To Serve is to Learn

Student involvement throughout schools should be an opportunity to experience the principles of democracy. Citizens in a democracy have a responsibility to serve the public good. Similarly, each student within a given school should serve the whole school body. Engaging students as partners fosters democratic learning. Focusing on a variety of actual opportunities students are engaged in right now, Table 15 introduces this idea, and a chapter in this *Handbook* explores new roles for students throughout the education system.

7) Students Are Responsible

Being required by society to attend school does not render students to be passive learners who are incapable of affecting positive change within their schools. Given increasing amounts of responsibility through technology and the Internet, schools must respond by increasing student responsibility. Meaningful Student Involvement is an avenue to do this. No longer merely a target or consumer of education, students are increasingly living democratic responsibility by presenting grievances, challenging inadequacies, and compelling authorities to change the education system. Schools can embrace this lean towards democracy building in education by embracing responsibilities for students and creating Student/Adult Partnerships throughout the education system.

7) The Future is Now

For a long time, policymakers, administrators and educators have been reluctant to fully embrace technology and its applications in classrooms. Now that those efforts are underway in earnest, the alarm is rising around student-to-student relationships and community-building throughout the learning environment. More people are speaking the language of mindfulness, project-based learning and other forward thinking pedagogies and methods than ever before. However, they're still talking about them in a future context. What we all need to realize is that the future is *now*, and that we must move forward in education to keep pace with society. That means moving forward to embrace Meaningful Student Involvement today, and tomorrow, and throughout the future.

This book is written for students, educators, community members, and all interested readers as an introduction to a burgeoning movement. It is meant to encourage students and adults to act together. The *Meaningful Student Involvement Handbook* does just that, and more, by providing a comprehensive vision for students as partners in school change through Meaningful Student Involvement.

Part I. Making Meaning with Students

Chapter 3: Introduction

Walking through the front doors, you immediately notice fresh, energetic paint covering the entryway to the school. As you step forward, a banner announces, "YOU Matter!" Suddenly, there's a voice on the loudspeaker announcing that it is time to move to your next class. It belongs to a student.

Imagine a school where democracy is more than a buzzword, and involvement is more than attendance. It is a place where adults and students interact as co-learners and leaders, and where students are encouraged to collaborate throughout their education. It's a school where adults value student empowerment and all students succeed through their active and authentic engagement.

The assistant superintendent and two students greet you at the office. Taking you on a short tour, you keep seeing vivid expressions of positive encouragement throughout the building, including high quality signs and posters you are told were made by students. As they walk you into a classroom, you immediately see groups of learners clustered into small groups, co-presenting nicely printed graphic planners to each other. A literature class, you can hear students talking about their own lives and relating them to characters in the classic book they are reading.

Envision classrooms where teachers hold student experiences as central to learning, and education boardrooms where students are partners in school change. Students evaluate themselves, their teachers, curricula, the school environment, and each other. When they are advocating for themselves, students aren't seen as adversaries, but as allies to educators who share a commitment to better education for all learners, including themselves.

Joining the workshop, you came for, you are surprised to find this district assessment committee is happening on a stage. The chairs are arranged in a circle, and instead of the whiteboard and projector and slides you expect, there are flipcharts and markers on several stands. After welcoming the group, the district's curriculum leader hands the meeting over to a group of facilitators. You are startled when they turn out to be two eleventh grade students, a ninth grader, and a sixth grader. After their brief self-introductions, they cajole the group into an icebreaker. You are suddenly expecting a very interesting session.

Ultimately, all people in the education system are engaged as equitable partners, each one fully invested and capable of affecting lifelong learning for all learners everywhere, all the time.

You learn the student tour guides and the student facilitators were all given classroom credit for their various duties. Planning, facilitation and reflection all happened through Student/Adult Partnerships, and there is a larger framework the school uses to situate these activities—and many more—into their learning outcomes and performance measures. You want to learn about this framework, and so you ask the assistant principal who originally walked you around the building. "This is Meaningful Student Involvement," he says, and quickly adds, "But you should really ask some of our other students about it instead of me." Walking out into the hallway, you interrupt a small group huddled around a locker. They give you a surprisingly thorough earful, but with a professionalism and succinctness you wish some teachers would adopt. "Oh, we're presenting the frameworks at a teacher training next week, so we're ready!" explained one of the group.

Taught by their peers, conducting self- and peer-evaluations, representing their own interests throughout school, and becoming meaningfully involved in myriad nontraditional roles throughout the education system has transformed this environment massively. Low-income students, English language learners, and students who historically dropout or are pushed out are engaged and re-engaged for the first time, substantially increasing their likelihood to succeed.

This is a picture of an ideal school that embodies Meaningful Student Involvement. This book explores what it looks like when schools embody student voice and choice throughout their entirety. It questions whether student engagement and ownership can be more than selling points for classroom curricula and learning assessments. The stories throughout these pages highlight resourceful and knowledgeable students and educators using strategic and goal-oriented learning to emphasis purposeful and motivated outcomes. Ultimately, it is a handbook that any educator or student can use to sharpen their abilities, deepen their understanding and ignite their desire to transform education for every student in every school, everywhere, all the time. This is *Meaningful Student Involvement.*

---

5 PATHWAYS TO AUTHENTIC STUDENT VOICE

1. **ACKNOWLEDGE:** Begin by acknowledging the real ways young people express themselves right now throughout their own lives, across their communities, and around our world. Youth voice happens all the time. Do adults want to hear what it is, or make it into what we want it to be?
2. **COMMIT:** Foster genuine commitment within your organization to engage young people beyond simply listening to what they say. Do adults want young people to be full partners?
3. **PROMOTE:** Create interest among constituents- including young people, adults, or seniors- to contribute beyond their voices. Are adults willing to allow them to come in on young peoples' own terms instead of our own?
4. **EMPOWER:** Position young people in sustained opportunities to impact change as real doers and decision-makers. Are adults ready to cede power, share power, and relinquish our power as adults?
5. **EXPAND:** Educate young people about the whole issue that affects them, not just what they already know. Are adults committed to building the abilities of young people to be full partners instead of minor players.

Table 1. 5 Pathways to Authentic Student Voice

Chapter 4: No Tabula Rasa

Within the boundaries of the education system people share a thousand purposes for its existence. Some insist on the purpose of schools being to create better citizens, while others think it is to make more productive workers. Others want to promote values and culture, while some want to build a secure future. Some people mix it all together, insisting school does all of that and more.

Within that messy blur, there's a lot that goes missing. Unfortunately for students, most of them are missing an understanding of the purpose of their education. They are literally schooled within a vacuum, being taught as if they are *tabula rasa,* or blank slates, that adults can project knowledge onto without their own conceptions for learning, teaching, and leadership today. The reality is that people who believe this are wholly wrong and completely misinformed. Those who work in schools and force students to attend schools who believe in *tabula rasa* are totally disingenuous.

These same teachers, principals, school support staff, and parents who believe that students are merely tabula rasa generally miss the point of education altogether. They are the ones who aspire to have and keep the things that are prescribed in life. Their roles in life do not hold meaning for them beyond a paycheck or position, and a place to spend their time during the day. When they do get home, time they could spend with their loved ones is spent in recovery from standardized abuse, or at least numbing the boredom of life. These people anesthetize the pain inherent in their lives with television and alcohol, video games and sex, the Internet and food. They live controlled lives. Their cycles of living without purposefulness makes them question the meaning of life, let alone the meaningfulness of schools.

For a long time, there have been exceptionally achieving students in schools, focused on academic performance and good behavior. They have been awarded with good grades and other recognition since the advent of public schools. Less recognized, but no less important, are other students who were not waiting for an invitation from adults in the education system to get involved in improving schools. These students have rallied against educational equality and inadequate schools for decades. The urgent reality being lived by these students and many others right now is dramatically different from the past many adults have lived.

Chapter 5: Grounded in Action

The idea that all students everywhere be meaningfully involved—all the time—may sound like an idealistic pipedream, but the examples in this book are not. Individual classrooms, buildings of all grade levels, and entire school districts are taking action that embodies Meaningful Student involvement right now. These practices exemplify **Meaningful Student Involvement**, which is the systematic approach to engaging students as partners in learning throughout every facet of education for the purpose of strengthening their commitment to education, community and democracy.

After researching thousands of cases and working with hundreds of schools in dozens of states across the United States and in Canada, I have found that Meaningful Student Involvement is the most direct pathway towards student engagement for all learners. I explore what that looks like in Table 6 of this book. Built on research- and practice-based frameworks, Meaningful Student Involvement encapsulates practices throughout education that actively engage students as partners, situates them within the larger context of continuous school transformation, and proves young people are an essential step towards transforming society.

Throughout this book there are examples to support each concept, and much more. For instance, I share the story of a local school board in Maryland where students have been engaged as full voting members of the school board for more than 25 years. (Fletcher, 2004) In California, a group of students led a district-wide evaluation of their teachers, curriculum, facilities, and fellow students. (REAL HARD, 2003) A program based in Washington state gives teachers a technology curriculum so schools rely on students to teach younger students, their peers, and adults how to use technology in the classroom. (Harper, 1996) Among the dozens shared throughout this book, these examples highlight some of the beliefs that inform the frameworks for Meaningful Student Involvement. Highlighting research from across the field of education and my own practice with schools across the US and Canada, this book is the most comprehensive publication I have written to elaborate on Meaningful Student Involvement, which is a unified theory of student voice. It identifies the best practices to promote the highest levels of theory and practice.

Some of the benefits of Meaningful Student Involvement include:

- Bringing fresh perspectives to school learning, teaching and leadership, including things going right, things that are challenging and potential solutions.
- Creating new energy and alignment between students and adults to improve the likelihood of successful school transformation.
- Promoting ownership among students and adults for school transformation.
- Sustaining meaningful support for teachers and other adults in the regular process of their positions throughout education.
- ✓ Providing educators with greater access to information about, and relationships with, marginalized student groups, families, and community groups. (Mitra, 2004; Cook-Sather, 2002; Fletcher, 2003b)

A. Listening to Student Voice is Not Enough

More than ever before, people today are talking about student voice. They describe the opinions, ideas and actions of students like they are static things that once shared, do not change. Student voice is being shared as a data source, an input in an information gathering activity. And student voice is simply being talked about for the sake of talking about it. However, it is not enough for educators to listen to student voice. Instead, students must become engaged in learning, teaching and leadership throughout schools in sustained, meaningful ways that demonstrate impact and outcomes. Fielding was perhaps the first to explore this transition in-depth and to promote moving students from passive informants to active partners in school improvement (Bragg, 2007). Holdsworth summarized a pasel of definitions a decade earlier though, writing that student voice is, "speaking out; being heard; being listened to; being listened to seriously and with respect; incorporating student views into action taken by others; and sharing decision-making, implementing action and reflecting on action, with young people." (Holdsworth, 2000b)

Unfortunately, though, many educators have specific expectations for what student voice should say, instead of simply listening to what students want to say for themselves. This is evident in definitions of the term from organizations like the Washington State Professional Educators Standards Board, which declares, "Student voice is the term used to describe students' expressing their understanding of their learning process." (WASPESB, 2009) This definition is clearly made for the benefit of adults in the education system, rather than students themselves, as it necessitates on "students' expressing their understanding" rather than students' saying what they want to how they want to about any component of the education system that targets them. Also, this definition centers on "the learning process," as if that were the only thing students know about in schools. Student voice is much more than this.

In a similar way, a student forum made of students just talking about schools is equivalent to using iPads in the classroom with no real instruction. Talking for the sake of talking is of no value to students, since it inherently incapacities them and minimizes their ability to affect change throughout schools. Learning and action must emerge from the genuine concerns of students, especially when they partner with adults by actively advocating for systemic school improvement, researching classroom climate, and teaching new approaches to learning and teaching. These activities cannot be wholly prescribed, either, since they must be navigated differently in every circumstance. Whatever form they take, if conducted through the frameworks of Meaningful Student Involvement, student voice can effectively demonstrate what schools should look like when the hearts, heads, and hands of students are infused throughout the process. But just as in building houses, no one builder works alone: Students must partner with adults, including teachers, administrators, counselors, and support staff, on the building crew.

In a demanding piece entitled "Make a Difference With, Not For, Students," Corbett and Wilson offered this sage warning:

> "Our proposition is that student role redefinition is a critical linchpin between adult reform and student success, and that failing to acknowledge this connection is a potentially fatal flaw in promoting our understanding of reform and in creating effective change initiatives." (1995)

This sounds an alarm that we would fail miserably if we did not seriously consider the very people who are most affected. Now, almost two decades after their warning, we sit in the ruins of many failed attempts at improving schools, blaming others without often considering our own complicity.

However, considering student voice specifically without seeing students as actors in improving education is limiting the inherent potential of students as partners, and denying the inevitable route schools are taking today. Corbett and Wilson's ongoing studies about the perspectives and roles of students in school improvement led to a powerful report about their work in Philadelphia called *Listening to Urban Kids: School Reform and the Teachers They Want* (2001). This book is like Cushman's *Fires in the Bathroom: Advice for teachers from high school students* (2003); its companions, *Sent to the Principal: Students talk about making high school better* (2005) and *Fires in the Mind: What kids can tell us about motivation and mastery* (2010); and Schultz and Cook-Sather's important book, *In Our Own Words: Students' perspectives on schools* (2001). Each of these books offers student voice in context of what can be done to improve schools. All of them also charge readers with acting for change.

There are many reasons schools must live up to the challenge that Meaningful Student Involvement presents, not the least of which being that students are more than the future: As many reports, books, forums and videos today show, they are the present.[1] More than ever before, students are urgently pressing teachers, administrators, and school leaders to respond to the challenges in our schools right now. This requires the radical reconceptualization of schools embodied by Meaningful Student Involvement. A movement has been percolating throughout education towards Meaningful Student Involvement for almost 15 years. In that time, I have discovered unlikely allies and found surprising opposition that I'll discuss in-depth later in this book.

However, I have also encountered many detractors within and throughout the education system. They have refuted the necessity of engaging students as partners in schools and denied the necessity of Meaningful Student Involvement. Some have suggested that Meaningful Student Involvement is about making students happy, pacifying unruly children, or letting kids run the school. I explore these and other barriers further in this book in Figures 18 and 20, and in several chapters.

Research cited throughout this book suggests that when educators work *with* students in schools—as opposed to working *for* them—schools become positive and powerful for students, adults in schools, and the entire school community. At the heart of Meaningful Student Involvement are students, whose voices have long been neglected, silenced, and even repressed by adults in schools. The stories here show how building equity between students and adults throughout the education system may be the key to successful learning, teaching, and leadership for all schools.

Despite this, it is still the norm to deny the belief that student voice should guide education, let alone consider that students should have substantive roles in schools that enrich their learning. Educators must reach students with lessons that are rooted in the experiences students live every single day. Grounding some part of these lessons in the educative processes they are subjected to daily only makes sense.

Yet, there is far from enough effort to engage students as creators, implementers, assessors, or advocates within their own educational experiences. As Canadian school reformer Michael Fullan wrote,

"When adults think of students, they think of them as potential beneficiaries of change... they rarely think of students as participants in a process of school change and organizational life." (1991)

Meaningful Student Involvement authorizes students and adults to act as partners throughout schools, and inherently relies on adult acceptance. (Cook-Sather, 2002; Cervone, 2012 ; Cervone & Cushman, 2002) It does that to acknowledge the genuine situation in schools by not denying that adults operate students for schools. That alone makes Student/Adult Partnerships a necessity, and student voice a constant presence.

There is a growing awareness that strengthening, supporting, and sustaining student voice fosters student engagement for all learners. Among the best understandings of the concept is the notion that student voice is not just the words and phrases that adults want to hear from students. Instead, student voice happens when groups of students collect in the hallway after class to talk about their teachers. It happens when impassioned students go to the school board meeting to demand funding for new textbooks. It happens when students regularly throw away tasteless, unhealthy food served in the cafeteria. Most students and adults would agree that those frequently are not meaningful experiences.

B. Essential Terms

Unfortunately, misconceptions about student voice and student engagement are growing. Well-meaning educators, politicians, and even students are attributing all sorts of peculiarities to the terms of *voice* and *engagement*, melding them with notions about student leadership, student achievement and school communities as a whole. It is vital that schools have common, working understandings of this work before they begin. The reasoning for this extends from how to effectively teach in schools today:

"Effective teaching looks effortless but is, in reality, grounded in depth: in a deep knowledge of teaching, learning, and subject matter; in a deep-seated commitment to developing and honing the craft of teaching; and in a deep conviction that every student and every student group has unique needs, idiosyncrasies, and talents. Explore, develop, or deepen the skills, strategies, and practices that can transform teaching and improve student learning." (Martin-Kniep & Picone-Zocchia, 2009)

Meaningful Student Involvement inherently requires a similar tact because it is inherently a large part of effective teaching.

In my time and action through elementary, middle, and senior high schools, as well as with education agencies at the district, regional, state, and federal levels, I have come to understand that it is essential to define and clarify the terms we use, as well as the work that is done by people who use these terms.

As I wrote above, **Meaningful Student Involvement** is a systematic approach to engaging students as partners in learning throughout every facet of education for the purpose of strengthening their commitment to education, community, and democracy. It is validating and authorizing students to represent their own ideas, opinions, knowledge and experiences throughout education to improve our schools—not just for themselves, but for every student and every adult to ever walk into education after they are involved.

Student engagement is any sustained connection a learner has to any part of the educational experience. This connection can be psychological, social, emotional, physical, or otherwise, so long as it's sustained. Student engagement is an outcome of Meaningful Student Involvement.

Student voice is any expression by any learner about education, learning, or schooling in general. Student voice is not *just* student choice, as there are many other ways to express voice.

As these definitions show, these three terms are not synonymous. Further in this book, I explore the research behind each concept in depth, providing substantive background to my definitions. In the meantime, it is important to know that involvement does not equal engagement; engagement is not the same as voice; and voice does not only happen through involvement.

I chose to name this conception Meaningful Student *Involvement* because that is what students are as soon as they walk through the doors of schools: they are involved. They are not inherently engaged—that requires their choice. Their voices are not necessarily listened to either. However, as soon as they enter the hallways, they are involved in peer-to-peer interactions, they are involved in using the school building's physical features, and they are involved in their classrooms. Student involvement simply happens.

Unfortunately, throughout the history of schools much of this involvement has been meaningless and belittling. Fifteen years ago, I wanted to elevate this involvement by recognizing the depth, breadth, purpose and potential of student involvement, thus I began studying and practicing it. This book features what I have come to learn from all the opportunities I have had to learn from students, researchers, educators, administrators, and concerned community members. It represents my interpretations, summarization, and conceptualization of the much of the wisdom, knowledge, ideas, reflection, concerns and criticisms I have heard throughout this journey. This understanding is helpful as you read this book and discover what Meaningful Student Involvement is and how it happens in schools across North America and around the world.

As an important side note, youth voice, as it were, cannot be engaged in schools. Once a young person walks through the doors of a public school building, they are automatically thrust into the role of learner, which we call Student. This is a public role that benefits society, like the roles of voter, public servant, or politician. The private roles of young people, including that of youth, child, kid, kiddo, yute, youngin', etc., are completely different from their role of student and should end when they walk through the doors of a school building. My work in schools leads me to seek to engage young people in the context where they become students, which is school. Therefore, I seek student voice. This is a subtle, yet important distinction.

This means Meaningful Student Involvement is not the same as...

- Student voice, which is any expression of any learner related to learning, schools, or education;
- Student engagement, which is the sustained connection a learner feels towards learning, schools, or education;

- Student involvement, which is any activity for students in schools;
- Pupil consultation, which is a systematic process for listening to students' opinions about school;
- Youth voice, which happens outside of the formal learning environments students are compelled to attend.

As we see increased interest in the entwined topics of student engagement and student voice throughout schools, it becomes easy to misunderstand the relationships between these topics and Meaningful Student Involvement. To help us understand that, it can be said that student voice can lead to student engagement through Meaningful Student Involvement.

---

[1] For examples of student-led projects focused on school improvement see soundout.org/listening.html

Chapter 6: A Short History

The student voice movement today is being presented as a new thing, something invented by ambitious students determined to improve their schools. However, this simply is not true. In classrooms and education programs scattered across North America and around the world, students have been naming their own intentions for education for decades. Over the last twenty years, this call has become louder and more urgent than ever. (Corbett & Wilson, 1995; Rudduck, 2007; Fielding, 2001) They have been working for democracy and social justice throughout education, and many times, calling for more empowered, engaged roles for students in all sorts of places (Kurth-Schai, 1988; Klein, 2003; Dzur, 2013). Table 15 highlights some of these roles.

Like many student voice advocates, I learned a lot from A.S. Neill's Summerhill School in the United Kingdom, founded in 1921 and a clear inspiration for Meaningful Student Involvement. However, further back than this was Russian author Tolstoy's foundational work focused on fostering freedom through schooling. In the 1850s, Tolstoy wrote an article entitled, "Who Should Teach Whom to Write, We the Peasant Children or the Peasant Children Us?". In it he proposed that students are the most effective teachers of other students, and that learning is most effective when it addresses real world situations. (Simmons, 1968) Tolstoy did not want to promote a method or structure for learning or schooling, either. While it did not succeed in Russia more than 160 years ago, Tolstoy's work influences my conception of Meaningful Student Involvement substantially.

Stories of meaningful involvement and deep student voice emerge throughout the history of American public education from the 1920s through the 1970s. In 1922, students at Mineola High School in New York protested the suspension of their senior class president. When she was suspended for skipping study hall, a disagreement between the students and the school led to a walkout. (*The New York Times*, 1922) Elsia Clapp, an educator in Arthurdale, West Virginia, pioneered a school there that was centered on the role of the student in education in the 1920s. From 1927 through the 1960s, teacher Grace Pilon developed the concept of "The Workshop Way." Pilon's approach has worked in thousands of schools by focusing on making students active agents in learning and teaching. Pilon wrote the Workshop Way depends "on an environment that provides equal opportunities to manage the same experiences in different ways" for elementary students. (Loflin, 2006) There are dozens of similar examples of singular teachers and individual schools that deliberately involved students in school functioning and other systemic ways.

As time passed, students started taking the lead. A vanguard organization of the hippie movement, Students for a Democratic Society, wrote a manifesto including democratic student involvement throughout the public education system in 1962. (Hayden, 1962) In 1968, on the day following the assassination of Rev. Dr. Martin Luther King, Jr., more than 250 African American students at William Penn Senior High School in York, Pennsylvania, refused to attend class. Instead the students quietly barricaded themselves in the auditorium of the school to commence Black Pride Day. (Wright D. C., 2003) More than 100 high schools across the United States were reported to have student-led campaigns focused on changing schools, according to a snapshot of student activism in 1971. (Erlich & Erlich, 1971)

That same year, the Montgomery County, Maryland Board of Education, adopted the following declaration:

> "Students must be actively involved in the learning process. Therefore, in each course and at each grade level, students shall be encouraged to participate in establishing grade goals, suggesting interest areas, planning classroom activities and appraising the courses. Student suggestions and recommendations concerning curricular offerings and opportunities shall be permitted at any time and shall be solicited by the professional staff." (Kleeman, 1972)

This is clearly a precedent for Meaningful Student Involvement. Also in 1971, the 16-student Task Force of Student Involvement for the North Carolina State Department of Education released a statement that said,

> "What students are saying is that they care about schools' they want to be contributors to the educational process, not just recipients. Educators greatest potential resource lies in taking advantage of this interest and channeling it into responsible areas of action." (Kleeman, 1972)

A concern over students' First Amendment rights has factored into much of this work for more than forty years. After strong forays into the subject of student voice through self-expression, clothes, print magazines and student-led organizing, several campaigns assailed schools for stifling student voice in the 1960s. This action led students towards many then-radical acts, including a student for a school board in Ann Arbor, Michigan[2], and launching a nationwide press for student-created publications[3]. In 1969, these actions culminated in the United States Supreme Court trial *Tinker v. Des Moines*. In *Tinker* a school district was sued after denying students the right to protest in their high school. The justices famously ruled, "Students do not shed their constitutional rights at the school house gates." However, the Court was not unanimous in their opinion. Framing many arguments against Meaningful Student Involvement that are still used today, Justice Hugo Black wrote in his dissent that he did not want to be part of,

> "a new revolutionary era of permissiveness in this country fostered by the judiciary... I wish, therefore, wholly to disclaim any purpose on my part to hold that the Federal Constitution compels the teachers, parents, and elected school officials to surrender control of the American public school system to public school students."[4]

Despite that ruling, many students and adults continue to struggle in order to ensure students have First Amendment rights in schools today.[5] The US Supreme Court also wavers in their support for student voice, alternating supporting students and denying their rights. This includes the 1988 *Hazelwood* decision, which ruled that student newspapers are not protected by First Amendment rights. (Verchick, 1991) In 2007, the Supreme Court ruled that schools can suppress student voice outside of schools as well, if students are at a school-supervised event. (Dickler, 2007)

Beane and Apple found that student voice work continued over the next three decades. They shared examples of students sharing in school design decisions along with teachers, administrators, parents, board members, and community organizations in Port Jarvis, New York, in 1972. Seven years later, students in Ulysses, Pennsylvania, elementary students and teachers debated and voted on a new rule for anyone caught vandalizing school property. They agreed that guilty student would spend free time over 3 days working with the custodian. In 1991, middle school students in Madison, Wisconsin worked together to create new social studies curriculum out of students' questions and concerns regarding the world. (Beane & Apple, 1995) As they are highlighted later in this book, my own research showed how these examples continued to grow from the 1990s into the 2000s. (Fletcher, 2005b)

Some individual cities have deep histories of student-driven school change, especially Philadelphia, Pennsylvania. According to Conner and Rosen, the city's pertinent history stretches back to 1967. That year, a campaign demanded new black history courses, no more police in high schools, and more black principals. To leverage their demands, 3,500 students walked out of school. Thirty-three years later, in 2000, thousands of students again walked out, this time rallying at City Hall and marching to the state education agency. The state took over their local school district and signed a multimillion dollar contract with a for-profit education management organization. In 2013, severe budget cuts to public education closed 23 schools and left those remaining schools without extracurricular programs, guidance counselors, librarians, and other vital resources. Thousands of students again organized a walkout to protest the cuts on the anniversary of *Brown versus the Board of Education*. All of this action was driven by students who struggled to learn about the education, leverage their community's energy towards positive change, and challenge the political and economic forces forcing change in area schools. The longevity of their struggle was driven by several organizations, including the long-standing Philadelphia Students Union, a student-driven nonprofit. (Conner & Rosen, 2013)

Today, as never before, these examples are less anomalous. Instead, they are coalescing and leadership is stepping forward to build a movement of students focused on improving education around the world. Across the United States today, this movement is made of groups like Student Voice[6]; the Pritchard Committee Student Voice Team in Kentucky[7]; and the Boston Student Advisory Council[8]. There are literally hundreds of other efforts too, including activities in local school buildings by organizations like Up For Learning[9] in Vermont, school district programs like New York City's Student Voice Collaborative[10], and individual educators like Donnan Stoicovy in Pennsylvania (McGarry & Stoicovy, 2014; Dzur, 2013) and Nelson Beaudoin in Maine. (Beaudoin, 2005) There are literally hundreds of other programs, education agencies, nonprofit organizations and individuals promoting this concept in other countries around the world. Especially strong work is happening in the United Kingdom, Chile, Australia and my native country, Canada. (Rudduck, Chaplain & Wallace, 1996; Fielding, 2001)

For more than a decade, I have been consulting and training individual schools, districts, and state education agencies to actively implement Meaningful Student Involvement. More than 300 schools across North America have launched efforts, all to varying effects. This book shares their processes, my learning and other outcomes from their action.

We must challenge the meaninglessness of being a student in schools today. Forced to sit in rows, learn facts through rote memorization, exhibit their mastery through standardized tests, and behave according to adult standards under threat of expulsion or imprisonment, schools are routinely harangued for what they inadvertently teach learners. Compliance, obedience and authoritarian submissiveness are often the silent assassins of creativity in young people today.

This treatment as *tabula rasa* makes students yearn for meaningful in school starting at the youngest of ages. Without that meaningfulness, they have a harder time identifying meaningfulness and purpose in throughout their lives. In the meantime, we must recognize the reality that strategically weaving meaningfulness throughout the education system meets the purpose of the Common Core State Standards. (McGarry & Stoicovy, 2014)

Leaving seven to nine hours in school settings every day to return home where their parents are beginning daily recuperation from their workaday lives, young people face the prospect that after thirteen years of their daily conditioning they get to face the same realities their parents do, day in and out. However, without adult role models who live in fully meaningful, purposeful ways, students are left to the devices of popular culture, mainstream media, and socio-economic norms to find their way in the world.

This forms a vacuum in society, a void where young people and adults lose their bearing on what matters to them, what matters to their families, and what matters to the world community as a whole. Entire generations have been raised without the prospect that there is a better life for everyone beyond the shallow materialism and hollow sentimentalism propagated by television shows, pop music, and junk magazines. Brought up to love conformity and honor authority, entire social classes reject the notion of transformative living or revolutionary thought.

The value of meaningfulness is that it harbors within it an inherent hope, a prospect that all things can be better in all ways. Finding meaning means naming purpose, finding belonging, or identifying pathways for living in any of its myriad forms. Meaningfulness is, by its nature, a restlessness and a specifically kind of urgency that insists that life is not merely what is right in front of us, but something more, something deeper—or more so, that life is what it is, and that there is meaning in that, too. That's the awesome thing about meaningfulness: it's entirely up to each and every individual to determine what the meaning is.

Schools should aspire to nothing less than helping students discern the meaning of learning for themselves and with adults as partners. This vision insists that learning is to be lived anew by every student everywhere all of the time. It is urgency combined with the reality that everything means something, and it stands in direct opposition to popular yet drab prospect that nothing means anything. This vision is the reason why meaningfulness is more important than ever before.

---

[2] Learn about Sonia Yaco running for the school board at en.wikipedia.org/wiki/Sonia_Yaco

[3] Learn about Youth Liberation Press at en.wikipedia.org/wiki/Youth_Liberation_of_Ann_Arbor

[4] Learn about *Tinker v. Des Moines* at uscourts.gov/multimedia/podcasts/Landmarks/tinkervdesmoines.aspx

[5] Learn about the First Amendment Schools at firstamendmentschools.org/freedoms/case.aspx?id=404

[6] Learn about Student Voice and Student Voice Live! at stuvoice.org

[7] Learn about the Prichard Committee Student Voice Team at prichardcommittee.org

[8] Learn about the Boston Student Advisory Committee at bostonpublicschools.org/student-voice

[9] Find about Up For Learning at upforlearning.com

[10] Learn about the Student Voice Collaborative at studentvoicecollaborative.com

FIVE STEPS TO CHANGE YOUR SCHOOL IMMEDIATELY

Step 1: Get motivated.
Start by figuring out what reality you want to change. Look at your school and see how closely its aligned to Meaningful Student Involvement. Let yourself get inspired, and build your knowledge so that inspiration stays motivated.

Step 2: Increase your knowledge.
Begin by getting educated. If you think you already know a lot about Meaningful Student Involvement, dig deeper and learn even more. See the bibliography of this book and read other authors focused on student voice, student engagement and Student/Adult Partnerships, too.

Step 3: Build your skills.
Get real. Figure out what you're capable of doing right now, and what you are not capable of doing right now. You must have the ability or be willing to develop the ability to affect the world around you. Get uncomfortable, NOW. Challenge yourself to do uncomfortable things in uncomfortable settings, and if you don't know how to do a thing, figure it out. If you can't figure it out, ask someone. If you can't find someone to ask, look further.

Step 4: Take action.
Action requires... acting. Without spending too much time planning, launch into employing the knowledge and skills you have and have acquired. Sometimes, the best way to move things forward is to simply get moving, deliberately and with intention. Do not accept the way things are. Anytime you face a roadblock, name it, walk to it, and confront it.

Step 5: Look back to go forward.
Whenever you think Meaningful Student Involvement is finished, take a moment to acknowledge what has been done. Accomplishments, barriers, obstacles overcome, and places students have made a difference should all come out. Celebrate what you've done. Don't quit – you're never really done.

Table 2: Steps to Change Your School Right Away

Chapter 7: A Crisis of Purpose

"The times are a changing." Forty years ago, Bob Dylan's song was shocking, provocative and powerful. Today it seems shocked, pretentious and spent. However, as a teacher from Oakland said in a SoundOut workshop, "Students have changed more in the last ten years than schools have in the last hundred." All that underscores the notion that education transformation is long overdue.

Educators, theorists and researchers have seen this too, with one examination boldly concluding that we must, "reconceptualize the roles of young people throughout society." (Kurth-Schai, 1988) More so, Paulo Freire's revolutionary exposure of the reality that the structure, processes and politics of school are oppressive to many learners is more relevant today than ever. (2004) However, despite all these years of sage voices and students changing, schools have not done a very good job of listening, let alone responding to these challenges and engaging with students as problem-solvers instead of problems to be solved.

Lots of people have wrestled with understanding why students continuously change so much, and how schools can stay relevant, including Rousseau, Froebel, Montessori and Dewey. Social forces like media infiltration, commercialism and technology have all been cited as sources that have changed the experience of learning in today's schools. Critical insights reveal deep concerns about the effects of marketplace commercialism and neoliberalism on schools. (Giroux, 1989)

However, as researchers, philosophers and educators search for answers, the drivers who fuel these changes have largely been ignored: students themselves. Collectively, we seem to not understand that all students, no matter their age, race, socio-economic background, culture or gender, are not just humans-in-the-making who merely echo and mirror adult concepts of them. (Kohn, 1993) Instead, they are human beings right now who have the capacities to embrace the world around them and within them. Instead of simply doing schools *to* students and *for* students, adults need to embrace the notion of educating *with* students as partners. With their ideas, concerns, wisdom and actions in present throughout the process, adults need to understand and negotiate why, how, when, where and what students learn. As Cook-Sather noted,

> "Since the advent of formal education in the United States both the educational system and that system's every reform have been premised on adult's notions of how education should be conceptualized and practiced. There is something fundamentally amiss about building and rebuilding an entire system without consulting at any point those it is ostensibly designed to serve." (2002)

Make no mistake: Students have one essential role in schools, and that is the position of learner. However, it is essential to see that role in context of the society that makes it matter. Like Dewey almost a century before him, Giroux believes, "In any democratic society, education should be viewed as a right, not an entitlement." (Giroux, 2014) Meaningful Student Involvement is a logical extension of that right, as it positions students as active, engaged (lowercase d) democrats within the education system. It helps define *new* ways students can learn in schools, while they become engaged in positively changing schools. The old ways have not worked well for some time, and their effectiveness is diminishing every day.

Traditional student involvement has taken several forms, including student government, extra-curricular programs and athletic activities. In some of the most progressive classrooms, schools and education agencies across the country, those activities have been extended to engage students in special committees, advisory boards and other opportunities. The dilemma with most all those activities is simple: It is disconnected from the essential role of students in schools. Devoid of classroom credit or meaningful evaluations of student learning, these activities dissuade most the student body in many schools from participating. Informal surveying conducted in many of the schools SoundOut has worked in has shown that fewer than twenty-five percent of all students in a school participate in any substantive school-based activity outside of the classroom.

Adding to that conundrum is the reality that many students do not connect with classroom learning topics, teachers or outcomes in any significant way. That is not a recent development: in the 1920s, Dewey proposed that schools design relevant learning opportunities for all students, which eventually led to the creation of career and technical education classes in many high schools. Dewey believed teachers do not merely "teach" as much as they help students learn and build on their experiences. (1948)

My conceptualization of Meaningful Student Involvement is ironically also informed by George Counts, who addressed Dewey directly by charging educators with implementing "truly progressive education" by engaging all students in learning through social change. (1978) Meaningful Student Involvement will drastically transform the educative process by situating students as the owners of their learning, partners in the education system, and fully engaged citizens throughout our democracy (Rudduck & Fielding, 2006). This meets McLaren's expectation that,

> "Schools should be sites for social transformation and emancipation, places where students are educated not only to be critical thinkers, but also to view the world as a place where their actions might make the difference." (2003)

By taking action throughout education, students can become critically inquisitive, culturally aware and civically adept. This is the ultimate expression of an engaged democratic education in a time of utmost need. (Giroux, 2014) It also elevates schools to the position that Kohn (1993) proposed when he wrote that students,

> "...after all, are not just adults-in-the-making. They are people whose current needs and rights and experiences must be taken seriously. Put it this way: students should not only be trained to live in a democracy when they grow up; they should have the chance to live in one today."

While some schools have adjusted their subject areas for modern interests, a large number still have not. Leadership, technology, modern politics and contemporary culture courses are not the norm in American high schools; worse still, these are rare topics in middle schools, and almost completely missing from elementary schools. Even in schools where these adjustments have happened, there is still often a crisis of disinterest among students.

Most activities that proponent student involvement suffer a *crisis of purpose.* Students and teachers alike do not know what these activities represent or demonstrate. Because of that, there is no real purpose for many students to become engaged throughout their education. This majority does not seek the rewards of traditional student leadership activities, and they do not yearn for the acknowledgment of being "star" students. This is the same majority of students who go to school just because somebody tells them to. Their moms or dads, girlfriends or best friends, or the truancy officer is there to remind them that they are not in it alone.

The good news is the answers to these problems have been shared no fewer than ten million times over the last one hundred years. The challenge is that we—educators, administrators, politicians, researchers, advocates, parents and voters—still have not learned to listen to them. The voices offering the solutions do not offer them in simple ways; rather, the answers are complex and idealistic, opportunistic and often inconvenient. Sometimes the answers present themselves as very sophisticated, substantive transformations; others, they are seemingly menial and insignificant to the people listening. However, each of these answers is a solution to the challenges schools face.

Where do these elusive "silver bullets" come from? The tests where unexceptional students performed exceptionally were intended to be an answer. Classes that ended up with high attendance and low achievement were supposed to be an answer. Teachers that every student loved, hallways where students want to "hang out", clothes that lots of students *wanted* to wear were all supposed to be wonderful answers. However, in a more complicated way, every time a student has griped about class, they have shared a solution. Every frustrated crumpling of paper, every exhibition of crying and storming from a room, every hallway fight, and even every school shooting has presented a solution to the challenges of schools.

Perhaps the most frustrating aspect of these solutions is that they have not been so convenient to us. Rather than staring us in the in the face, they are staring out the window or down at their cell phone - where they are often text messaging a friend about how boring this class is. So, it is not clear how to learn from student voice. However, there is an answer in the words and actions of students.

Somehow, somewhere along the way many adults forgot to listen. Or we actively plugged our ears. Worst still, a small group of adults, the masters of education, learned how to manipulate student voices, turning them into opportunities to strengthen our assumptions, keep our jobs, maintain our schools, and build our reputations. Perhaps most heinously, a small (and actively growing) group of adults learned how to use student voice *against* students, using their words, deeds and ideas to keep them from becoming active partners throughout the educational process.

Around the world, more educators, researchers, students and advocates are rallying for Meaningful Student Involvement than ever before. They are studying the phenomenon in Washington state (Chopra, 2014), China (Yang, 2010), Brazil (Dotta & Ristow, 2011), Nepal (Dahal, 2014), Kenya (Chemutai & Chumba, 2014), and beyond. They are implementing programs in the United Kingdom, Australia and South Africa. They are facilitating programs across Vermont (Beattie, 2012), Alberta and Colorado. So many people are doing so much. Cook-Sather identified three assumptions underlying much of this work:

- Students have unique perspectives on learning, teaching and schooling;
- Their insights warrant not only the attention but also the responses of adults; and,
- They should be afforded opportunities to actively shape their education. (Cook-Sather, 2006)

To find out what students think is meaningful, start by listening to student voice. Not just the token few, either: surround yourself in the muck and mire of daily student lives. Stand in the hallways and just listen. Go to the cafeteria and simply hear. Make provocative statements to groups of students and soak up the responses, positive and challenging. But do not stop there, because your job is more essential than that. Adults and students who carry the mantle of Meaningful Student Involvement are charged with being more than friends, more than colleagues, but actual partners. Learn why throughout the rest of this book.

3 REASONS STUDENTS DISENGAGE	
1. **TEACHING**	Students are taught to disengage. Between teachers who are too busy to care, or who are too overwhelmed to focus on them, and lawmakers too beholden to give students the supports they need to succeed, many students are actually taught to disengage. That come from the culture surrounding them, including TV, the internet and music; schools they attended, including teachers and curriculum; and the social safety net that allows them to disengage.
2. **RESIGNATION**	Some teachers have given up on many students. Driven by standardized testing, mandatory evaluations, pre-scripted programs, and byzantine policies, many school social workers, teachers, elected education officials, and others have given up on many of the students they're supposed to serve. Instead of believing "students are the future", they treat students like merely numbers to achieve testing goals, and as ineffective contributors to the economy, civic society, and world around them.
3. **FAILURE**	Traditional schools fail today's students. Classroom curriculum, testing and assessment, and even traditional extracurricular activities fail to teach many students today. Too reliant on student complacency and obedience, many schools fail to foster student thinking, implement accurate strategies, or create successful cultures that engage students. This is happening in epidemic proportions in many, many communities, especially affecting low-income youth and youth of color.

Table 3. 3 Reasons Students Disengage

Chapter 8: Shared Responsibility

Meaningful Student Involvement is a shared responsibility of every adult involved anywhere throughout the education system. This ranges from classroom teachers to district office receptionists, state superintendents to school building managers. Each person with any authority of any kind within a school is responsible for engaging students as partners in learning, teaching and leaders (Conzemius & O'Neill, 2001; Beattie, 2012; Mitra, 2008). Table 15 introduces these roles.

When educators, administrators and other adults throughout the education system own Meaningful Student Involvement in this way, they can then share responsibility with students themselves. Students should not be held responsible for Meaningful Student Involvement if adults do not first take ownership. That does not mean they cannot take responsibility; it does mean that if students advocate, clamor, or otherwise agitate for it, adults throughout education are inherently and explicitly obligated by their professional ethics to act upon these calls (Mockler & Groundwater-Smith, 2015). That does not mean adults cannot begin without students' calls for Meaningful Student Involvement, either.

As it is launched and underway, Meaningful Student Involvement continuously acknowledges the diversity of students by authorizing them to represent their own ideas, opinions, knowledge and experiences throughout education. It does not accomplish this passively, either: instead, educators are challenged to constantly address their own biases in engaging student voice. These biases are illustrated in Figure 21 of this book. By doing this, Meaningful Student Involvement practitioners can substantively acknowledge what Fielding and Rudduck identified as the three main tensions in this work: power relations between teachers and students; the commitment to authenticity; and the principle of inclusiveness. (Rudduck & Fielding, 2006)

The authority students inherently have presents students with the ability to tell their own stories in their own language and abilities. Authorization is one difference between engaging students as partners and simply involving students (Cook-Sather, 2002). Simple involvement is not inherently meaningful for students. This involvement is typical throughout the history of schooling, and because of that, schools and the entire education system need new frameworks through which to view learning, teaching and leadership (Smyth, 2006). These frameworks are provided by Meaningful Student Involvement.

Students need to be partners throughout the entirety of the education system, and not just in a theoretical way. (Fielding, 2001; Jackson, 2005) To experience involvement in a meaningful way, students need to work alongside adults as co-planners, co-researchers, co-teachers, co-evaluators, co-decision-makers and co-advocates with adults. Infused throughout each of these roles is co-learning, co-creating and critical thinking. The frameworks for Meaningful Student Involvement can be realized in the entire education system, from the individual classroom to building leadership, district administration to the state board of education and the chief school officer for the state, to state legislators and the Congress, to the national education department and the leader of the country. (Mitra, 2003 & 2008; Holdsworth, 2000a; 2000b; Brasof, 2015) The United Nations, all nations and every single government and entity providing education, provisioning learning, administering school support, or educating educators can and should be promoting Meaningful Student Involvement.

When asked, students consistently describe how they arrive to obtuse, confusing notions about the purpose of school. (What Kids Can Do, 2003; Corbett & Wilson, 1995; Klein, 2003) Instead of addressing their confusion, well-meaning adults routinely employ the *means* of schooling without identifying the *ends*; they educate students without knowing why. In the meantime, schools position students to receive this education without ever exploring *why* these things should matter *with* students themselves. Developmental psychology has shown clearly that from school age forward young people of all ages have the capacity to develop sophisticated understandings of the educational undertakings they participate in. (Mitra, 2004) This book highlights many examples of this. Unfortunately, policy and practice in schools today have not kept up with that research, and the practices are still largely anomalous.

Research reveals that the success of school transformation will be demonstrated through students' reflections about schools. We will know schools are improving when students demonstrate the outcomes we seek, and this will be revealed in academic achievement. (Comfort, Giorgi & Moody, 1997) That reality alone shows how the role of the student within the education system is that of the essential partner. (Toshalis & Nakkula, 2012) The most direct avenue to Student/Adult Partnerships is Meaningful Student Involvement. (SooHoo, 1993)

As a research-driven model, Meaningful Student Involvement effectively reveals the evolving capacities of children and youth in the environments where they spend the large majority of their days: schools. (Fletcher, 2003b) It centers on developing constructivist approaches for students to participate in roles as researchers, planners, teachers, evaluators, systemic decision-makers, and advocates in schools, for schools. Adults in schools, including teachers, administrators, and support staff, as well as parents, are central to Meaningful Student Involvement. By building partnerships for better curriculum, classroom management, and formal school improvement, Meaningful Student Involvement recognizes the necessity of engaging all adults within the learning environment as partners to students. Focused professional development for staff and learning opportunities integrated throughout the school day for students allow the whole school to change.

By reinforcing critical thinking, problem solving, civic participation, and an appreciation for diverse perspectives, Meaningful Student Involvement allows students to apply essential "soft skills" learning to real world issues that affect them. It represents a shift away from the perspective of students as passive recipients of adult-driven education systems by positioning young people in education-related environments as learners, teachers, and leaders. See Table 22 in this book for examples of what that can look like. The model provides schools with concrete, customizable tools to do this, too. Meaningful Student Involvement is not just an idea whose time has come—it is a new reality that schools must face.

Chapter 9: Transforming Schools

In the confined spaces of schools today, we may be accidentally nurturing myopic perspectives within many students. Devoid opportunities to deeply interact, assess, critique and transform the world around them, large numbers of learners are living within themselves. They are not learning the value of belonging, place-based identification, or connectedness to something larger than themselves. Through my projects in schools, I have heard more and more students interpreting their school experiences as negative, limiting and authoritarian. None of these perceptions are necessarily wrong, either. They reflect actual experiences students are having right now.

Meaningful Student Involvement offers practical, observable frameworks that actively foster Student/Adult Partnerships throughout the education system. It acknowledges the complexities of life by infusing lived experience throughout schools. It does this because all learners have an innate desire to mold their learning and the world they live in. No matter what their ability or socio-economic status, starting at the youngest young age all learners everywhere are learning what matters, why it matters, and how it should matter to them. This is an important part of every young person's growth. However, by increasingly educating students in the vacuum of consumerism and routinely segregating them from their larger communities because of their ages, schools are defeating this important growth.

There are many ways to transform schools today. Engaging students as partners may be the most direct route to improving student achievement though. As Nieto found (1994), when students begin the process of becoming partners, they actively move from being passive recipients. Connecting with adults by sharing themselves as full humans, students feel investment and ownership they would not otherwise, causing them to attach to the learning and teaching experience that much more effectively. Perhaps more important though, Meaningful Student Involvement actively combats student isolation, age segregation and the traditional perception of schools as insular, disengaged institutions unaffected by the larger systems and communities to which they belong. As Counts said more than 80 years, ago,

> "Place the child in a world of his own and you take from him the most powerful incentives to growth and achievement. Perhaps one of the greatest tragedies of contemporary society lies in the fact that the child is becoming increasingly isolated from the serious activities of adults... Until school and society are bound together by common purposes the program of education will lack both meaning and vitality." (Counts, 1978)

Meaningful Student Involvement unites schools and society together in building students' commitment to education, community and democracy. It does this by powerfully, purposefully and positively injecting students as partners throughout all elements of the education system (Kurth-Schai, 1988; Cervone & Cushman, 2002; Holcomb, 2006). Table 15 shows exactly what that can look like.

This is why transforming the education system is an aim of Meaningful Student Involvement. Because of that, we cannot address it as a giant, ambiguous blob that is hard to see and even harder to become engaged within. It means seeing the parameters and possibilities of the system, understanding its form, function and outcomes, and working with intention to foster

Student/Adult Partnerships to meet Teddy Roosevelt's challenge of doing what they can, where they are, with what they have.

This means seeing everyone who could potentially be involved in Student/Adult Partnerships, including, but are not limited to: students, teachers, parents, student support staff, non-certificated staff, building leaders, school coaches, district administrators, district leaders, school board members, state/provincial administrators, state/provincial leaders federal administrators researchers, advocates/activists, independent consultants, trainers education-focused nonprofit staff, other nonprofit staff, and others.

It means understanding all the places where Meaningful Student Involvement could happen, including, but are not limited to: classrooms, hallways, extracurricular spaces, cafeterias, building leadership offices, teacher offices, sports facilities, whole entire school buildings, district administration, district boards of education, district leadership offices, provincial/state leadership positions, provincial/state administration offices, federal administration offices, federal leadership positions, local/national/international education-related nonprofits, and in the homes of students and adults in education.

The activities throughout the education system that can be driven through Student/Adult Partnerships are so vast that its almost purposeless to begin listing them. However, it is important to note that the first activity is always learning. From there, activities include, but are not limited to: school planning, classroom teaching, school evaluation, testing and assessment, policy-making, research, curriculum, classroom management, dropping out, restorative justice, sports and much more. There is a longer list that looks more in-depth further on in this book.

There are more than those parts to Meaningful Student Involvement though, and that's why we address the entirety of the education system.

A. New Vision

Although they could serve as essential partners in schools, students are not routinely, systemically, or systematically engaged in the process of school transformation. Instead, their role is continuously relegated to that of "recipient." To better relate to their out-of-school lives, schools must reposition all students from being mere recipients of pre-constructed knowledge delivery vehicles towards being co-creators of explorative educational processes. Students must have more substantive positions for learning in order for *any* school transformation to be effective. This makes Meaningful Student Involvement a necessity for the future of education.

The greatest challenge facing schools today is not simply the achievement gap. It is the crisis of disconnection. It is disconnection from learning, from curriculum, from peers, from adults; it is disconnection from relevance, rigor, and relationships; it is disconnection from self and community; it is systemic disconnection. While it does not only affect schools, is does plague schools in a special way.

The cure to disconnection is meaningfulness. Defined as "the quality of having great value or significance", just about anything can be meaningful in our lives. After conducting a two-year long action research project in Washington State's public schools, I collected more than 3,000 examples of times when learners said they experienced meaningfulness in schools. (Fletcher, 2001) It was from this basis that I began developing my model of Meaningful Student Involvement.

Meaningful Student Involvement happens when the roles of students are actively re-aligned from being the passive recipients of schooling to becoming active partners throughout the educational process. Meaningful Student Involvement can happen throughout education, including the classroom, the counselor's office, hallways, after school programs, district board of education offices, at the state or federal levels, and in other places that directly affect the students' educational experience. Real learning and deep purpose take form through Meaningful Student Involvement, often showing immediate impacts on the lives of students by authorizing them to have powerful, purposeful opportunities to impact their own learning and the lives of others.

Every school can be fully meaningful for every student all the time. Anything less than that is selling our students short, and our society, too.

B: Fully Meaningful Schools

How meaningful can schools be? The following is a brief examination of the best practices adults and students are creating, implementing, sustaining, critiquing, and expanding upon in order to herald Meaningful Student Involvement around the world. They are all explored further throughout this book.

Foster Meaningful Involvement for ALL Learners

Some buildings are eliminating tokenistic student involvement opportunities entirely. All students in all grades in all schools need to experience meaningful involvement as a practical, tangible component of their daily educational experience, without the tokenistic gesture of representation and the passive activity of voting being at the middle of their day. Instead, concrete experiences of dialogue, peer-driven conflict resolution and interactive learning are infused and integrated throughout learning across the democratic culture. I explore what this can look like in Table 6 of this book.

No More Tokenism

An increasing number of educators understand that there should be no single seats for high school students on building-, district-, or state-level committees. Instead, all school committees at all levels should be operated in a way that deliberately engages all students as equal partners, including using meeting techniques that are engaging, and having equitable positions on those committees, including numbers and representative power. (Thomson, 2011)

Student/Adult Decision-Making Rules

When educators learn to use school rules as interactive educative tools for determining social interactions schools can engage students and adults collectively in determining appropriate outcomes for infractions.

Student-Driven Learning

Self-guided educational practices are already the norm in some "alternative" schools; let's make this practice normative throughout all levels of schools. There is a possibility in the relationships between all students and teachers to have all K-12 students design their own individual academic programs, and to utilize those experiences as educational and democratic processes. Rather than seeing this as a situation where adults are "handing over the keys to the car" to a 16-year-old, let's use student-driven learning in a constructivist fashion from kindergarten forward.

Constructivist Democratic Learning

Engaging students takes a deliberate process that should begin in their youngest years and extend through high school. It should build on students' previous knowledge and be imbued by their cultural norms. In kindergarten learners can facilitate peer-to-peer conflict resolution, personal decision-making and democratic group learning experiences; by fourth, fifth and sixth grades students can conduct original research on their schools, complete regular self- and teacher-evaluations, and participate in building-wide decision-making activities; by high school young people should have established clear and equitable relationships with adults throughout schools in order to participate in full Student/Adult Partnerships.

Reciprocal Accountability

The era of adults measuring student achievement without some form of mutual measurement is over. When some teachers started mocking the power of students in the early 2000s teachers across the nation flipped out, finding their names and classrooms rated by anonymous users calling themselves students. Educators still haven't identified a way *en masse* to use tools like this as teaching opportunities, but there has been some headway. And while assessments of student behavior have often been focused on negative perspectives, schools are finding ways to acknowledge positive student behavior and learning through student-led conferencing. So, there is progress towards reciprocity- but educators must continue to move forward with students as partners.

Full-Court Press

All student expression, positive, negative and otherwise, must be allowed space and opportunity within schools, and used towards teaching and learning. By embracing diverse and divergent student voice, educators can embrace the potential of learning led by students and learn new ways to relate to, teach, and encourage themselves and everyone in our communities. This is a full-court press for Meaningful Student Involvement.

Equity and Equality

A common assumption among educators is that all student involvement should be actualized as complete equality. However, equity is often the just, fair and righteous route to take. Equity is about fairness in schools, equality of access in learning, recognizing inequalities throughout education and taking steps to address them. It is about changing school culture and structure to ensure equally accessible to all students.

Make Meaning from Life

Curriculum should be based in every students' experiences of living their daily lives as well as preparing them for tomorrow so that schools meet the purpose of enriching the present as well as enlightening the future. This validates the ideas, experiences, wisdom and knowledge young people have, ultimately positioning their voices as central throughout learning, which in turn reinforces the depth and meaning of democracy. (Brennan, 1996) This will secure learning for life, and a commitment to democracy that is unparalleled.

Public Or Nothing At All

Democracy is inherently meaningful. Private schools and charter schools can be blatantly antithetical to the democratic levers of public control over public schools, as they generally operate with privately elected boards of directors or fully autonomous presidents. Admittedly, public schools generally behave as if they're out of the purview of the masses; however, forceful, peaceful and powerful advocacy by students and parents will ultimately lead to stronger controls.

There are many other ways Meaningful Student Involvement is happening in schools around the world today. As an introduction though, this highlighted some of the best practices. The next chapter shares some essential understandings that should be in place for these actions to happen.

ESSENTIAL QUESTIONS FOR MEANINGFUL STUDENT INVOLVEMENT

- Do you believe students are fully competent to be co-creators of their own learning? Teaching? Leadership?
- Do you understand that students can change the world *right now* and not merely in some unforeseeable future?
- Do you see how students need skills that go far beyond the content of most curricula?
- Do you believe that students want to learn, but often they lack the what they need to spark their passion as life-long learners?
- Do you understand that students have more than a voice? That they have energy and actions that can benefit everyone throughout education, and they should be engaged?
- Do you believe that every student has unique talents, wisdom, knowledge, interests, opinions and ideas that should inform schools and the function of education?
- Do you understand the value of students developing their metacognitive skills and make their thinking visible through Meaningful Student Involvement?
- Do you see how all students are creative and can teach adults important things about learning, teaching and leadership throughout the education system?
- Do you believe that, if given the chance and the right support, all students in every school can become more than they ever thought they could be?
- Do you understand that once students begin to see their talents and gifts, have their voices validated, and take action to improve schools they will grow in confidence and ability?
- Do you see that schools should places of joy, engagement, learning and play for all students and all adults?
- Do you believe that all adults throughout the education system could benefit all students more by asking more questions and offering fewer answers?
- Do you understand that all adults throughout education can and should model what learning, failing, grit & perseverance look like for students?
- Do you see why the most important question any adult in any part of the education system can ask any student is, "What do you need?"
- Do you understand why the entirety of every part of education needs to be transparent for students?

* Adapted from Wright, 2013.

Table 4. Essential Questions I. For Essential Questions II, see Table 21.

Part II. Student Voice and Student Engagement

Chapter 10: Introduction

With more and more people increasingly jumping on the bandwagons of student voice and student engagement, it is becoming increasingly important to define, refine and understand what it is that we are talking about. It is important to critically examine the assumptions informing a lot of this conversation and action, as well as the implications, impacts and processes throughout.

Student voice and choice and student engagement are an entryway into Meaningful Student Involvement. However, they shouldn't be seen as the beginning and end of the conversation. The larger topic at hand is the role of students in schools and whether the education system should continue to promote students being passive recipients of adult-driven learning. See Table 22 in this book for examples of what that can look like.

Unfortunately, in many ways the ideas of student voice and choice and student engagement are being used as a surrogate for actual Meaningful Student Involvement. This happens when adults...

• Insinuate that student voice and choice is the best thing, everywhere, all the time;
• Provide students with limited opportunities to share their voices or limited opportunities to make choices;
• Take away the context for why voice and choice matter by misapplying strategies;
• Assume that student voice and choice are the key to learning in classrooms and beyond.

When teachers decide that students should determine what, how, when, where, why and with whom they are learning, they are reinforcing a notion of power, control and authority in learning and teaching. Suddenly, students are being told it's their power, while in reality, control still rests in the hands of adults who have long been answered with "leave it to the professionals," meaning administrators and policy-makers.

A lot of well-meaning people are throwing around phrases without really understanding what they are talking about. People are using student voice as a synonym for student engagement. All the while, they are discussing activities that are the exclusive domain of either concept as if they were. That is problematic for a few reasons. Before this book examines why that's the case, the following several chapters examine research-determined definitions for each term.

Chapter 11: Defining Student Voice

For many years, researchers and practitioners defined student voice according to their own intentions for the activities and outcomes. It was often along the lines of student agency and purpose in education, or otherwise a movement towards action and increased abilities for learners (Mockler & Groundwater-Smith, 2015). This chapter explores different meanings and understandings of student voice, and presents my own definition of the term.

Mitra wrote that student voice is, "the focus on the design, facilitation and improvement of learning." Similarly, a high school principal in Seattle suggested, "[Student voice is] the active opportunity for students to express their opinions and make decisions regarding the planning, implementation, and evaluation of their learning experiences." (Rogers, 2004) One of my longtime allies, Dr. Dennis Harper of the international nonprofit organization GenYes, built a classroom program specifically designed to empower students. In a paper about the topic he wrote, "Student voice is giving students the ability to influence learning to include policies, programs, contexts and principles." (Harper, 2000)

Researchers have taken the concept in many directions, identifying many implications, ideas and avenues for student voice. One suggested that student voice is "literal, metaphorical, and political" (Britzman, 1992). This allows us to understand several things: What a student says counts as student voice; What a student does is student voice, and; The meanings behind what students say and do are student voice.

In 2004, SoundOut began defining student voice as "the individual and collective perspective and actions of young people within the context of learning and education." (SoundOut, 2004) After working with the schools I had, I discovered this could include, but is not limited to, active or passive participation, knowledge, voting, wisdom, activism, beliefs, service, opinions, leadership, and ideas. Student voice reflects identity, and comes from a person's experiences, ideals, and knowledge. As my experiences working to promote student voice expanded, I found that any person who participates in a process of learning, including every single student in every classroom in any grade, has a voice that should be engaged in schools. That means that student voice is for pre-kindergarten students, elementary students, junior high and middle school students, and high school students (Knowles & Brown, 2000). It can also come from students of color, low-income students, low-achieving students, high-performing students, ESL/ELL students, special needs students, and gifted students. Table 10 shows initial ways this can happen.

Continuing my examination of student voice, I found a variety of literature suggesting that student voice has locations throughout the curriculum (Grace M. , 1999), culture (Mitra, 2003), climate (Libbey, 2004; Galloway, Pope, & Osberg, 2007) the entire education community (Fielding, 2001), and when appropriately dismantling the school/community binary, throughout life in general (Alvermann & Eakle, 2007). Armed with that knowledge, my own experience showed me that since every adult working in education effectively has authority over students, every adult effectively has an ethical responsibility to listen to student voice. (Freire, 1998; Mitra, Frick, & Crawford, 2011) That includes classroom teachers, building leaders, school support staff, school board members, district and state school leaders education agency officials, education policy-makers, curriculum makers, education researchers, and politicians. (Joselowsky F. , 2007) My experience with student voice left my disenchanted though, as many adults seemed pleased to simply listen to student voice and then talk about student voice, reading reports and sitting around fishbowl-style conversations between students. They were not obligated to do anything with student voice, and as much research has shown, this is the norm in this topic (Mockler & Groundwater-Smith, 2015).

When brought together, these understandings of student voice cast a massive net over a lot of different assumptions, presumptions and biases. The challenge of each of these different perspectives is that none of them holds all the others, and because of that, all of them exclude something else.

Informed by all these definitions, along with my experience, I define student voice as any expression of any student, anywhere at any time about learning, schools and education. (Fletcher, 2014)

A. Social Justice

Growing up, my family experienced situational poverty and occasional homelessness. In my teenage years, once we had settled in the Midwestern United States, I was hired by a neighborhood nonprofit to co-teach in a summer program for young people who lived in Omaha, Nebraska's public housing projects. The program, called "You're The Star!", was developed alongside Augusto Boal's notable approach called "Theatre of the Oppressed." My director, Idu Maduli, became a lifelong inspiration whom I sought to mold my work with young people after. Idu was Omaha's premier African American theatre director, and taught classes citywide for years.

Idu taught me a lot, not the least of which being a love of learning and teaching. I developed a deep appreciation for the history of the predominately African American community where I eventually grew up for a decade. I also learned the elements of social justice from my work with Idu. Social justice, which is the deliberate empowerment of oppressed people within a system of intentional or coincidental injustice, can be fostered throughout education in many ways. (Banks, 1998) Through its focus on social justice, Meaningful Student Involvement holds multicultural education at its heart.

From my young efforts in social justice education, I transitioned to youth development programs with historically disengaged children and youth. Working in out-of-school learning programs in low-income communities and communities of color, the places I mentored, tutored and taught often reflected my own upbringing in a socially, economically and emotionally depressed community. However, I was enthralled to facilitate student empowerment outside and within the education system. In my first AmeriCorps term, I worked with Kurdish and Iraqi refugee students in the Midwest. For the first time, I observed the elements that made successful student learning, and discovered intersections leading to student empowerment. Since then I continued exploring the topic, and today, I understand that student empowerment is the attitudinal, structural, and cultural process whereby learners gain the ability, authority, and agency to make decisions and implement change in their own lives and the lives of other people, including students and adults. (Vavrus & Fletcher, 2006)

That centers student empowerment and social justice in the heart of Meaningful Student Involvement. I hold that the frameworks, considerations, concepts and applications explored throughout this book can affect every student in every school across every nation and around the world. As several others have posited, Student/Adult Partnerships are student empowerment and social justice in action. (Beane & Apple, 1995; Cervone & Cushman, 2002; Beaudoin, 2005; Mitra, 2006; Fielding, 2010; Beattie, 2012)

Considering my own background, it should come as no surprise that I merged my undergraduate studies in critical pedagogy with my graduate and professional studies focused on student voice. After studying works by Paulo Freire (Freire, 2004), Michelle Fine (Fine & Weis, 2003), bell hooks (hooks, 1994) and Peter McLaren (McLaren, 2003), Henry Giroux (Giroux, 2013) and others, I began examining some of my basic assumptions about student voice. I explored the reasons why student voice is so frequently qualified by adults, and saw how adults selectively choose which students to listen to and which to ignore, consciously and unconsciously. Looking for the faces of the low-income young people and youth of color I worked with throughout my career, I saw very few of them being invited to share their voices. Yet, as these young people (myself included) got in fights, cheated on tests, vandalized classrooms and dropped out of school, I also heard them call out. This was reinforced by other critical literature, too. (McDermott, 1998; Rubin & Silva, 2003; Cook-Sather, 2007)

However, it was my mentor Henry Giroux whose definition of voice resolved these differences for me. According to McLaren, Giroux says voice "refers to the multifaceted and interlocking set of meanings through which students actively engage in a dialogue with one another." (McLaren, 2003) Together, McLaren and Giroux built an early understanding of the potential for student voice to affect social justice in education. (Giroux & McLaren, 1982) Wanting to simplify and expand common understanding of student voice, I believe it is important to hold the intent of Giroux's definition by holding a lot of different ideas and critical conceptions inside of the term.

This is all meant to illustrate the various ways our concepts of social justice are informed. The term can be intensely personal and even private for some people; strongly academic and institutional for others. Neither is wrong, and both are right: To truly understand social justice deeply, we must personally identify with it and be informed by others' experiences, too.

Social justice and student voice meet at the intersection of Meaningful Student Involvement, providing powerful, positive and purpose-filled opportunities for historically disengaged students to drive active, substantive and transformative change throughout education. Who can ask for more?

Chapter 12: Defining Student Engagement

Student engagement is increasingly seen as an indicator of successful classroom instruction (Kenny, Kenny, & Dumont, 2005), and is increasingly valued as an outcome of school improvement activities. Students are engaged when they are attracted to their work, persist in despite challenges and obstacles, and take visible delight in accomplishing their work. (Schlecty, 1994) Student engagement also refers to a "student's willingness, need, desire and compulsion to participate in, and be successful in, the learning process." (Boma & et al, 1997)

In several studies, student engagement has been identified as a desirable trait in schools; however, there is little consensus among students and educators as to how to define it. (Farmer-Dougan & McKinney, 2001) Engagement is used as a synonym or closely aligned concept with participation, motivation, attachment, self-regulated behavior, anti-social behavior, thoughtfulness, ownership, belonging, connectedness, and investment in school. (Fredricks, Blumenfeld, & Paris, 2004) In my practice, have even seen the phrase student engagement used synonymously with obedience, compliance and adult control.

Other definitions usually include a psychological and behavioral component. Student engagement is used to discuss students' attitudes towards school, while student disengagement identifies withdrawing from school in any significant way. (Douglas, 2003) Several studies have shown that student engagement overlaps with, but is not the same as, student motivation. (Sharan, Shachar , & Levine, 1999)

The term student engagement has been used to depict students' willingness to participate in routine school activities, such as attending classes, submitting required work, following teachers' direction in class, and performing well on standardized tests. (Brewster & Fager, 2000; Chapman, 2003) That includes participating in the activities offered as part of the school program (Natriello, 1984) and student participation in school transformation activities. (Fletcher, 2005a)

[Students] who are engaged show sustained behavioral involvement in learning activities accompanied by a positive emotional tone. They select tasks at the border of their competencies, initiate action when given the opportunity, and exert intense effort and concentration in the implementation of learning tasks; they show generally positive emotions during ongoing action, including enthusiasm, optimism, curiosity, and interest. (Skinner & Belmont, 1993)

Another study identified five indicators for student engagement in college. They included the level of academic challenge, active and collaborative learning, student-faculty interaction, enriching education experiences and a supportive learning environment. (Kenny, Kenny, & Dumont, 2005) My research has demonstrated that student engagement is fostered through the active and sustained infusion of student voice throughout the educational environment, including learning, teaching and leadership in schools. (Fletcher, 2005a)

Indicators of the absence of student engagement include unexcused absences from classes, cheating on tests, and damaging school property. (Chapman, 2003) The opposite of engagement is disaffection. Disaffected [students] are passive, do not try hard, and give up easily in the face of challenges... [they can] be bored, depressed, anxious, or even angry about their presence in the classroom; they can be withdrawn from learning opportunities or even rebellious towards teachers and classmates. (Skinner & Belmont, 1993)

Despite many educators' insistence, student disengagement not caused by students themselves. Instead, it is the result of ineffectual teaching, poor learning environments (including climate and culture), and student disaffection, among several other factors that I summarize in Tables 3 and 5, and explore more in Chapter 12.

Students can be engaged in one place, at one time, in one activity with one other person; or in several places with many people addressing several issues. What engages one student might cause disaffection in the next, leading to disengagement. Recognizing these variations among activities is essential for any school that seeks to engage learners, since their interests, abilities, desires and affection are as diverse as they are. Student engagement is more diverse than many sources currently recognize.

A. Requirements

In listing their definitions of student engagement, many studies list requirements that must exist for student engagement to occur. These studies consistently imply that educators actively create the conditions that foster student engagement. The first step to whole-school improvement in the area of student engagement is for the entire building faculty to share a definition of student engagement (Berardi & Gerschick, 2002), and ensure it reflects both the perceptions of students and adults. The late researcher Richard Strong, a key advocate for student engagement, found there are many steps to ensure student engagement happening throughout education. They include adults—including teachers, principals, and others—clearly articulating learning criteria and providing students with clear, immediate, and constructive feedback; clear and systematic demonstrations to students of the skills they need to be successful, and; demonstration of engagement in learning as a valuable aspect of their personalities. (Strong, Silver, & Robinson, 1995)

Relationships between students and adults in schools, and among students themselves, are a critical factor of student engagement. Students know what teachers think of them, and their relationship clearly affects their achievement and behavior in school, especially when they think teachers expect them to fail. (Wilson & Corbett, 2007; Quaglia, Fox, & Corso, 2003) This is especially true among students considered to be at-risk and without other positive adult interaction. (Tyler & Boelter, 2008; McCombs & Pope, 1994) There are several strategies for developing these relationships, including acknowledging student voice, increasing intergenerational equity between students and adults in schools, and sustaining Student/Adult Partnerships throughout the learning environment. (Fletcher, 2005b) A variety of teaching approaches can enhance student engagement to varying effects. While teacher-centered methods and content focused methods seem counter-intuitive, they can work. (Turley, 1994) Obviously, student-centered and interactive or participative methods create conditions that give rise to student engagement. (Mitra, 2003) Some educators and instruments identify dozens of everyday indicators of student engagement that are observable, including hand-raising, technology usage and verbal interactions with peers. Focusing on students spending time on-task, these approaches can lead educators to overemphasize engagement as a teaching strategy. However, they can foster mock participation, leading students to pretend to be on-task while they are not really engaged in learning. (Slavin, 2003; O'Neill, Horner, & Albi, 1996) Kohn observed that research consistently shows "...the amount of time a student spends on a task 'is not so consistently related to achievement as it may seem." (Kohn, 2007)

The reality is that student engagement is not the measure many educators believe it is. In the 1980s, Fred Newman's longitudinal research on high schools uncovered that student engagement is not an indicator of academic achievement. (Newmann, Wehlage, & Lamborn, 1992) This means that a student can be deeply engaged in a topic, whether history or physics or Spanish, and still not succeed in learning assessments or evaluation mechanisms. Unfortunately, this finding has seemingly been lost in the sands of time as educators and advocates reach for the kernel of inevitable success through this notion.

B. Assessing Student Engagement

Student engagement is seen as both a way students learn and an outcome from student learning. Assessing student engagement is seen as an essential step towards a school becoming a successful place for student engagement. (Chapman, 2003; Fredricks & al, 2011) Much of these assessments should focus on the abilities of classroom teachers to engage students. Consequently, this has been proposed as an element of teacher certification and is seen as an increasingly essential component of teacher preparation curricula. (Cook-Sather, 2002; Cook-Sather, 2001)

There are concerns that definitions and assessments of student engagement are often exclusive to the values represented by dominant groups within the learning environment where the assessment is conducted. (Hurtado, 1999) Studies have also suggested that gauging student engagement among minority populations within a school is central to a school's overall assessment of student engagement. Relationships between students and adults are one of the best predictors of student engagement (Osterman, 2000), and researchers in these activities have identified several elements of their activities that overlap findings Student/Adult Partnerships. (Cervone & Cushman, 2002; Rubin & Silva, 2003; Cook-Sather, Bovill, & Felten, 2014)

There are several methods to assess student engagement. They include self- reporting, such as surveys, questionnaires, checklists and rating scales. Using direct observations, work sample analyses, and focused case studies are options. (Chapman, 2003) There is an increasing amount of interest and commitment among researchers and educators to use students themselves as assessment designers, evaluators and assessors all focused on student engagement. This handbook will show later that this is aligned with Meaningful Student Involvement. Studies using this "students as evaluators" model consistently report high levels of efficacy and depth in their findings, and researchers consistently attribute these outcomes to the participation of student evaluators. (Fletcher, 2003b)

C. Student Engagement in the Future

Critics have long been concerned about the lack of student engagement in schools. As far back as the 1930s, educational leader John Dewey proposed a radical transformation of schools centering on student engagement. That led to the creation of career and technical education courses over the next ninety years, all in the name of student engagement. (Dewey, Experience and Education, 1938) In the early 1990s, Jonathan Kozol inadvertently suggested this had fallen apart in the current school reform climate, saying, "[W]e have not been listening much to children in these recent years of 'summit conferences' on education, of severe reports, and ominous prescriptions. The voices of children, frankly, have been missing from the whole discussion." (Kozol, 1991) With these longstanding and powerful indictments, it is important that all schools continue to evolve towards becoming more engaging, more meaningful and more powerful learning environments for all students. Meaningful Student Involvement offers many avenues for engaging all learners as partners, ultimately fostering their engagement. Table 6 explores some of these avenues.

3 *MORE* REASONS STUDENTS DISENGAGE	
4. **EXPECTATIONS**	Teachers expect students to change. Rather than acknowledging that students are changing and society is different now, most educators expect students to change to meet today's schools. This is carryover thinking from an old education model, which sought to mold students into the types of learners teachers were capable of teaching. It is a disingenuous perspective, because the future depends on nimble thinking, transformative action and creative realities.
5. **GOALS**	Student engagement isn't really the goal. When most educators talk about student engagement, they're actually talking about student compliance and obedience. They want students to comply with the expectations, values, perspectives, and realities of educators, not those students arrive to schools with. Educators often couch their expectations by talking about activities being student voice and choice, but in reality, they only make programs for students who comply with educators' expectations or desires. This is seeking student conformity, not student engagement.
6. **OVER-ENGAGED**	Students are already engaged. Whether educators want to see it, all students are already engaged right now. They are 100% human, choosing where, how, when, and why they want to engage. They might be engaged in things educators don't approve of, including sex, drugs, and rock-n-roll, or any of a plethora of other activities (smoking, gangs, video games, graffiti, fighting, basketball, driving, etc.). This shows that student engagement isn't limited to things educators approve of them doing; student engagement isn't just compliance. It's any sustained connection a student must education, learning and schools. Simply because students aren't engaged in classes or programs, students aren't automatically disengaged. Instead, educators should meet students where they are at, instead of insisting they come to where adults want them to be.

Table 5. 3 More Reasons Students Disengage

Chapter 13: Student Engagement and Student Voice

It is important to understand that I define student voice differently than most. As I addressed above, student voice is any expression of any learner about anything related to education. Because of this, it can include a student speaking at a school board meeting, co-writing a curriculum with a teacher, or leading a community-wide forum on schools.

However, it can also include students texting the answers to quizzes to each other during class; fighting in the hallways; or smoking behind the school building. These are expressions of learners relating to education. This puts bullying in the same league as student government; research in cahoots with graffiting; and dropping out in league with graduating. Each is an expression of student voice. Student voice does not need adults to agree with it, incite it, define it, or appreciate it; it simply is what it is.

The second thing to understand is that while my definition of student engagement is derived from many others, I define it more simply as any sustained connection a learner experiences in the course of education. With that definition, we can understand how student engagement happens through healthy student/adult relationships, as well as through a positive school climate and meaningful coursework. We can also see how specific subjects, methods, attitudes and cultures can foster student engagement. This definition does not reject negative student engagement either, as students can be sustainably connected to stealing, drugs and alcohol, sex, skipping school, or other activities that are not socially acceptable that can occur within a school environment.

Because of these definitions, it is important to understand that neither student voice or student engagement are inherently positive or negative. Neither one is exclusive to activities adults approve of, needs specific platforms to exist, or is the exclusive domain of one type of student or another. Neither one inherently leads to better grades, more effective performance on standardized tests, or more successful students.

However, looking across activities being promoted as student voice and student engagement today, you might think otherwise. You might think student voice is homogenized and sanitized as the students who they put forward say things to adults just the ways adults want to hear them, when they want to hear them, and from students they want to listen to. You might think student engagement happens only simply when adults get the results they want to see from students. The education media regularly promotes classroom-based approaches that get students to do the things adults want them to with the results adults want to see. While this is one form of student engagement, it is not the only one.

The challenge with all this is that by seeing it all as the same thing, adults and students alike actually diminish, negate and serve to silence and stifle authentic student voice. I explore several pathways to authentic student voice in Table 1. If students are constantly sharing their voices, why aren't adults simply listening to what they are already saying? Is it that we do not really want to hear what they are saying right now? It is as if we want to squeeze their genuine concerns into convenient, bite-sized and acceptable blurbs that fit within our agendas. If students are engaged in many things throughout the schooling experience, why aren't we examining those things for the attributes of learning, teaching and leadership we hope to foster throughout schools? There is so much we can learn from students right now that we are simply ignoring because student voice and student engagement does not currently meet our expectations.

We can do better than this. Meaningful Student Involvement turns the microphone around by making the student the examiner as well as the examined by turning the feedback loop into an engine for school transformation.

---

3 WAYS TO MAKE SCHOOL MEANINGFUL FOR *ALL* LEARNERS

Research shows many ways students become engaged in schools. However, when the goal is Meaningful Student Involvement for all learners, everywhere, all the time, there are specific avenues to ensure meaningfulness.

Mindsets for Educational Success

Our mindsets obviously affect our realities. Many students never learn that, or develop the mindsets they need for educational success. They don't know how their thoughts affect their realities. Many have never seen the formula showing how thoughts drive actions, actions create outcomes, outcomes affect beliefs, and beliefs create thoughts. We can END the dropout crisis by teaching every student what mindsets are and how they work, and help them understand how mindsets affects their lives right now (Dweck, 1999). My research and work in schools has shown me that teaching students about educational mindsets, they can also learn about learning, the education system, about learning, and about Meaningful Student Involvement.

Reinvest Wholly in Every Student.

Activists grapple with ending the school-to-prison pipeline while educational leaders struggle with ending the dropout crisis, at the same time parents wrestle with their kids slipping away and employers aren't getting the employees they want into their workplaces. Reinvesting in every single student means revisiting the idiom that "Students are the future" and acknowledging that isn't enough. We can end the dropout crisis by divesting from standardized testing, mandatory evaluations, pre-scripted student curricula and programs, and byzantine school policies *en masse*. Instead of supporting outdated, outmoded thinking, we'd embrace what Dr. King called "the fierce urgency of now" by reinvesting wholly in every student, everywhere, all the time. (Germond, et al, 2006)

Invigorate Every School, Organization and Community With Meaningful Student Involvement Everywhere, All The Time.

Almost all students everywhere are routinely, habitually, and systematically segregated from adults throughout our society. Their learning, social lives, work opportunities, and cultural settings are separate and apart from adults. We can invigorate everywhere throughout our society with the full involvement of students in everything, all the time.

Table 6. 3 Ways to Make School Meaningful for All Learners

Chapter 14: Student Voice and Meaningful Student Involvement

Figure 1. Options for Students Changing Schools

Now that we understand student voice as an all-encompassing reality in schools, it might be easy to simply side-step its relevance to Meaningful Student Involvement. Don't dismiss it too quickly though, since student voice is the very energy at the heart of Meaningful Student Involvement. For a long time, educators and researchers have used the term student voice to discuss the specific phenomenon of students changing schools. While I differentiated that in-depth throughout this chapter, I want to honor the ideas many have had about student voice in the past by further exploring the connections and disconnections between student voice and Meaningful Student Involvement.

As identified by many writers in the past (Fielding, 2001; Rudduck, Chaplain, & Wallace, 1996; Holdsworth, 2000b; Fine & Weis, 2003; McLaren, 2003), student voice can and should be a powerful voice in the process of changing schools. However, many ideas about student voice reinforce my belief that it is simply any expression of any student anywhere about education and learning. The challenge of this reality is that student voice does not inherently require schools to change, and if it does demand change, student voice does not make improvement necessary. Instead, it can lead to less-effective schools, less-safe environments and merely short term impacts, if anything at all.

When ignored, student voice does not necessarily change education at all. Students who channel student voice towards self-destructive or anti-social behavior are on a similar trajectory as students who have their voices tokenized or infantalized by well-meaning but poorly informed adults throughout schools. That is because student voice does not require adults to change. Perhaps the most challenging reality of student voice is that sharing it does not inherently build the capacity of students to participate in school improvement or be sustainably engaging anywhere in the education system. It does not require students to change. Part of the engaging reality of education is that it calls individuals to a higher place within themselves and helps them understand their interdependence with all of society and the world around them. When that is missing, education is a shallow, rote routine merely followed by obedience and not enthusiasm.

Meaningful Student Involvement focuses exclusively on students becoming sustained, effective agents of change throughout the education system. The many elements expanded on in this book support and sustain these positions. They include the reality that Meaningful Student Involvement is infused into education system-wide action for school improvement; fosters deep student/adult commitment; promotes whole school transformation; sustains deep learning by students and adults; and expands possibilities for students and adults.

This means not setting up students to assume they can fix schools along, nor does it allow them to believe their voices are magic forces that are repressed by oppressive teachers. It does not give adults the luxury of tokenizing students or let them placate upset parents by having a student present at a meeting without any ability to affect change. It also does not separate student voice from the process of formal classroom learning; instead, it makes it integral.

Instead, it incorporates students in holistic, practical and meaningful ways. Adults are required to acknowledge their appropriate amounts and types of responsibilities, while students are compelled to assume more authority, purpose and interdependence than they have been granted for more than a century.

The following image, Figure 1, compares student voice and Meaningful Student Involvement by highlighting some of the options for students changing schools.

Chapter 15: Where Meaningful Student Involvement Factors

As this section has illustrated, the approaches explored throughout this book can go by many names. However, taken as a whole and understood in the larger context of systemic school improvement, many other concepts fall away. Student voice gets lost in a cacophony of busyness; student engagement swirls together with other goals and strategies in the din of reformers. As I will show repeatedly throughout this book, Meaningful Student Involvement does not happen in isolation; rather, it is the implementation of interrelated strategies and activities that are infused with other efforts directed towards increased school success for all students. It factors largely in the school transformation movement today because it holds many grandiose, yet incomplete, ideas by carefully melding them all into a powerful strategy for the future.

Meaningful Student Involvement inherently emerges with urgency by embracing critical capacity and enhancing the requisite enthusiasm that is not necessarily part of either student voice or student engagement.

It is meant to embody the implicit challenge inherent in Freire's observation that,

> "Knowledge emerges only through invention and re-invention, through the restless, impatient, continuing, hopeful inquiry human beings pursue in the world, with the world, and with each other." (Freire, 1970)

Meaningful Student Involvement is distinct from both student voice and student engagement because it encapsulates each, but is not only either one. Instead, it holds a lot of approaches, supports and outcomes that go far beyond either. With Student/Adult Partnerships at the center, approaches like service learning, place-based education, applied learning, democratic education, civic engagement, constructivism, and more become more than mere classroom activities. Seen through the lenses of Meaningful Student Involvement, they become part of a pedagogy of engagement that embeds all of them, along with student voice and student engagement, in a larger project focused on education, community and democracy with power, purpose and possibilities at the core. That is what makes it meaningful, vibrant and essential for modern times and throughout the future.

However, it is not the entire picture. The rest of this book expands on this reality by showing what is required, what happens and what the outcomes are from infusing this powerful, positive action throughout the education system.

Part III. Frameworks for Meaningful Student Involvement

Chapter 16: Introduction

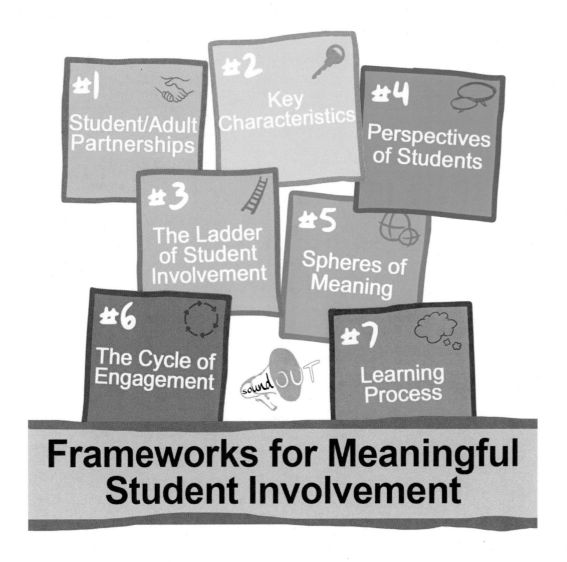

Figure 2. Frameworks for Meaningful Student Involvement

For some people, the most important aspect of Meaningful Student Involvement is that it just feels right. Through the course of my work, I have spoken with state superintendents and national education leaders, retired teachers, educational researchers, grant administrators, and taxpaying, voting community members who all believe engaging students as partners throughout education. When asked why in front of a crowd, many will say something about research or what they personally saw or did. However, one-on-one, many will simply say that it's just the right thing to do.

Part Three details different frameworks that can draw forth a *feeling* of meaningfulness. After my literature review and subsequent multi-year action research project, I structured these frameworks from the patterns I saw recurring in more than 3,000 examples. Since then, I have used these tools to teach, evaluate, and advocate for Meaningful Student Involvement with tens of thousands of students and adults around the world. They may be able to guide you too.

As illustrated in Figure 2 above, the following section explores six different frameworks for Meaningful Student Involvement. The first framework is *Student/Adult Partnerships.* While this term has been used and explored in-depth before, this framework sets a reasonable bar for understanding the motivations, ideals and outcomes of these unique relationships. The second framework is the *Cycle of Engagement.* Based in my research on Meaningful Student Involvement (Fletcher, 2001; 2003; 2003b; 2005a), the Cycle is elucidating a simple process for student engagement that when utilized repeatedly results in more secure Student/Adult Partnerships. Examining the *Key Characteristics of Meaningful Student Involvement* is the basis of the third framework. These research-based attributes form a powerful narrative for action and provide a basis for understanding Meaningful Student Involvement in context of school leadership, student achievement and beyond. The fourth framework is the *Ladder of Student Involvement.* Providing an essential platform for student engagement, this tool helps classroom educators, school leaders and others determine how, where and why students are involved. Many of these frameworks are reflected in the fifth framework, *Perspectives of Students.* This framework provides an essential understanding of how adults see students throughout education and what that could look like. The sixth framework is called the *Spheres of Meaning.* It succinctly summarizes where, how and what Meaningful Student Involvement does, and how each of those elements interact. The last framework is called the *Meaningful Student Involvement Learning Process*, and it summarizes the main aspects students and adults need to understand to be able to effectively foster this approach.

If an opportunity has Student/Adult Partnerships at the core, they are meaningfully involving students. If the five elements of the Cycle of Engagement are present—including listening, validating, authorizing, action and reflecting—and are being met repeatedly, an opportunity is meaningfully involving students. If the key characteristics described earlier are present throughout an opportunity, students are being involved. The Ladder of Student Involvement can show how different opportunities can reflect the most meaningful forms of student involvement, as well as the least meaningful. When adult perspectives of students are honestly acknowledged and accordingly addressed, involvement can be meaningful. The Spheres of Meaning should be interlocked and are dependent on each other, and the learning process is essential to implementing Meaningful Student Involvement.

In the past, democratic society relied on schools to prepare students for the future. It was enough to simply teach students about civic life, ensure their recollection of core curriculum, and enrich learners with adult-determined extra-curricular courses and activities. However, the changing social dynamics and structures in our society require adults to recognize that the future is now. The access many young people have to information, their ability to generate and distribute learning, and the impact children and youth have on the world around them has never been so pronounced as it is today. We all need to learn to use these tools to build democracy.

Fostering an actively democratic culture in education that has the potential to engage all students in every school, it is essential to do more than *listen* to student voice. (Mitra, 2003) The democratic principles underpinning many nations today suggest nothing less than complete equity between students and adults. As this book aims to illustrate, these principles actually make Student/Adult Partnerships essential for the future of communities and democracy.

Chapter 17: Framework 1—Student/Adult Partnerships

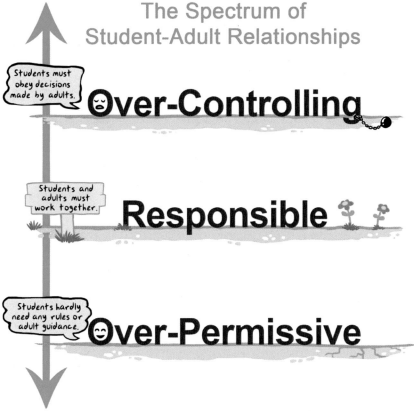

Figure 3. Student-Adult Relationships Spectrum

That app does not use authentic student voice to improve learning. That assessment does not promote deeper student engagement. Those devices do not build meaningful involvement. Only Student/Adult Partnerships can do that.

The first framework for Meaningful Student Involvement is that of Student/Adult Partnerships. Their importance cannot be overstated. However, before understanding what they are, it is important to understand what Student/Adult Partnerships are not. (Oldfather, 1995)

Following are several aspects of Student/Adult Partnerships. The first is a typology of different relationships between students and adults today, along with different ways adults categorize students in schools today. The second aspect is made of elements of Student/Adult Partnerships, while the last aspect explored in this framework is the difference between meaningful and *non*-meaningful student involvement. When potential partners understand these aspects, they can form Student/Adult Partnerships that are sustainable, effective and meaningful for everyone involved.

A. Types of Relationships between Students and Adults

Understanding the different types of relationships students and adults can have with each other is vital to Meaningful Student Involvement. There is not one simple way all adults interact with all students all the time. Instead, there is a wide spectrum. Additionally, it is important to understand how those interactions are manifested in classrooms, principals' offices Student/Adult Partnerships are neither over-controlling and over-permissive. Figure 3 shows how the following three relationships between students and adults interact with each other.

1. Over-controlling student-adult relationships

Over-controlling student-adult relationships occur when adults react to a negative perception or misconception of students, including their freedoms, rights and responsibilities. Taking the guise of concern for students, over-controlling student-adult relationships are defined by distrust, fear, or willful misunderstanding of students. This type of relationship can lead to students being infantilized by teachers, counselors, administrators, and others throughout schools, made to feel like infants who are incapable or subhuman. Over-controlling schools can lead to locked doors, coded language, filtered Internet, and choices made for students that rely on force to implement.

2. Over-permissive student-adult relationships

Over-permissive student-adult relationships are the opposite end of the spectrum, when adults assume students have too much ability. This can reflect a misguided attempt by adults in schools who think the best of students or want to be their friends. However, this is a disingenuous relationship as well, in the same sense that we would never give a 16-year-old the keys to a car and expect them to teach themselves how to drive. This type of relationship is often labeled of as student empowerment, despite actually incapacitating some students' abilities to exercise power in their own learning or with others. Over-permissiveness may take the form of ill-trained, under-informed students acting without adult input. Fortunately, the ideal relationship might be the most realistic and responsive.

3. Responsible student-adult relationships

Responsible student-adult relationships are typified by Meaningful Student Involvement because they train students and adults about responsibility in terms of *being able to respond*, or being *Response-Able*. Response-Able student-adult relationships require adults to become able to respond appropriately to the demands of engaging students throughout the education system. This type of relationship fosters Student/Adult Partnerships. Providing issue- and action-specific learning opportunities, engaging student wisdom, and saying "no" when it is appropriate are key. Adults become allies with students by working with they, instead of for them.

B. Ways Adults Treat Students

Following are four basic ways that all adults throughout the education system treat students today. Further in this book I explore more ways in depth.

1. **Students as Objects**: Adults treat students as inanimate objects, exercising arbitrary and total control over them. All classes, programs and activities throughout education are done TO students.
2. **Students as Recipients**: After deciding what is best for students, adults determine needs, prescribe remedies, implement solutions and evaluate outcomes with little or no student input. All classes, programs and activities are FOR students.
3. **Students as Resources:** Adults see students as capable of sharing student voice, listening to students while they are planning, implementing and evaluating classes, programs and activities throughout the education system.
4. **Student as Partners:** Students and adults are actively engaged in equitable partnerships where they share authority, ability and accountability. (Innovation Center, 2005)

The last basic way is the foundation of Meaningful Student Involvement: Student/Adult Partnerships.

C. Elements of Student/Adult Partnerships

The following elements were identified to help adults and students understand what Student/Adult Partnerships behave throughout education. When students are genuinely supported in schools, Student/Adult Partnerships can be successfully brokered in schools. Many of these elements were originally identified by 500 students and adults from across the United States

1. Authentic Engagement

Authentic engagement for students is required for Student/Adult Partnerships. The first way to do this is be making it real: Open the doors for real Meaningful Student Involvement right now throughout education. Allow students to address every variety of educational activity that affects them by learning to listen, validate, authorize, mobilize, and reflect on schools. Seek nothing less than full Student/Adult Partnerships for every learner in school, and encourage students to expect meaningfulness. That means not letting any member of the school community be apathetic, whether they are students or adults. I explore several pathways to authentic student voice earlier in this book in Table 1.

2. Mutual Respect

Respect is mutual between students and adults, and when you give it, you receive it. Creating a culture of respect shatters stereotypes based on age for both students and adults. Students respect adults in schools who listen and ask challenging questions. You can find examples in Tables 4 and 21. Creating a culture of respect provides all people—both students and adults— the opportunity to act on their dreams and learn from their mistakes.

3. Positive Communication

Adults must listen up and students must hear, because an honest and open exchange of ideas is crucial. Students are best heard when adults step back and students speak up, and adults are best heard when they are straight forward and explain where they are coming from. All people's ideas and opinions in schools are valuable to the educational process and the educational system, and each must be heard.

4. Active Investment

Meaningful Student Involvement takes time. For adults, it's important to remember that investing in the future is accepting that students are leaders today. Students and adults must first set their fears aside and take a chance on each other. Adults must provide students with the information, education and support they will need to succeed, and should strive to develop their own ability to engage students. Strong Student/Adult Partnerships require patience and courage.

5. Meaningful Action

Count students in by making it meaningful. When decisions about students are made, they should be made with students. All adults in schools should strive to be allies to students by not acting as adversaries. Adults need to support students in taking on responsibility based on what they can do, not what they have done. Reflection helps everyone appreciate the importance of their education—for themselves, for their communities and for their lives. In Student/Adult Partnerships, students and adults must hold each other accountable for all their decisions and actions. Students and teachers should continually reflect on, analyze, and challenge the impact of schools in their lives.

When students are genuinely supported through Student/Adult Partnerships, Meaningful Student Involvement can be successfully fostered. Many students, educators, parents, and other advocates have argued that any form of student involvement is inherently meaningful for students, as if there is inherent meaning in being involved. That may be true, if only because there is meaning in not being involved. Many students have reported that not being involved in student government activities, sports, extracurricular clubs, and other traditional forms of student involvement affected their self-esteem, cultural identity, and critical thinking, ultimately negatively impacting their engagement as students.

D. Understanding Meaningfulness

Meaningfulness is an entirely subjective experience that varies almost entirely from person to person. We each make our own meaning in life all the time, sometimes consciously and often unconsciously. The same is true of students.

Whether something is meaningful to anyone is affected by several things. Who we are individually, where we are at, and what we are doing all affect meaningfulness. This is our personal context. The people and places around us provide a cultural context that affects whether we see something as meaningful or not. The signs and language people use affects our perspective of meaningfulness, as do the media and technology at hand. Finally, biology and psychology affects our interpretation of whether something is meaningful to us.

All that is to say that every student determines what is meaningful for themselves. In my studies, I have found that students in schools are largely responsive to a set of factors that allow them to determine whether something is meaningful for themselves. These factors include:

- **Purpose**: Why are students involved?
- **Type**: Which form of involvement is chosen?
- **Action**: What specific ways does involvement happen?
- **Intent**: What tare the driving reasons students are involved?
- **People**: Who is involved?
- **Place**: Where does involvement happen?
- **How**: What are the avenues for involvement?

These questions emerge in a variety of research, especially the vital work of Michael Fielding, who asserts almost two dozen other questions as well. (Fielding, 2001) There are other questions throughout this book, including Tables 4 and 21, too. Through my projects, I have found the factors represented here are vital for personal, group and organizational examination by both students and educators. There is something more at the heart of this though.

To be meaningful, student involvement must challenge and re-define the ideas of power, control and authority throughout the education. Meaningful Student Involvement calls schools to a higher purpose. Students are positioned as generators of knowledge, co-makers of culture, and co-facilitators of learning. They are fully acknowledged as real partners to all adults throughout education through equitable treatment to adults in schools. These are the roles students need to have in schools, and this is what makes involvement meaningful.

1. Choice and Voice Are Not Enough

There is an increasingly popular formula in the student empowerment movement that is undermining Student/Adult Partnerships. More and more, well-meaning educators and school leaders are talking about student voice and student choice, and implying that simply listening to student voice and giving students choices will lead to student empowerment. (Booth, 2013) Unfortunately, choice and voice are not enough to count as meaningful.

Instead, students need to understand that their voice happens in a context of something larger than themselves, and that their choices affect more than themselves alone. The context they should know is that their schooling affects them, their classroom and school, and the education system as a whole, our communities at large, and all of the democratic experiment we share and benefit from every day. Similarly, there are thousands of micro- and macro-levels individual choices students make throughout the day. These choices affect themselves, their peers, the families, neighbors, public servants and all of society every single time they make them.

Meaningful Student Involvement provides the context and larger picture for all students in every classroom throughout every school in every community all around the world. There are six expectations for all Student/Adult Partnerships that occur through the frameworks of Meaningful Student Involvement. All students and adults will:

1. Assume responsibility for their education and can articulate the purpose of schools.
2. Learn to be collaborative and act responsibility throughout their school and learning experiences.
3. Communicate creatively and effectively with others to sustain meaningfulness.
4. Demonstrate integrated, critical and applied learning through action and reflection.
5. Examine and inquire consistently throughout their educative experiences.
6. Through action, show depth, breadth and deep understanding about the focus of schooling.

Holding each other mutually accountable through these expectations is vital for students and adults. Pulling together broad student voice from a variety of peers, students apply the expectations throughout their daily learning, enabling them to practice real-world applications immediately in their schools. Educators link theory to practice by actively applying Meaningful Student Involvement in their daily classroom practice or administrative activities. Everyone throughout the school learns to bridge differences on purpose through recognizing each other in ways they may not otherwise. The capacity of the entire school community is increased as these frameworks for Meaningful Student Involvement are infused throughout everyone's mutual experiences. All of this challenges the habit of segregation among age groups that our schools have become accustomed to. It also combats the false competitions among students and between students and educators and builds mutuality through shared learning and community building.

2. Meaningful or Un-Meaningful Involvement
It is vital to understand when student involvement is and is not meaningful.

When is student involvement not meaningful?

- Students are regarded as passive recipients in schools, or as empty vessels to be filled with adults' knowledge.
- Students view skills as something they are either born with or not, and adults do nothing to change that viewpoint.
- The contributions of students are minimized or tokenized by adults by asking students to "rubber stamp" ideas developed by adults, or by inviting students to sit on committees without real power or responsibility.
- Students and adults view challenges as something to avoid and something that reveals their lack of skills.
- Student perspectives, experiences or knowledge are filtered with adult interpretations.
- Students and adults avoid challenge and tend to give up easily when they meet it.
- Students are given problems to solve without adult support or adequate training.
- Adults see student involvement as a statement of their inadequacy and take it personally by getting defensive.
- Students are trained in leadership skills without opportunities to take on real leadership roles in their school.
- When they meet barriers or setbacks, students and adults blame each other and get discouraged.

When is student involvement meaningful?

- Students are allies and partners with adults in improving schools.
- Students and adults know that every school can always improve.
- Students have the training and authority to create real solutions to the challenges that schools face in learning, teaching, and leadership.
- Schools, including educators and administrators, are accountable to students themselves.
- Student-adult partnerships are a major component of every sustainable, responsive, and systemic approach to transforming schools.
- Students and adults know schools change through hard work
- Schools persistently embrace challenges as opportunities to keep growing.
- Students understand that effort is an essential tool that leads to them becoming more effective learners, and educators acknowledge effort duly.
- Adults view involvement as a meaningful opportunity for students that is useful for them to identify areas for school improvement and as something to learn from.
- Students and adults work together to understand setbacks and barriers as something to grow from and work harder towards next time.

Currently, some schools talk about students as consumers. This is not a meaningful approach, because it ultimately reduces learning to consumption, as if students simply need to show up and digest whatever adults give to them.

In the same way that you go to the store, buy what you need, and leave, addressing students as consumers implies the conveyor belt approach to teaching, learning, and leadership in schools is okay, and as stagnant student achievement rates show worldwide, it is not. Engaging students as partners requires their meaningful involvement throughout the entirety of the education system, from research to planning, teaching to evaluation, decision-making to advocacy.

The remainder of these frameworks show how this happens in different ways, starting with the Cycle of Engagement.

15 ACTIVITIES TO FOSTER MEANINGFUL STUDENT INVOLVEMENT

1. **Teach** students about multiple perspectives regarding issues in education.
2. **Train** educators about the difference between Students as Recipients and Students as Partners.
3. **Facilitate** students understand the education system, including what it is, how it operates, who is in it, where it fails and when it succeeds
4. **Develop** opportunities for students to share their unfettered concerns about schools and education with adults
5. **Create** formal positions for students to occupy throughout education
6. **Create** curriculum with students as partners in identifying, planning, and critiquing
7. **Co-design** learning plans with every student
8. **Encourage** all students to find a student mentor to introduce them to the culture and traditions of the school.
9. **Explore** yearlong school day calendars with students to see how they affect students and others.
10. **Engage** students in designing and redesigning schools
11. **Encourage** nontraditional student leaders to co-teach regular classes with adults
12. **Allow** students to become active partners in school budgeting
13. **Give** students positions to become classroom teaching assistants
14. **Partner** student teams to teach courses
15. **Acknowledge** students teaching younger students in lower grade levels with classroom credit

Table 7. 15 Activities to Foster Meaningful Student Involvement. See Table 8 for more.

Chapter 18: Framework 2—The Cycle of Engagement

Figure 4. The Cycle of Engagement

Meaningful Student Involvement is not a magical formula or mysterious bargain with students—but, it does not just simply happen, either. When consciously conducted throughout the education system, meaningfully involving students can lead to strong student engagement.

I have identified a series of patterns that occur in nearly all activities students identify as leading to their engagement. The following *Cycle of Engagement* is one of those patterns. In its simplicity, the Cycle gives adults a practical pathway to their daily relationships with students.

By following the *Cycle*, interactions in schools can transform from passive, disconnected activities into a process promoting student achievement and school improvement. It is a continuous five-step process that can be used to assess current activities, or to plan future programs.

Figure 4 shows what the Cycle of Engagement looks like, and how the steps in the Cycle are related to each other. The following explanations provide more information about each step. Examples and more information about each of these actions are shared further on in this book.

A. Listen

Many educators fill their days with hearing students, but never truly take time to listen to student voice. True listening requires enormous skill, especially in education systems that routinely devalue the voices of students. It does not help that students are often not interested in sitting down in a room doing an adult-style one-on-one conversation with structured question/answer interviewing techniques. The process of listening begins when adults take responsibility for their personal beliefs and assumptions about students in schools. They acknowledge the barriers and limitations Meaningful Student Involvement faces in their educational settings, whether a classroom, office, boardroom, or agency; and identify the cultural expectations of schools.

This shows that Meaningful Student Involvement inherently requires more than simply listening. Providing a platform for student voice to be heard can be challenging. Listening to students can happen in personal conversations, classroom discussions, agenda items in meetings, or through written reports and studies. It happens when there are both informal and formal practices in place that require adults in schools to listen to students.

These may include classroom-based activities such as journals, check-ins, and group discussions, as well as schoolwide activities such as student forums, online websites, and other venues. Sometimes the most successful student voice listening activities happen when adults are not directly conversing with students. Listening to students while acknowledging multiple intelligences can lead to spectacular results, and is explored further in this book. Doing activities, walking or making things, and using the Internet are options. Creating things through graffiti art, printmaking, stencils, writing, or recording music are very useful for group discussion and can provide appropriate space for one-on-one discussions take place too (Armstrong, 2009).

These activities should be backed by policies to eliminate barriers to engaging students as partners. The policy and practice supporting Meaningful Student Involvement should be invented and re-invented according to location, as each school community has unique cultures, supporting factors, and barriers that affect Meaningful Student Involvement. (Robinson & Taylor, 2013) These barriers are examined in Figures 18 and 20, and in several chapters further on in this book.

B. Validate

To become engaged, adults must validate the opinions, ideas, experiences, wisdom, questions, actions, and reflections of students. When they speak about education, students are accustomed to being ignored, denied or ridiculed. It is imperative that students hear adult feedback as sincere, including adult criticism. Disagreeing with students lets them know that adults in schools actually heard what was said, think about it, and have their own knowledge or opinions they think is important to share with students. It means students are important enough to treat as fully human.

When students speak, it is not enough for adults to simply nod their head. Validating students does not mean automatically agreeing with students, either. It is important to offer students sincere comments, criticism, or feedback. Disagreeing with students allows young people to know that you actually heard what was said, that you thought about it, and that you have your own knowledge or opinion which you think is important to share with them. Students must know that education is not about autonomous authority, and that a chorus of voices inform learning, teaching and leadership throughout the education system. Students should be acknowledged for their contributions, whether positive or otherwise, in appropriately meaningful ways. I explore this validation further on. It also means that rather than condemning or denying students opportunities for meaningfulness because of their culture, identity, attitudes, or academic achievement, they are uplifted and supported further in their involvement.

Validation means more than adults nodding their heads and murmuring, "Oh yes." Instead, it means acknowledging students by paraphrasing what they have said in simple terms to check adult understanding. Meaningful Student Involvement teaches students that democracy is not about autonomous authority, and that a chorus of people, including students but not exclusive to them, is responsible for what happens throughout our education systems.

C. Authorize

Every day, students in schools are repeatedly ignored, condemned, denied, or abandoned because of their identities. Democracy inherently requires ability, which comes in the form of experience and knowledge. Authorizing students means going beyond the traditional expectations you have hold for student by actively providing the learning opportunities, creating the positions, and allowing the space they need to be partners in schools.

Engaging students partners requires *ability,* which in the education system comes in the forms of *positioning* and *learning.* Providing students with authority means going beyond traditional roles for students in classrooms by actively providing the learning opportunities they need to affect substantive change within the education system. It is essential that adults provide students with the opportunities they need to be authors of their own narratives through deliberate positioning in either formal or informal roles. Authorizing involves adults in schools going beyond assumed expectations of students by providing the learning opportunities they need to affect change in their own learning, their schools, and the entire education system. It means creating the sustainable opportunities students need and creating space for students to be equitable partners with adults in all areas of schooling. Ultimately, authorizing students to be partners in schools requires that adults rearrange the ways we teach, lead, and learn throughout schools.

D. Act

Transitioning from passive participants to active learners and leaders throughout education requires students taking action to create change. Mobilizing students with new authority allows them to affect cultural and systemic educational transformation, and encourages educators to acknowledge students as partners. See Table 20 for examples of what this can look like. Action can take many forms, but so long as it engages students as partners in schools as explored throughout this book, it is Meaningful Student Involvement.

Transitioning from passive recipients of schools to active and equitable partners throughout the education system requires students to actually taking action to create change. Mobilizing requires motivating, implementing, and sustaining action. Students with authority in schools affect cultural, systemic, and personal transformation in their own lives and the lives of others. It also encourages adults throughout the education system to actively acknowledge students as partners throughout schools. See Table 20 for examples of what this can look like.

E. Reflect

Meaningful Student Involvement cannot happen in a vacuum that affects only students or the immediate situation. Educators and students should take responsibility for learning through involvement by engaging students in conscious critical reflection by examining what was successful and what failed. Students and adults can also work together to identify how to sustain and expand the *Cycle of Engagement* by effectively returning to the first step above. Student reflection on Meaningful Student Involvement can build the capacity that students must be effectively engaged throughout education.

Individually, these steps may be happening right now in schools. However, when they do happen it is rare that they are connected with formal teaching, learning, or leadership throughout schools. It is even less likely that they are connected with one another. The connection of all the steps in the Cycle is what makes partnerships between students and adults meaningful, effective, and sustainable.

15 *MORE* ACTIVITIES TO FOSTER MEANINGFUL STUDENT INVOLVEMENT

16. **Co-create** professional development with students to teach teachers about students
17. **Explore** with students how to create meaningful classroom evaluations of themselves
18. **Partner** with students to create evaluations of classes, curriculum, teaching styles, and schools
19. **Train** students how to evaluate teacher performance
20. **Create** opportunities for students to lead parent-teacher conferences
21. **Develop** positions for students to participate in curriculum selection and design committees
22. **Advocate** with students for school boards to have full-voting positions for students
23. **Create** enough positions for students to be equally represented in every education committee and meeting
24. **Facilitate** students creating and enforcing culture change in schools, including behavior policies
25. **Partner** with students in school personnel decisions
26. **Work** with students to organize public campaigns for school improvement
27. **Create** opportunities for students to fully join all existing school committees
28. **Give** students data and information so they understand why and how schools are changing
29. **Allow** students to educate policy-makers about challenges in schools
30. **Encourage** students with formal and informal opportunities to present their concerns

Table 8. 15 More Activities to Foster Meaningful Student Involvement. See Table 7 for more.

Chapter 19: Framework 3—Key Characteristics

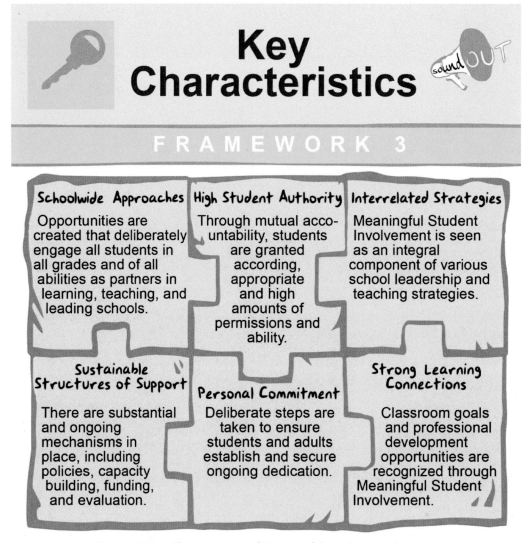

Figure 5. Key Characteristics of Meaningful Student Involvement

The cure to disconnection is meaningfulness. Meaningful Student Involvement happens when the roles of students are actively re-aligned from being the passive recipients of schools to becoming active partners throughout the educational process. Real learning and real purpose take form through Meaningful Student Involvement, often showing immediate impacts on the lives of students by actively authorizing each of them to have powerful, purposeful opportunities to impact their own learning and the lives of others.

Figure 5 illustrates the key characteristics of Meaningful Student Involvement, and the reality that they're interdependent on each other like a puzzle. The following section explores how they are consistently identified in schools where students and adults commonly agree that there are high levels of Meaningful Student Involvement. Each characteristic is illustrated further in this book.

A. Schoolwide Approaches

All students in all grades are meaningfully involved throughout their education, including their learning experiences, classroom management, interactions with peers and adults throughout the school, and ongoing throughout their educational careers. This may include becoming engaged in education system-wide planning, research, teaching, evaluation, decision-making, and advocacy. It may also mean partnerships between students and adults in learning communities; student-specific roles in building leadership, and; intentional programs designed to increase student efficacy as partners in school improvement.

B. High Student Authority

Students' ideas, knowledge, opinions and experiences in schools and regarding education are actively sought and substantiated by educators, administrators, and other adults within the educational system. Adults' acknowledgment of students' ability to improve schools is validated and authorized through deliberate teaching focused on learning about learning, learning about the education system, learning about student voice and Meaningful Student Involvement, and learning about school improvement (McCombs & Whisler, 1997). This characteristic should reflect a schools' commitment to sustainable Student/Adult Partnerships, comprehensive planning and effective assessments that measure shared and individual perspectives and outcomes of Meaningful Student Involvement.

C. Interrelated Strategies

Students are deeply infused into ongoing, sustainable school transformation activities through deliberate opportunities for learning, teaching, and leadership throughout the educational system. In individual classrooms, this can mean integrating student voice into classroom management practices; giving students opportunities to design, facilitate, and evaluate curriculum; or facilitating student learning about school systems. In the Principal's office, it can mean students' having equitable opportunities to participate with adults in formal school improvement activities. On the state school board of education it can mean students having full voting rights, and equal representation to adults. Whatever the opportunities are, ultimately it means they are all tied together with the intention of improving schools for all learners all the time. Each of these strategies should be integrated with a building's school improvement plan, the district improvement policies, the state education reform laws, and federal law, as well as all levels' regular policies and procedures. This ensures sustained collaboration among stakeholders, especially students.

D. Sustainable Structures of Support

Policies and procedures are created and amended to promote Meaningful Student Involvement throughout schools. This includes creating specific funding opportunities that support student voice and student engagement; facilitating ongoing professional development for educators focused on Meaningful Student Involvement; and integrating this new vision for students into classroom practice, building procedures, and district, state and federal policies.

Sustainability within schools cannot be seen solely through a structural lens; instead, it must happen with the intermixing of culture and structure. The previously described characteristics deal with the former; this characteristic addresses the latter. These structures of support may include student action centers that train students and provide information to student/adult partners; curriculum specifically designed to teach students about school improvement and student action, and; fully-funded, ongoing programs that support Meaningful Student Involvement.

E. Personal Commitment

Students and adults acknowledge their mutual investment, dedication, and benefit, visible in learning, relationships, practices, policies, school culture, and many other ways. This builds community and connection among partners who may have previously seen "the other" as different and separate, both in intention and action. That may be specifically true among low-income students, students-of-color and low-achieving students in buildings where predominately white, upper-income and/or high achieving students have been perceived as having greater value or more importance than other learners.

Meaningful Student Involvement is not just about students themselves, either. It insists that from their pre-service training through retirement, all adults throughout the education system—including teachers, administrators, paraprofessionals, counselors, and others—see students as substantive, powerful, and significant partners in all the different machinations of schools. When they have this commitment, adults throughout education will actively seek nothing other than to fully integrate students at every turn.

F. Strong Learning Connections

Classroom learning and student involvement are connected by classroom credit, ensuring relevancy for educators and significance to students. Meaningful student involvement should not be an "add-on" strategy for educators - it should be integrated throughout their daily activities. Classroom teachers should acknowledge exceptional projects and involvement by students with credit, just as they acknowledge service learning activities - because Meaningful Student Involvement is a service learning activity. The difference is that students focus on schools. This deliberate connection ties together the roles for students with the purpose of education, thoroughly substantiating Student/Adult Partnerships and signifying the intention of adults to continue transforming learning as learners themselves evolve. Table 16 in this book shows how that can happen.

Considerations

Meaningful student involvement can help meet the goals of learning in all schools by dramatically re-envisioning the roles of students throughout education. These characteristics can help schools establish strong foundations that engage students as partners and sustain Meaningful Student Involvement
for all learners, everywhere.

Chapter 20: Framework 4—Ladder of Student Involvement

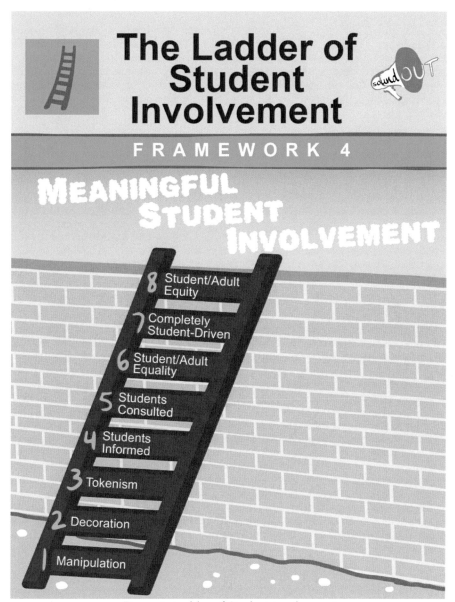

Figure 6. Ladder of Student Involvement

For a long time, the only formal role for young people in society was as a learner who attended school to meet society's expectations. That is changing. Right now, and more than ever before, students increasingly have positions throughout education beyond being the passive recipients of adult-controlled classrooms; instead, they are serving schools as decision-makers, planners, researchers, and more. However, there is still a long way most students to go before they experience Meaningful Student Involvement.

It is essential to understand there are boundless ways for students to be involved throughout the education system. With an absence of critical literature that examines those boundless ways, in 2001, I turned to the work of sociologist Roger Hart. (Hart, 1997) I adapted the Ladder (Fletcher, 2003) for schools from Hart, who originally adapted the Ladder from Arnstien (1969). Hart proposed that the pinnacle experience for children in organizational decision-making was to initiate action and share decision-making with adults. My interpretation soon differed from his.

As illustrated in Figure 6, I adapted the *Ladder of Student Involvement in Schools* to reflect the practical structure of schools today. While there are ideal structures that are enacted in exceptional schools, I want to encourage students and adults to examine *why* and *how* students are involved throughout the education system today. Each individual activity students are involved in throughout the education system, from local classrooms to national departments of education around the world, can be measured against the Ladder of Student Involvement.

Before exploring the Ladder in-depth, its important to understand that this is not meant to position one relationship as better than all others, or that a classroom, school or education system can be one way all the time. Instead, it is to help understand the gradient ways students are involved throughout schools.

Rung 1. Manipulation

In nations around the world, students of specific ages are compelled by law to attend schools. Once they are there, students receive grades, scores and other acknowledgements of their academic performance and behavior. Some people automatically say these are examples of adults manipulating students. However, if students understand why they are forced to attend schools and agree to the democratic nature of compulsory education, the manipulative nature of these arguments is dismantled.

Similarly, if students fail academically or socially in many schools, they will receive failing grades. Success is awarded with good grades, and there is a clear line for failure that is acknowledge with low grades. There are alternatives to manipulating students to performing to adults' expectations, too. This act minimizes learning into an exchange based off control and compliance, rather than authentic learning from effective teaching. Classroom teachers might manipulate students into behaving how they want them to, while non-certificated or paraprofessional staff can manipulate students by offering them exclusive rewards for good behavior. School leaders sometimes manipulate students by coercing student leaders to sway other students with threats of poor letters of recommendation into college, or noncompliant students with threats of expulsion.

The challenge of this rung is that students are forced to attend without regard to interest. This is true of general school attendance and school board meetings. Grades, praise, or prizes are used to manipulate students. The reward to manipulating students is that students experience whatever they are attending, whether a class, special program, athletic event or otherwise.

Often this gives adults further rationale for continuing activities. Manipulating students cannot be meaningful. See Table 22 for some examples of what that can look like.

Rung 2. Decoration

Moving up the Ladder, adults use students to decorate their actions throughout the education system. This happens whenever adults affix students to something they want to do for themselves, but insist on having students participate because it is school related. For instance, press conferences, school open houses and education foundation fundraisers often decorate with students. Similarly, decoration can happen in classrooms when a teacher really wants to cover a topic regardless of students' needs or desire. At this point, teachers simply decorate their time with students in order to collect a paycheck for the day. School leaders might have students sit with them during a press conference to say acceptable things, or allow a positive message to be spray painted onto the school building with their approval. Afterschool workers and paraprofessionals can decorate with students by not allowing students to make any decisions about programming, but forcing them to attend in order to say students were there. Districts may launch programs to tell students about education reform initiatives simply to claim students know about what they are going through while they are going through it, without allowing students to say anything critical or otherwise respond substantively. For specific activities, see Table 10 in this book.

The challenge is that the presence of students is treated as all that is necessary without reinforcing any sort of meaning in their involvement. Students do not have to learn in classrooms or from activities where they are decorations, because the intention truly is not for them to learn. Instead, it is for adults to fulfill their agenda while students are in attendance.

The reward may be that student presence is a tangible outcome that demonstrates adults have some thought in mind regarding student involvement. Using students as decorations cannot be meaningful.

Rung 3. Tokenism

Students are tokenized when adults involve them simply to say students are involved, rather than having a genuine desire to engage them. In these circumstances, students receive no information, have no input and are not given opportunities to learn anything of substance. Instead, they simply attend and adults claim credit for their participation. Some students will say their entire school experience reflects this reality. When adults invite students to be ushers at professional education conferences, they are tokenizing students. In an instance where a teacher takes a vote in a class ostensibly to decide on the next activity they are going to do, but then makes a decision completely different from what the students choose, that teacher is tokenizing students.

In these circumstances, meaningfulness is challenged because students are used inconsequentially by adults to reinforce the perspective that students are involved. Tokenizing students can teach them their perspective is irrelevant, and that their attendance is all that is necessary for adults. It can also teach students to tokenize other people for different reasons, including women, people of color and otherwise.

The reward to this approach is that it may validate student attendance without requiring adults take any effort to go beyond that simple approach. Tokenizing students cannot be meaningful.

Rung 4. Information

Rung four is the first actual opportunity for meaningful involvement to happen for students in schools. When adults tell students what is happening in schools and let students share their attitudes, opinions, ideas, knowledge, wisdom and actions, schools are beginning to form the basis for meaningful involvement. They are treating students like information sources, as informants. This can happen in classes where teachers survey students about their learning styles or options in making curriculum; in student athletic programs where coaches facilitate connections between sports with learning through structured reflection; and in state or provincial education agencies that host programs to gather student voice about learning.

The challenge of this rung is that adults do not *have* to let students impact their decisions. There could be a mass of student voice pointing in one direction, but adults maintain their authority and choose to go a different direction. Worst still, they do not feel accountable to students and might not actually tell students about why they made the decisions they made and why they excluded students.

The reward may be that students impact adult-driven decisions or activities while adults maintain control. Informing adults can be meaningful if the activity reflects the Characteristics of Meaningful Student Involvement examined in this book.

Rung 5. Consultation

Consulting is a specific job, different from coaching or being an informant. When adults in education recognize students are experts who can inform schools greatly, they can engage students as consultants. This can happen informally in a classroom or extracurricular program when an adult asks students their opinions on topics throughout education, including what happens, why it happens, who is involved or when it happens. When students share student voice to respond to these kinds of questions, adults may or may not act upon their guidance. The important part, though, is that students consult the process. Outside school time education programs can consult with students by inviting them to participate in staff hiring processes, while some school boards currently consult students by having ex-officio or special roles for students on their boards.

The challenge of Rung 5 is that students only have the authority that adults grant them, and are subject to adult approval. While this can feel safe for adults, it can also reflect an inability of educators to prepare students to be responsibly and ethically engaged in schools. Similarly, this approach to student involvement can also feel disingenuous to students since it does not reflect their sincere capacities and desires.

The reward to this rung is that students can substantially transform adults' opinions, ideas, and actions while adults maintain control. Consulting adults can be meaningful for students if the process reflects the Cycle of Engagement explored further in this chapter.

Rung 6. Equality

On the sixth rung, students are fully equal with adults while they are involved in a given activity within schools. This is a 50/50 split of authority, obligation, and commitment. There is not specific recognition of the developmental differences between grade levels or students and adults, and that's not "bad", per se. Opportunities for student involvement aren't necessarily distinguished between grade levels, academic achievement, social groupings, or other factors, either.

The challenge of this rung is that without continuous acknowledgment of their needs, ideas, wisdom and actions, students may lose interest and become disengaged quickly in activities that do not reflect this rung. Thoughtful facilitation focused on self-applying skills learned through meaningful involvement can help students apply lessons learned to other situations that are not meaningful.

This same rung can allow students to experience full power and authority in relationship to each other and with adults. This rung can also foster the formation of basic Student/Adult Partnerships.

Rung 7. Self-Driven

On the seventh rung, which is completely student-driven, adults are not situated in positions of authority. Instead, they are there to support students in passive or *very* behind-the-scenes roles. This gives students the platform to act in situations where adults are apparently indifferent, apathetic, or disregarding towards students, or students are not seen with regard for their contributions, only for their deficits. This can happen when students form self-teaching groups to examine topics teachers do not address in class or otherwise, or when students create extracurricular clubs that reflect their desires without adult leadership.

The challenge of this rung is that in this way, self-led activities by students can operate in a vacuum where the impact of their actions on the larger school is not recognized by the entire school community. A "school community" is all the people who intimately attach to a school building, including the teachers, administrators, students, and the students' families. In this community, student-led activities may not be seen with the validity of activities led by students and adults together too (Weiss & Huget, 2015).

However, approaches to meaningful involvement that reflect Rung 7 can allow students to experience high amounts of self-efficacy. Developmental, cultural, social, and educational experiences led by students may be extremely effective too, both for themselves, their peers, and their school communities as well.

Rung 8. Equity

When students are completely equitable with adults, the activity they are involved in occupies the eighth rung of the ladder. Equity allows for this to be a 40/60 split, or 20/80 split when it's deemed appropriate by students and adults together. Everyone involved is recognized for their impact in the activity, including students and adults, and each has ownership of the outcomes. Equity between students and adults requires conscious commitment by all participants to overcome the barriers involved, and positions adults and students in healthy, whole relationships with each other while moving forward through action and learning. This can lead to creating structures to support differences by establishing safe, supportive environments for equitable involvement. In turn, this may lead to recreating the climate and culture of communities, and lead to the greatest meaningfulness of student involvement.

Exploring the Ladder

It is important to recognize that the Ladder is not meant to represent the involvement of every student in every school all at once. It's also not support to show the entire experience of one student throughout their day. Instead, it should be used to plan and assess each specific instance of student involvement. That means that rather than say a whole classroom is rung 4, several students could be experiencing that they are at that rung four while others are experiencing that they are at rung six.

For a long time, determining which rung students occupied was left to perspective and position: If an adult believed the students on their committee were at rung 6, and the students believed they were at rung 8, they simply agreed to disagree. The following rubric can help provide a clearer explanation of what student involvement looks like.

Roger Hart, a sociologist for UNICEF who developed the original *Ladder of Children's Participation* in 1994, identified the first three rungs as representing forms of *non*-participation. However, while the first rung generally represents the nature of all student involvement in schools with the threat of attend or fail, as Table 16 shows, there are more roles for students than ever before throughout the education system. Rungs 6, 7, and 8 generally represent Student/Adult Partnerships, which are intentionally designed relationships that foster authentic student engagement in schools. With this knowledge in mind, the rungs of the Ladder can help students and adults throughout education identify how students are currently involved in schools, and give them goals to aspire towards.

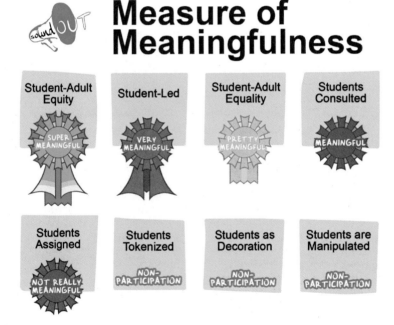

Figure 7. Measure of Meaningfulness

Inspired Action

As Figure 7 shows, the Ladder model can inspire action that validates students by authorizing their involvement throughout the education system in different ways. When students initiate action and share decisions with adults, partnerships flourish. Later in this book there are examples of specific ways that students and adults can work together to realize that vision. See Table 9 for specific ways to use the Ladder.

As I describe earlier, simply calling something meaningful does not make it so. Saying that students are complex is an understatement; saying that schools need to be responsive to their complexity seems overly simplistic. However, according to the Ladder, many educators may be treating students in disingenuous, non-empowering ways without even knowing it.

Among student voice researchers and practitioners who have learned about and studied this model, there is an important argument about the Ladder. There is been a debate raging about whether Hart was off-based regarding the pinnacle experience for young people in decision-making. Many people wondered if it is best for adults to initiate activities and share decision-making with young people; whether it is best for young people to initiate and direct decision-making in their activities; or for young people to initiate activities and share decisions with adults. It was his research that led Hart to conclude that child-led experiences where best for all involved. (Hart, 1997)

I have been serving schools with my Meaningful Student Involvement hypothesis for more than a decade and teaching about the Ladder model the entire time. After spending several years implementing each of the rungs on the Ladder in classrooms, boardrooms, offices, and other spaces throughout the education system, I have come to understand that Hart was not acknowledging the unique environments and cultures of schools when he created the Ladder. Unfortunately, many practitioners of student voice in schools today do not acknowledge it, either.

In recreating the Ladder for schools, I wanted to accommodate these understandings. However, instead of merely installing alternative words or shuffling around different words to other places, I have added wholly new concepts to the ladder. Illustrating the differences in involvement like this can help adults and students critically examine the myriad ways involvement happens throughout schools focused on decision-making and much more. However, it's essential to consider the unique environments of schools and the different ways involvement happens there as opposed to the community at large. It's essential to understand where students and adults are at and where we can *really* go with Meaningful Student Involvement. As soon as we begin using it, we assume responsibility for interpreting and re-interpreting this Ladder every time we use it to provide much needed information to keep modifying Meaningful Student Involvement.

HOW TO USE THE LADDER OF STUDENT INVOLVEMENT	
Don't **Use The Ladder To...**	*Do* **Use The Ladder To...**
• Set expectations for educators • Assess a whole school • Show students how powerful they can be • Give a teacher a score for how well they've engaged students • Set a single standard for activities throughout a student program • Evaluate a whole quarter of classes as a group • Empower students to call out teachers' behaviors in front of a class • Rank or rate classes, teachers, extracurricular activities or schools • Plan a single day of activities about schools in general • Justify a limited or narrow way of thinking about student involvement in a class or program	• Create conversations throughout schools about student involvement • Teach every student in a school about ways teachers might treat them • Encourage teachers to engage every student in their classes or activities • Teach teachers different options they have for ways to interact with students • Plan for the greatest engage of the greatest number of students within a program • Individually assess students' perceptions of a single day of class • Foster safe student/teacher conversations designed to improve their classroom practice • Develop ongoing, safe and supportive strategies for school improvement • Establish and sustain opportunities for students and teachers to work together to improve specific classes, teachers, extracurricular activities or schools • Support sustained, expansive and responsive activities throughout education

Table 9. How to Use the Ladder of Student Involvement

Chapter 21: Framework 5—Adult Perspectives of Students

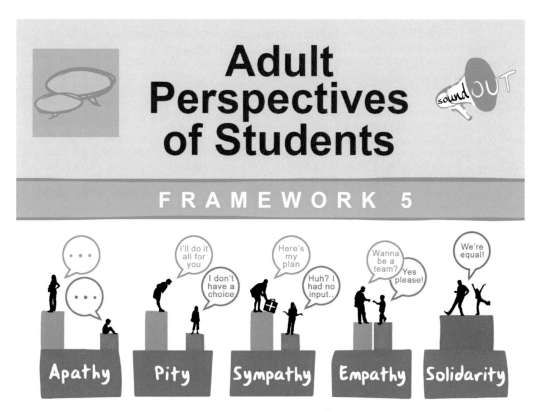

Figure 8. Adult Perspectives of Students

Adults have a lot unique motivations to become teachers, paraprofessionals, administrators, counselors, and school support staff. However, few of these motivations are as strong as our perspectives: If adults see students as needing or wanting us in any way, we can pretty much justify any activity that creates, fosters, and sustains learning for students.

The way we *see* students determines how we *treat* them. The way we treat students determines the outcomes of our activities with them. It can be hard when we are in the middle of our busy careers and work to stop and reflect on our perspectives of students. Adults' perspectives of students are informed by countless factors; however, I have seen five distinct perspectives of students emerge. Reflected in Figure 8 above, the following section explores these perspectives.[11]

1. Apathy

The first way adults can perceive students is with apathy. This occurs when adults deliberately choose to be indifferent toward students. This is different from *antipathy*, where one person does not know the other person exists. However, in schools, adults implicitly know students exist. Consciously choosing not to see them meaningfully is what determines whether adults have an apathetic perspective. This can happen in many ways, including school decision-making affecting both individual students and entire schools. Both students and adults can (and do) express apathy toward students. When an educator chooses not to listen to students' regular complaints about their teaching style and instead continues to teach the ways they always have, they are being apathetic toward students.

2. Pity

Pity happens when adults perceive students from the top down, making students the essential person to help without acknowledging the benefits they receive. Pity makes adults think they are completely superior to students in all ways, including intellectually, morally, and culturally. Adults view students as completely incapable of providing anything for themselves, and see students as fully dependent on adults. By positioning adults in positions of absolute authority, pity dehumanizes students by suppressing their self-esteem and incapacitating their self-conceptions of ability and purpose. Knowing what's best for students, adults in schools frequently do things to students without regard for whether students know what is happening, why it's happening, or how its relevant to their lives. This is pity towards students.

3. Sympathy

Perceiving students with sympathy is alluring to many adults. Sympathy disengages students from actively creating knowledge or resources by singularly positioning adults to give without acknowledging they are receiving anything in return. Sympathy is another top down perspective. It allows adults to give to students what they apparently cannot acquire for themselves, whether material, time, money, or otherwise, and to do that from a position of compassion. Beginning to acknowledge that students need to understand why they are doing what they do, principals might post their formal school improvement plan on the internet and invite students to view it. However, students aren't engaged as actors in the plan, instead being targeted as the recipients of change. Posting the plan demonstrates sympathy towards students.

4. Empathy

Reciprocity is at the core of an empathetic perspective of students. This viewpoint allows adults to see students are giving something as well as receiving it. Each person acknowledges the other as a partner, and each person becomes invested in the outcomes of the others' perspective. Empathy is rooted in equity and reciprocity. A professional development session that engages students as teacher trainers allows students to share their authentic voice with educators while allowing educators to gain valuable insight from students. This mutual exchange demonstrates empathy with students. I explore several pathways to authentic student voice in Table 1 of this book.

5. Solidarity

Complete solidarity comes from the perspective that students are not different from adults simply because of their age. Instead, it allows for complete equity by fully recognizing the benefits and challenges of Meaningful Student Involvement, and engaging students and adults in complete partnerships. These relationships between adults and students operate from a place of possibilities rather than deficits. Solidarity may be the most challenge image to conjure in education, since it makes both students and adults equally vulnerable and beneficial.

A. Considerations

There are many important considerations to recognize about adult perspectives of students. Following are two of the most important:

1. Adults do not maintain one perspective of all students all the time. While there are predominate perspectives, there are also exceptions to the rule. When confronting challenging perspectives, it can be important to acknowledge the exception, if it is positive.
2. These perspectives are not about good and bad—they just are. Adults simply cannot operate in complete empathy towards students all the time; likewise, students should not be expected to care for every single adult they ever meet.

Using these perspectives of students as a starting point, the challenge for adults becomes whether we can consciously, critically, and creatively reflect on our attitudes, behaviors, and ultimately, our perspectives. While we do this, it is our obligation to keep an eye towards further developing our practice to be more effective in the work we do.

Meaningful Student Involvement actively engages students throughout their schools and the education system. As they stand today, most student voice and student engagement programs only serve to help students learn about the absence of their effect on adults and their lack of power. They often reinforce the belief that the roles of young people throughout society are determined for them, and they simply need to accept what is coming down the line. These historical approaches to student voice and student engagement have brought our schools to where they are now. By manipulating, tokenizing, and exploiting individual students' perspectives on any given topic in education, and by seeing students in pitiful or sympathetic ways, entire generations of young people have been disengaged in schools. I explore some reasons for student disengagement in Tables 3 and 5 of this book.

While this prognosis is grim, the models in Part Three also showed another way. Learning about student-led involvement as well as equality and equity between students and adults demonstrates practical theory to inform practice. Perhaps more importantly, Part Three examined personal steps each student and adult in schools can take by transforming their perspectives from apathy towards empathy and solidarity. This is the hope represented by Meaningful Student Involvement, that schools can move from being done *to* students towards being done *by* and *with* students. That's the future of learning.

---

[1] This section was previously published as Fletcher, A. (Aug 2011) "Keeping an Eye Out: How Adults Perceive Students," *Connect*, No. 190. p 27-28.

Chapter 22: Framework 6—Spheres of Meaning

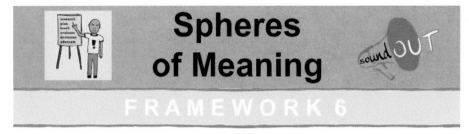

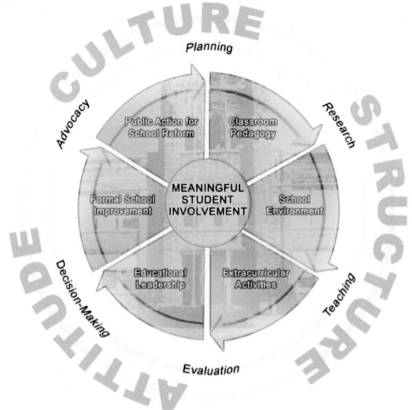

Figure 9. Spheres of Meaningful Student Involvement

Meaningful Student Involvement is not a stand-alone activity. Educators and school leaders commit to fostering Student/Adult Partnerships that transform the hearts and minds of school communities through initiatives that concentrate on the well-defined need to integrate roles for Meaningful Student Involvement throughout education. Taking a whole systems approach to addressing that challenge, individual classrooms, whole buildings, or entire districts emphasize new designs, materials, processes, tools, policies, or any combination, in order to address multiple problems surrounding student engagement and student voice. These strategies should be integrated, dealing with key issues throughout the school community.

Figure 9 above illustrates the systems approach of Meaningful Student Involvement. It reflects three spheres of activity where I have seen and worked with schools as they integrate students as partners throughout education. They are the Core Sphere, which illustrates the places where Meaningful Student Involvement happens; the Nesting Sphere, which shows which activities I have consistently found foster Meaningful Student Involvement throughout the education system; and the Surrounding Sphere that emphasizes the elements of the education system that hold the keys to transformation.

There are two commitments represented in Figure 9: The first, a commitment to aligning Meaningful Student Involvement with systems thinking, and second, a commitment to demonstrating practical, pragmatic ways to move theory into action.

There are three Spheres of Meaningful Student Involvement that should be recognized.

A. Core Sphere: Locations

The Core Sphere of Meaningful Student Involvement is comprised of several locations for where students can be engaged as partners in learning, teaching and leadership. While I have identified specific activities throughout the school where student voice happens, this specific sphere reflects a larger systemic approach to integrating students as partners throughout the education system. There are six sections in the Core Sphere that show where Student/Adult Partnerships are formed and affected.

1. Classroom Pedagogy

This is the crux of teaching, learning, and assessment in all schools. Teachers study, practice, and critically examine pedagogy, often identifying places where student voice can strengthen their practice. Pedagogy includes curriculum and informal assessments, as well as teaching styles and learning tools including technology and textbooks. Meaningful Student Involvement should be reflected in the ways teachers teach, classrooms are managed, and learning is assessed, starting in classroom and rippling throughout the entirety of the system.

2. School Environment

The environment for teaching, learning and leadership throughout schools is determined by many factors including relationships, relevance, rigor and responsibility. The environment includes relationships between students, including bullying and peer helpers, as well as student-teacher relationships, and relationships between every adult throughout education. Meaningful Student Involvement informs all relationships between students and adults throughout schools and the education system, from school counselors to principals to district staff to the state school board.

3. Extracurricular Activities

Student government, clubs, sports, and any other activity not directed by classroom learning happens in extracurricular activities. Extracurricular activities include anytime a student spends in school when they are not earning credits, including clubs, sports and student government, as well as cafeteria time, library usage, theater and more. The efficacy of out-of-classroom learning should be deeply informed by Meaningful Student Involvement by embracing students as active drivers of activities, opportunities and outcomes through extracurricular functions of all kinds.

4. Education Leadership

Building principals, local and state boards of education, district and state education agency staff, and federal politicians fall into this category. Meaningful Student Involvement should be infused through equitable partnerships with education leaders, and should not negate, deny or otherwise silence any students. Leadership activities include building administration, teacher committees, district policy-making including school boards, state administration including grant administration, professional standards, building assessments, program reviews, and formal assessments of student learning. Decision-making efficacy, ongoing relevance and empowered outcomes can all happen through Meaningful Student Involvement throughout these processes.

5. Formal School Improvement

Every K-12 public school must strive to constantly improve, innovate and transform to meet the needs of today's students and tomorrow's society. This includes data-driven assessments of school performance; qualitative evidence of student and adults' opinions about school achievement; analysis and data; prioritization of issues according to research-demonstrated outcomes; whole school planning; student/adult partnered implementation; and ongoing monitoring by students and adults that re-informs the process of assessments. To do this, Meaningful Student Involvement is infused throughout formal school improvement plans and actions by integrating students as partners. This process can lead students and educators towards powerful outcomes for all learners.

6. Public Action for School Transformation

Students around the world are asserting themselves into local, state, national and international dialogues about education transformation and other essential conversations about schools. They are doing this by engaging as public citizens who are leading student organizing, participating in community-led school transformation and other active protest movements. Meaningful Student Involvement can be an engine of this action, serving to embrace and empower students through deep learning and substantive outcomes that sustain their roles throughout time.

The six components of the core sphere hold almost all activities that occur throughout education. That is because *every* adult throughout the education system can benefit from Meaningful Student Involvement. When adults throughout the education system realize and enact that, more and more students will have room to become meaningfully involved.

From here, it becomes vital to understand that Meaningful Student Involvement cannot happen within a silo or simply through one channel. Instead, when understood as needing nesting, the Core Sphere is seen as a poignant place to begin—not end.

B. Nesting Sphere: Actions

The Nesting Sphere of Meaningful Student Involvement is made of the roles through which research and practice consistently demonstrate positive, powerful outcomes. I call it the Nesting Sphere because these activities hold the Core Sphere intact by nurturing Student/Adult Partnerships in action, rather than just in concept. Meaningful Student Involvement is both conceptual and practical, and not simply an either/or dichotomy.

These six roles form a typology that can be infused throughout schools on both personal/individual levels, and the community/collective levels. They can be seen as both a progression through a linear continuum of action, and as a hodgepodge from a variety of perspectives that depend on where you are looking from. I identified them in my initial research on student involvement almost fifteen years ago. They are meant to reflect the majority of the times students said involvement mattered most to them.

I expand on each of these greatly further in the book; this section is merely an introduction.

1. Students Planning Education

When you are observing the second sphere, the first role you should understand is student as planner. Students of all ages are capable of planning a variety of activities throughout education. Any student can participate in planning on personal and community levels in activities that affect just them, or ones that affect everyone throughout a school district or beyond. The possibilities of students as planners align well with the first sphere, as each of those locations requires planning of some sort.

2. Students Researching Schools

The second role has to do with examining any component of education, from why it happens to how it's delivered, and all points in between. This research can be practical, where Student/Adult Partnerships examine what is happening throughout education and why it is happening. Practical research generally includes questionnaires, surveys, interviews, observations and/or discussion groups. Students researching schools can also focus on theoretical research, where they read research archives, published academic journals and other sources to device their own theories about learning, teaching and leadership.

3. Students Teaching Classes

The arch of time has consistently shown that French philosopher Joseph Joubert was right when he philosophized that to teach is to learn twice. When students teach students, when students teach adults and when students teach themselves, they learn far more effectively than through any other approach. Whether focused on building skills or sharing knowledge, students can devise their own lessons plans or partner with teachers; they can deliver curriculum and facilitate coursework; they can co-teach, tutor, or self-lead learning. This is not just *some* students, either: it is every student. Every student has the capacity to teach and learn from themselves and other students.

4. Students Evaluating Education

Stepping into roles as evaluators shows students they have substantive perspectives that other students and adults need and want to know. Students are already evaluating their schools every single day by showing up metaphorically and practically. Given opportunities to systematize and expand on those evaluations, they can help inform practical action and transform stagnate learning into active, dynamic and meaningful involvement for themselves and their peers.

5. Students Making Decisions

Research has consistently shown that students want more opportunities to be involved in making substantive decisions about what happens to them in schools. Confronted with individual choices daily, students also want systemic decision-making opportunities that move beyond the A/B binary and towards the complex, real-world decisions made so often by adults for them. This can happen on every level throughout the education system, and effectively engage every single student as partners in the process.

6. Students Advocating For Education

When they are first confronted with the picture of students advocating for education, many adults automatically assume there is no one better to stand up for schools than the beneficiaries. However, the challenge of this is that students often do not understand themselves to be benefiting from schools. Learning about things that matter to them and discovering ways to stand up for what they believe in is a lifelong skill that will enrich everyone, especially students in schools.

This six roles can wrap around the hearts of students and adults alike, weaving through their imaginations the possibilities and hopes of learning, teaching and leadership throughout schools. Concentrated by their alignment with a place in Core Sphere, these roles can invigorate and enhance the meaning of student involvement wherever it happens. However, they become truly enriched when viewed from the perspective of the Surrounding Sphere.

C. Surrounding Sphere: Realms

The outer sphere of Meaningful Student Involvement are the realms for transformation. Individually, each of these reflects a different way that summarizes the major areas of action. Collectively, they form a distinct pathway for students, classroom teachers, school leaders, education agency officials, and others throughout the education system as well as community partners. This sphere seeks to infuse student voice with power, purpose and belonging throughout the entirety of the education system, but does so by showing the main drivers in each location throughout schools. Each of these realms can become apparent to anyone who is observing them, when they know to look for them. Students can see the culture of schools in their everyday interactions with peers and adults; teachers can see the structure of schools in their pedagogy and practice throughout the day; leaders can see the attitudes of individuals in every location and activity throughout the system.

1. Culture

Apparent throughout the everyday functioning of the education system, culture is made of the beliefs, habits values, visions, norms, systems, and symbols within a specific and definable school community. Culture is shown in the ways people talk with each other; the nonverbal communication they use; the clothing they wear and the ways they decorate themselves, and more. The physical places throughout school systems reflect the culture of education, whether considering the hallways, classrooms, cafeterias, student commons, principals' offices, school boardroom, or other places. If a space is highly formal, it might demonstrate a culture of tradition and determination. If a space is decorated with student art and graffiti, it might represent informality and looseness.

The culture of schools is reflected in student involvement. It is important to understand that culture is in the eye of the beholder also. If a classroom is filled with slouching, bored-looking students who are sloppily dressed and mumbling to each other, an adult may assume that the teacher is ineffectual and the students are disengaged. However, listening to student voice could show these same students are reclining comfortably while deeply engrossed in brainstorming and problem-solving a classroom issue.

Similarly, vandalism and bullying in schools is also an indication of whether students feel meaningfully involved or not. If Meaningful Student Involvement is apparent in school culture, bullying will be mitigated. All students of all ages are well capable of expressing themselves and their opinions, experiences and ideas in schools and about education in healthy and positive ways, given substantive opportunities to do that. Without those opportunities, students are left to identify ways to express themselves. While these may take the form of articles in the school newspaper or impassioned speeches at school board meetings, Meaningful Student Involvement these do not make. Instead, these are temporary and constrained expressions. So are vandalism and bullying in schools.

The culture of a school that has embedded Meaningful Student Involvement is distinctly reflective of that reality. The elements of Student/Adult Partnerships become increasingly obvious in every relationship between every student and each adult within a school building, and beyond that into the entire education system they belong to. The key characteristics of Meaningful Student Involvement appear eventually will appear with such frequency in classrooms, hallways and throughout schools that they will be indistinguishable from the school culture. The very perspectives of adults will have transformed wholly, and every student in every school will be seen and engage as partners.

2. Structure

Where culture reflects the intangible, yet observable components of Meaningful Student Involvement, the structure of schools is made of the named activities, policies, strategies, processes, allocation, coordination, and supervision of people throughout an education system. The structure of the education system has traditionally appeared rigid, inflexible and hardened to the realities and needs of modern society. With compartmentalization of jobs throughout these old-fashioned structures, teachers were responsible merely for teaching the subjects they are responsible for; principals were responsible for managing their teachers; and others throughout the education system were similarly divided by purpose and outcomes. This worked in a society that treasured conformity and uniformity over creativity and entrepreneurship. However, coordination and communication between different players in these education systems was limited, and the real needs of students were wholly ignored. Standardized curriculum and assessments were the norm, and a fixation on efficiency increased classroom sizes while allowing a large percentage of students to dropout and/or be funneled through the school-to-prison pipeline. Regardless of their position in schools, students were always seen as the passive recipients of adult-driven planning, research, teaching, evaluation, decision-making and advocacy in schools. See Table 22 of this book for examples of what that can look like.

An emerging structure in schools is focused on smaller learning environments. This approach allows more specialization to meet student needs or desires by giving educators more leeway to make decisions for themselves. A large urban school that once had 5,000 students might be split into four small schools, each one focusing on a different learning area, including a liberal arts school, a social good school, a technology and engineering school, and a performing arts school. This approach can work to foster Meaningful Student Involvement rapidly and specifically among different populations of students. However, it can be expensive and limited by a district's size or budget. Additionally, since there are no guarantees, these smaller schools can also use a traditional structure on their scale.

A third type of school structure overlays both previous types of structures—traditional and small schools—within a single school building. This can allow educators to act as experts in their own fields of teaching and leadership, while allowing students to experience Meaningful Student Involvement in teaching, learning and leadership. Without deliberate facilitation and high-level coordination by school leaders, struggles can emerge among students who are experiencing meaningful involvement, and there can be distinct senses of challenge and competition between the meaningfully involved and those who do not experience that meaningfulness. These challenges can be met though, as according Student/Adult Partnerships can nurture wide-ranging student engagement, while the structure of the school maintains its alignment with the school improvement planning process.

3. Attitude

Attitude is made of the opinions, actions, knowledge and beliefs of individuals. The attitudes within an education-oriented environment are made of every individual within those environments. Attitudes determine the outlook a person has on the world around them, and as such they influence the course and outcomes of all teaching, learning and leadership throughout the education system. Attitudes belong to all layers of a person's identity, whether it is their role in schools as a student, teacher, paraprofessional, janitor, school board member, or bus driver; as a member of a racial or ethnic group; whether a person is an English Language Learner, is fluent in multiple languages, or is a non-English speaker; and whether a person identifies as poor, working class, low-income, middle income or high income. Self-perceptions of academic achievement drive students' attitudes, while adults in schools perceptions of professional efficacy drive their attitudes as well.

Student attitudes affect every component of their school day and educational experience. This includes their social standing, academic achievement, classroom and out-of-classroom behavior, as well as Meaningful Student Involvement. If a student has an attitude that allows for them to be in a partnership with adults throughout the education system, they will be much more effective than the student who is limited to believing they must resist Student/Adult Partnerships. Similarly, adult attitudes affect every component of Meaningful Student Involvement.

If students look around a classroom and do not see themselves, they will not have attitudes that will lead towards Meaningful Student Involvement. If adults throughout an education setting constantly use diminutive and limiting language about students or simply do not discuss students at all, they cannot foster Meaningful Student Involvement. When students feel threatened with punishment for expressing their perspectives, wisdom, ideas, criticisms and knowledge about schools and education at large, they cannot be meaningfully involved. If teachers constantly experience disengaged and apathetic students, they may not attempt to meaningfully involve learners in their classrooms. Students and adults need to work together to identify what attitudes look like when they reflect Meaningful Student Involvement. Planning for action should center on fostering the proper attitudes for Meaningful Student Involvement.

D. Habits of Meaningful Student Involvement

Fostering the attitudes needed to support Meaningful Student Involvement requires intention and action. The following attitudes form the habits of Meaningful Student Involvement. They reflect the highest attitudes and best potential individual habits required. To support every student in every school becoming meaningfully involved throughout every facet of the educational system, every part of the education system from kindergarten classrooms to the president of the country should foster these habits among students and adults alike.

- **Trust:** Mutual trust is required, including trusting oneself and trusting others, whether its students trusting other students, students trusting adults, adults trusting students, or adults trusting other adults.
- **Inclusiveness:** Intentionally reaching out to every student and every adult throughout a school or district or state agency should be a habit of all meaningful involvement.
- **Commitment:** Everyone shares a commitment to build and support Student/Adult Partnerships for every student.
- **Reciprocity:** Forming a habit of sharing with others what is shared with you is a key to meaningful involvement.
- **Challenging:** Students should take on challenges throughout the educational process and across the entire education system by partnering with adults.
- **Equality:** No student is more deserving or naturally needing meaningfulness in education than any other student.
- **Grit:** Working hard to improve schools benefits each of us and every generation after us.
- **Learning:** We learn valuable lessons we would not otherwise by serving our schools, communities and society at large through Meaningful Student Involvement.
- **Equity:** Adults should not do anything *to* or *for* students; they should do everything *with* students, or create opportunities for students to do it on their own.
- **Transformation:** Schools are places where students will continually grow and change, and because of this they will continually grow and change to support students. They will do this through Meaningful Student Involvement.
- **Humility:** Students and adults are humble and accept that there are things about themselves and what they do in schools that can be transformed through Meaningful Student Involvement.
- **Accepting:** Creating space for students to provide critiques instead of criticism requires adults become accepting of difference and acknowledging of ongoing change.

These attitudes are vital for individuals the education system to adopt, including students and all adults no matter what their roles. Our attitudes inform the deep beliefs every person has about teaching, learning and leadership—no matter what their age. These beliefs drive student and adult decisions and behavior in schools. The attitudes behind Meaningful Student Involvement are about looking at education in terms of creating value for everyone involved instead of adults alone. This is an engaging and necessary approach in today's dynamic society that continues to transform every single day.

Summary
These three components form the surrounding sphere of Meaningful Student Involvement. They form the container that the core sphere and nesting sphere rest inside of. Without addressing these components, the other spheres will not and cannot be meaningful. I expand on these components in depth later in this book.

Each of these spheres is wholly interactive with the others, and provides a view into the heart of Meaningful Student Involvement.

10 STEPS TO TRANSFORM YOUR DISTRICT OVER TIME

1. **Infuse** Meaningful Student Involvement into every school's improvement plan, everywhere and for every student.
2. **Teach** all students about education as a process, as an institution and as a democratic responsibility.
3. **Educate** every teacher in every school about all aspects of students' cultures.
4. **Create** opportunities for students to co-lead federal, state and district educational policymaking.
5. **Establish** every student as an active, empowered and engaged partner in every aspect of schools and throughout the entire education system.
6. **Engage** every educator in exploring the roles of discrimination throughout education.
7. **Develop** standard opportunities for all students to research education, in either elementary, middle or high school.
8. **Promote** widespread understanding of adultism throughout the education system.
9. **Foster** policies, professional development, student training and other sustainable supports for Meaningful Student Involvement.
10. **Challenge** all student tokenism in all education settings, everywhere, all the time.

Table 10. 10 Steps to Transform Your District Over Time

Chapter 23: Framework 7—Learning Process

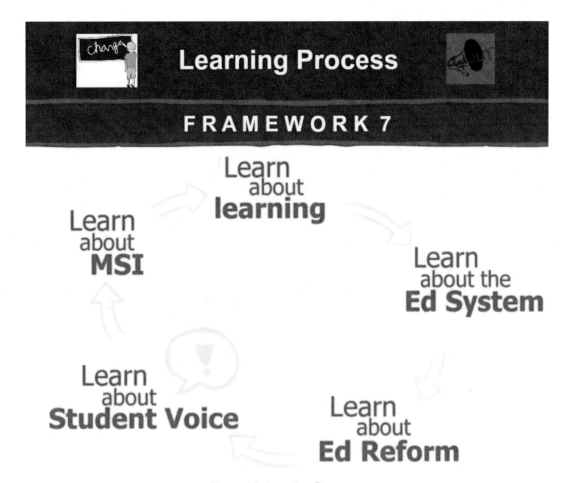

Figure 10. Learning Process

What does it say that after eight, ten, or even thirteen years of formal schooling most students cannot explain the process of education in that they participate in? SoundOut believes that every student should be able to verbalize what they are a part of when they come to school. This is what Giroux calls sharing the "language of possibility." (McLaren, 2003) For that reason, the Meaningful Student Involvement Learning Process is the final framework.

The notion behind the Learning Process shown in Figure 10 above is pinned to Delpit's essential theories focused on social justice in education. Addressing the neoliberal myth that all students benefit from free-range education practices, Delpit promotes the practice of teachers "decode" the white, middle-class culture that pervades schools. (Delpit, 1988) Meaningful Student Involvement seeks to decode the middle-class structure and adulist restraints that are pervasive throughout the entire public education system. Dismantling the entrenched systems of power and authority throughout the education system, Meaningful Student Involvement relies on students learning about all aspects of education. This requires decoding and the end of the assumption that any action in schools is good action. It also combats the belief that any student voice is good student voice by acknowledging where students are at now, and naming new places they can go.

This Learning Process is designed to maximize student learning while realizing their involvement potential throughout the educational system. Each of the following components of the Learning Process is neither a step nor an end in-and-of-itself. Instead, each is an interlocking platform that can serve to ensure the meaningfulness of student involvement.

Starting in kindergarten and extending through twelfth grade, students should have the opportunity to expand their capacity to be meaningfully involved throughout education. The following Learning Process, as illustrated in Figure 10, represents a constructivist perspective, in the sense that it is essential for past student learning to be acknowledged to build upon and progress. Regardless of the grade a student experiences Meaningful Student Involvement, their previous knowledge about education should be assessed and built upon.

A. What Learning Focuses On

To foster Meaningful Student Involvement, learning should focus on five areas shown in Figure 10. Students and adults should:

- Learn about learning;
- Learning about the education system;
- Learning about education reform and transformation;
- Learn about student voice, and;
- Learn about Meaningful Student Involvement.

Of course, each of these can be studied independently, but without an understanding of each a complete picture of possibilities and purpose might not be complete. Additionally, each of these should be studied before, during and after different activities (See Table 7 for activities). As illustrated in the Cycle of Engagement, reflection is essential for learning through Meaningful Student Involvement.

1. Learning

Learning is no longer the mystery it once was. We now know that there are different learning styles, multiple learning supports and a variety of ways to demonstrate learning. To be meaningfully involved, students must understand those different aspects as well.

Students have the mental capacity to learn about learning from the very beginning of their intentional educative experiences. From those pre-school years through graduation, schools can be fostering student learning about learning. This means helping students understand what learning styles are, how they function and what good it does to recognize them. It means providing students with countless opportunities to explore different learning styles in addition to encouraging them to self-identify their own predominant style. It also means allowing them multiple opportunities to re-assess their learning style, build empathy with learners who identify with other styles and expand their capacities to successfully learn through other avenues.

As students build their capacity to learn about learning, more opportunities should be shared that expand their understanding of what learning is, how learning happens and what learning does. Through this constructivist approach, students can incorporate learning from life and learning in classrooms, reinforcing the relevance of the teaching/learning process and self-education. This is illustrated in Figure 17.

2. Education System

The complexities of schools are not known to many adults. Theoretical and moral debates, funding streams and the rigors of student assessment are overwhelming to many administrators, as well as teachers and parents. Many adults cannot name everything involved in an education system, either. An education system is the entire set of activities, individuals, places and outcomes set into motion for students to learn. It is made of everything that goes into schools from local, state and federal sources. These include the laws, policies, and regulations; funding, resource allocations, and procedures for determining funding levels; district, state and federal administrative offices, as well as school facilities, and transportation vehicles; human resources, staffing, contracts, compensation and employee benefits; books, computers, teaching resources and other learning materials; and many other elements. (Glossary of Education Reform, 2013)

For students to be meaningfully involved in schools, they must have at least a basic knowledge of what is being done to them and for them, if not with them. At the minimum, students should know there is a current system for educating young people, and they are part of it. They should understand grade levels and student grouping, e.g. elementary, middle, and senior high schools as well as the purposes of grading, testing, graduation, and dropping out. Students should understand the ways curricular topics work together to form a liberal arts education, as well as the relationship between classes, schools, districts, state education agencies, and federal education departments. Students should have a wide understanding of who the individuals are throughout the education system, from individual students to teachers, principals, superintendents, governors, state education leaders, legislators, and federal leaders. The connections between graduation and life after high school, e.g. college, work, and income levels, should be made clear, as well as the relationship between public schools, basic education and the democratic society we live in.

3. Education Reform

The unending process of school transformation is heavily influenced by economic trends, cultural attitudes, socio-economic backgrounds and political beliefs. Understandings about the nature of democratic governance and social justice play into school leadership, too. There are many practical avenues for students to learn about formal and informal school improvement measures, especially by becoming meaningfully involved within those activities. Sometimes there is no better avenue for understanding than through active engagement in the subject matter, and school improvement may be one of those areas.

4. Student Voice

While it seems intuitive to understand the voices that we are born with, unfortunately many students seem to lack that knowledge. Whether through submissive consumerism, oppressive social conditions or the internalization of popular conceptions of youth, many students today do not believe they have anything worth saying, or any action worth contributing towards making their schools better places for everyone involved. Even if a student does understand their voice, it is essential to expand that understanding and gain new abilities to be able to become meaningfully involved.

5. Meaningful Student Involvement

While Meaningful Student Involvement is not "rocket science", it does challenge many students. After so many years of being subjected to passive or cynical treatment, many students are leery or resistant towards substantive engagement in schools. Educating students about Meaningful Student Involvement means increasing their capacity to participate by focusing on the skills and knowledge they need. Only in this way can they be effective partners, and fully realize the possibilities for education today and in the future.

When the Learning Process is complete, schools should use what the evolving capacities of their student body to re-inform the next process, as students in the cohort will certainly be able to become meaningfully involved in yet more expansive ways! This is the re-invigorating challenge of Meaningful Student Involvement: As students are always evolving, so should schools. That should not equate the end of tradition; instead, it should mark the beginning of a transformation that never ends. That is what learning is all about.

B. Additional Areas for Learning

The five areas of the Meaningful Student Involvement Learning Process show a general process for what students and adults should learn about to prepare for and engage in throughout different activities. There are additional areas participants can learn about.

1. Learning about Ourselves

Wrapped up in this deconstruction is an understanding of who is involved in Meaningful Student Involvement and throughout the education system at large. Students can learn about who they are individually, which situates their voice in the center of classroom curriculum. They can learn about who other students are, individually and as student bodies; who teachers are personally and professionally; who the administrators and support staff are supporting them throughout the education system; and other adults who benefit their learning, teaching and leadership. Nobody should be left out of this function, whether students are examining the individuals within their own buildings or the people who constitute their local school boards.

2. Learning about Roles

Starting from the youngest ages, students should have a functioning understanding of the roles involved directly in their education. As they progress through grades, this understanding should expand until they completely understand the myriad roles throughout education, as well as their functions, activities and outcomes. This should include the roles of students; parents; school support staff, paraprofessionals, non-certificated staff, and adult volunteers; secretaries, adult tutors, coaches, librarians, classroom assistants, and parent representatives; teachers, teacher leaders, and teacher coaches; counselors and mental health specialists; building administrators including the principal or headmaster and assistant principals; district administration including staff and leaders; state administration and the chief school officers; elected officials like school board, superintendents, governors, state legislators, and the state supreme court; and federal officials, including the department of education, congress and national leader.

Students should learn about the specific roles they are interested in, going to focus on, on set to partner with through Meaningful Student Involvement. For instance, if a student team is working with a group of teachers, education professors and a teachers union representative to promote students going into the teaching profession after they graduate, they should understand the role of the teacher. This should happen beyond a superficial way, too: Students should know "what it takes to be certified as teachers; how teachers are affected by policies and requirements in choosing how and why they teach a certain way; what specific instructional methods are commonly used by teachers and which seem to work best; how educational research informs new instructional approaches, or how certain kinds of professional development can improve teaching effectiveness in a school, among many other things." (Glossary of Education Reform, 2013)

3. Learning about Functions

Many people have broad opinions about what the functions of the education system are. Before we think about the functions of the system though, we must name exactly what the education system is and does. Understanding the moving pieces of the education system, it is easier to understand that the function of the education system has several parts:

- To make sure that new generations learn what previous generations know, and expand on it as necessary;
- To help young people move from living with their families to living in the wider society;
- To intentionally and coincidentally socialize students to the culture, attitudes and values surrounding them;
- To help people find what roles they are going to have in society;
- To drive society and social reform through focus on specific topics and people, like English language learning and low-income students. (Haggar, 2013)

Once a student understands these functions of school and the education system, they can be more effective agents of change throughout that system. (Fielding, 2001) Without a full understanding of the functions of education, students will merely be yelling into a vacuum while trying to get it to stop. Table 10 explores some ways classroom teachers, club sponsors, athletic coaches and others can make every day meaningful for students.

13 WAYS TO CHANGE CLASSROOMS EVERY DAY

Everyday Respect All Students, Everywhere, All the Time
1. **Memorize:** Learn students' names and use them frequently.
2. **Stylize:** Make the learning environment reflect students' intentions, hopes and dreams for education, learning and the classroom itself.
3. **Utilize:** Show students you're interested in them through deliberate interactions, thoughtful words and kindness.
4. **Operationalize:** Teach students about and foster Student/Adult Partnerships to flip the traditional passive student roles they may assume.
5. **Dualize:** Actively demonstrate what Student/Adult Partnerships can look like in teaching, classroom prep and cleanup, classroom expectations and more by working with a student partner *as often as possible.*
6. **Strategize:** Daily throughout the entire year engage students in deliberate conversations about meaningfulness, student involvement and school improvement.

Build School Belonging and Student Ownership
Students can become meaningfully involved in your class by...
7. Evaluating lessons
8. Creating learning materials
9. Facilitating activities for their peers
10. Co-teaching with teachers
11. Being peer mediators
12. Tutoring younger students or peers
13. And contributing in other areas.

Table 11. 11 Ways to Change Classrooms Every Day

Chapter 24: Comparing the Frameworks

These Frameworks can provide essential guidance to involve students as partners. They always interact; often compliment; and even occasionally contradict each other, all to provide Meaningful Student Involvement practitioners with useful, challenging and enlightening avenues to transform education. Each can be used to teach; plan; evaluate; make decisions; research; and advocate for Meaningful Student Involvement.

The Frameworks for Meaningful Student Involvement are:
1. Student/Adult Partnerships
2. Key Characteristics
3. Perspectives of Students
4. The Ladder of Student Involvement
5. Spheres of Meaning
6. The Cycle of Engagement
7. Learning Process

Framework 1 lays the basis for conscientious, practical relationships between students and adults throughout schools. It shows the appropriate amount of authority and potential within these relationships, and lays a foundation for strong Meaningful Student Involvement. Framework 2 holds the potential of student involvement high by relating the most obvious features of meaningfulness to the structure and puprpose of schools today. By examining the ways adults see students, Framework 3 allows adults to reveal their underlying assumptions that may undermine, demean or otherwise betray their attempts at meaningfully involving students. Similarly, Framework 4 places the individual activities that students are involved in within a model to understand why different approaches work, flounder or fail. Framework 5 demonstrates some of these interrelationships by relating what, how and why students are working to improve schools. In Framework 6, a process for engaging others can expose the potential of involvement to transform schools, while Framework 7 shows how individuals can learn from involvement.

These frameworks interact by constantly creating opportunities to overtly and subtly navigate a variety of different spaces and concepts within and across the education system. For instances, the Spheres of Meaning contain three main areas for action: Core Sphere, Nesting Sphere, and the Surrounding Sphere, all of which reflect the Characteristics of Meaningful Student Involvement. In the core sphere, we learn that public action, classroom pedagogy, school environment, extracurricular activities, educational leadership and formal school improvement being the main locations for meaningfulness. But with the characteristics, we discover those general activities need to be reflected in specific ways. Similarly, the frameworks show us that adult perspectives of students are always present in different ways on the Ladder of Student Involvement, and that both of those inform the learning process. Table 9 shows varying approaches to employing the Ladder.

Meaningful Student Involvement is intricately woven together through action, theory and outcomes. The Frameworks can guide and inform the systems thinking behind this by compelling students, educators and others towards substantive action everyday throughout the entirety of the education system.

Part IV. Benefits of Meaningful Student Involvement

Chapter 25: Introduction

Rather than being a pie-in-the-sky goal with lofty ideals and purposeless implementation, Meaningful Student Involvement has very concrete benefits. Part Four shows many of the benefits of using the frameworks from Part Three. The inherent outcomes of Student/Adult Partnerships are elaborated here as the Aims of Meaningful Student Involvement, while the attributes demonstrate what actionable outcomes look like. After that, research-proven outcomes are made explicit.

For the first decade of my work in this field, I heard a basic question emerge every time I mentioned student voice. Faced with the suffocating effects of federal education laws, educators across the United States continually asked, "Why does student voice matter?" Sometimes it is a rhetorical question, sometimes facetious, usually it was honest. Educators simply wanted to know what advantages there are to engaging students as partners in learning throughout education.

Following is a summary of reasons why Meaningful Student Involvement matters, and why Student/Adult Partnerships are changing schools right now.

AIMS OF MEANINGFUL STUDENT INVOLVEMENT

1. **Deepen** learning for all students in every school, everywhere, all the time.
2. **Engage** students at all grade levels and in all subjects as contributing stakeholders in teaching, learning and leading the entire education system.
3. **Expand** the expectation of every student in every school to become an active and equitable partner throughout education.
4. **Promote** a core commitment within all members of the school community—including teachers, administrators, school staff, parents, community supports and others—to meaningfully involve students as learners, teachers and leaders throughout every part of schools.
5. **Provide** students and educators with sustainable, responsive and systemic approaches to engaging all students throughout education, committing to the reality that as society constantly changes, schools should too.
6. **Acknowledge** the experience, perspectives and knowledge of all students.
7. **Engage** adults as allies and partners with students.
8. **Foster** appreciation of student perspectives, experiences and knowledge and avoid adult interpretations.
9. **Recognize** the right, responsibility and need for students to experience ownership of their learning, schools and the entire education system.

Table 12. Aims of Meaningful Student Involvement

Chapter 26: Aims of Meaningful Student Involvement

There must be active intentions that are not afraid to accomplish big goals by going through deliberate process. Considering the history of public education, it is vital to build democracy and empowerment. Through reflection and brainstorming, I have identified the following Aims of Meaningful Student Involvement to fulfill these expectations in powerful ways.

1. Deepen learning for all students in every school, everywhere, all the time.

Effective learning is deepened learning. Deepened learning is life transforming, paving the road for a lifelong commitment to expanding personal knowledge and skills that allow people to change their lives and make a difference in the world. Every person is capable of making a difference in the world in a positive, powerful way. The first aim of Meaningful Student Involvement is to foster deepened learning for all students in every school, everywhere, all the time. To do this, students will become partners in every facet of education. Simultaneous to deepening their learning, Meaningful Student Involvement will strengthen learner commitment to learning, community and democracy.

Meaningful involvement builds the access that learners must the tools that build their literacy. They gain access to the materials they need to transform education as well as the people who make schools function, operate and change every single day. This may mean high school students partnering with a district program director to conduct research to benefit a grant application that will establish an outreach program for area elementary students. It could include English language learners from Latin America working with a curriculum committee to select the best literature for Spanish language classes for non-native speakers. Eighth grade students may develop and facilitate an outreach program with their school counselors to introduce and integrate incoming fifth grade students into their middle schools. Graduating seniors might write deeply reflective and evaluative reflections summarizing their learning journey as part of their graduation requirements and develop substantive, meaningful documents to share their recommended best practices, tips and tools with teachers in specifically designated student-led professional development days. Kindergarten students might participate in design activities for a new school building that replaces their current one. The access that is implicit throughout these activities might include high usage of technology; interactive sessions with adults from a variety of backgrounds in the education system and throughout the community; and the ability to identify what they need to learn for themselves.

Students engagement soars through Meaningful Student Involvement by building their sustained connections throughout the learning experience. Every activity they are involved in focuses on applied learning that positions them as problem solvers who directly contribute to making a positive, powerful and effective difference throughout education. They design learning activities, determine learning objectives, and facilitate their own learning experiences and those for other students, too. Co-learning with adults, in Meaningful Student Involvement students experience substantial opportunities for self-assessment, too, as they constantly explore their own intentions, abilities, successes and challenges throughout the process of change.

The process of Meaningful Student Involvement also emphasizes student expression. Deliberately establishing Student/Adult Partnerships requires high levels of communication, and to do that students have many opportunities to build their verbal, written, artistic and other forms of appropriate expression. All these types of intentionally infused into the process to reach the multiple engagement styles of students, which mirror multiple intelligences. Written expression, storytelling, multimedia presentations, building and making, and creative/artistic outlets are all key to making a difference in schools and substantiating student learning through meaningful involvement.

Questions to Ask

- When can students *not* learn from student involvement?
- Why are students limited to receiving classroom credit only for activities when adults approve of the learning they experience?
- Which learners are not experiencing Meaningful Student Involvement right now? Why not?

2. Engage students at all grade levels and in all subjects as contributing stakeholders in teaching, learning, and leading in schools.

There are no "across-the-board" limitations, such as race, gender, socio-economic status, school size, or subject matter, or developmental roadblocks, like age, academic performance or physical disabilities that prohibit Meaningful Student Involvement. Educators in all grade levels are equally charged with the responsibility of infusing hope into learning. Meaningful Student Involvement also extends across and integrates within all curricula, challenging the social studies teacher equally with the physical education teacher.

Unfortunately, there is an unspoken belief that only *some* students can be involved in schools. Requirements around academic participation, behavior and teacher permission often coincide with racial and socio-economic gaps between students who participate and those who do not. The adult educators who sponsor these opportunities also frequently mirror those gaps, all of which combine to demonstrate a "student involvement gap" that is much like the academic achievement gap present throughout many schools today.

Even in schools where there are largely homogenous student bodies, there are still disparities among students who are involved and those who are not. These can shake out along the lines of parent involvement, historical family cultural attitudes towards education, and teacher support for student engagement.

Questions to Ask

- Which students are allowed to become meaningfully involved in your school?
- Which students and adults are they allowed to become involved with?
- Which students are not meaningfully involved?

3. Expand the expectation of every student in every school to become an active and equitable partner throughout education.

Traditional roles for student participation in schools can be perceived as limiting in many ways. Meaningful Student Involvement acknowledges the central role students have in educational transformation by building the capacity of schools for meaningful involvement.

In the history of schools, students were expected to be the merely passive recipients of adult-driven education systems. See Table 22 of this book for examples of what that looked like. They were to show up when adults want, learn the topics that adults wanted, and behave the ways that adults expected them to. However, technology has heralded many changes that schools have not adapted to. Schools are wrestling to succeed through immersing students in Internet usage and the tools that allow them to access greater success. Sure, there may be computers in every classroom and Internet throughout every school, but many teachers still have not learned to actively engage students as partners in learning, teaching and leadership throughout education. (Wankel & Blessinger, 2013) This is what students today demand to make their learning relevant.

Learning, teaching and leadership should be integrated into every classroom for every student, no matter their grade level, subject matter, or academic ability. Every student can learn, every student can teach and every student can lead. Table 10 shows some ways that can happen. That means that even the most disaffected learner still has opportunities to make decisions about their own learning and other students' learning. It means that transient students get to evaluate teachers and curriculum. It means that all students get to research learning, plan activities, and be active partners no matter what their status in schools.

Some researchers have been using the phrase "Student/Adult Partnerships" lately to describe any occasion where adults engage student voice deliberately in schools. That is an excellent way to build interest in the concept. The unfortunate part, though, is that it minimizes the potential of what students could be doing throughout schools. Partnerships are not easily entered into relationships that should be thrown around for feel good activities. Instead, if we consider the background of partnerships in law, we can understand Student/Adult Partnerships as fully active, mutually invested opportunities for each party to recognize the full humanity of the other. Students need these activities with adults starting when they are young so they can build their skills and knowledge across the span of their education careers. There is a challenge when adults treat partnerships as equal though, because students *are not* equals to adults. While they are full humans with a wealth of knowledge and abilities, they do not have the same knowledge, abilities, or experience of adults. This necessitates creating equitable partnerships between students and adults. Equitable Student/Adult Partnerships are vital for many reasons, not the least of which being that they recognize the uniqueness of each party involved. They validate the perspectives or students with romanticizing them, at the same time as they recognize the appropriate authority of educators and support staff throughout the education system.

Raising our expectations for students should go far beyond academics, because it is not just the academic life of the student affected by schools. Student/Adult Partnerships appropriately elevate student voice, as well as the roles of students and adults throughout the education system.

Questions to Ask

- What do students' current roles throughout education say about adults' expectations for students?
- Whose responsibility is it to build student engagement for all students?
- Should everyone involved in the lives of students be charged with changing their perceptions of students?

4. Instill a core commitment within all members of the school community—including teachers, administrators, school staff, parents, community supporters and others—to meaningfully involve students as learners, teachers and leaders throughout schools.

This happens in collaborative, community-building classrooms, kindergarten through twelfth grade, where student/teacher partnerships are valued as primary tools for teaching, learning and leading. From the earliest grades all students are taught critical thinking and active leadership, and are engaged as purposeful learners who embrace multiple, diverse perspectives.

In a democratic society that relies on engaging people every day in their civic duties such as paying taxes, taking care of public spaces and voting, it is vital to establish the basis of that engagement. Public schools in the United States are supposed to serve that very basis, as they are in many nations around the world. United States president Franklin Roosevelt once said, "Democracy cannot succeed unless those who express their choice are prepared to choose wisely. The real safeguard of democracy, therefore, is education."

The problem comes when students and adults throughout the education system do not share that intention. There must be a mutually agreed upon understanding that this is the commitment we should all share, and that understanding should be fostered among everyone involved in schools in any way.

Meaningful Student Involvement is a logical way to educate students about the role of schools in democracy; the absence of these opportunities speaks well for the opposite.

Questions to Ask

- What difference does it make if students are committed to Meaningful Student Involvement?
- What difference does it make if administrators are not committed?
- How can you instill commitment in others without manipulating them?

5. Provide students and educators with sustainable, responsive, and systemic approaches to engaging all students throughout education. As our society constantly changes, so must schools.

Meaningful Student Involvement transforms schools into places where students can make significant contributions alongside educators and administrators. This activity takes place within an educational context where adults and young people are equal contributors to a continuous learning process focusing on school change.

Sustainability is frequently thought about in an ecological sense: We must protect, preserve and ensure the health and wellbeing of our environment to secure a successful future. The same is true of Meaningful Student Involvement. The environment students learn in—including the places, people, activities, cultures and outcomes—must be thought about in a global sense focused on the preservation of assets while eliminating the bad things that adversely affect learners. Since they strike the proactive, positive relationships that embody healthy education, Student/Adult Partnerships are the hallmark of sustainable schools.

Responsive approaches to education require constant and deliberate innovation, transformation and critical thinking. The challenge of responsiveness is that it cannot merely come from educators who are responding to their own concerns. As the focus of education, schools should be responsive to students, too. This does not mean giving in to every single concern students have about their peers, teaching, the curriculum, the climate, or schools overall. However, it does mean acknowledging every single thing students say. Adults habitually qualify, negate, deny, or silence students' concerns. To meet this aim of Meaningful Student Involvement, this must change.

As Table 11 showed earlier, Meaningful Student Involvement aims to ensure the systemic transformation of education to ensure successful Student/Adult Partnerships. Examining the entirety of the education system for locations where Meaningful Student Involvement can happen is essential. Everyone from students through the federal government's leader of education should focus on engaging students as partners in their efforts, no matter what they are. Aside from individually engaging students, educators and administrators should ensure they are ensuring Meaningful Student Involvement throughout policy and practice as well by actively creating roles, infusing opportunities and securing their colleagues' investment for engaging students as partners.

The final requirement for this aim is constant change. Emerging from the notion that Meaningful Student Involvement is never *done*, this concept challenges students and educators alike to work together to ensure evolutionary action. Given the transformative nature of society, it is essential that education keep pace. This can only happen when Meaningful Student Involvement is invented, examined and re-invented for every successive generation of learners and educators. As Freire wrote,

> "Those who authentically commit themselves to the people must re-examine themselves constantly. This conversion is so radical as not to allow for ambivalent behavior... Conversion to the people requires a profound rebirth. Those who undergo it must take on a new form of existence; they can no longer remain as they were." (1973)

This unwillingness to remain as they were is what differentiates Student/Adult Partnerships from regular student-adult relationships. These partnerships inherently challenge the status quo in schools, and more importantly, throughout society. They demand both partners actively see each other anew by allowing the other to make mistakes, learn and grow from their interactions and partnership. Adults who are incapable of allowing students to be different than their expectations are incapable of Meaningful Student Involvement. No adult in the education system should be so intransigent.

Questions to Ask

- What are the barriers you can envision to meaningfully involving students throughout the education system?
- How do your own beliefs narrow the possibilities for Student/Adult Partnerships?
- Do opportunities to transform your practice in education excite you or challenge you?

6. Acknowledge the experience, perspectives and knowledge of all students.

Using sustainable, powerful and purposeful school-oriented roles, acknowledge the experience, perspectives and knowledge of all students. Instead of creating special, one-time opportunities where student voice can misrepresent the multiple perspectives of diverse student populations, Meaningful Student Involvement charges educators with the responsibility of engaging all students in dynamic roles with the on-going task of creating and fostering success in schools.

This means there is space for both traditional student leaders and nontraditional student leaders, as illustrated in Figure 22. As Christensen wrote, "All opportunities for leadership and contribution must be encouraged and embraced if schools are going to utilize students as resources for leadership." (Christensen, 1997) Both traditional and nontraditional student leaders have excellent attributes that are relevant to Meaningful Student Involvement. However, there is more space than that. Every single student of every age in each grade throughout every school should be meaningfully involved throughout their education and the entirety of the education system. Different from throwing the doors open and posting flyers throughout the hallways saying, "Come One, Come All," this requires deliberately reaching out to diverse students and diverse adults throughout the education system. Diversity does not mean setting quotas of student athletes, student leaders, honor-roll students, class clowns, faux nerds, real nerds, cheerleaders and longhaired students—although it does not exclude that, either. To practically engage every student as a partner in education, there needs to be given practical, pragmatic efforts to reach students across racial, cultural, gender, religious, academic, and economic barriers with emphasis that lasts throughout Meaningful Student Involvement.

Starting in the youngest grades, all students can experience opportunities to experience the Cycle of Engagement in action. Researching education, planning schools, teaching, evaluating, decision-making and advocating should be woven throughout their educational experiences. Rather than standing up only for themselves and their own interests, students should have opportunities to expand their perspectives by getting to know, tolerate, embrace and engage diversity among their peers and with adults throughout the education system.

Part of this acknowledgment is learning to see students as the makers and builders of knowledge, and adults as the facilitators and stewards of learning. This repositioning challenges the entrenched beliefs many educators have and should not be taken lightly. However, it should not be dismissed, either. It's through this mutual challenge that educators, administrators and other adults throughout schools can activate and sustain Meaningful Student Involvement.

Questions to Ask

- Have you ever asked students their perspectives on major issues in education, such as school funding, testing and assessment, and teaching styles? Did you lead them, or simply let them share their own thoughts?
- Do your students opinions about education differ from your own in substantive ways? Why or why not?
- Can you do anything to acknowledge student perspectives besides simple verbal cues?

7. Engage adults as allies and partners to students.

Today, schools routinely treat students as passive recipients of education, encouraging the perspective of students as empty vessels that need to be filled with teachers' knowledge. However, there are alternatives. Some schools are using students as informants to tell them what students like and do not like; others are giving students the reigns to their learning and entrusting them with the keys to the castle of education. Meaningful Student Involvement is different from both of those approaches because it positions students as partners who are actively, wholly engaged throughout the entirety of teaching, learning and leading throughout the education system.

Meaningful Student Involvement does not cast students as the sole authors of their educational experiences. Research and experience have repeatedly proven that is not wholly beneficial to students or the democratic society we share. Instead, adults can have all kinds of roles in engaging students as partners, including facilitating, training, teaching, challenging, developing ideas, advising, mentoring, standing up with, or even standing up for students. (Bragg, 2007) Meaningful Student Involvement even encourages adult allies to do things on behalf of students when it is appropriate—and throughout the current education system, that is often the case. The challenge for adults within Meaningful Student Involvement is to not do *for* students what that can do *with* students.

Empowering adults to become allies and partners to students requires helping them see students as part of the solution, instead of seeing them as a problem to be solved. It is important to distinguish this difference, if only because it is foreign to many educators, administrators, parents and community workers focused on education. Seeing students as a problem to be solved is a deficit model that is entrenched in the belief that young people are not full humans. Instead, many adults throughout the school system today see students as "adults-in-the-making" (Kohn, 1993) who are not capable, desiring or deserving of the right to make decisions for themselves, let alone for other students.

It takes a deliberate effort for many adults throughout the education system to see students in a different light than what they have been traditionally cast. Colleges of education, education publishing companies, professional development trainers, policymakers and other facilitators of adult capacity building throughout the education system routinely demean, neglect, deny and incapacitate students. Wholly neglectful of the people they are charged with serving, these entities cannot be demonized for their roles in traditional student involvement, as they are merely perpetuating the larger culture they have inherited and the culture they are part of. However, if promoting Meaningful Student Involvement is going to be successful, all adults throughout the entirety of the education system must become engaged as allies and partners to students.

This can happen by using the same efforts that engage teachers as classroom experts and parents as community partners, and expanding, innovating and transforming these practices to bring in other adults and to also include students as substantive contributors throughout all parts of the education system.

Questions to Ask

- Can you envision having a 50/50 partnership with every single student you interact with every day, week, month, or year?
- Are there different kinds of partnerships you are in with adults? Are all partnerships equal?
- What gets in the way of engaging students as allies right now?

8. Foster appreciation of student perspectives, experiences and knowledge and avoid adult interpretations.

When considering students as allies to educators, adults may be tempted to act as translators for student voice. Concerned that students are not capable of speaking "education-ese", these well-meaning administrators, researchers, advocates and teachers reword students' ideas, interpret them, or otherwise differentiate between what students actually said and what adults believe they meant. Adults do this because we do not believe that the raw data represented by student voice has actual value in the space of education policymaking, classroom teaching, building leadership, or school improvement. We do that because we do not trust students at face value; without extracting what we think students are saying, without reframing it into concepts, ideas, or beliefs we share, we think student voice is foreign, alien, or juvenile. (Table 14 sharing what accurate framing can look like.)

The challenge here is not that students do not have valuable things to add to the conversation, but that adults do not have the ability to solicit the perspectives, experiences, knowledge and wisdom of students without filtering, analyzing, or otherwise destabilizing their expressions. We must accept that responsibility and build our capacity to do this important work. We must stop bastardizing student voice.

I do not use that word lightly. To bastardize student voice, adults take it away from its author or speaker. In reality, we routinely corrupt how students share their voices, however it is expressed. Sometimes inadvertently, sometimes intentionally, adults debase students by adding new elements, their own ideas, moving their own agendas and forcing their own beliefs through the actions, ideas, experiences, and wisdom of students. Bastardizing student voice this way is not necessary, appropriate, or relevant to Meaningful Student Involvement.

All adults throughout the education system need to learn that all students of all ages have the capacity and the ability to speak for themselves, albeit to different extents. Often this capacity may be undermined by the disbelief of otherwise good-hearted adults who honestly believe they know what students think. Meaningful Student Involvement creates appropriate platforms for students' experience, ideas and knowledge of schools, without filtering those words through adult lenses. Students can learn about the schools they attend, the topics they should learn, the methods being tested on them, the roles of educators and administrators, and much more.

Questions to Ask

- How do you interpret student voice right now?
- Does the idea of adults bastardizing student voice offend you? Why or why not?
- Where can you practice simply listening to student voice today, without interpreting or bastardizing it?

9. Recognize the right, responsibility and need for students to experience ownership of their learning, schools and the entire education system.

For years, many adults scoffed at playground games, make believe and games of tag, believing child's play was infantile filler without the merit of formal teaching. Research is increasingly showing the value of taking play seriously. Today, it is still challenging to most educators and school leaders to believe that students have an intrinsic desire to learn, at least the ways that adults want them to. Yet, both psychological and educational literature have repeatedly demonstrated that when students' right to owning their own learning is embraced, learning is more substantial and effective. (Stefanou, 2004; Newmann, 1992)

Given appropriate education and authority, students have many places where they can exert their ownership rights within schools. Meaningful Student Involvement is premised on the belief that educators, school leaders and other adults throughout the education system can and should recognize student ownership. As far back as the 1970s, there were educators promoting student ownership of homework assignments, tests, self-evaluation, self-review/peer review/teacher review, and student feedback. (Erlich & Erlich, 1971) Those exact same topics are raised today. More than a decade ago, I found a dearth of imagination about this topic when I researched my first monograph on the topic, *A Meaningful Student Involvement Idea Guide*. In that piece I advocated to acknowledge student ownership through self-directed learning, student/teacher team teaching, student-designed courses and curriculum, student-driven school needs assessments, student-led teacher training, and staff hiring, among many other activities. (Fletcher, 2001)

Since then, I have come to understand that student ownership is deeper still than positioning students to lead learning, teaching and leadership opportunities throughout schools. Within the hearts and minds of all students around the world right now—no matter what their economic, academic, social, cultural, religious, language, gender or racial identities—is an inherent desire to expand their abilities, capacities, wisdom and experiences, thereby creating the world they want to live in.

In talking about student ownership, many adults have attributed increased student engagement and student investment in schools to physical materials. They believe that learning tools like the laptops or tablet computers, Smart Boards, and networked printers in all classrooms, as well as schoolwide course-management systems are all that is needed. Other people believe it's a teachers' approach to learning that affects student ownership, concentrating on shifting to project-based learning, the addition of advanced placement courses, and increased academic rigor for all students. Still other educators express faith in the vestiges of what were considered vital practices in democratic education in the past, including classroom voting, whole school meetings, student courts and similar mechanisms.

All of those tools and practics require context, and have often been used without one. Instead, they are used for the sake of building student ownership, but even that is done without context. Meaningful Student Involvement is meaningful because it is contextualized by its definition:*the systematic approach to engaging students as partners in learning throughout every facet of education for the purpose of strengthening their commitment to education, community and democracy.* Placing learning at the center of action ensures meaningfulness, which a lot of the activities mentioned above did not do explicitly.

Pedagogy is at the heart of the student learning experience in schools, and student learning is the goal of all schools. Meaningful Student Invovlement acknowledges that by building the capacities of educators to engage students as partners in learning, in turn by infusing Student/Adult Partnerships throughout the education system. This can logically leads to progressive, democratic, open, free, experimental, or alternative learning. Educational methods and ideologies that are constructivist, holistic, or learner-centered; or specific innovations such as whole-language learning, discovery-based science, or authentic assessment all hold opportunities for meaningful involvement. Experiential and applied learning methods, service learning and activist learning, collaborative and group teaching all support the daily practices of teachers whose natural instinct is to treat children with respect. Meaningful Student Involvement provides frameworks for going further.

Questions to Ask

- What does student ownership mean to you in practical ways, right now?
- Can or should students have full and complete ownership over learning? Teaching? Leadership?
- Does student ownership need to be assessed?

Chapter 27: Attributes of Meaningful Student Involvement

When examining what the benefits of Meaningful Student Involvement are, these attributes become apparent throughout the opportunities students and adults are engaged in. In her study, Chopra (2014) found that these attributes are key for determining the presence, power and potential of Meaningful Student Involvement.

- **Indicators.** There are the observable indications that Meaningful Student Involvement has had an impact on students and adults within the activity at hand and throughout the larger educational environments where those involved regularly occupy. Ultimately, Meaningful Student Involvement should be seen across the entirety of the education system.
- **Learning.** The complex learning skills developed by students should be assessed in meaningful and substantive ways, whether through demonstration or proof. Students and adults should also receive credit for their learning through involvement.
- **Partnership.** Partnerships should be observable and students and adults should be taught and shown how to actively demonstrates them. These partnerships should reflect respect, communication, investment, and meaningful involvement, and should occur among students, between students and adults, and throughout the education system.
- **Equity.** Meaningful Student Involvement actively promotes powerful student voice without discrimination. There are practical, appropriate steps taken to ensure the active engagement of every student without bias towards academic achievement, race, gender, socio-economic status, language, or otherwise.
- **Infusion.** Students should be integrated throughout the various school improvement, education reform and systems transformation work happening within classrooms, throughout schools and across the education system. The practical ways to infuse them have been implemented and are visible in a variety of ways (Wood, 2005).
- **Quality.** In Meaningful Student Involvement, students are validated through substantive and systemic interactions with adults, deep relationship-building in Student/Adult Partnerships, and pragmatic action with their peers leading to observable outcomes. Quality comes through planning, research, training, evaluation, action and advocacy, all of which are embedded in the process of Meaningful Student Involvement.
- **Evidence.** When students are engaged as partners throughout education, there is measurable and effective evidence of Meaningful Student Involvement. If evidence of impact is not present, the activities have not been meaningful. Some are shown in Table 12 of this book.

These attributes portray the possibilities of Meaningful Student Involvement. If this were a paint-by-numbers picture, the attributes would be the numbers. The following research-based outcomes show what the colors that students and adults use to create action.

Chapter 28: Research-Based Outcomes

Many educators intuitively understand Meaningful Student Involvement and believe that valuing, validating, and empowering students in democratic learning environments is important. While intuition is important, the modern climate of education calls for scientific research to support new approaches to student learning. As a student in Colorado said, "We can give you respect. We are able to understand the issues. We can think for ourselves. It's our education. If we have a say, it will make a difference." (Forum for Youth Investment, 2002)

For more than two decades though, well-meaning adults throughout the educational system saw students merely as sources of information they needed to extract. As evidenced by the following passage from Kozol, these researchers covered both conservative and liberal perspectives.

> "We have not been listening much to children in these recent years of 'summit conferences' on education, of severe reports, and ominous prescriptions. The voices of children, frankly, have been missing from the whole discussion." (Kozol, 1991)

However, they did open the doorway to students being taken more seriously. As research of student voice morphed into participatory action research and student-led studies[12], more researchers began addressing students as agents of school reform. Learners began to become advocates. Simultaneously, classroom work across the United States and worldwide began morphing through the service-learning methodology, activist learning, and more action-oriented processes that actively embrace the power of students to transform learning, teaching, leadership and more.

Luckily, there is a growing body of evidence to back up these education transformations. With sources ranging from academic studies from around the world to a recent study from the Centers for Disease Control and Prevention (CDC, 2009), potentiality, possibilities and probabilities are seen as keys to the doorway to tomorrow. The following chapter highlights many other sources, while Table 12 of this book shows a variety of evidence in literature surrounding Meaningful Student Involvement.

Student/Adult Partnerships are urgently needed throughout education for many reasons. A recent examination of the Philadelphia Student Union summarized one part of the need for students to take action to change schools, reporting,

> "Student voice is critical not just because students have the greatest stake in schools and school systems and not just because their first-hand experiences can help us understand the real life consequences of policies and practice, but also because students are uniquely positioned to challenge neoliberal logic... [B]y flipping the script, establishing broad-based alliances, and demonstrating historical vigilance on issues that matter, the Philadelphia Student Union shows how students can take on critical leadership roles in the struggle for educational equity." (Conner & Rosen, 2013)

As Table 12 shows, there is a growing body of substantial evidence suggesting numerous benefits to Meaningful Student Involvement (Fletcher, 2003b). The recipients of those benefits range include individual students who participate and others who are not directly involved;

adults who are directly involved and others who do not; and the school system as a whole. (Osberg, Pope, & Galloway, 2006; Cook-Sather, et al., 2014)

When considering what impacts Meaningful Student Involvement has had, it is necessary to look across the entirety of the body of evidence supporting what is happening. Partnering with Seattle Public Schools in 2007-08, I trained eight high schools on Meaningful Student Involvement and supported students and adults as they formed Student Equity Teams in several schools. Learning about student voice, diversity and racial equity in education, these students taught me many lessons. Using some of what I learned, I have adapted and expanded on the evaluation findings from the program. Today, I use them to encourage people in education to map the extent and quality of Meaningful Student Involvement.

TYPES OF EVIDENCE SUPPORTING MEANINGFUL STUDENT INVOLVEMENT

Evidence of Engagement	Schools actively demonstrate how students and adults are actively engaged as partners in multiple locations throughout education.
	Students and adults can effectively describe and demonstrate how they are actively engaged in school, throughout the education system, and/or in transforming learning, teaching and leadership.
Evidence of Planning	Schools actively demonstrate how plans have been put in place in response to the frameworks for Meaningful Student Involvement.
	Students and adults can effectively describe and demonstrate how plans have been put in place in response to the frameworks for Meaningful Student Involvement.
Evidence of Learning	Schools actively acknowledge learning through the frameworks for Meaningful Student Involvement with suitable acknowledgment for students and adults who are engaged.
	Students and adults can effectively demonstrate what they have learned and identify how their learning has been acknowledged.
Evidence of Impact	The school, education agency or nonprofit can describe and demonstrate what the impacts of Meaningful Student Involvement have been.
	Students and adults who have been involved can describe and demonstrate what the impacts of Meaningful Student Involvement have been.
	A wider group of students and adults throughout the education system can describe and demonstrate what the impacts of Meaningful Student Involvement have been.

Table 13. Types of Evidence. See Figure 11 for an illustration of this in action.

---

[12] For examples of student-led research about education see soundout.org/studentresearch.html

Chapter 29: Research Supporting Meaningful Student Involvement

While studies have clearly shown that students are most likely to be engaged in learning when they are active and given some choice and control over the learning process, many teachers rely on student passivity, rote learning, and routine in instruction with young people of all ages. (Goodlad, 1984; Yair, 2000) Newmann's studies on student engagement have shown that students make a, "psychological investment in learning. They try hard to learn what school offers. They take pride not simply in earning the formal indicators of success (grades), but in understanding the material and incorporating it in their lives." (1992) The connection between student engagement and partnering with students has been made, but is still largely ignored across the United States and around the world. (Mitra, 2003; Fletcher, 2005a; Beaudoin, 2005; Cook-Sather, 2002; Fielding, 2001)

Empowered student voice in educational reform is increasingly identified as critical to the successful implementation of specific academic programs and projects (Ericson & Ellett, 2002; Wilson & Corbett, 2001; Cook-Sather, 2002; Beresford, 2000). In response to these urgent calls for Meaningful Student Involvement, some educators and community workers are infusing student voice into educational planning, research, instruction, and evaluation.

The documented benefits of Meaningful Student Involvement are wide-ranging. In one compilation of youth involvement case studies from around the world (Golombek, 2002), several programs recited similar reasons for deepening youth involvement in their programs. Reasons included youth developing leadership skills, adults earning young peoples' trust, and increased engagement of young peoples' capacity to make a difference in their communities. Another study found that through meaningful involvement young people experienced relevancy of learning, empowered voice, meaningful skill-building, and affirmation from adults and their peers (Zeldin & Price, 1995). Through Meaningful Student Involvement, students learn metacognitive skills, becoming more skilled at self-directed learning and classroom-based learning by becoming more capable of improving the quality of their own work. (Ontario Literacy and Numeracy Secretariat, 2007)

Studies indicate that young people who are engaged in meaningful community activities are more likely to understand civic engagement, political socialization, and how passive citizenry can be manipulated by political ideologues (Bellig, 2000; Evans & Anthony, 1991). Research has also found that young people engaged in service to their school are more likely to be actively engaged in their communities throughout their lives (Lesko & Tsouronis, 1998; Constitutional Rights Foundation & Close-Up Foundation, 1995). One study of the impacts of young people on adult-led organizations found that engaging youth as active decision-makers benefited organizations in positive ways that included clarification of purpose and mission, program improvements, and more directly meeting community needs (Zeldin, et al., 2000).

How student voice is interjected and towards what ends is a question of intention. Giving students a voice entails more than asking young people for periodic comments or feedback during an externally controlled process (Onore, 1992). Studies exploring schools as communities for learning through service to others report increased student cooperation, enjoyment of the learning environment (Sparapani, 2000), quality increases in student work and better grades (Follman, 1998), and heightened participation in classrooms (Loesch-Griffin, et al., 1995). Studies show that meaningfully involved students have more positive relationships with teachers, and can be successful allies in the classroom (Houghton, 2001; Weiler, et al., 1998). Research examining engaging students as researchers found that individual youth development, furthering community empowerment, and organizational capacity building are all outcomes of engaging youth in community organizations (Harvard Family Research Project, 2002), while research on students conducting meaningful classroom evaluation shows significant correlations between students' ratings of teachers with their own learning gains (Scriven, 1995). Studies have shown that students lead parent conferences are a successful method for increasing student ownership in learning (Hackman, 1997). Reports show that voter participation and civic engagement can be enhanced if students were members of local school boards (Keating, 1995). Furthermore, research indicates that students want to be involved in school board activities, such as significant school planning, choosing curriculum, hiring teachers, and deciding policy (Patmor, 1998; Marques, 2001; Kaba, 2001). Research also found that students participating in meaningful activities such as school accreditation processes and school reform conferences are less cynical and apathetic because they "were really listened to and had impact" (McCall, 2000).

While this documentation covers a wide breadth of potential opportunities, more research is needed on the role of student voice in building engaged citizenry. Absent are cross-examinations between the experience of meaningful youth involvement in community organizations and Meaningful Student Involvement in schools. I have not found any research that examines the direct correlation between any of these forms of Meaningful Student Involvement and academic achievement. Other issues such as the academic achievement gap, racial, ethnic, religious and socio-economic diversity in student involvement also need further investigation. Nevertheless, this brief overview demonstrates that research in this area is burgeoning and with proper guidance can further contribute to structural means to significantly involve young people in many of the decisions that directly affect their lives, schools, and local communities.

Jackson (2005) promotes six reasons why Meaningful Student Involvement makes sense. They are:

- **Educational values**: Valuing the learning that results when we engage the capacities of the multiple voices in our schools
- **Community values**: School communities characterized by collaborative, aspirational, optimistic and high challenge cultures.
- **Rights**: Students are a significant voice in schools
- **Social responsibilities**: Young people have rights and responsibilities now enshrined in international law
- **Legitimacy**: The authenticity of student perspectives about learning and school community
- **Pragmatics**: If students are not allowed to change what they do, then we will never
- transform learning.

This is not so much a measure of importance as it is potential. It is meant to help students and educators to see that the effects of Meaningful Student Involvement reach beyond simply impacting one student; more so, Meaningful Student Involvement can actually impact entire schools. When students experience sustainable, meaningful involvement, school improvement will have greater outcomes throughout the education system. (Rudd, Colligan, & Nalk, 2008; Skinner & Belmont, 1993) Parent involvement and community engagement can actually be improved by infusing student voice throughout school improvement planning, too (Mitra, 2006).

EFFECTS OF MEANINGFUL STUDENT INVOLVEMENT

When the focus is on...	It Affects...	And May Cause...
STUDENTS	Learning: Academic achievement, attendance rates, graduation rates, ethnic/racial/socio-economic/gender gaps, lifelong learning, and more.	Greater interest in academic achievement, gains in test scores, higher graduation rates, increased student engagement.
STUDENTS AND ADULTS	Relationships: Purpose, ownership, community, engagement.	Higher levels of ownership, increased belonging and motivation, identification with educational goals.
	Practices and procedures: Education planning, classroom teaching, learning evaluating, school research, and education decision-making.	Adults hear new perspectives about schools; allyship and partnership become norms; greater acceptance of programs and decisions.
STUDENTS, ADULTS AND SCHOOL SYSTEMS	**Policies and laws:** Regulations that govern participation, funding, etc.	Regular, fully authoritative positions on committees and boards; ongoing funding, development, and support for student involvement.
	Culture: Student and educator attitudes, learning environments, social interactions.	Positive and productive climates; new human resources emerge as students share responsibility; stronger relationships between students and adults.

Table 14. Effects of Meaningful Student Involvement (See Appendix 1 for Research Sources)

Chapter 30: Impact on Learning

A logical entry point for engaging students as partners is in classroom learning. Take further, when this approach is incorporated throughout learning and relationship-building in schools, it is more impactful on both students and adults. When it's deeply brought into learning, relationships, practices, and policies, it will surely affect the culture of education. In turn, not only does it affect students and adults, but it affects the entire education system. It is only logical to assume that will produce the greatest number of outcomes. Stories throughout the rest of this book support that assumption. Meaningful Student Involvement can be a powerful and effective force for school improvement, increasing students' commitment to their own achievement as well as to school goals and making schools, in turn, more responsive to the characteristics and needs of their students.

Meaningful Student Involvement does not force students to assume responsibility for every aspect of their learning and development. Instead, it assumes that educators are capable of facilitating students' gradual assumption of responsibility. Through direct instruction, students build their knowledge of education, learning, teaching, leadership, student voice, the education system at large, school improvement, and Meaningful Student Involvement. Educators teach students about the functions of education research; school planning; classroom teaching; learning evaluations; systemic decision-making; and advocacy.

By establishing strategic Student/Adult Partnerships, educators can model and guide lifelong learning and determined action for school improvement. As Mitra writes,

> "[B]y assuming responsibilities and enacting decisions that have consequences for themselves and others... participating students develop a broad set of competencies that help them prepare for adulthood." (2004)

They collaborate with learners in collegial learning communities, emphasizing every students' ability to create positive change. They also give students plenty of opportunities for positive independent work that is deliberately chosen for its impact. This is not make-busy work or filler; instead, both students and adults understand that it is integral to the purpose of Meaningful Student Involvement. Again, adults deliberately model for students that they do this, too, as a course of their regular work in education as well as for the purpose of meaningfully involving learners. Finally, regular opportunities for reflection and sharing among students and between students and adults emphasize mutual learning and deep impacts. All of this can lead to deepened learning, which is the foundational aim of Meaningful Student Involvement.

Chapter 31: Impacts on Development

Beyond learning, there is a space in all schools where the development of social and emotional skills is key. Some schools continue to refer to this as child development or youth development, while others call this social/emotional learning. Mitra's studies (2004; Serriere & Mitra, 2012; Mitra & Serriere, 2012) have found that a key outcome of what I describe as Meaningful Student Involvement was youth development. Specifically, Mitra and her colleagues found the following attributes present as a result:

- **Agency:** Acting or exerting influence and power in a given situation
- **Belonging:** Developing meaningful relationships with other students and adults and having a role at the school
- **Competence:** Developing new abilities and being appreciated for one's talents (Mitra, 2004)

Exploring them further, Mitra suggests that student voice increasing student agency by increasing their abilities to articulate opinions to others; constructing new student identities as change makers; and developing a greater sense of leadership. She says student voice fosters students' sense of belonging by developing relationships with caring adults; improving interactions with teachers; and increasing students' sense of attachment to their schools. Finally, she states that student competence is improved because student voice activities promote students "critiquing their environment; developing problem solving and facilitation skills; and getting along with others." (Mitra, 2004)

In a report on the well-respected and long-running Vermont Governor's Institute on Public Issues and Youth Activism, researchers identified twelve developmental attributes that were enhanced through student-led action to improve education and communities. The Insitute recruits academically high performing students to foster their leadership development and community action. The attributes found by the researcher included intellectual rigor, self-education, critical analysis, personal voice, emotional nurturance, diversity acceptance, healthy expression of emotions, safety and appreciation, shared power, and the ability to use appropriate power. (Ungerleider & DiBenedetto, 1997)

Another study reported that students experience increased responsibility for their own self-learning as well as their peers because of Meaningful Student Involvement. This was caused by increased student capacity for critical thinking and an overall reduction in disruptive behavior, all because of the process of engaging students as partners throughout education. (Ontario Literacy and Numeracy Secretariat, 2007) The finding that students' skills can be vitally employed in school improvement, but are habitually underutilized, is continually documented in a number of studies. (Fine & Weis, 2003; Nieto, 1994; Wilson & Corbett, 2001; Shultz & Cook-Sather, 2001)

In my work focused on promoting student voice through SoundOut, I have identified the following skill building and knowledge-sharing areas becoming developed when schools are committed to Meaningful Student Involvement. I have found when developing plans to build Student/Adult Partnerships, it is vital to consider capacity building for everyone involved. However, I have also seen the following skills and knowledge grow through activities focused on other issues, but naturally nurturing of these areas. See earlier in Part Four for how skills and knowledge development relate. My book, *The SoundOut Workshop Guide for Student/Adult Partnerships* (Fletcher, 2015) shares the following training activities focused on these areas.

A. Skills Developed through Meaningful Student Involvement

Following are skills developed through the various approaches to Meaningful Student Involvement explored throughout this book.

- **Self-engagement**: Instead of seeing engagement as just a result of action, Meaningful Student Involvement builds students' abilities to self-engage in activities they care about.

- **Stereotypes**: Students learn to identify what stereotypes are across differences, whether academic performance, age, race, gender, sexual identity, or otherwise. They also learn to embrace difference and engage diversity as a positive school for transformation.

- **Media bias**: Students examine all sorts of media for its biases and perspectives, and build their ability to interpret and monitor information constantly.

- **Learning about learning**: Having a basic understanding of why schools teach what they do the ways they do is a key to learning through Meaningful Student Involvement. All the skills and knowledge available about schools and education are irrelevant if students do not understand why and how they are doing what they are doing.

- **Being authentic**: Faced with opportunities to become "miniature adults" or assume other identities, Meaningful Student Involvement encourages students to learn who they authentically are and what they authentically care about throughout education.

- **Leading through adapting**: Being able to plan and adapt pathways to Meaningful Student Involvement is vital, and should reflect the needs and contexts where it's happening.

- **Collaboration and partnerships**: Forming intentional partnerships requires skills in effective participation in groups, including both being involved and facilitating.

- **Decision-making and Conflict resolution**: Meaningful Student Involvement supports positive, powerful opportunities for co-decision-making between students and adults.

- **Co-learning**: Students and adults need to learn to be deliberate co-learners by building their skills in collaboration and teamwork. Meaningful Student Involvement fosters co-learning skills through applied learning opportunities and reflection.

- **Learning about the education system**: Historically seen as the targets or subjects of the education system, Meaningful Student Involvement actively engages students as partners throughout the system. This requires students needing to learn what the education system is, how it operates, what the inputs and outcomes are, and other variable factors.

- **Critical thinking**: Increasing and honing the ability of students to be critical partners in learning, teaching and leading is key to creating new knowledge, which is a central outcome of Meaningful Student Involvement.

- **Language and jargon**: Applying diverse learned terminology, students are encouraged to embrace useful jargon and dismiss meaningless language.

- **Learning about student voice**: Going beyond assuming that students have enough knowledge about themselves and how to express themselves, Meaningful Student

Involvement builds students' knowledge and skills to express their ideas, knowledge, action and outcomes throughout the education system.

- **Listening**: As part of the Cycle of Engagement, students can become excellent listeners to each other, adults, younger students, and people throughout their educational communities.

- **Feedback techniques**: Learning to listen to and provide constructive feedback is a vital skill for Meaningful Student Involvement, especially while encouraging others to do the same with specific tools.

- **Learning about Meaningful Student Involvement**: Students learn to see how, when, where, why and what they are involved in. They learn about roles for students as partners, equity and equality, and more at the center of Meaningful Student Involvement.

- **Power, trust and respect**: Through meaningful involvement, students learn to identify others' understanding of these key concepts and critically examine the role of power, trust and respect throughout education.

- **Action planning**: The importance of Meaningful Student Involvement is highlighted by the skills to know where to begin and how to develop learning-infused, education-oriented initiatives.

- **Problem solving**: Students learn how to name the different types of problems they face at school and understand the impact Meaningful Student Involvement can have on the way schools solve problems. They also learn which problems are theirs to solve alone and which they should solve with adults as partners.

- **Learning about school omprovement**: Learning about different components of schools, student voice and their meaningful involvement is important. However, learning to apply that learning to making schools better for everyone is key. Students learn formal, informal, strategic and situational methods to make schools better for everyone, including other students.

- **Addressing roadblocks**: Students learn to look in-depth at education and see where language abilities, cultural disparities, academic abilities, age and other factors affect Meaningful Student Involvement. Applying meaningfulness throughout their learning experience is a result of this skill.

- **Letting go and taking charge**: Through Meaningful Student Involvement, students and adults learn to take responsibility for their roles. Understanding what roles, rights and responsibilities each group has is key, especially for creating agreements that lead to actionable outcomes.

- **Fostering ideal partnerships**: Reaching equity between students and adults is an outcome of meaningful involvement that is central for everyone involved. Students learn to foster these ideal partnerships in practical ways through learning and action.

- **Reflection**: Discovering different methods to reflect and examine their experiences through Meaningful Student Involvement, students gain the ability to make meaning from any activity in their lives. I explore meaning making in Table 6 of this book.

These skill and knowledge sets are important for taking action to transform schools through the Student/Adult Partnerships inherent in Meaningful Student Involvement.

Chapter 32: Impact and Implementation

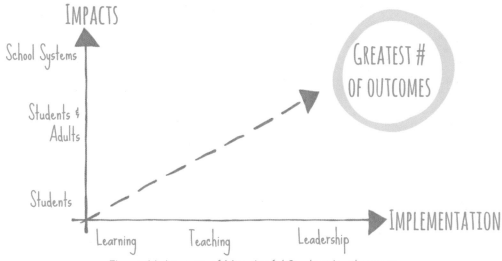

Figure 11. Impacts of Meaningful Student Involvement

From my practice in schools across the nation, I have observed a relationship the number of people affected by Meaningful Student Involvement and the overall outcomes from the actions taken. Similarly, I have seen that deeper implementation of Meaningful Student Involvement leads to greater outcomes, too. In Figure 11, I have illustrated what happens when these two aspects meet: outcomes will be the greatest when they affect the highest number of people through the broadest implementation.

As illustrated in Figure 11, as we consider the who is impacted by Meaningful Student Involvement it becomes easy to discern three primary audiences:

- **Students**, who as individuals are the primary focus of schools. These are any learners who are in the primary learners within a learning environment. In most schools, they're divided by grade levels or ages; topic, subject or issue areas; and/or performance, ability or other arbitrary determinations.

- **Students and Adults**, who as a combined group of individuals form the culture of a school. Adults may include any role within and throughout the entire education system, including classroom teachers and building leaders, as well as cafeteria workers and janitors, and district program staff as well as school board members.
- **School Systems**, which summarizes the entire collective group of people, processes and policies that drive the education structure in countries around the world. Depending on the community, these systems can include pre-school and higher education institutions, as well as the officials, staff and students within and throughout the systems.

The activities that happen throughout education can best be summarized as learning, teaching and leadership. Those three elements should happen in every part of school systems, including classrooms, hallways, libraries, education agencies and elsewhere. If officials aren't learning, they aren't improving schools. If students aren't leading schools, they aren't learning what democracy truly is. Every person throughout the education system teaches themselves and others, and when that stops, education has failed.

Earlier, I suggested that each opportunity to involve students throughout the education system should aspire to be meaningful for students. However, it is important to note that the actual impact of any form of student involvement depends on the number of students directly involved in the activity, the type of activity being undertaken, and the long-range sustainability of the project beyond the involvement of a specific student or students.

Part V. Planning for Meaningful Student Involvement

Chapter 33: Introduction

There are many ways that Meaningful Student Involvement can happen throughout the education system. (Fielding, 2001; Fletcher, 2001 & 2003; Rudduck & Flutter, 2004) The entirety of the system can engage students as partners who are treated with respect, open communication, investment, and meaningful action. There are practical opportunities for all students to experience meaningful involvement, too. One of those opportunities is through planning in education, including individual classrooms, whole schools, every grade and every ability level. Through intentional design and systemic commitment, every learner can experience Meaningful Student Involvement in education planning (Tomlinson & McTighe, 2006)

In individual classrooms, students can be partners in classroom planning, behavior management, curriculum planning, and classroom teaching. They can also participate in classroom evaluation focused on themselves, their peers, and their teachers. On the building and district level, students can be meaningfully involved in staff hiring and firing, school siting and building design, and budgeting. For more examples of district involvement, see Table 10 in this book. On the district, state, and federal levels, students can be partners in policy-making through committees and school boards, research design and delivery, and presentations both online and in print. On each level students can also be meaningfully involved in project planning, advisory positions, teacher education, and many other activities.

Students in every grade level can be meaningfully involved, too. Elementary, middle or junior high, and high school students can be engaged as partners. Additionally, out-of-school students, dropouts and pushouts can be engaged, as can graduates. (Smyth, 2007) A practical consideration of which kinds of students are going to be engaged must be considered too. I have found academic achievement is often a cloak to stifle diversity in student voice activities, masking racism, sexism, socio-economic discrimination and more. Meaningful Student Involvement rebalances this by establishing equitable partnerships among students, as well as between students and adults.

Considering how students will be involved is vital in planning Meaningful Student Involvement. All students should always be involved throughout the education system as learners first. Students have many different opportunities when they are involved. Whether they receive credit or not, or if they are volunteers or paid participants in an activity is one question, while other factors affect engaging students as partners include considering whether students are given rights to be advisors to a project, full members in a committee, less-than-full partners in an activity, or simply representatives of other students without a full voice.

When schools engage students, they should consider the investment they are willing to make in Meaningful Student Involvement. They should consider whether they are going to pay staff for additional activities, whether they are going to engage older students by providing classroom credit or other meaningful incentives, or if they are going to involve community volunteers or staff from education nonprofit organizations.

Meaningful Student Involvement focuses on shared responsibility for learning. Focusing on shared responsibility "creates shared clarity of thought, direction, and purpose. Reflection helps people learn from what they've done in the past and identify better ways of accomplishing their goals. Collaboration brings people together to share ideas and knowledge." (Conzemius & O'Neill, 2001) That is why the process of reflection is so important to Meaningful Student Involvement, as evidenced by the Cycle of Student Engagement.

The clarity of thought, direction, and purpose needed to take action for Meaningful Student Involvement means that students teachers, school administrators, support staff and every adult in schools needs to be working together to constantly learn, teach and lead *each other.* True Student/Adult Partnerships require that each of these people—especially students—need to know the best instructional and leadership practices. One exploration of these relationships suggested of students that,

> "They would have to understand the purpose, role, and value of assessments and data-gathering techniques; use wisdom, commitment, and professional expertise to set results-based goals; and use the data to inform continuous practice improvement." (Conzemius & O'Neill, 2001)

We must also consider whether the activity is a new circumstance that never existed before, or if it's an existing circumstance students are being brought into. It may also be a student-led concern, and that should be considered too (Weiss & Huget, 2015). The length of the activity is a factor as well, as the difference between an activity that takes one day, one that takes an entire school year, and one that is sustained in the lifeblood of the school is entirely different (Tomlinson & McTighe, 2006).

The number of students who are engaged as partners ultimately affects the meaningfulness of student involvement too. Meaningful Student Involvement can also be measured according to whether it's a small group, a class or a club, the whole school, or an entire district.

Chapter 34: People to Consider

There are innumerable people who can be affected by Meaningful Student Involvement, no matter where it is happening, who is involved or what it is addressing.

Among the many stakeholders, it is vital to understand exactly how Student/Adult Partnerships can be most effective. Fielding addresses this when he wrote,

> "the inclusion of student voice can be achieved in a variety of different methods that allow multiple opportunities for students to be included in the planning and decision-making about their own learning environment but that it will be the leadership of the principal that ultimately determines which school-based decisions will be inclusive of student voice." (Fielding, 2001)

Following is an examination of some of the people who are affected by Meaningful Student Involvement, including students, the principal, and others throughout the education system.

A. Students

All students everywhere, in every grade and every school, should experience Meaningful Student Involvement every day. Individual students determine whether they're meaningfully involved. You are in ultimately in charge of your own education because you can actively choose whether or not you are going to actively participate and learn in schools. Younger and older students actively and passively influence other students' decision-making. This can be meaningful if it's done intentionally to make schools better. Many schools have active programs that draw out "traditional student leaders" by identifying certain skills or abilities students have. Despite having a range of abilities, these student leaders are mostly focused on activities that affect students only. However, a growing number of student leaders have an increasing amount of ability to affect the whole education system. There are also nontraditional student leaders whose influence over their peers' decision-making has not been acknowledged in school. This is illustrated in Figure 22.

B. Local Schools

Guiding children is one of the most important jobs of parents; this is especially true in schools. Parents can also passively or actively decision-making. As their students' most vital advocates, parents are also the first partners that students have in schools. Teaching parents about Meaningful Student Involvement and ensuring their ability to advocate for it is essential.

Support staff, paraprofessionals and adult volunteers are vital for Meaningful Student Involvement. Secretaries, adult tutors, coaches, librarians, classroom assistants, and parent representatives may influence student decision-making. Paraprofessionals are people who are hired to work in schools to help students and teachers be successful.

Everyday students are subjected to a range of decisions made by teachers about grading, curriculum, behavior management, and relationships with students. Teachers are also responsible for executing others' decisions. They are key for integrating Meaningful Student Involvement into curriculum and classroom management, as well as the regular climate of schools. Among the faculty at a school are teachers whose experience, knowledge, or influence gives them ability, authority, or position to make decisions for other teachers. These teachers may lead grade-level or curriculum areas, participate on special committees, or influence decision-making in other ways. They are essential for Meaningful Student Involvement because they teach younger teachers and lead many processes. As allies, teacher leaders can drive the adoption and development of Meaningful Student Involvement throughout education, especially in local buildings, but extending in districts and throughout state or provincial governments.

Students often go to counselors to ask questions, seek advice, and talk to when they need a supportive adult in school. While they often guide student decision-making with classes or life after high school, counselors may also help students make decisions about life in general. This makes their role in Meaningful Student Involvement essential, since they can help young people remain conscious of their roles as partners to adults throughout education.

In many schools, principals need assistants to guide behavior management, budgeting, staff supervision, curriculum, and other areas. They affect students by doling out punishments and rewards; guiding student activities; and in other ways. This potentially positions them as key proponents for and benefactors of Meaningful Student Involvement. Securing their ongoing commitment to engaging students as partners is key. The commonly acknowledged "leader" of a school, whether a principal, headmaster, or lead learner, is responsible for most areas of school operations, including many of the assistant principal roles listed above. They also publicly represent the school; mediate conflicts among students, staff, parents, and community members; and interact with district, state, and federal authorities. They set the schoolwide agenda for improvement and transformation, and ensure the ongoing commitment of adults and students to Meaningful Student Involvement.

C. School Districts

Officials on the district level administer programs, funds, rules and regulations given to them by their superiors. In some states districts are simply counties (Maryland) or large regions. New York City has more than ten districts. District offices may also be known as a local education agency, or LEA. As the leader of a given area or group of schools, superintendents are often the first elected official in the chain of decision-making affecting students. Sometimes they are appointed by the district school board or city mayor. They act as the figurehead and authority of all education-related issues within their physical area of authority.

The district school board are elected officials get recommendations from the public and the superintendent to deliver their range of decision-making authority. They set the budget and agenda of schools, assign students to schools, make rules and policies, set learning standards, and more. This is only more essential if there are students engaged on the school board, because adults in these situations regularly interact with students in nontraditional ways that are intended to be partnerships, as illustrated in Figure 22. Meaningful Student Involvement can move them there.

For specific activities in a district, see Table 10 earlier in this book.

D. Education Agencies

In regional and state education agencies, adults may have a variety of roles as program administrators, data evaluators, education researchers, teacher trainers and leadership. Regional education agencies are in-between organizations that may offer professional development, administrative guidance, or funding to districts and local schools. These offices have different names, including Educational Service Districts (Washington); BOCEs (New York); or Regional Service Centers (Texas). Their support for Meaningful Student Involvement can ensure local district and building adoption, provide essential adult professional development, create new programs and opportunities, and many other things.

On the state level, education employees are responsible for administering federal and state programs designed to meet the goals of schools. Also known as the state education agency or department of education, in several states this may include or be a Office of Superintendent of Public Instruction. These officials interpret state and federal policy requirements, implement programs, research schools and conduct many other activities as a backbone for districts and local schools. Their support for Meaningful Student Involvement may ensure fiscal and policy support, as well as develop a political will.

These agencies are led by a state education leader. The state education leader may be elected or appointed; they may also work equally with the state school board and governor, or independently. They may also either serve as the political leaders of public education, or be directly appointed to ensure that the state governor is following political will in schools. They are responsible for guiding the implementation of the rules, regulations, laws, budgets, and programs of the state legislature; in some states, the governor; and the federal government. This person may be called the Chief Education Officer, or the Superintendent of Public Instruction (SPI). State education leaders can set the tone for the education culture of a state, and as such they are essential for Meaningful Student Involvement.

The state school board is an elected group of officials that overseas all schools and ensures the state's adherence to federal rules and regulations. Students can be meaningfully involved as full voting members elected by their peers are responsible for a full slate of activities, issues, and outcomes. They may engage students as members of their board, too, thereby serving as essential role models of Meaningful Student Involvement.

The state school board may or may not have the support of the state governor, legislature, or state supreme court. These are all state-level officials who are responsible for setting state priorities and funding for education, as well as ensuring local, state, and federal compliance with education laws. Their roles directly affect K-12 schools every single day, and as such their support for Meaningful Student Involvement is vital.

E. Federal Agencies

In the United States, there are a variety of adults in federal agencies who can benefit Meaningful Student Involvement. Their support cannot be understated. The United States Secretary of Education is the individual official responsible for setting and implementing the President's education agenda. They operate the United States Department of Education, which is the federal agency responsible for administering the budgets, rules, and regulations of the Secretary of Education and the Congress. Responsible for allocating funding throughout the education system and ensuring the President's education agenda is being fulfilled, the Department has countless roles throughout the process of educating students, guiding schools, evaluating outcomes and building public will. All of this can and should be informed through Meaningful Student Involvement.

The United States Congress is made of elected officials who are responsible for setting the President's educational policy recommendations into motion, in addition to supplementing their states' policy with additional funding. Held accountable by their local constituents and other national forces, these politicians could ensure the fidelity and sustainability for Meaningful Student Involvement throughout the future. Their roles cannot be overstated. Similarly, the United States Supreme Court justices are appointed to make sure the government, including schools, districts, states and the federal government, complies with the Constitution and Bill of Rights through their interpretation of the law.

The President is the elected official who is ultimately responsible for setting national educational priorities that affect all public schools. With a single pen stroke, they could implement Meaningful Student Involvement with any amount of force throughout any level of education.

F. Other Adults

There are countless other adults who are affected and who can affect Meaningful Student Involvement. These include nonprofit education organizations, including membership groups like the PTA, teachers unions, and others, as well as community-based organizations that augment, enhance, or balance the roles of schools throughout society. They also include education publishers, who are the companies that develop the educational materials used in schools. Assessments, curricula, books, computer apps, and many other tools could be transformed vastly with Meaningful Student Involvement.

Chapter 35: Places to Consider

Meaningful Student Involvement can happen in every location throughout the education system. It is important to consider these places for many reasons, including that it promotes realistic expectations for adults and students involved. If a teacher wants to involve students in meaningful ways, they might consider their classroom as the first focus for action. That same teacher might look towards changing state education agencies by partnering with an administrator in their state capitol. There are many different locations to keep in mind.

Practically any location throughout education could meaningfully involve students, including the classroom, the counselor's office, hallways, after school programs, district board of education offices, at the state or federal levels, and in other places that directly affect the students' experience of education. The following list shows a variety of places where Meaningful Student Involvement can happen.

A. Classrooms

While student voice happens all the time in classrooms, meaningful involvement does not. Student voice happens when students talk to each other and teachers, as well as student behavior, attitudes, and actions. The student sharing their life experience is sharing student voice, just like the student cheating on a test or bullying. Meaningful Student Involvement can happen through classroom management and curriculum delivery, class evaluations, and creating the culture of classrooms.

B. School Boardrooms

Students can present ideas, share concerns, and sit through school board meetings just like adults. When school boards involve students as representatives of their peers, they are listening to student voice. However, meaningful involvement means students having full-voting, fully participating positions on school boards. When students are partners on school boards, they are not treated tokenistically either. Instead, they are respected for their individual perspectives and not expected to represent all students.

C. Hallways

When a student graffitis on a wall that, "Mrs. Jones Sux!", they are sharing student voice. So are students who gossip, form cliques, and share lockers. Meaningful Student Involvement can happen informally throughout schools all the time, with or without adult supervision and/or approval, as well. However, students can be strategically engaged as partners in fostering safe and supportive student culture as it's expressed in hallways through nonviolent communication training, peer mediation programs, and other educational opportunities and informal positioning.

D. Afterschool

Meaningful Student Involvement in afterschool activities can happen in all sorts of programs, both educational and recreational, in school and otherwise. Students can plan, evaluate, facilitate, research, advocate, and more for the activities designed to serve them. As partners, they promote education for all learners.

E. Clubs

Clubs and other extracurricular activities give the appearance of being an appropriate outlet for student voice. However, students may glean from their experiences in clubs that their voices are at best tokenized if not entirely ignored by adults in schools. Engaging students as partners can include students earning credit for extracurricular activities or otherwise being acknowledged for their contributions, and the intentional positioning of students as partners in learning. Club activities will be integrated into learning and supported throughout the school day to be an effective avenue for Student/Adult Partnerships.

F. District offices

District, regional education units, and state education agencies can engage student voice throughout their processes. Grant planning, delivery, and evaluation; policy creation and evaluation; school improvement planning; building assessment; and many more locations throughout education administration are some locations. See Table 10 for specific examples.

G. Technology Departments

Meaningful Student Involvement in education technology begins with simply listening to students in teaching. Further, student voice can be engaged by having students teach students and teachers about technology; students maintain and develop educational technology infrastructure in schools; and students design ed tech policies on the building, district, state, and federal levels.

H. Playgrounds

When students are partners on playgrounds, playing and conflicts have purpose that can be captured for learning. Observing, but not facilitating, playground interactions allows adults in schools to help students navigate where and how to use their voice appropriately in interpersonal relationships, as well as schoolwide applications.

I. School Committees

Meaningful Student Involvement in education committees can happen within school buildings, at district and state levels, and at the federal level. Students can participate as full partners in policy-making, grant distribution, curriculum selection, teacher hiring and firing, and more.

J. Cafeteria

Engaging students as partners in the school cafeteria extends far beyond student complaints about food quality and fighting. Students are rallying schools to provide healthy choices, improve menu selection and pricing, and eliminate competitive foods from their buildings.

K. Building design

Meaningful Student Involvement can be engaged throughout building design processes and in all grade levels. From design to redesign to improvement to reconstruction, students can inform, co-design, and implement building planning in all areas.

L. School culture

The attitudes, policies, and structures of education may change when students are engaged as partners. Culture includes the spoken and unspoken norms in a school, as well as the beliefs, ideas, actions, and outcomes of students and adults. Engaging student voice deliberately can improve all these things for everyone in education.

M. Art Room

Creative arts can help students foster alternative thinking, diverse decision-making, and broadened cultural understanding. Within art—including creative and performing arts—are new opportunities for elementary, middle and high school students, allowing them to identify for themselves their identity, their voice and opportunities for Meaningful Student Involvement.

N. Assembly

When students and adults partner to present academic, arts and social activities in school assemblies, Meaningful Student Involvement can emerge. Creating effective opportunities for information distribution, school spirit, knowledge-building opportunities and other activities, assemblies can grow Student/Adult Partnerships in many ways.

O. Computer Lab

Students can teach teachers, partner with educators and do many other things to transform computer education, both in terms of building and maintaining computers, computer networking and software. There are times when students can lead teachers, and other times when teachers can facilitate student learning.

P. Library and Media Center

Helping to determine what resources are available, planning student programs, researching and evaluating services, and many other activities within school libraries and media centers reflect Student/Adult Partnerships. Meaningful Student Involvement can be present throughout the entirety of information services in schools.

Q. Music Room

Creative expressions and disciplined learning provide offer opportunities for Meaningful Student Involvement. The music room offers chances for students to work with teachers to foster learning and teaching, while music activities can give students chances to lead with teachers as partners.

Chapter 36: Issues to Consider

Student voice has been unfairly framed as simplistic and reactionary by some of the very programs intended to promote it. Limiting students to discussing what comes to their minds first, these activities make it sound like students can only talk about bathrooms, cafeteria food, and the colors used at the homecoming dance. Planning the winter dance, setting the price for Valentine's Day candies, and deciding the new school colors are decisions some schools allow student voice to influence or even drive.

Meaningful Student Involvement amplifies student voice much further than this. There are literally countless issues throughout the education system where engaging students as partners can be crucial for success, and yet rarely happens. By moving through the frameworks for Meaningful Student Involvement, students and adults can work in partnership to address countless issues across the entirety of the education system, ranging from curricular areas to identity, the physical plant to the societal purpose of schooling. (Checkoway & Richards-Schuster, 2006; Rubin & Silva, 2003; Mitra, 2003) Following are some of these issues. Throughout the rest of this book, there are explorations of grade-level implementations of Meaningful Student Involvement, as well as approaches to curriculum, and identification of opportunities through specific curricular areas including math (Anthony, Ohtani, & Clarke, 2013) and social studies.

Politicians, community groups, and the media may focus on the flavor of the month when it comes to improving schools. Meaningful Student Involvement averts that curse by focusing on ongoing, sustainable and intentionally transforming schools beyond any one single issue. The following list is just a beginning of what can happen though.

The issues presented here are all tied together, interrelated and inseparable. Here, I only present them as lists for the ease of reading; remembering the ways they weave together is essential to considering each issue. This list can be used to teach everyone involved in Meaningful Student Involvement about some of what's at work in schools today. It can also be used to critique student voice, expand Meaningful Student Involvement and subvert the popular over-simplification of education today.

Overarching Issues

Issue 1. Goals of Education and Student Success

Defining the purpose of schools focuses the direction of schools, teachers, and students. (Brennan, 1996) While some originally intended for public education to provide basic learning for successful democratic citizenship, others saw schools mainly as a way to support the economic workforce. Today, educational goals and success have become defined by student performance on standardized tests, in addition to measures like student attendance and graduation rates. While these might be part of the purpose of education, many school reformers are seeking ways to broaden the goals of education to include students' social, emotional, and intellectual development, as well as helping students gain the skills needed to build a better and more democratic world. (Dewey, 1948)

Issue 2. Voice and Engagement

The question of who has control and authority in schools has long been answered with leave it to the professionals, meaning administrators and policy-makers. However, as more people push for participatory structures throughout the government, there are also efforts toward more participation throughout the educational system. Creating opportunities for meaningful involvement for students, teachers, and parents is growing in many communities, while the federal government is increasingly asking how and where nontraditional voices can be engaged in decision-making. Businesses, community organizations, mayors, and others want roles, too. This is a topic that many people can rally around.

Issue 3. Charter Schools

In most states that have them, charter schools are schools that are publicly funded and privately operated (outside of the typical school district), and which students and parents can choose to attend instead of the local public school. Charter schools are all different, some are experimental and innovative, while others are very traditional but with longer hours. Studies are mixed about the benefit of charters, but the issue is becoming one that dominates education today. Many political leaders are supporting the creation of more and more charter schools, while those opposed believe charter schools take the most engaged parents and students, leaving the least engaged to stay in the regular public schools.

Issue 4. Educator Hiring

Hiring adults to work with students throughout the education system is generally done by adults. However, Student/Adult Partnerships in hiring teachers, administrators, and other adults in schools can help foster environments that are more responsive, safe, and supportive for students and adults.

Issue 5. School Advocacy

Student-led school advocacy and Student/Adult Partnerships can include school protests. When adults do not engage student voice in meaningful ways throughout the school environment, students may feel compelled to make their voices heard by adults. Meaningful Student Involvement in protest means equitable decision-making, non-tokenizing roles for students, and full involvement throughout all facets of protesting.

Issue 6. Democracy and Representation

When adults stand on either side of a school building a poke sticks at each other in the name of improving schools, they frequently lose sight of students. Who is represented in these conversations; what do they represent; and who do they represent? Students should have essential roles to ensure their interests are represented, as well as the interests of their families, communities and cultures. This should happen throughout every conversation about education.

Issue 7. Class and School Size

The number of students to teachers, called student/teacher ratios, has been shown to affect how well students learn. Many advocates call for smaller class size, while others claim size makes little difference. School consolidation, where small schools in local communities are merged into a single large school for a large surrounding area, has been happening since the 1940s. Now many of those larger schools are being closed, such as in New York City, to create smaller schools.

Issue 8. Political rallies

Meaningful Student Involvement in political rallies extends far beyond simply using young people to decorate adult causes by engaging students as partners in planning, facilitating, and participating throughout political activities. These can include rallies, committees, conferences, and more.

Issue 9. Technology in Schools

The issue of schools maintaining their relevance in the face of technological developments is not new. In the 1950s the US became engulfed with the Cold War, and schools were forced to innovate their educational goals with the supposed purpose of keeping America competitive with the Soviet Union. Today the issue of how to teach about technology in schools continues, as some schools limit access to the Internet, raising concerns about free speech, while other schools are increasing their use of technology in the classroom. Virtual schools and online classes are becoming more and more common, and many educators believe the future of education is found in technology.

Issue 10. Principal's Office

Meaningful Student Involvement in the principal's office has an important role in decision-making on the personal level and affecting the whole student body. In addition to advocating for themselves, students can work with building leaders to affect school improvement through Principal Advisory Councils and other formal and informal mechanisms.

Issue 11. Grant Evaluations

Evaluating the efficacy of the grant-making designed to serve them positions student voice to impact learning beyond the classroom. Adults gain important skills and perspectives, as well as energy for implementation, while students gain important understanding about the purpose of funding for their learning.

Issue 12. School Year Planning

Looking over the scope of learning activities gives students insight into how education operates. Engaging students as partners to drive school year planning provides a collaborative basis for Student/Adult Partnerships by giving students purpose in schools.

Issue 13. School Budgeting

Engaging students as partners in complex education budgeting gives student voice a purposeful outlet to affect the school system. Educators and administrators can gain important insight to the effectiveness of decision-making and implementation.

Issue 14. Policy Making

Policy-making includes legislation at any level, grantmaking guidelines, program requirements, program regulations, and initiatives by school boards, mayors, superintendents, or governors. More than one student voice campaign has the motto, "Nothing about me without me." They are frequently addressing about education policy-making, which is often done to and at students rather than with them. Always the target of formal decisions in schools, students are rarely engaged in the processes that affect them most. Meaningful Student Involvement in policy-making includes familiarity with education-specific jargon, as well as opportunities to address issues important to them, modify adult-driven policies, and partnering with adults to assess effectiveness.

Leadership Issues

When students participate in the formal activities of policy making, committee memberships and school improvement, they can be meaningfully involved in school leadership. This is more than simply attending school events. It is becoming actively engaged as fully equitable partners with adults in the guidance, deliberation, visioning and outcomes of the educational process for much more than the individual student. Oftentimes, Meaningful Student Involvement in school leadership can affect hundreds, if not thousands of students. Engaging students in these activities includes opportunities for them to be involved in decision-making, research, planning, evaluation, co-learning and advocacy.

Issue 15. Teacher Quality

Teacher quality is one of the biggest issues being discussed now by teachers unions, politicians, and teachers themselves. Many are saying that we need to determine who is a good teacher and who is a bad teacher. What some are saying is that when students are not succeeding in schools at sufficient rates, it must be the teachers' fault. While teachers certainly have impact on their students, outside factors are also a big issue, including poverty, home life, and the outside community. Getting rid of teacher tenure (which gives teachers extra support from being fired) and firing low-performing teachers based on student test scores is the new approach taken by districts around the country.

Issue 16. Time in School

The length of the school day has been a popular topic for decades, especially in recent years. Recent brain research has shown youth have different sleep needs than adults, while it's been popular to say that students in the US have less seat time than students around the world (as a matter of fact, this is incorrect: while students in some countries have more days of school than the US, most of those countries have shorter school days that results in less seat time). The length of the school year is also a consideration, as some advocates are determined to add more seat time by replacing traditional summer breaks with more frequent shorter breaks throughout the year. The amount of years a student needs to attend school is also an issue, as more public education leaders consider a "P16" system essential: pre-kindergarten through college graduation.

Issue 17. Scheduling

The schedule of a school often drives the learning and curriculum in the school. The traditional 45-minute period of high schools, for instance, means that projects and activities are harder to do and fit within that time, as is traveling outside of the school for field trips or connecting with the community. Block schedules often have 1.5 or 2 hour blocks of time for classes, which provides some of these opportunities. Other schools provide classes for part of the time and give students self-directed learning time to pursue projects that earn them credit.

Issue 18. School Processes

Everything that is not governed by formal school policies is controlled by formal and informal processes and procedures. The forth location for Meaningful Student Involvement is in school processes. This includes what topics such as what students do when arriving at school, riding school buses, school lockers, activities in the cafeteria, absences and truancies, student illnesses, school material usage, qualifications for participation in extracurricular programs, cell phone usage, and many more activities. Engaging students in these activities includes positioning them as problem-solvers and decision-makers, planners and evaluators.

Issue 19. School Planning

Meaningful Student Involvement in school planning includes students equitably partnering with adults to create school culture, plan school activities and operations, promote school improvement, and design the physical building. All education processes and procedures that teach students with intention and purpose can exemplify meaningful involvement.

Issue 20. School Climate

The way a school is physically built and looks affects school climate as much as the interactions among students and between students and teachers. Engaging students as partners in school climate does not mean handing over the schools to students for them to learn on their own. Instead, it means acknowledging they are already leading building climate, whether adults admit it or not. Educators can move from passively allowing students to lead school culture to actively encouraging them for taking responsibility for it through learning opportunities focused on their roles. While doing that, schools can use the Characteristics of Meaningful

Student Involvement to substantially enhance individual and building-wide culture.

Issue 21. Extracurricular Activities

While it seems obvious that Meaningful Student Involvement should drive extra-curricular activities, it is not always true that is the case. Adults in charge of extra-curricular activities may rely on the tradition of having students be passive recipients of their leadership in order to operate their activities. For this reason, in the case of most clubs, teams, and other activities, it is important to position Meaningful Student Involvement directly guide the operation of these activities. This allows students and adults in schools to answer many essential questions for extracurricular activities, including when, where, how, and who is engaged in the activities. There are essential questions elsewhere in this book, including Tables 4 and 21.

Issue 22. Education in the Media

It is increasingly popular to quote students in education articles. Engaging student voice in the news includes that, as well as student-created articles for mainstream websites and newspapers, student-led video, student school twitter feeds, and other news distribution channels.

Issue 23. Funding Priorities

Traditionally funded by taxpayer dollars at the local, state, and (at a smaller level) federal level, in recent decades schools have actively sought funding from corporations, philanthropic foundations, and private donors as well. Funding basic education is an increasing issue in times when government support is waning, and as a result teaching materials and school buildings are becoming neglected or worn out. Teachers often purchase supplies out of their own pockets, or simply go without in communities where schools are underfunded. In affluent school districts students generally have access to better materials and teachers get paid high salaries, affording those students better educations. In turn, this reinforces the so-called academic achievement gap that is used to separate students. Calls for equitable funding are frequent, and have found mixed success.

Issue 24. Out of School Time

Offering activities after school, in the evenings, on the weekends, and throughout the summer are common in some schools, while other schools do not provide them at all. Tutoring and mentoring, sports and extracurricular clubs, and other learning or social experiences are out of the norm for many students, as their families or their schools are fiscally incapable of participating. Schools and communities could come together to devise creative ways to offer these opportunities to all students, regardless of income.

Issue 25. Discipline

Partnering with students to make classroom guidelines, school policies, and district regulations is how adults can foster Meaningful Student Involvement in discipline. Student courts are another approach, as is having students lead remediation and conflict resolution. Simple activities designed to prevent, intervene, or respond to challenging student behavior can give appropriate and necessary credence to students as partners. Doing this can make learners essential contributors to substantive activities within the normal learning environment of the classroom. In turn, this allows them to understand themselves as essential actors, which allows their transition from passive recipients of adult-led education towards Student/Adult Partnerships promoting learning, teaching, and leadership for all.

Issue 26. Community Connections

Meaningful Student Involvement can substantiate community connections throughout the education system. Place-based learning happens in classroom activities rooted in local things, including the unique history, environment, culture, economy, literature, and art of a specific place. Because of their knowledge and familiarity with the places they live, place-based learning is an ideal avenue for engaging students as partners. This can include methodologies such as service learning and adventure education. Serving as more than mere puppets of well-meaning adults, students who are engaged as partners can serve as true liaisons between the school and the community. This allows schools to genuinely benefit from all of any communities' inherent assets, apparent or hidden.

Teaching and Learning Issues

When students are meaningfully involved in teaching they have opportunities to teach other students through facilitating learning, curriculum planning, evaluation, and other means. They can teach each other, they can teach younger students, they can teach teachers, and they can teach school administrators.

Issue 27. Teacher Training

When students teach teachers about youth culture, student rights, learning styles, and other topics important to them in schools, Meaningful Student Involvement can be present in teacher training. Students can also co-facilitate learning opportunities for adults focused on the critical study of power, language, culture, and history as they are related to Meaningful Student Involvement, ultimately and appropriately teaching teachers to value that their experiences and contributions to education. (Giroux & McLaren, 1982)

Issue 28. Teacher Development

Thinking about what teachers learn and how they learn it is important to making schools work better. The idea is that more and better opportunities for support, mentorship, and professional development for teachers will lead to better teaching and improved teacher quality. In some countries, teachers have far less teaching time than in the United States, and have more time to plan with other teachers and observe the teaching of others. Half of all teachers leave teaching within their first 5 years, and new teachers have a steep learning curve.

Issue 29. Class Evaluation

When students evaluate themselves, their teachers, their peers, the curriculum, physical classroom, or other parts of the school, they are sharing student voice. Evaluations that are designed, facilitated, implemented, and studied by students are an avenue for meaningful involvement to happen. Facilitating student learning, action, and reflection on the process of conducting student evaluations can help ensure meaningfulness.

Issue 30. School Research

Students who research their schools examine learning, behavior, funding, policies, and more for efficacy and purpose. Both sharing and collecting student voice, engaging students as partners in school research can help identify gaps and secure data in ways that many adult researchers cannot. It can also be a powerful opportunity to teach students about the practical application of research in schools.

Issue 31. Special Education

The questions facing special education include the labeling of students, funding the support services that special education students receive, and mainstreaming special education students throughout the school population. There are concerns about disproportionate representation of males and students of color as special education students, as well as equal access to support for such learners. Charter schools and other schools of choice are sometimes criticized for weeding out special education students since they have more leeway in which students they accept.

Issue 32. Curriculum Planning

Curriculum planning can be made richer and more effective with student voice. By participating as partners, students can help decide topic areas, curricular approaches, teaching methods, and other essential parts of the process. Student voice can be most effective in equal partnerships through regular curriculum committees, as well as individual teacher planning.

Issue 33. Curriculum

The question of who decides the curriculum in schools has a big impact on what goes on in schools. With influences ranging from textbook companies to politicians, and from school boards to businesses and more, schools and teachers somehow have to sort this out and provide a meaningful learning experience for students. The federal government, along with a coalition of private organizations, is supporting the concept of Common Core State Standards that would create the same standards throughout the country, and many governors have urged their states to follow them. Meaningfully involving students in the curriculum allows teachers to engage students' attitudes, experiences, beliefs, ideas, actions, and outcomes as central to learning. (Grace M. , 1999) By identifying the central role of classroom curriculum in promoting Meaningful Student Involvement, schools can re-position student leadership by moving it from the purview of eloquent or gifted students towards the experience of the proverbial "every student". This can allow learners to invest in learning, deepen their experience of curriculum, and secure the power of learning throughout their lives.

Issue 34. Sports

Adult responses to student voice in school sports have varied. When Meaningful Student Involvement is integrated into these activities, students can drive team climate in positive direction, set high standards for performance, teambuilding, and sportsmanship, and create positive experiences for all participants.

Conclusion

All these places for Meaningful Student Involvement do not matter if they are not acknowledged or drawn upon. They do not allow for apathy or disregard by educators, either. They *do* challenge teachers and administrators to get honest about their desire to teach, lead, and learn with students. From that place all things can change, always, throughout every one of our schools for every student. *That* is Meaningful Student Involvement. These are some of the issues students can address in schools as you consider what to change and how to work with adults. By learning more about these issues and taking firm stands, young people can contribute to the conversation and take action in sophisticated, relevant ways that make you a partner in working with adults to improve your school.

Chapter 38: Meaningful Student Involvement

Through my research and practice, I have identified several different strategies that students and adults have taken for integrating Meaningful Student Involvement throughout education. These strategies are to:

1) Establish necessity
2) Raise awareness
3) Build capacity
4) Advocate action
5) Change attitudes
6) Modify procedures
7) Transform policies
8) Develop structures
9) Challenge indifference
10) Transform cultures

The following section explores each of these strategies and shares an example of what they look like in schools.

1) Establish Necessity.

By the time the average student leaves high school they have at least 12 years of experience in schools. In many professions, anyone who has that much time under their belt is seen as an expert—especially teaching. However, young people are usually the last ones consulted for their knowledge. The first strategy to foster Meaningful Student Involvement is to establish necessity. Either through the necessity of their experience, unique knowledge, or investment in making schools better, the necessity of engaging students as partners throughout education is easy to make.

One hundred students and teachers from three high schools in Washington gathered for SoundOut's Changing SPACES retreat sponsored by the Washington State Office of Superintendent of Public Instruction. The retreat engaged students and adults as partners in critically examining the cultures of their schools. They reflected on learning, teaching, and leadership in schools, and presented exciting plans to the principals from their school to make school a more engaging place for students. This helped establish the necessity of Meaningful Student Involvement in several communities where there was no emphasis beforehand.

2) Raise Awareness.

Raise awareness and get on the radar by using peer education, media, and learning activities to raise awareness among students and throughout the community. There are many ways to reach popular media including the Internet and print such as newspapers and flyers. Many students are making Facebook pages or zines about the issues they care about.

For several years, the Office of Student Engagement in Washington charged students with the awesome responsibility of teaching their peers about education transformation. Student2Student was a statewide effort to raise awareness and enthusiasm among incoming ninth graders about the new graduation requirements that affected all learners. While they were serving as excellent teachers, these students have also provided proof positive to adults that peer education matters. In the process have they raised the profile of Meaningful Student Involvement.

3) Personalize the Process.

Meaningful Student Involvement requires educators to see students individually, and to create a variety of opportunities that are appropriate for each given student and responsive to their individual needs and their desires for their educational experience. This means that sometimes activities will focus on individual students doing individual things to improve their own education; other times, large groups of students will do large scale activities to impact the entirety of the education system; and everything in between. There is no one formula for all students everywhere. Instead, there are many, many ways that every student in every building can be engaged as partners all of the time.

Working with a large membership-based national education organization, I developed a nationwide program for engaging students as education policy advocates. The activities in the program helped learners identify what they were most passionate about, where they could leverage their passions, and how they could learn what they needed to know to successfully transform education. After testing it in dozens of communities across the country, the organization decided not to implement the program. "It is too burdensome to require our members to work with so many students individually," they reported back to me. This helped me learn about one of the main barriers of Meaningful Student Involvement, which is capacity. Later in this book I share how to identify whether that is a genuine barrier. This story illustrates the reality that personalizing the process takes investment of a variety of resources, including time.

4) Build Capacity.

Building individual capacity means helping people increase their knowledge about a given subject, such as Meaningful Student Involvement or the specific subject addressed by an activity. It also means developing the skills of students and adults to successfully engage students as partners. That includes communication, teamwork, conflict resolution, and other action-focused skills, as well as planning, reflection, and critical thinking skills. Building the capacity of a school, district, government education agency, or nonprofit organization includes creating and training students for strategic positions, as well as conducting regular evaluations and holding challenging, but necessary, critical conversations about Meaningful Student Involvement.

SoundOut has been providing Meaningful Student Involvement-focused skills development and program planning for young people and adults across the United States, Canada, the United Kingdom, Australia, and Brazil for almost a decade.[13] Working with adults, I have focused on promoting three primary areas of professional development: Readiness training, operations training, and outcomes assessment. Individual training topics in this area have included Student/Adult Partnerships, Student Voice 101, Making Student Involvement Meaningful, and much more. For students, I have led training activities on all ranges of Meaningful Student Involvement, including all those mentioned above. Building capacity has also taken the form of developing strategic relationships within a school, agency, or organization in order to ensure there is a strategic champion within the environment where students are to be engaged as partners. In addition to training and relationship management, capacity building has also included developing strong avenues towards action, like small streams feeding into a river. These avenues can take the form of individual action affecting a classroom; multiple classrooms affecting an entire school; several schools affecting a district, and several districts affecting the state or province where they are located.

5) Advocate Action.

Use action as a tool for learning. Paulo Freire infamously challenged activism without learning throughout his expositions on learning. (Freire, 1973; 2004) He encouraged community organizers to see beyond simply acting for the sake of doing something, writing,

> "Critical reflection on practice is a requirement of the relationship between theory and practice. Otherwise theory becomes simply 'blah, blah, blah,' and practice, pure activism."

Rather than merely theorizing the possibilities of student voice, it's important to actually do something.

For students in the Seattle Student Equity Project, awareness was not enough. On a contract with the Seattle School District Equity and Race Relations Office, I worked with ten high schools to establish student-driven advocacy and education projects for their peers and teachers focused on diversity, race and Meaningful Student Involvement. The projects took awareness to the next level by giving students the avenues and creating a platform for real action. In one school, students developed an ongoing, student-led club focused on integrating English Language Learners' experiences and knowledge into classes. Students developed trainings for students and teachers, and led annual evaluations for two years focused on their concerns. Because of the students' advocacy, the Seattle School District eventually adopted a policy allowing *A People's History of the United States* by Howard Zinn to be used to teach history.

6) Change Attitudes.

American cultural anthropologist Margaret Mead made the essential point that adults must show young people that they can and should be taken seriously when she wrote,

> "The young, free to act on their initiative, can lead their elders in the direction of the unknown... The children, the young, must ask the questions that we would never think to ask, but enough trust must be re-established so that the elders will be permitted to work with them on the answers."

When we change the way that students feel, we change the way they learn. Provide substantive training and other opportunities for students and adults to reflect on their experiences throughout the education systems and we can consequently change other students' feelings too, as well as other adults throughout the education system. Encourage critical exploration as well as action-oriented outcomes.

While dreaming of changing schools is a first step, the Alberta Ministry of Education's Student Engagement Initiative called SpeakOUT sees more value in changing the way people feel about students. Partnering with the provincial ministry to provide a focus on Meaningful Student Involvement, I helped the SpeakOUT team create vibrant opportunities for students throughout the province to share their thoughts about schools, and then share that data with decision-makers in government. Through dialogue among students and adults, SpeakOUT continues to provide young people with opportunities to reflect and dream of new realities for themselves and their schools. Further, they are creating dynamic new ways to infuse Meaningful Student Involvement throughout the education system.[14]

7) Modify Procedures.

It is not enough to simply talk about Meaningful Student Involvement. Instead, it is imperative to actually *do something.* Change the processes and activities of your class, school, district, or state to actively engage students as partners throughout the education system.

Students at Eagle Rock School in Estes Park, Colorado, are included in staff meetings and help determine curriculum. A philanthropic effort of Honda Motor Company, the school focuses on engaging high school students who didn't succeed in traditional schools. Student representatives are elected to attend staff meetings and bring up issues students find important, contributing equally to any conversation had by adults at the school.[15]

8) Transform Policies.

There is an old adage that says, "Keep your feet on the ground and your eyes on the sky." Transforming the policies of the education system illustrates this deeply. Working in Student/Adult Partnerships, young people can transform education policy in K-12 classrooms, throughout schools and across the entirety of education systems. They can research effective school policies, evaluate current guidelines and rules, and rewrite policies reflecting their knowledge and observations.

With a history extending into the 1970s, over the last several years the Boston Student Advisory Council, or BSAC, has newly engaged students in effective efforts that informed, formed and implemented district-wide policies in Boston Public Schools. The national nonprofit organization Youth On Board, located in the Boston area, helped the district redesign the program, creating new mechanisms that actively engage students in decision-making. Since the 2006-07 school year BSAC has convened meetings twice monthly; met with the Superintendent and members of the School Committee to offer their perspectives on high school renewal efforts regularly; and informed their respective schools about issues affecting the entire city. A recently-positioned student representative from BSAC on the Boston School Committee has increased the profile of the group, as well. Their decision-making has led to a variety of policy changes affecting schools across the city, with their leadership guiding a new cell phone policy and a "lockout policy" affecting truancy, with new efforts focused on school attendance. (Joselowsky, 2007)

9) Develop Structures.

Keep in mind that creating a great rule, guideline, or law is largely worthless if there is no way to implement it. Many schools already have financial constraints when it's decided to embark on the journey towards Meaningful Student Involvement for all learners. It can be essential for there to be money and a program behind the policy you are advocating.

Through their Student Leadership and Involvement Office, Anne Arundel County Public Schools in Maryland coordinated the superintendent's Teen Advisory committee for more than twenty years. Composed of two students from each of the district's high schools, they met with district officials four times annually. Student input from this committee has led to changes such as providing dinner for students in the evening high school program and revising course curricula to better facilitate service learning projects. Today, their responsibilities have been rolled into the work of the Chesapeake Regional Association of Student Councils.

10) Challenge Indifference.

Labeling students as apathetic implies that they choose not to be otherwise. However, in schools that routinely discourage students from becoming meaningfully involved in their own education, what looks like apathy is actually a conditioned response.

Consider the variety of people who are indifferent to students today. They are young, middle age, and older; they are wealthy and poor, suburban, rural, and urban; and they are educated as well as under-educated. Challenging indifference to Meaningful Student Involvement means acting for yourself and with others.

11) Transform Cultures.

The old song might have been more effective if it had implored young people to, "Teach your teachers well..." Education, advocacy, and action promoting Meaningful Student Involvement can start at the youngest age. Make sure that many educators, parents, and younger students are affected by Meaningful Student Involvement. Make opportunities for the larger education community to become meaningfully involved together, learning and doing and transforming schools together. When all education partners come together, Meaningful Student Involvement can change the entire education system.

It is hard to truly track the long-ranging effects of cultural change, especially when it comes to Meaningful Student Involvement. However, one state's program shines above all others across the country. For almost 10 years, dozens of schools in Vermont have participated in UP for Learning, formerly known as Youth and Adults Transforming Schools Together (YATST). (Beattie, 2012) The program's leader, Helen Beattie, has carefully stewarded a variety of approaches to engaging students as partners throughout education. "Changing a school's culture is a painstaking process, grounded in respectful discussion, not blame, and building upon strengths," Beattie said of the process. (Cervone, 2012) It is the commitment to that process that is at the heart of successful Meaningful Student Involvement.

---

[13] Learn related to this skill-building and knowledge-sharing, in Fletcher, A. (2013) *SoundOut Student Voice Curriculum.* Olympia, WA: CommonAction.
[14] Learn about Alberta Education's SpeakOUT program at speakout.alberta.ca
[15] Learn about Eagle Rock School at eaglerockschool.org

Chapter 39: Preparing for Meaningful Student Involvement

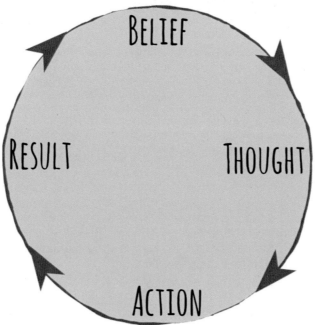

Figure 12. Developing Mindsets

No member of the education system—students, teachers, support staff, administrators, politicians, parents, or voters—is born knowing how to meaningfully involve students. It is important to prepare all parts of schools for Meaningful Student Involvement. Establishing the basis for developing might include teaching about the mindset model shown in Figure 12. According to research by Dweck (1999) and others, this approach supposes that our beliefs inform our thoughts; thoughts drive our actions; actions lead to results, and; results inform our beliefs. By understanding how our mindsets inform our realities, this model can inform how we prepare for Meaningful Student involvement.

Following are several steps that can be taken throughout the education system. They can be facilitated by students, along with teachers, administrators, support staff, and education partners from throughout the community. (Walker & Logan, 2008)

A. Meaningful Mindsets

Before beginning, both student and adults who are targeted for involvement should have mindsets that are meaningful. As illustrated in Figure 12, our mindsets are what determines how we act, interact and perform in certain circumstances. They are made of four parts: Our thoughts, which inform our actions; our actions, which lead to results; the results, which produce beliefs; and our beliefs, which drive our thoughts. Every student and adult should learn this cycle before engaging in Meaningful Student Involvement opportunities.

According to Dweck (1999; 2006), there are two primary types of mindsets that affect students and adults in schools. The first is a fixed mindset where people see skills as something they are born with; challenges as something to avoid; effort as something it takes when you are not good enough; feedback as something personal; and setbacks as something that is discouraging. The second type is the growth mindset, which tells people that skills come from hard work and can always be improved; challenges cause people to grow and we should embrace them; effort is essential and important; feedback is something to learn from; and setbacks are a wakeup call to make us work harder next time.

Preparing students and adults for Meaningful Student Involvement requires a culture that supports growth mindsets within the immediate opportunity, looking to grow them throughout the education system. According to Dweck's research, the right kinds of praise and encouragement—for effort applied, strategies used, choices made, persistence displayed, and so on—yields more long-term benefits than telling them they are "excellent" when they succeed. (Dweck, 2010)

B. Preparing Students

Most students have lived a lifetime of routinely being told their voices do not count and their actions do not make a difference. This happens overtly and subversively. Adults set expectations for them; make rules to govern their behavior; create punishments to control their actions; implement punitive measures when they break the rules, and; award behavior they find compelling. Because of this, most students have no idea how to be meaningfully involved in schools. However, almost every student of any age is highly capable of detecting when something is not meaningful for them.

The goal of preparing students for Meaningful Student Involvement is to foster highly engaged partners who are committed to education, community and democracy. Students should consider what they can do for other students more than themselves and want to inspire their peers to do the same. Ultimately, they should feel strongly about all aspects of education and know they are personally vital to their own education, as well as the system of schooling they are involved in.

Preparing students can include...

- Going through each of the components elaborated on earlier in this book as the Meaningful Student Involvement Learning Process.
- Assessing the current status of any student involvement in their classroom, school, district, or state is essential to establishing a firm foundation for student engagement.
- Being absolutely clear with them about the purpose or why you want to meaningfully involve them, work with students and other adults to ensure mutual understanding.
- Making sure students know what your expectations are for their involvement, support their complete investment by having them create mutual accountability measures for Student/Adult Partnerships.
- Facilitating Meaningful Student Involvement requires students and adults actively remembering their purpose by not getting distracted by the process.
- Developing mutual understandings of the roles of students and adults in their activities, Meaningful Student Involvement encourages everyone to be clear and consistent in their expectations.
- Following the Cycle of Student Engagement explained earlier, students should have opportunities to be listened to by adults; validated for their beliefs; authorized to take action; act on their concerns, interests, abilities, ideas and wisdom; and reflect on their involvement.
- When activities are done, students should complete the Cycle of Engagement working in Student/Adult Partnerships to apply their reflections to the next Cycle, starting with listening.

C. Preparing Adults

Meaningful Student Involvement requires students and entire schools be engaged. However, it is really important to ensure that adults are engaged, too. No matter what their roles, all adults should foster and build their abilities to meaningfully involve students. This allows every member of the school community to be a partner to students and transform education. It also strengthens the capacity of schools to foster Meaningful Student Involvement for all learners in all schools, everywhere, all of the time. I explore this concept in earlier in Table 6. As Mitra wrote,

> "Before youth can be accepted as important players in school decision making, the concept of student voice must gain acceptance among powerful stakeholders in the school." (Mitra, 2006)

The same holds true of Meaningful Student Involvement.

Preparing adults can include...

- Providing professional development for all adults throughout the education system centered on Meaningful Student Involvement and Student/Adult Partnerships helps teachers, administrators, support staff, parents and others focus on collaborating with students beyond simply listening to student voice.
- Encouraging everyone to form substantive Student/Adult Partnerships throughout the education system, from individual classrooms to the state board of education.
- Establishing and maintaining positive, empowering Student/Adult Partnerships in order to help dissolve barriers of perceived authority and encourage more open dialogue.
- Celebrating Meaningful Student Involvement through student-led parent conferences, student assemblies and media outlets, and school open houses.

- Naming a clear vision for Meaningful Student Involvement in order to transform student perceptions of their own purpose, power and possibilities through strong, consistent messages actively promoted throughout the school, agency or education system as a whole.
- Having robust, adaptive and continuously improving processes that actively aim for every student in every classroom throughout every school becoming actively engaged in Student/Adult Partnerships and Meaningful Student Involvement. Table 10 shows some ways that can happen.
- Developing regular and substantial structures in classrooms, schools, districts, state agencies, or otherwise that support Meaningful Student Involvement throughout the education system.
- Creating specific student discussion areas, regular student congresses/forums/conferences and having real and enforceable open-door policies are all ways to encourage meaningful involvement for students.
- Challenging the restraints of the school year calendar and the 9 to 5 business day in order to support Meaningful Student Involvement.
- Allowing natural student development of ownership and investment rather than thrusting students into roles and opportunities they might not want or be ready for.
- Supporting teachers and school support staff with regular and ongoing capacity building activities, including reading materials, classroom tools, professional events and other supports that foster Meaningful Student Involvement. See Table 6 for activities.

D. Preparing Schools

Facilitating Meaningful Student Involvement inherently means being willing to change the ways a school thinks about student voice, student engagement and Student/Adult Partnerships. Your classroom, club, program and school should always demonstrate commitment to Meaningful Student Involvement by...

Preparing schools can include...
- Forming a group with a substantial number of students to partner directly with building or agency leadership, whether at the school, district or state levels whose roles are role is linked to education quality and curriculum issues and not merely token issues approved by adults.
- Establishing an independent student committee or student council, led by students and supported through Student/Adult Partnerships, in order to inform, drive, mediate, and motivate Meaningful Student Involvement throughout education.
- Making student schedules central to setting meetings and assigning sufficient time and space for them to be involved.
- Creating new policies to sustain the practice of Meaningful Student Involvement
- Collecting data as it shows how students, peers, adults and the larger school are affected by Meaningful Student Involvement activities.
- Building specific budget line items that support the implementation of Meaningful Student Involvement throughout the education system, whether starting small or large.
- Facilitating regular training for students and adults on Meaningful Student Involvement to introduce and strengthen skills, knowledge and commitment.
- Documenting policies and procedures that supporting Meaningful Student Involvement, and making those documents know to students and available to them in order to assure accountability to students and adults throughout the education system and beyond.

- Enforcing mutual accountability can mean having a regular coordinator or liaison for Meaningful Student Involvement report to a high-level administrator with the position is incorporated into a school's or nonprofit's organizational chart.
- Surviving a significant change of leadership at the school and being available to succeeding classes of students throughout the school.
- School-driven work can include gathering groups, organizations and/or student communities within the school to assist with designing, implementing, sustaining and/or evaluating their Meaningful Student Involvement activities through conferences, workshops and/or local outreach.
- Forming new networks and coalitions within schools, around districts, across states, throughout nations, and across the world can support Meaningful Student Involvement. Gathering like-minded students and adults and organizations form networks leads to support and coalitions for advocacy. Tangible action, practical outcomes, and meaningful activities form and transformation the bonds that unite them.
- Ensuring there are appropriate, meaningful, sufficient and effective ways to meaningfully involve students throughout your classroom, school, district, state or nation.
- Preparing adults to intentionally share increasing amounts of authority with students throughout the course of activities.
- Focusing everyone involved to stay centered on characteristics, not individuals; transformation, not reform; and courage, not corruption.
- Making space for all students to become meaningfully involved and not just the loudest or best performing students.
- Working with fellow adults throughout the education system to increase support and commitment to Meaningful Student Involvement.
- Establishing a specific and committed space for activities to be held.
- Building a schoolwide commitment to Student/Adult Partnerships and Meaningful Student Involvement through messaging, workshops, assessments and ongoing activities that target all members of the school community.
- Creating an ongoing mechanism for meaningfully involving students in assessment processes that report frequently how student views have helped the school, district, state or nation to improve.

E. Preparing the Education System

Seeing that every individual classroom is part of a school that affects Meaningful Student Involvement, Student/Adult Partnerships require readying all the parts, components and colleagues possible. This preparation can focus on curricular areas within a school, feeder schools within a district, multiple districts within a city, multiple cities within a state, and so on. The education system includes the individuals listed above, as well as the formal and informal policies and practices, the curriculum, and so forth. Education systems can demonstrate Meaningful Student Involvement by...

Preparing the education system can include...
- Analyzing ways in which schools can engage students through equitable partnerships with adults throughout education.
- Demonstrating strong connections between academic learning and meaningful involvement.
- Examining the underlying causes and effects of Meaningful Student Involvement throughout education (see Table 13 for examples).

- Engaging all students in every school all of the time through Meaningful Student involvement.
- Requiring authentic engagement instead of tokenism, decoration and manipulation.
- Teaching how students about student voice, learning, the education system, school transformation and learning through action. Explore several pathways to authentic student voice in Table 1 of this book.
- Demonstrating how Student/Adult Partnerships actively, powerfully and purposefully transform learning, teaching and leadership throughout schools.
- Providing resources to transform education in ways that benefit all students, all adults and all communities in constant win/win situations.
- Inspiring and empowering students and adults to constantly work together to make Meaningful Student Involvement reality for everyone, everywhere, all of the time. I explore this idea in Table 6 earlier in this book. [16]

These different parts of preparing students, adults, schools and systems for Meaningful Student Involvement can deeply influence the meaningfulness, outcomes and sustainability of Student/Adult Partnerships throughout learning, teaching and leadership across the entirety of the education system. That intentionally is a key to meaningfulness, and builds opportunities for the future as well as answers needs in the present

---

[16] This list was adapted from Banks, J. A. (1997). *Educating Citizens in a Multicultural Society.* New York: Teachers College Press.

Chapter 40: Considering the Ethics

There are no guaranteed outcomes in Meaningful Student Involvement, in Student/Adult Partnerships, or any part of education as a whole. Adults throughout the education system have to approach every opportunity to meaningfully involve students as a new or renewed opportunity to positively, powerfully and meaningfully impact the lives of students and foster a healthier democracy—no matter how big or small their activities appear. From this position, it becomes obvious that the ethics of Meaningful Student Involvement must be considered by everyone involved. (Hill, M. as cited by Bragg, 2007; Booker & MacDonald, 1999)

When planning opportunities, it is vital to consider the purpose of Meaningful Student Involvement, and whether the opportunities presented are actually in the interest of students. In that consideration, it is important to remember that students themselves can make the determination about whether they care about something—after they understand the degrees of possibility, mentioned earlier in this book.

Students will want to understand the costs and benefits to being meaningfully involved in deciding whether or not an opportunity matters to them. They should understand whether there are costs for becoming meaningfully involved or not becoming involved in something. They should also know upfront whether there are benefits to being involved. Students should know whether there are privacy or confidentiality issues, and if there are choices for how they are represented.

In planning Meaningful Student Involvement, adults should keep in mind who is involved and who is excluded, and why. Student/Adult Partnerships should focus on disengaged students and students who are historically disconnected throughout their schools and the education system, including those with physical impairments, homeless students, and students in minority populations within the school. Students who are historically disengaged in schools believe they are only there because they have to be, and are determined to leave as soon as they can. They generally do not like being at school, and learning does not appear to be exciting for them. Disengaged students often watch the clock, act bored, or only do the minimum required amount of work. They may want to graduate, but because they have too many sick days or turn in too few assignments, they probably cannot graduate on time. These students appear not to like any teacher or get along with other students, but they keep coming to school regardless. I explore reasons for student disengagement in Tables 3 and 5 of this book.

Students and adults should clearly understand what the requirements of the funding for their activities are, and what impact that has on their partnerships. There should also be clear conversations about what types of acknowledgment students are going to receive, whether that is class credit, some form of pay, or an award or scholarship.

The nature of Meaningful Student Involvement has been carefully expanded on throughout this book. Educators and school leaders need to carefully consider the characteristics, the Cycle of Engagement and other tools throughout this book in order to determine how they are going to involve students. Because of its difference from their daily educational experiences, students should know what kind of mutual accountability they can rely on through Student/Adult Partnerships. Students and adults should be clear on what they can actually contribute through Meaningful Student Involvement, whether in the planning and design, implementation, evaluation, or other steps for implementation and assessment. Careful consideration should be given to identifying safeguards and checks and balances among students and between students and adults throughout the activities as well.

To ensure Student/Adult Partnerships, the aims and implications of all activities with students should be clearly explained and examined with students and adults who are participating. For instance, I share the "Aims of Meaningful Student Involvement" in Table 11 of this book. There should be written documentation available in students' native languages, and preferably written by students for students. If jargon and "education-ese" are used, there should be easy reference sheets for students to refresh themselves on the definitions.

Throughout activities, students should have opportunities to give their repeated consent until they are fully invested in the outcomes they are creating. They should fully understand their rights to refuse to be involved, too. Adults should remain conscientious of the informal pressure they can exert over students, and keep that to a minimum. There is a balance between adult assignments in Meaningful Student Involvement and students' consent, and that should be present throughout all activities.

Throughout the course of Student/Adult Partnerships, everyone involved should know whether their creations, products and processes are going to be shared with others. Students specifically should have opportunities to reflect on their actions and outcomes. Everyone involved should also be aware of who the audience for this sharing is, whether it is other students, adults throughout an immediate school community, academics, community partners, education policy makers, the public, parents, etc.

The final ethical consideration for Meaningful Student Involvement may be the most important: the impact on students directly. Participants should know how Meaningful Student Involvement affects students through its impact on thinking, policy and practice throughout education. Students should also be the ultimate judges of whether their perspectives, actions, ideas, knowledge and wisdom are accurately conveyed, and should be able to share that with the people who administered the Meaningful Student Involvement activities or opportunities.

Part VI. Meaningful Student Involvement in Action

Chapter 41. Introduction

When students begin to realize that the *way* they learn is keeping them from *what* they are actually supposed to be learning, the situation in schools can get tense. Around the world today schools are promoting transparent, engaging relationships between adults and students in schools by engaging young people in designing, implementing, assessing, advocating, and making decisions about education. When this is done, students become partners, allies, and companions in school improvement.

However, resolving that tension does not happen easily or fast. After strategic planning and preparation, it is vital to be intentional in setting Meaningful Student Involvement in action. Table 14 highlights some considerations, approaches and activities to use that accomplish that goal.

FRAMING MEANINGFUL STUDENT INVOLVEMENT

Confer With Students
Work with students to brainstorm on-going lists of things students want to transform in schools. The more they learn about education, the more they will see to transform.

Build Individual and Group Capacities
Consider whether students need to shore up specific skills or knowledge in order to be effective in their involvement. Do they need more strength in communication, conflict resolution or social media? Can their knowledge of curriculum planning, grading or education grants be enriched? Use formal and informal assessment to identify opportunities.

Create Classroom Task Forces
Selecting topics from the brainstorm list, encourage students to work together to assess, research and facilitate on that education topic. If you are thinking, "too much valuable class time off the curriculum or content," find a way to connect school improvement activities to the educational standards your school follows.

Assess Student Needs, Wants and Ideas
Work with students to create several statements for a unit of study to gauge student interest in specific school improvement issues. Then use a scale to allow them to self-determine where the most interest in the class is.

Share Options and Self-Evaluations
Give students plenty of options in types of school improvement projects and also collaborate with your students in identifying the criteria, activities and outcomes for each project. Having ownership, students can use the criteria to evaluate themselves during and at the end of the project. Self-evaluation should reflect deeply on learning, teaching and leadership throughout the education system.

Table 15. Framing Meaningful Student Involvement

Chapter 42. Beginning with Purpose

There is no one single way to begin meaningfully involving students. It cannot be said enough that every single student needs to experience avenues and opportunities that suit their specific learning styles, lifestyles, backgrounds and other diversities. There are some activities that open the doorways to Meaningful Student Involvement. They do not form a system, constitute a curriculum, or guarantee any results. Some schools have used some individual activities over and over, while others combine a variety of them successively. (Brasof, 2009) However, when utilized in the context of engaging students as partners in learning throughout the education system in order to improve the education system, these activities can move towards Student/Adult Partnerships for all students, everywhere, all of the time. (Cheminais, 2013)

A. Activities to Foster Meaningful Student Involvement

With the locations above previously as the large areas where Meaningful Student Involvement can be infused throughout the education system, it is important to acknowledge that "a journey of a thousand miles begin with a single step." Following are some of the single steps in schools. For a more comprehensive list, see Table 7.

1. Student-Led Parent Conferences

Students facilitating parent conferences with their teacher as a supportive partner in the process. In preparation, students evaluate their learning, and as an outcome, co-create plans to continue and expand their learning.

2. Student Forums

Large gatherings of students focused on improving schools, also called student congresses, can help create momentum for Meaningful Student Involvement and an initial surge of interest in engaging student voice throughout education.

3. Student Government

These groups include student councils, associated student body, etc. These are representative decision-making structures that operate in many primary and secondary schools. Frequently providing token opportunities, many address social activities and other superficial topics. In a small but growing minority of schools, they are increasingly working for the larger purpose of school management, evaluation and student engagement by moving past representative governance and towards Student/Adult Partnerships.[17]

4. Self-Directed Learning

Students, in partnership with teachers and parents, implement learning plans in specific subject areas, developing learning goals and meeting assessment criteria throughout.

5. Curriculum Committees

Students participate in committees which advise staff on a variety of issues including their personal experiences, classes, internships, research opportunities and career assistance.

6. Learner Leaders

In the United Kingdom, these students are elected by their peers to regularly represent their interests at governor's meetings, which are roughly equivalent to district school boards.

7. Student-Teacher Team Teaching/Student-Run Classes

Students work with teachers to facilitate classroom learning in subjects that they have expertise in, including history, business and science. Students teach their peer groups or cross-grade courses.

8. Hiring Committees

As partners with adults throughout the hiring process, students are involved in interviewing and selecting teachers, principals, district and state education agency staff.

9. Student Evaluations

Students provide input and considerations for teachers and administrators regarding the effectiveness of curriculum, quality of teacher instruction methods and student voice in the classroom.

10. Student/Peer Evaluations Of Classroom Performance

Students provide constructive feedback regarding student-led teaching and presentations, as well as behavior and learning attitudes.

11. Student Designed Courses And Curriculum

Teachers train students to research, plan, design and evaluate regular course curriculum throughout schools, and students partner, lead, or join committees to design courses and curricula.

12. Classroom Curriculum

Steeped inside of the classroom curriculum, Meaningful Student Involvement can be embedded in learning through research, planning, teaching, evaluation, decision-making and advocacy, all focused on education. Core curriculum and other topics can all hold this effort.

13. Training For Student Decision-Makers

All students are engaged in constant and meaningful decision-making opportunities in their own education, schoolwide and community issues. Schools train students and adults to be effective and empowered members of decision-making groups.

14. Student-Based School Needs Assessments

Students voice their concerns and praise on topics including school climate, student ownership and teacher/principal responsiveness.

15. Student-Led Teacher Training

Students facilitate professional development for teachers including (but not limited to) service learning, diversity and using technology in the classroom. Students' teaching is evaluated by teachers and administrators in attendance, and guided by supporting adults.

16. Student Action Committees

Diverse student groups reflect the attitude and ability of students throughout the school regarding a wide-range of topics, including class offerings, school activities and teachers, adult coordinators and peer leadership.

17. Learning To Learn

Teaching students about learning styles and multiple intelligences can foster Meaningful Student Involvement in numerous ways by empowering students to take charge of their own learning.

18. School Or Site Councils

Students engaged in community-wide discussions about school policy. Students have full membership, and are empowered to go to meetings by the validation of their concerns and beliefs. Students are encouraged to push for what they need and want in their education.

19. Student Self-Assessments

Students can learn about state standards and use them to establish their own learning goals, creating rubrics and other measurements to assess their own performance.

20. School Design

Either through focus groups, design charrettes or other forums, students have opportunities to contribute to building design, redesign and supplying with equipment. As the users of most school features, students can be invaluable partners in evaluating, planning and researching school design.

21. Technology Integration

As the learners who will employ many of the apps and other technology tools available to schools, students can participate in identifying and planning usage, as well as making decisions about purchases and implementation, and evaluating implementation.

22. Communications

Students can be key implementers in school communications by using texts, podcasts, diaries and blogs, conversations, presentations, surveys, assemblies, websites, notice boards, meetings and forums to connect with their peers. Not just information sources, students can also plan, facilitate, evaluate and advocate for communications too.

23. Circle Time

Using horizontal relationships between students and adults, circle time gives everyone a chance to dialogue openly and generate new thinking and action as co-learners

24. Teacher Tutors

On a regular, scheduled basis students have a designated time and place within the classroom to actively consult teachers and other adults in the education system. Given as much input as possible, students must understand what is being requested of them, and must not be used as tokens in the decision-making process. Students should know the outcome from every teacher tutoring session.

25. Principal Advisory Councils
These are structures for students to become regularly involved in the affairs the school, working in Student/Adult Partnerships with principals, headmasters, administrators, and others.

26. Best Practice Clubs
Students learn the basics of schools and school improvement and devise classroom evaluations reflecting their concerns, ideas, thoughts and considerations. Then, they voluntarily attend classes during their study halls or lunch breaks. While there, the best practice club members evaluate the class and take notes. Afterwards, they offer teachers feedback on their curriculum, delivery, classroom management skills, the classroom climate, and other issues, such as diversity and equality.

27. Student Takeover Day
Young and old students in the United Kingdom have an opportunity once a year to work with adults for the day and become involved in decision-making. Children benefit from the opportunity to experience the world of work and make their voices heard, while adults and schools gain a fresh perspective on what they do.[18] This can be extended throughout K-12 and across the education system, with students actively engaged throughout building leadership, district and state education administration, and beyond.

Closing
When facilitated effectively, these activities can move towards Meaningful Student Involvement by helping create a positive school climate, which in turn creates stronger relationships between adults and students, an increased sense of responsibility, increased interest in school and increased success for all learners.

B. Teaching Techniques to Foster Meaningful Student Involvement

Classroom learning and Meaningful Student Involvement are deeply connected, ensuring relevancy for educators and significance to students. This deliberate connection ties together the roles for students with the purpose of education, thoroughly substantiating Student/Adult Partnerships and signifying the intention of adults to continue transforming learning as learners themselves evolve.

No single teaching technique, method, approach, style or ideology encapsulates Meaningful Student Involvement. However, several different methods can be used to enhance, enrich, encourage and enliven student involvement throughout learning, teaching and leadership. For individual activities, see Table 7.

1. Anytime, Anywhere Learning
With the assumption that through access to knowledgeable teachers and constant access to technology, Anytime Anywhere Learning gives schools permission to infuse technology with learning, and vice versa. This can lead to fully capable students who can drive learning and teaching. By emphasizing school improvement, this approach can also lead to Meaningful Student Involvement.

2. Blended Learning

Blended learning combines different ways of teaching and learning in lesson plans in order to teach students more effectively. It enables and empowers educators to adapt and transform their lessons in order to reach students more powerfully. Focusing largely on technology and interactive learning approaches, including service learning, experiential education and environmental education. Meaningful Student Involvement can be at the heart of each of these approaches through planning, research, teaching, facilitation, evaluation and decision-making. It is great for the practice of teaching, increasing students' access to knowledge, promoting social interactions between learners, developing personal agency in students, using classroom resources more effective and being highly adaptable. (Osguthorpe & Graham, 2003)

3. Civic Education

Civic education provides opportunities for students to learn the values, ideals, actions and outcomes of shared social, political, cultural and economic lives. The elements of citizenship education include awareness, knowledge, conscientiousness, sharing, activity and responsibility. Meaningful Student Involvement can be at the center of civic education.

4. Classroom Management

Classroom management is a consistently important issue to educators and students in the area of Meaningful Student Involvement, although for different reasons. Teachers often report they want to use meaningful involvement as an incentive to make students behave better; students often report that if they were meaningfully involved, classroom behavior would not be an issue. When considering the variety of issues that are tied together within student behavior, it may seem important to address it through school improvement approaches. However, what Meaningful Student Involvement promotes is consideration and understanding of the contexts of challenges in schools. This includes the overall issue of student engagement and the different ways different students are engaged throughout learning, teaching and leadership.

5. Community Engagement

Meaningful Student Involvement can foster healthy, successful community engagement. Community engagement is any sustained connection a community has with the larger community of which it is a part of. Because of their knowledge and familiarity with the places they live, community engagement offers strong possibilities for Student/Adult Partnerships. This can include methodologies such as service learning and adventure education. Serving as more than mere puppets of well-meaning adults, students who are engaged as partners can serve as true liaisons between the school and the community. This allows schools to genuinely benefit from all of any communities' inherent assets, apparent or hidden. Meaningful Student Involvement can substantiate community connections throughout the education system. Happening in classroom activities rooted in local things, including the unique history, environment, culture, economy, literature, and art of a specific place, community engagement provides powerful opportunities for Meaningful Student Involvement.

6. Differentiated Instruction

Tailoring teaching to individual students' needs happens through differentiated instruction. Teachers use this approach to meet students' individual learning needs and aspirations. Differentiated instruction can include self-led learning time, integrated technology usage, modified curriculum and assessments, or modified teaching approaches. It can foster Meaningful Student Involvement when it infuses student authority and student voice throughout learning and teaching.

7. Formative Assessment

Formative Assessment is a process-driven process happening in learning and teaching to determine how students are performing. Through formal and informal procedures, formative assessments can provide teachers with information during the learning process to modify teaching and learning activities to improve student attainment. Meaningful Student Involvement can be a key factor in formative assessments, because it reflects, suggests and sustains the learning trajectory throughout learning, teaching and leadership. Formative assessments typically involve qualitative feedback (rather than scores) for both student and teacher. These focus on the details of content and performance instead of the outcomes of testing. Studies have shown that formative assessment practices that meaningfully involve students can help all learners. The results are most dramatic with struggling or disengaged students. (Chappuis & Chappuis, 2002)

8. Inquiry-Based Learning

By asking students to discover knowledge on their own with guidance from their teachers, inquiry-based learning can be deeply integral to Meaningful Student Involvement, both in the classroom and throughout the education system. Working from the assumptions that every teacher of every subject can share equal responsibility for teaching and evaluating skills, educators can infuse inquiry-based learning in schools today by creating performance rubrics focused on student competencies, and by making skills-oriented growth sixty percent of their grade. Any classroom can be on the path to supporting inquiry-based learning, in turn nurturing Meaningful Student Involvement for every learner. (Markham, 2013)

9. Learning Communities

Martin-Kniep (2008) wrote that learning communities must infuse learners as well as teachers, administrators, parents and other adults, because "students have firsthand experiences that affect their learning and their thinking." (Martin-Kniep, 2008) By engaging students as partners throughout education teachers can foster learning communities between adults and students, throughout their classrooms and throughout entire schools and districts. Learning communities engage participants in caring deeply about learning; feeling free to take risks; challenging each other and raising the expectations of everyone; respecting and valuing perspectives other than their own by seeking and valuing every member's input; intentionally seeking to do the work better, and; aggressively and continually building capacity of each member to work smarter. (Martin-Kniep 2004) By using these attributes as the basis of learning communities with students and adults, schools can foster Meaningful Student Involvement as well.

10. Mindsets

A mindset is the way someone thinks about something. A growing body of research and literature has shown that students' mindsets determine educational effectiveness, school culture and much more. Figure 12 from earlier in this book shows how deeply mindsets affect Meaningful Student Involvement. By focusing on the intersection between mindset and strategy, educators can help students learn a practical framework for identifying opportunities so they can proceed from promising ideas to practical actions in schools. Whether seeking to start a school improvement campaign or infuse a meaningful mindset into their current classrooms, students can learn directly from the firsthand experience of other students who've experienced meaningful involvement throughout education. This shift of mindset begins by immersing students in school improvement activities that share knowledge, build skills, and launch students into Student/Adult Partnerships that transform learning, teaching and leadership and own their own education.

11. Participatory Action Research

Engaging students as researchers who examine teaching, learning, leadership, or anything to do with education is called participatory action research, or PAR. Student researchers actively work to transform education during and after their research, and reflect throughout the process. Meaningful Student Involvement happens when PAR emphasizes co-learning among students and between students and adults, and embeds action with stated learning goals focused on students experiencing and transforming schools in new ways. See Table 17 for some research topics explored by students. (Morgan & Porter, 2011)

12. Project-Based Learning

Organizing educators and other adults into teams with students as partners focused on learning outcomes for everyone positions project-based learning as a key avenue towards Meaningful Student Involvement. Project-based learning centers classroom learning goals on creating, implementing and assessing projects led by students. When project-based learning position students as partners with educators, these Student/Adult Partnerships can be made of varying ages, abilities, genders and interests that collaboratively decide how the teams function to achieve student learning.

13. Restorative Justice

Restorative justice is a student-led approach to resolving conflict in schools. When facilitated right, it holds Meaningful Student Involvement at the center, positioning students as planners, facilitators and evaluators throughout the entirety of the process. Where many previous conflict resolution programs in schools were adult-led and student-driven, restorative justice programs elevate student voice by increasing student agency through positioning learners as strategic owners of the entire process. Students can call for restorative justice, plan its implementation, facilitate the process and submit their feedback afterwards. Restorative justice moves students to engage with each other in powerful, responsive ways. The philosophy and practices of restorative justice bring students who misbehave into structured, safe and supportive conversations with students who are affected by their misbehavior. This teaches accountability and interdependence while repairing the harm that was caused and prevents future behavior of a similar fashion, as students become more responsible for their actions and responsive to the climate of the learning environment.

14. Serving Learning

Treating students are seen as partners instead of recipients in service learning, this method can foster Meaningful Student Involvement when it is focused on transforming education. Service learning, which infuses classroom learning with meeting real community needs, can be ideal. Working with adults as partners, students must identify challenges, research the issues, identify and create strategies, facilitate action, and infuse reflection throughout activities.

(Fletcher, 2004) Some approaches position students in each strategy for Meaningful Student Involvement, while others focus on enhanced Student/Adult Partnerships through service. Whichever way it goes, it's important for activities for focus on school improvement.

15. Youth-Led Organizing for Education Reform

Working with adults as allies, students across the United States are stepping outside schools to organize youth and communities to improve schools. Leading sophisticated campaigns, they are compiling signature petitions, picketing school boards, holding teach-ins, and doing more to insist schools pay attention to social justice, promote equity among students, deconstruct the school-to-prison pipeline, and more.

16. Whole Child Approach

The whole child approach is a distinct strategy for education today. Built on professional collaboration among students, between students and adults, and among educators, administrators and others, the whole child approach partners people from different perspectives in order to affect the entire student, rather than piece by piece. Schools that seek to meet the basic student needs of safety, belonging, autonomy and competence are more likely to foster authentic student engagement.

Infusing Meaningful Student Involvement into their approach, the whole school approach encourages adults in schools to act in accord with school goals and values through Student/Adult Partnerships that develop social skills and understanding for everyone involved. Students and adults consequently contribute to the school and community and achieve goals together, including culturally, socially and academically. Schools and communities must work together to ensure that student needs are met on all levels, including fundamental levels of health, safety, and belonging. (Dalton, Churchman, & Tesco, 2008)

Each of these approaches to teaching can provide educators with strategic and deliberate opportunities to infuse and sustain Meaningful Student Involvement in their classrooms. There are many nuances and subtleties in these approaches that can only be learned through years of practice and professional development. Meaningful Student Involvement might only emerge in some of these approaches after that time. However, it might be on the surface of the approach, too, and simply be waiting to be called forth.

---

[17] Learn about transforming student government from School Councils UK at schoolcouncils.org
[18] Learn about Takeover Day at childrenscommissioner.gov.uk/takeover_day

Chapter 43. Strategies for Meaningful Student Involvement

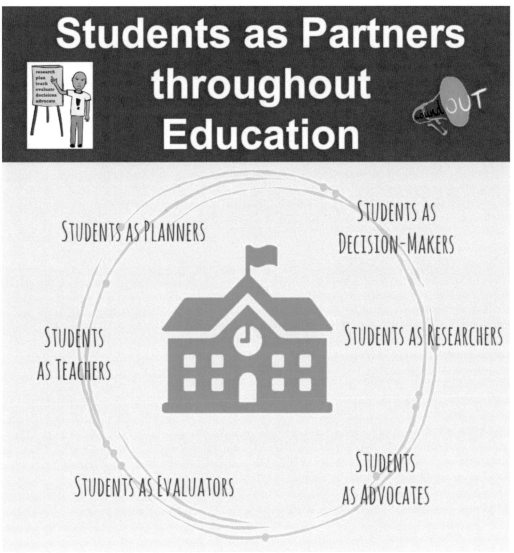

Figure 13. Students as Partners throughout Education

Of the many themes that consistently arise when I talk with students about meaningful involvement, two stick out beyond the rest. One theme is relevancy: when students really feel motivated, when they really feel connected, engaged and meaningfully involved, they are addressing issues that are relevant to them. It is truly challenging to define relevancy, specifically when the term has been thrown around so easily over the last several years. I have learned from students themselves that relevancy reflects the places, spaces, and motivations of students; it includes their interests, their passions, and their identities.

The other theme deals with breadth: Students want the things they participate in to reach wide and far, and to be surprised by their impact. These activities are not limited to any one specific avenue; rather, they occur throughout regular classroom curriculum, building leadership activities, and extra-curricular programs. See some examples in Table 7.

Students regularly identify these roles as meaningful. Instead of serving as mere information sources, they are developing ownership by participating in the design, facilitation, assessment and re-conception of more than just student involvement; their target is nothing less than improving schools and all student learning.

Considering the second theme and the way it weaves into the first, another pattern that emerged in my research on Meaningful Student Involvement makes a lot of sense. Forming a clear understanding of the strategies for engaging students as partners throughout education, this pattern, as illustrated in Figure 13, became apparent to me as I examined the thousands of activities students said were meaningful to them in activities related to improving education. They want distinct roles that allow them to research education in all its component forms; plan learning, teaching and leadership throughout the school system; teach each other, teachers and others; evaluate learning for its various values; make substantive decisions affecting themselves and others; and advocate for the schools and education transformation that matters to them most.

The following examples show Meaningful Student Involvement in action, and show how Meaningful Student Involvement promotes academic achievement, supportive learning environments, and lifelong civic engagement, as well as many other benefits. These stories from across the nation illustrate the broad practice of Meaningful Student Involvement throughout education today, and hint at wider possibilities in the future.

SUMMARY OF STRATEGIES FOR MEANINGFUL STUDENT INVOLVEMENT

Students as Researchers
- **Interview** students, educators and alumni about their classroom experiences;
- **Conduct** surveys to examine student opinions about budget priorities;
- **Study** student records from earlier eras.

Students as Planners
- **Participate** in teacher, principal, superintendent or other staff hiring processes;
- **Write** or rewriting classroom curriculum;
- **Join** a school committee for a grant focusing on redesigning current facilities.

Students as Teachers
- **Teach** students regular class lesson plans;
- **Tutor** younger and older students, or teachers;
- **Facilitate** professional development opportunities for teachers and other staff.

Students as Evaluators
- **Create** and utilize self-evaluations of learning and conduct for classes;
- **Devise** and implement student evaluations of curriculum, teachers, or classes, etc.;
- **Evaluate** school climate, culture, perceptions, spirit, etc.

Students as Decision-Makers
- **Join** school improvement committees as full members;
- **Accept** elections to school boards;
- **Co-create** classroom norms, behavior outcomes.

Students as Advocates
- **Conduct** a schoolwide email campaign to call for healthier school nutrition;
- **Picket** school boards to change racist school mascots;
- **Create** a student voice movement in a school or district.

Table 16. Summary of Strategies. Table 15 introduces these strategies.

Chapter 44. Students as School Researchers

Meaningful Student Involvement engages students as researchers of the educational settings, practices, beliefs, and outcomes that they are subject to. When students research their schools, they can become critical consumers of the institutions that affect them most. (Bragg, 2007) In participatory action research, or PAR, students participate in research design, execution, analysis, and writing about schools, environments, the teaching and learning process, and more. (Morgan & Porter, 2011) Meaningful Student Involvement in education research turns the microphone around, making the student the examiner as well as the examined, and turns the feedback loop an engine for school change. This is essential for meaningfulness and for Student/Adult Partnerships. (Fielding & Bragg, 2003)

Some areas in education for students as school researchers include:

- **Classrooms**: Students can examine student, teacher, and district decision-makers' interest in a given subject; student engagement in class; the efficacy of a specific way of teaching; factors that encourage learning and barriers that prevent learning; how to deal with noise in the classroom; what they would like more and less of in lessons; different ways of grouping students; peer support in learning; best ways of starting and ending the lessons; ways of catching up if students do not understand or if they miss work.
- **Administration**: Students can analyze current student involvement practices in a school; district policies regarding the active engagement of current school partners such as nonprofits, parents, or businesses; or activities of designed to meet school improvement goals.
- **Culture**: Students can compare student/administrator/teacher/parent perspectives of Meaningful Student Involvement; the effects of education about education on students; or student/teacher/administrator/parent attitudes towards student achievement, and much more.

As education researchers, students become critical thinkers and engaged participants in learning. The following examples focus on students engaged in research design, execution, analysis, and writing about schools, environments, the teaching and learning process, and more. Their work represents a critical step towards Meaningful Student Involvement.

One of the most important keys for Meaningful Student Involvement is the consistent support and willingness of adults to integrate students in all aspects of schooling, including teaching, learning, and decision-making. The role of Student/Adult Partnerships is central to involving student as education researchers.

Stories of Students as Researchers

The following stories illustrate how supportive learning environments can foster deep academic understanding, and therefore achievement, for all students.

Story 1: Students Speak Up

In Ontario, student teams across the province from grades seven through twelve participated in the Students as Researchers pilot project facilitated by the Ontario Ministry of Education's student voice program. To foster Student/Adult Partnerships in school and classroom activities, participants were taught about collaborative inquiry. The program emphasized hands-on learning in order to directly enhance student engagement.

Early outcomes confirmed that students were very engaged in this project and wanted to practice and apply research skills. They had questions they were interested in exploring and quickly became ready to take responsibility for seeing local projects through, especially in the interest of helping their peers. According to the Ministry's student engagement team, Students as Researchers forums involving more than 250 student/teacher teams were planned. All project teams shared their findings with their own school, their local school board and the Ontario Ministry of Education.

That final presentation happened at the Students as Researchers Conference in Toronto in February 2012. Students' constantly suggested learning life skills like research and critical thinking were vital to them now and in the future, and the conference was intended to provide new ways to gather student perspectives and incorporate students' views into school policy and directives.

This effort to involve students in research focused on Student/Adult Partnerships. Through these unique relationships, students worked alongside teachers, mobilizing student knowledge to solve serious challenges in their schools. These teams developed shared responsibility for the quality and conditions of learning and teaching, both within specific classrooms and throughout their entire school communities. Topics addressed by the teams included effective bullying and racial harassment policies; barriers that Aboriginal youth face as they transition to our school; support for girls sports; increase self-esteem in young women; and eliminating homophobia at school. (Jacob, 2012; Students as Researchers Conference, 2014)[19]

Story 2: Real Change in Schools

A high school principal in Bear Valley, California, wanted to explore student views of learning, so she started a student-research program. The group focused on the questions including,

- Do our school restructuring activities really make fundamental changes in the learning process?
- Do students throughout our school value school restructuring activities the same as adults?
- Does all of our work have an impact in the classroom?

As part of the yearlong study, the student researchers participated in a twice-weekly course that focused on their work, and consequently, the students became the driving force in the data collection and analyses. Students conceived the methods used and led the data collection work. In their study, the student researchers collected data from 200 of the school's 1,600 students. They worked with 27 classes, and conducted focus group discussions with 150 students. Ultimately, the students presented their findings to professional researchers from across the country. The findings showed that students define success in different ways, with a strong theme focusing on students' diligence and balance. Students recognized the importance of motivation, good study habits, a balance between school and work, involvement in school life, being organized, and simply putting forth the effort to succeed.

The student researchers also explored learning outside of school, how students learn best, and the school's effect on student learning. The project coordinators state that "the lessons of this project occurred on two levels: what the students, staff, and parents learned from the data, and what we all (adults) learned about engaging students as researchers in a topic that is relevant to them." (Kushman & Shanessy, 1997)

Story 3: Saving Money

In Poughkeepsie, New York, high school students conducted research on their district's budget crisis as part of a government class. After designing a survey for students on what should be included in next year's school district budget, student researchers hand-tabulated and analyzed data from 596 completed surveys - over half the student body. District board members then had student-created data from that survey to highlight exactly what students thought should be included in next year's school district budget. When the Board of Education passed its budget for the coming school year, they introduced an unprecedented line item: $25,000 for "student-led initiatives." (What Kids Can Do, 2003)

Story 4: Graduation Roadblocks

Students at a high school in Denver, Colorado, explored why many of their peers didn't graduate. Their goal was, "...to change statistics, and to make [our]... school of excellence where all students learn, graduate, and have the opportunity to go on to college." Their report outlines findings from more than 700 student surveys, national education research findings, and a proposal for school transformation. (Jovenes Unidos, 2004)

Story 5: High Quality Education

Four school districts are participating in a student action research program as part of the Education and Advocacy Project, coordinated by the Youth Action Research Institute in Hartford, Connecticut. This program is a model program that engages students in identifying and researching issues that affect the quality of education in their schools and elsewhere in the state. The program, for fifth and six graders, has nine teachers participating who are integrating student driven action research into their classrooms using cooperative learning methods into core curricular activities. The project's methods and goals include assessing the effects of PAR on students, educators, and the overall school communities involved. (Berg, 2007)

Considerations for Students as Researchers

With the recent national debate on scientific research in education, Participatory Action Research can provide educators with a refreshing approach to classroom research. PAR is designed to allow the perspective of students to constantly inform and help navigate the goals of schools, and better inform educators' practices consequently. Perhaps this is better for schools than traditional forms of scientific research. By listening to the experiences, opinions, ideas and knowledge of students, PAR provides a responsive, urgent analysis of schools, as well as a validating avenue for Meaningful Student Involvement. Meaningful Student Involvement in education research can be the opportunity many students need to speak on behalf of their own learning and education as a whole.

STUDENT RESEARCH TOPICS

These are actual topics researched by students. Find reports and more at SoundOut.org

- Communicating school improvement to students
- Engaging us with scientific practices: Science by students, for students
- Expanding educational access to students of color
- Interest, identity, culture and learning
- Connecting learning inside and outside of schools
- Teaching and learning by students
- Connected classrooms
- Gender equity in science education
- Gender identities in small schools
- Learning through tinkering with computers
- Making reading matter
- Do I HAVE to? Math for middle school students
- Flipping classrooms from students view
- Challenging us to behave better
- Motivating at-risk students to share our voices
- New student leadership
- Student participation in education
- Teach us like it matters: Best teaching practices

Table 17. Student Research Topics

---

[19] Learn more about Ontario's student voice program, Speak Up, at ontario.ca/speakup

Chapter 45. Students as Educational Planners

Education planning happens in many different avenues, with several different considerations. Students can be partners in planning throughout education, whether selecting textbooks, determining classroom behavior guidelines, or participating in the physical design process for a new building. There are two forms of Meaningful Student Involvement in education planning. The first form is individualized education planning, which is planning that affects only the student who is involved. The second form is institutionalized education planning, or planning that affects large numbers of students or the entire student body.

Individualized Education Planning

Imagine if you will, before the beginning of the school year, every educator receives a file. The student, their previous teachers, and their parents all participated equally in creating this file. In it is a description of the child, learning goals and objectives for the year, specific learning needs and focus areas, and past evaluations of the student is learning, completed by the student, their previous teacher, and their parents. This Individual Education Plan, or IEP, is developed with every student, regardless of age, grade, ability, or achievement, focusing on the student as a partner in his or her own education. While there are currently few schools developing IEPs for every student, the effectiveness of this approach to education planning has been echoed for many years. Students with disabilities have been using these tools successfully in many schools, with large increases in students' focus and motivation, more support for students in mainstream classrooms, and more. The responsibility of a student's progress is not just on the shoulders of the adults, but shared with the student. The student becomes eager to track his progress in specific IEP objectives, such as reading speed and accuracy, sentence writing and paragraph skills, math fact fluency, self-control behaviors and self-advocacy.

Institutionalized Education Planning

Educators and students alike face a variety of barriers to Meaningful Student Involvement in institutionalized education planning, especially as illustrated in Figures 18 and 20. Educators often exclaim that students have the "wrong" attitudes, are immature, and ill equipped for the responsibility of large-scale school planning. Students say that educators act intimidated by students, or do not value their experience. The following examples offer hopeful glimpses into classrooms and schools where those barriers have been addressed and overcome.

Engaging students as partners in education planning illustrates how a variety of everyday school activities, including building design, curriculum development, personnel management, personal learning plans, can embody Meaningful Student Involvement. I am not talking about oft-told stories of students planning dances or fundraisers either. Instead, this chapter concentrates on students writing curricula, designing new school buildings, and developing programs affecting entire state education systems. That is how Meaningful Student Involvement improves education for *all* learners. I explore this concept in Table 6 of this book.

Through my research and experience, I have learned that education planning can have global effects on students. Rather than just affecting them students who are directly involved, engaging students as partners in education planning can affect all students in the specific environment the planning affects. (Rigolon, 2011) Through education planning, every student in every school can have opportunities to positively participate in, gain from, and affect schools. Many educators and research studies have shown me that Meaningful Student Involvement in planning requires training and reflection in order to meaningfully validate and authorize students to create change. It also inherently requires the participation and investment of those most affected; this means that taking time to educate students about their involvement ensures successful planning.

One of the very realistic challenges to engaging students in school improvement is identifying their motivation for participating. Some students might be participating in education planning activities simply to earn credit or for other external factors. Whatever their reason for participating is, when activities meet the characteristics of Meaningful Student Involvement, any student can experience the benefits of meaningful involvement.

Meaningful Student Involvement engages students as education planners by ensuring that they know what, how, why, where, when, and how effectively they are learning. This includes students designing curriculum, planning the school day, co-creating new school designs, or other activities that build upon their experience, education, ideas and opinions.

As I explore throughout this book, places in schools that can engage students as educational planners include:

- **Classrooms**: Students co-design curriculum with teachers; create project-based learning opportunities for themselves and their peers; and set personal learning goals.
- **Administration**: Students develop policy development or adjustment recommendations; students participate as full members in the formal school improvement process.
- **Culture**: Teachers and students co-create classroom behavior standards; teachers participate in professional development settings to learn student/teacher partnership activities

Stories of Students as Planners

Understanding different activities and approaches is integral to engaging students as educational planners. The following stories illustrate a variety of approaches to Student/Adult Partnerships in school planning.

Story 7: Writing Curriculum

Way back in 1972, students in Buffalo, Atlanta and San Diego were reported to be paid stipends for working as members of school district curriculum writing and review teams. These students participated fully in decision-making, evaluating and advocating for what they saw was best in classes both in their schools and throughout their districts. (Kleeman, 1972)

Story 8: Engaging Students on Purpose

During the 2007-08 school year students at the Black Hills High School in Tumwater, Washington, participated in the hiring of their future principal. Meeting after school, students were able to tell district hiring officials exactly what they wanted in their future building leader. The students respectfully and deliberately pressed the officials about standardized tests, student-principal interactions, and community building within their school. Taking root in the school's Student Engagement Team, the students had been preparing for the meeting for several months. In addition to participating in the hiring process, participants, who are self-selected, have conducted building-wide surveys and testified before the Education Committee of the Washington State House of Representatives.

They continually encourage educators to move to working *with* students instead of *for* them. This level of participation in planning encourages students to see ahead of their own time in schools. Members of the Student Engagement Team have planned schoolwide forums for the 2008-09 school year, and their advisor has stated her commitment to maintaining membership open to all students at the school. Towards the end of the school year final candidates for the principal position at the school had the opportunity to answer students' questions directly, and when they were interviewed the panel included a student from the Team.

Speaking of the Team, Bob Kuehl, the Human Resource director of the Tumwater School District, said of the Student Engagement Team, "They are very insightful of the needs of a school from a student's perspective and they are very candid about their opinions and thoughts... They have a lot of strong feelings that need to be heard and used." This type of commitment is exactly what Meaningful Student Involvement can—and should—foster among all partners throughout a school. (Barton, 2008)

Story 9: Designing a School Building

An eighth-grader student was a member of the high school building design committee for a small school district in rural Texas. The committee, which reported to the school board, was creating plans for a new high school building. One of the main issues the student raised was the monotony of the current school's environment. "Why does the library have to have plain tables and chairs? They are so boring. Why cannot we have sofas or armchairs? And why do all the tables in the cafeteria have to seat ten people? Can there be tables for four?" The student said the experience helped them "understand how the school board and planning committee works." It also changed the students' self-perception and made them want to be more involved in what was going on in the school. (Borden, 2004)

A growing number of schools are providing "regular" students with the opportunity to be involved in individualized education planning after recognizing the effectiveness of the approach. In these situations, student-designed learning practices require flexible goals students can take ownership in.

Story 10: Planning High School Learning

Students at Science Leadership Academy in Philadelphia, Pennsylvania, are responsible for planning their learning throughout their high school careers, on the individual and group levels. Working in Student/Adult Partnerships throughout their school, teachers and administrators trust that students will ask when they need help. Students have responsibility for completing tasks and meeting deadlines in their project-based, inquiry focused classrooms. Demonstrating learning in several ways, students admit they are often challenged of staying on task, but see it as a lifelong skill. "You know what you should and you should not do," says one student. "You just got to realize it's gotta get done sooner or later." (Schwartz, 2014)

Story 11: Action through PICI

Lewis and Clark High School in Spokane, Washington, offers a course called Practicum in Community Involvement (PICI) that engages students in developing their own year-long learning project. Students must incorporate certain elements into their project, including research, action and reflection, and identify a community mentor to guide them in their learning. Students' responses to their experiences grow increasingly sophisticated and powerful, with students regularly exclaiming, "This is the only reason I made it through my senior year." (Fletcher, 2005b)

Story 12: Learning Units for Teachers

A small middle school in Orange, California, was brought to life with an exciting project that engaged students as researchers. In addition, the school decided to take the research to the next step, and invited the student researchers to start participating in curricular planning meetings. Students planned and constructed learning units with several teachers, and met with their principal to press for changes in school rules and militaristic physical education practices. (SooHoo, 1993)

Story 13: Students in School Redesign

A public alternative high school in Bothell, Washington engaged more than 100 students in a new school planning process. A team of student facilitators led a schoolwide forum, developed a report from their findings, and shared the report with the whole student body, with teachers, and with the local school district. In response to their findings, students are invited to join the formal school planning team, with their findings incorporated in the new school plans, including school facilities, teaching practices, and decision-making processes. (Fletcher, 2004)

Story 14: Students Launch a School

One student group in the Bronx, New York, took Meaningful Student Involvement in education planning to the next level. Sistas and Brothas United, or SBU, worked with school district officials to create a small school focused on educating students for social justice. SBU worked to improve their own schools for several years. They rallied and researched, and as one student said, "[We] got a lot of stuff fixed, that gives me a sense of power." The students flexed their power in another direction. They worked with the district and a coalition of organizations to start a new high school called the Leadership Institute for Social Justice. Through partnerships, the school trains students to be leaders who take charge of their schools and communities. Yearly Community Action Projects give students the skills they need to act in their communities. (What Kids Can Do, 2003)

Story 15: Elementary Students Revise Curriculum

In Cheney, Washington, a classroom-based program engaged first-grade students in developing a curriculum. Their teachers believed that if students helped to create the curriculum, the class dialogue about this process would shed light on how to make learning experiences more cohesive and purposeful. The teachers began by teaching students a unit, and then had students recreate the lesson plan. (Nelson & Fredrick, 1994)

Considerations for Students as Planners

As many schools grapple with the need for effective school transformation practices, few are actually asking their primary constituency: the students. Later in this book you can read about the closely related topic of Meaningful Student Involvement in education decision-making, including students on school boards and school site councils. However, the future of Meaningful Student Involvement in education planning includes student participation on school improvement teams and in state, district, and local school program planning processes.

These opportunities will ensure the sustainable and effective influence of students in schools into the future by creating important avenues for students to impact the school classes, programs, and other activities that affect them the most.

Asked recently about Student/Adult Partnerships focused on improving the elementary school she leads, principal Donnan Stoicovy of State Park, Pennsylvania said this about students as planners:

> "...[I]t should not be what we think they should know. It should be what the kids want to know. Besides that, teachers do not have all of the answers or knowledge. Together, as teachers and students, we accomplish so much more together. Having that openness to learning from each other and engaging in deliberation to solve problems is so important for the survival of a democracy. It is the gift we can give to our students and our future. (Dzur, 2013)

Connecting student-led planning to democracy is the key to Meaningful Student Involvement (Weiss & Huget, 2015).

DEMOCRATIC PURPOSES OF EDUCATION

The goal of public schools should always focus on the primary role of anyone in society, which is that of citizen. First and foremost, if you live in a society and contribute to it, you are a citizen of that society, whether that is acknowledged or not.

When they enter the door to schools, students are participating as citizens in society. Their purpose in schools is more than to simply become adults or workers. Instead, it is what W.E.B. DuBois challenged when he wrote,

> "The ideals of education, whether men [sic] are taught to teach or plow, to weave or to write, must not be allowed to sink into sordid utilitarianism. Education must keep broad ideals before it, and never forget that it is dealing with Souls and not with Dollars."

Meaningful Student Involvement narrows the broad ideals of student voice and targets students on democracy building in education. Some of the democratic purposes of education include:

- **Discovering**—Exploring one's own abilities and desires, and determining what their abilities are to fulfill their desires.
- **Learning**—Deliberately setting about expanding, critiquing and transforming one's abilities to fulfill their desires according to their own discovery and assessment.
- **Belonging**—Joining a larger community of learners, students have powerful opportunities to self-identify who they are, who they aren't and how they fit into society they are part of.
- **Purpose**—Through discovery and learning, students can also identify what they stand for and what they stand against, what matters to them and what doesn't, and so forth.

There are many other purposes of education in general, but when it comes to democracy its vital to recognize the powerful, positive potential of Meaningful Student Involvement in schools.

Table 18. Democratic Purposes of Education

Chapter 46: Students as Classroom Teachers

"There is, in fact, no teaching without learning." (Freire, 1998) This is as true for students as it is for adult educators. However, since teaching is not the exclusive domain of adults, we know that not only wise people or graduates from higher education capable of learning things this way (Martin-Kniep, 2005). Neither are computers or video games the only places where young people teach each other.

Everyday classrooms everywhere are lit up with the frenetic energy of students teaching one another to say words, understand concepts, and learn formulas. Meaningful Student Involvement embraces that energy by guiding students through a process of learning about learning, learning about teaching, and teaching each other.

Several out-of-school youth-serving programs have engaged young people as teachers for more than 100 years. Organizations including 4-H, the Girl Scouts and the Boy Scouts have long relied on the merits of youth-led classes to teach young women and men of all ages significant life lessons and invaluable skills. This approach has been valued for generations, witnessed by the many indigenous communities who have entrusted young people with teaching their peers for thousands of years and been supplemented by the American colonists whose first schools employed young teachers, who in turn gave the responsibility of teaching to their younger charges. Famed pioneer teacher Laura Ingalls Wilder was 15 when she began teaching. While young people teaching generally ceased in schools with the advent of advanced teacher education in the early 1900s, pockets of activity continued. The 1960s "free school" movement recognized the value of students teaching students, and many instituted the practice as everyday experiences for young people. Throughout the past 30 years the concept of students as teachers has gained momentum as more professional educators are beginning to see its effects.

There is a plethora of research supporting the effectiveness of engaging students as teachers. A variety of findings shows how teaching results in better learning than being taught in traditional methods. When students prepare to teach other students, learning suddenly involves active thinking about material, analysis and selection of main ideas, and processing the concepts into one's own thoughts and words. (Morgan J. , 2011) Also, the superiority of student-led teaching is specifically marked for students below the median in ability.

Most importantly, moving students to the front of the classroom moves young people from being passive recipients to becoming active drivers of learning. We know that learning is a lifelong process that requires a variety of inputs; Meaningful Student Involvement effectively engages students as intentional drivers of that process. Engaged as partners, students can strengthen, expand, and deepen their learning through teaching. Teaching is equally mindset and ability: As Table 12 in this book showed earlier, students must develop their capacity for teaching by believing in themselves and developing their skills.

While peer tutoring, cross-age tutoring, and student-driven conversations are popular in classrooms, it is rare for adult educators to actually turn classroom control over to students, or to share that control equally with students. Meaningful Student Involvement shows how courses which are co-taught with students can be powerfully engaging for peers, younger students, and adult learners. Engaging students as teachers can be a radical departure from the rigid norms of learning and teaching that many people, including adults and students, are accustomed to. Therefore, it is vital for adults to examine their own perspectives about this engagement of students as partners in teaching before attempting to facilitate it with students.

Meaningful Student Involvement engages students as teachers as a way to strengthen students' learning and teachers' efficacy. Students can experience a variety of significant classroom teaching experiences, such as partnering with teachers or peers to deliver curriculum, teaching fellow students in lower grade levels, or teaching adults. They also participate in choosing the activities and content of their lesson plans. See Table 7 for examples.

Places in schools that can engage students as classroom teachers include:

- **Classrooms**: Student/adult co-teaching teams are used; student-centered methods are integrated throughout a classroom; multiple intelligences are honored throughout the class.
- **Administration**: Teachers participate in professional development focused on student voice and Meaningful Student Involvement, student-led training for teachers
- **Culture**: Model student-driven learning throughout education and engage students as co-learners and co-facilitators of staff professional development activities.

Meaningful Student Involvement recognizes the importance of acknowledging the knowledge of students, and charges them with the responsibility of educating their peers, younger students or adults. Students teaching students is not meant to undermine the influence or ability of adult educators: instead, it uplifts the role of educators by making their knowledge and abilities accessible to more students. A growing body of practice and research from the education arena reinforces the seemingly radical belief that students can teach students effectively, given appropriate support from their adult teachers.

Stories of Students as Teachers

The following examples show students serving as teaching assistants, partnering with teachers or peers to deliver curriculum, teaching peers or students on their own, or teaching adults in a variety of settings. (Kirk, 2014)

Story 16: Community that Leads

PS 205 is a K-5 in the Bronx, New York that sought to develop new approaches to school improvement. Working with Communities for Learning, a nonprofit organization based in Floral Park, New York, students became meaningfully involved in the development and ongoing operation of a learning community that included multiple students, teachers, parents and administrators. With an existent history of staff-identified professional development, school/community partnerships and a strong principal/leader, the building seemed to be an ideal community, and the development of a learning community focused on school improvement seemed suspicious to many participants.

Teachers saw the learning community as another example of temporary professional development, and students appeared confused by the opportunity to work and interact with adults. However, through a series of guided critical reflection and development sessions for all team members, including students as partners as shown in Figure 13, the team transformed their own expectations and those of the school-at-large. Student-inclusive data collection and analysis led the learning community to identify differentiation a focus for the 2007-08 school year. Members of the Community That Leads project are participating in collegial inquiry, developing an understanding of how this process may be used to promote learning while also deepening their own learning around differentiation and language development.

According to Martin-Kniep, research projects can be a core of learning communities, ultimately influencing practice throughout the learning environment. She writes,

> "Students possess tremendous experience and expertise in the areas of teaching and learning. Their experiences as learners in schools are far more grounded in reality than are those of most adults... They live teaching and learning every day." (Martin-Kniep, 2008)

Story 17: Students Teaching Teachers

Student trainers can be effective trainers for other students and/or adults. For instance, students can lead trainings around a special curriculum, such as interpersonal violence or environmental issues. On Vashon Island, Washington, students from StudentLink, the local alternative high school facilitated a service learning training event for teachers and youth workers from their community. Over two days student trainers taught about the basics of service learning, implementing a project, and assessing youth voice. (Fletcher, 2001)

Story 18: Teacher Academy

Twelfth grade students at Mt. Pleasant High School in Providence, Rhode Island, can join a teacher academy and team up with students in a local teacher education program to give presentations on educational philosophy to high school students. The high school students researched important educational philosophers and wrote personal statements of educational philosophy. The two groups revised papers together, and were able to effectively critique peer research based on what they knew about the classroom. The cooperating college professor reported that this experience helped dispel stereotypes his teacher education students had held about urban high school students. (Mt. Pleasant High School, n.d.)

Considerations for Students as Teachers

While a growing number of educators recognize the validity of students' thoughts about schools, few see students actually being players in addressing those concerns. Engaging students in teaching fills a three-fold gap in student learning. 1) It develops empathy between students and teachers, making students more understanding of teachers' jobs while making teachers more aware of students learning needs. 2) It makes learning more tangible and relevant for students, specifically for students without the ability to access other "real-world" learning opportunities. 3) It empowers students to approach the problems they identify in their classrooms through critical analysis and applicable solutions. Engaging students as teachers is more than simply teaching new tricks to an old dog. It challenges the old dog to teach others, and to allow the younger pups to teach themselves.

ROLE MODELING GOOD TEACHING

As they learn to teach, students should have adults role model effective teaching, and learn effective ways to teach others. They should be able to...

- **Grow:** Understand, find, use, evaluate and share effective tools that enhance and support instruction that leads student achievement;
- **Act:** Facilitate and support collaborative, action-oriented learning environments that promote to innovative, improved learning, teaching and leadership;
- **Foster:** Provide for learner-centered environments that use technology to meet the individual and diverse needs of learners.
- **Facilitate:** Teach the use of tools that support and enrich classroom approaches fostering higher-level thinking, decision-making, and problem-solving skills through student voice.
- **Advocate:** Make sure their peers and teachers take advantage of quality tools and experiences and promote improved learning and teaching through Meaningful Student Involvement.

These are all skills and knowledge that students and educators can partner together to attain or enhance by providing hands-on training.

Table 19. Role Modeling Good Teaching

Chapter 47. Students as Learning Evaluators

On one level, teachers are always listening to students' opinions, checking for comprehension, and whether they have accomplished a task. Another level is reflected in the barrage of student surveys conducted, and the myriad education books that tokenize students' opinions with quotes from students on their covers.

Meaningful Student Involvement calls for something more, something that is deliberate, empowering, far-reaching and sustainable. Engaging students as evaluators calls for educators to develop practical, applicable feedback opportunities where students are encouraged to be honest, open and solution-oriented. Students find specific investment in evaluation when they can see tangible outcomes, and have some measure of accountability from the systems, educators, or situations they are evaluating.

Over the course of a school year, teachers might want a variety of evaluations from students. These may include:

- An occasional large-scale forum where the opinions of students in one or all grade levels are canvassed;
- Creating a regular pattern of evaluative feedback in lessons; or,
- Facilitating a series of one-to-one or small group discussions, how members of a specific sub-group of students (the disengaged, high-achievers, young women, young men, or students not from the majority culture in the surrounding community, for example) are feeling about their learning experiences; or shaping a new initiative in the classroom or school.

By involving students as evaluators, schools can develop purposeful, impacting, and authentic assessments of classes, schools, teachers, and enact accountability and ownership for all participants in the learning process. Effective evaluations may include student evaluations of classes and schools; student evaluations of teachers; student evaluations of self, and; student-led parent-teacher conferences, where students present their learning as partners with teachers and parents, instead of as passive recipients of teaching done "to" them.

Experience shows that student voice is best understood through the personal experience of all students in all schools, everywhere. We have discovered that critical self-examination leads to deeper perspectives about Meaningful Student Involvement, which allows the evolution of action to be responsive to ever-transforming student populations in schools. We have also found that research-based tools can successfully guide practice in Meaningful Student Involvement, and engaging students in evaluation can help develop those tools.

When this kind of evaluation is new to a school, teachers may feel apprehensive about talking with students in a way that changes traditional power relationships within the school. Teachers may feel challenged by empowering students for many reasons, including feeling disempowered to make decisions in their own classrooms. In response to what is perceived as some schools' inadequate understanding of the experiences and opinions of students, community groups and education organizations across the nation are engaging students as evaluators. Adults work with students in these programs to design evaluations, conduct surveys, analyze data and create reports to share with fellow students and educators.

Meaningful Student Involvement is tantamount to putting mutual respect and communication in motion between students and educators in schools. Meaningful Student Involvement also requires the investment from educators and students. Many student voice programs have simply thrown the job of sounding out at students, without showing students the degrees of possibility for the input and action of young people. Some neglect the necessity of two-way dialogue, of collaborative student/teacher problem solving, and of truly student inclusive, interdependent school change.

Meaningful Student Involvement in education evaluation gives students and educators the impetus to establish constructive, critical dialogues that place common purpose and interdependence at the center of the discussion. When dissent is encountered, appropriate avenues for resolution can be identified. When inconsistencies and prejudice are revealed, intentional exposure and practical understanding is sought. When educators strive to engage the hope students have for schools, they can foster students' growth as effective evaluators who actually impact the processes of learning, teaching and leading. In turn, students will offer vital lessons for educators and the education system as a whole.

Meaningful Student Involvement engages *students as evaluators* delivering purposeful assessments of their classes, teachers, and whole school. Students can also evaluate themselves or facilitate student-led parent-teacher conferences, where students present their learning as partners with teachers and parents, instead of as passive recipients of teaching done "to" them.

When this kind of evaluation is new to a school, teachers may feel apprehensive about talking with students in a way that changes traditional power relationships within the school. Teachers may feel challenged by empowering students for many reasons, including feeling disempowered to make decisions in their own classrooms. In response to what is perceived as some schools' inadequate understanding of the experiences and opinions of students, community groups and education organizations across the nation are engaging students as evaluators. Adults work with students in these programs to design evaluations, conduct surveys, analyze data and create reports to share with fellow students and educators.

Following are some of activities that engage students as evaluators.

- **Classrooms**: Students assess themselves, their peers, teachers, curricula, and classes, recommending changes and acknowledging expectations on teachers and administrators.
- **Administration**: Students are engaged with administrators in evaluating the effects and outcomes of meaningfully involving students throughout school decision-making.
- **Culture**: Students compare student/teacher relationships and perspectives of respect throughout school.

Stories of Students as Evaluators

When they have opportunities to evaluate learning, teaching and leadership, students can take deeper ownership and feel a wealth of belonging in their classrooms, schools and communities. The following stories offer illustrations for how that happens.

Story 19: Evaluating Learning

Middle and high school students in New York City participated in a student evaluator program for the Teens as School Volunteer Tutors Project. Together with an adult evaluation facilitator, they decided to interview two groups of subjects: an adult group made up of school professionals and the tutors' own parents and a student group made up of both tutors and their tutees. The student evaluators devised interview forms, agreed on interview assignments, and drew up a time line for completion.

Story 20: Evaluating a District

In 2003, high school students in Oakland, California, designed and collected 1,000 report card surveys evaluating teaching, counseling, school safety and facilities at three local high schools. They compiled their findings, analyzed the results, and made concrete recommendations in an exciting, comprehensive report. The introduction to the report states,

> "There are 48,000 youth in Oakland's schools that are experts—who are in class every day and who have a lot to say about how the schools are run and how to improve our education... [E]veryone wants to hear from the teachers and parents - but what about the students? Who asks our opinion? Why do we feel shut out, like no one cares what we think?"

Story 21: Voluntarily Evaluating Classes

Students at Lexington High School in suburban Boston wanted to work with teachers to improve teaching and learning in their classes. Forming the Best Practices Club, they volunteered to go into classrooms and sharing watch how teachers delivered their lessons. After that, they sought to create a dialogue between students and teachers about good classroom practice. They created and used an observation tool with open-ended questions on topics like the classroom atmosphere, teaching for understanding, etc. After that, they facilitated student-teacher meetings and workshops to share their findings, and led schoolwide workshops on best teaching practices they discovered.

Story 22: Building a Case for School Improvement

A range of students participated in a Bay Area School Reform Collaborative project. One school invited students to share their views on what needed to be changed, and how to accomplish those changes. The students then joined teachers to analyze the data gathered. They found that there were five main concerns students raised, including better communication between staff and students, higher quality teaching, and better counseling and support. The students then presented these findings to their teachers during an after-school meeting. The reform leadership at the school was amazed by the way the student evaluators maneuvered the concerns of other students, carefully making sure adults understood what each concern truly was. The students learned about how to conduct research on an important issue in their school and how to present that information to teachers. Many students reported that participating in the evaluation process improved their self-opinions and provided opportunities to develop meaningful interactions with adults at school

Considerations for Students as Evaluators

Engaging students as evaluators should not mean replacing any other evaluations. Instead, it should be seen as an additional information source. This is true whether students are evaluating themselves, their peers, classroom curricula, school climate, or their teachers directly. Student evaluations should not replace teacher evaluations. This is an important reality to consider.

Another important consideration is that students in all of the stories above where not simply thrown evaluations and expected to do wonderful things. Instead, they were partnered meaningfully with adults, taught about what they were evaluating, and facilitated through the entire process. This is essential for honoring student learning as well as whatever is being evaluated.

Chapter 48. Students as Systemic Decision-Makers

"Schools are compulsory for about ten years of a person's life. They are, perhaps, the only compulsory institutions for all citizens, although those with full membership in schools are not yet treated as full citizens of our society..." (Brennan, 1996)

Maybe it is only ironic that students recognize that situation immediately and consequently offer resistance to Meaningful Student Involvement. When presented with opportunities to make significant decisions in their schools, students almost always test adults through parroting teachers and others; saying only what they think adults want to hear; and testing adults by offering the most outlandish possibilities. In the most dramatic form of resistance, students simply refuse to do things they have been taught to believe should be done for them. (Kohn, 1993)

Pushing paper across tables and going through the motions of decision making without practical applications is no one's idea of a good time, or good learning. Yet many schools actively promote this approach in their student governments, allowing students to choose the themes for school dances year or the colors on this year's yearbook cover, but not giving them any say in decisions that have more serious implications. School curriculum, policy, and climate are more meaningful leadership areas for students. In addition to making decisions that affect themselves and their immediate peers, students can participate in boards of education, grant making, and school assessment at the district and state levels. Find more examples of district-level action in Table 10 of this book.

The purpose and practice of engaging students as decision-makers throughout education is made obvious through Meaningful Student Involvement. In our practice, students identify multiple spheres where decision-making occurs in schools every day. Then they explore the intention and meaning of those activities. They examine common practices in decision-making, and analyze the impacts of those practices. To cap the process, students explore some of the most frequently identified skills needed to successfully participate in decision-making in schools.

Working with students as partners throughout the education system as shown in Figure 13, I have uncovered how Meaningful Student Involvement in decision-making can occur throughout education, affecting individuals, schools, and the entire system every day. Research has shown how students are uniquely positioned in their personal development to be attentive to the ethical implications of educational decision-making. The other essential consideration of this practice is that leadership skill development cannot be the exclusive domain of traditional student leaders.

Embedded in Meaningful Student Involvement is the assumption that all education decision-making should be democratic in its nature. It should not merely be an exercise, but a reality that engages, challenges, and expands students' understanding of democracy in their education and throughout their lives. Table 18 shows why this matters.

Scheduling, project choices, lunchtime options... many adults maintain that students today are inundated with decision-making opportunities in schools. However, there these types of choices provide little opportunity for students to learn about the real effects of decision-making on other people. Unfortunately, many schools approach student decision-making with a disregard for the responsibility our democracy gives every individual to become active, effective decision-makers. It is as if giving the car keys to a 16-year-old were enough for them to learn to drive—but we know it's not. Similarly, giving menial decision-making opportunities to students is not enough to teach them to make good decisions.

Traditional student leadership opportunities have proven to not be well-situated to provide powerful opportunities for learning. While these activities do already exist in many schools, the teachable moments implicit in these activities are generally lost to the insignificance of the decisions that are to be made. Students should analyze those activities, as well as identifying new opportunities for engaging students as partners in education decision-making. Find examples of what these activities look like in Table 7.

Educators should critically reflect on their own decision-making practices as well, whether those affect a classroom, a grade level, a school, or a community. In order to support students as partners educators must examine the decision-making opportunities within their own spheres of responsibility. When reflecting, facilitators might consider what decisions students were asked to make when they attended elementary, junior or middle, and high school. They might think about which decisions are left to students now, which are the exclusive domain of adults, and what is actually done in partnership with students? In their own practice today, educators should consider how they work with students to make decisions. By exploring one's own assumptions about decision-making, educators can more effectively challenge students to do the same.

Meaningful Student Involvement engages *students as systemic decision-makers.* There are many levels of decision-making that happen in schools. They include decision-making in individual classrooms, whole schools, citywide and regional districts, state education agencies, and the nationwide education system.

There are a number of local schools where student involvement in decision-making is becoming the norm. Many districts have had policies that support student involvement for decades, although few are deliberately enforced. Almost half of all states have some form of student involvement in their decision-making, while there are few opportunities for students to be directly involved in federal education decision-making.

I have identified two main approaches to student involvement in education decision-making:

1. Involve students directly in an existing adult activity, such as a special task force, school site council, on the board of education, or with an instructional leadership team.
2. Set up an activity just for students, such as a student advisory board or a peer mediation group.

In some cases, both approaches are incorporated. For example, having students on an adult task force and having a student action forum where students identify important issues the school should address. Remember that there is no single right approach; each situation will always be different.

Places in schools that can engage students as systemic decision-makers include:

- **Classrooms**: Students participate in classroom management and resource allocation. They are taught consensus skills and encouraged to participate in decisions affecting themselves, their peers, their families and their communities.
- **Administration**: Positions are created for students to participate as full members of all school committees; training and cultural awareness activities are taught to all new students and adults in the school; there are committees for students only to make decisions, as well.
- **Culture**: Students are authorized to mediate decisions; spaces are created for student decision-making; student forums are facilitated by and for students throughout the school environment.

John Dewey, the father of modern progressive education, delineated a course of learning that is easily adaptable for student involvement in education decision-making. (Dewey, 1948) The following *Pathway for Meaningful Student Involvement in Decision-Making* is modified from Dewey's original course.

1. All students should have validating, sustainable, opportunities that they are interested in to make decisions about their own learning and education as a whole.
2. Decision-making opportunities should engage students in solving genuine problems and making substantial decisions that will promote critical thinking skills.
3. Students should possess the knowledge and ability needed to make informed decisions.
4. Students and educators should be responsible and accountable for developing responsible, creative action plans to implement decisions.
5. Students should apply these plans, reflect on the decisions and outcomes, and be charged with continually examining, applying, and challenging this learning.

Stories of Students as Decision-Makers

Rather than belaboring the necessity of engaging students in education decision-making, the following vignettes start with exemplary models, and are followed by research summaries from across the United States. These stories offer a glimpse into the increasingly well-defined role of students as school decision-makers.

Story 23: Learning through Social Justice

The Social Justice Academy in Boston is doing powerful work engaging students as decision-makers. Through sixteen student-created committees, students are involved in a variety of functions throughout the school, covering everything from school decor to student/adult relationships. According to one study,

> "[E]ach week an entire period is devoted to committee meetings and advisories; committees meet once a week for fifty minutes and have two teachers acting as advisors. Twice a month, two student representatives from each committee meet with [Youth On Board] staff for team-building activities and sharing of committee information." (Joselowsky, 2007)

Youth On Board is profiled later in this publication, along with other organizations supporting Meaningful Student Involvement in schools.

Story 24: A Bright Star Among Peers

NOVA opened as a public alternative school in Seattle, Washington, in 1970. Their unique curriculum offers students the opportunity to learn through democratic school governance. Committees govern the school through consensus-based decision-making. Membership is voluntary and includes both staff and students, each of whom have an equal vote. Teachers serve on one or more committees, and model leadership skills. Student participation in committees gives them a stake in their education, and encourages responsibility in their personal lives.

Story 25: Infusing Students Everywhere

Federal Hocking High School, located in rural Stuart, Ohio, gives students an equal place at the table when faculty hiring decisions are made, when curriculum is chosen, and when class offerings are determined. A former principal recently commented that,

> "Students often find themselves preached to about values instead of practicing them. That's why our efforts have been to focus on practice rather than exhortation. Everything we do, including classroom teaching practices, school governance, students' experience... out of school, assessment, even the organization of the school day, is done with an eye toward developing democratic community." (Wood, 2005)

Students are also given full responsibility for all student events and various school programs, and a student serves on the local school board. (Haynes, 2014)

Story 26: School District Partners

The Boston Student Advisory Council is a citywide body of student leaders representing their respective high schools. BSAC, which is coordinated by the administered by the district office in partnership with a nonprofit called Youth on Board, offers student perspectives on high school renewal efforts and inform their respective schools about relevant citywide school issues. In addition to personal skill development and knowledge building activities for their 20-plus members, BSAC students have strongly influenced district policy-making about cell phone usage, truancy, reducing the dropout rate, and more. The students also have regular dialogues with the district superintendent and school board members in order to maintain personal proximity to important decision-makers in the district.

Story 27: Built into the District

The Denver Student Board of Education is a group of 30 students who represent the fifteen high schools in the city. They are charged to serve as leaders in their schools and represent all students at the district level. Students create projects that affect their local schools and report back on them to the district. They have also created a curriculum that is used in several high school leadership classes. However, these students have to ask permission to speak to their regular board, and that does not happen frequently.

Story 28: Students on Committees

The responsibilities of local school site councils vary across the nation; however, many are responsible for creating and reviewing school improvement plans, making funding decisions, and hiring principals and administrators. Many have regular voting positions for students; some have representative non-voting positions only. In Gonzales, California, students on Gonzales High School's Site Council have full voting rights, often making decisions on curricula, services for special needs students, teacher training, and more. There are 2 students on an 8-person board.

Story 29: All-City Student Engagement

Most schools nationwide have some form of student government. It is important to give students a voice in school issues and a chance to learn leadership and organizational skills. However, it is also important to give student governments real responsibility, and to remember that students can address education issues beyond those that students specifically. In Oakland, California, Oakland Unified School District has a unique program called the All-City Council Governing Board (ACCGB). It is comprised of eight student-elected student representatives and represents six different high schools. The students coordinate district-wide events, and represent OUSD students at various community and district events. Currently, student representatives on the ACCGB meet regularly with the state administrator to propose school improvements, and position themselves on district-wide decision-making committees.

Story 30: Elementary Students Leading Action

Elementary students are often lost in the fray when it comes to substantive student voice. Through her school's work focused on Meaningful Student Involvement, a school leader in Pennsylvania has successfully engaged students as policy-makers who are molding school culture and driving positive Student/Adult Partnerships every day. Donnan Stoicovy, the lead learner at Park Forest Elementary School in State College, Pennsylvania, created a student-led constitution process at her school in 2012. That year, students from kindergarten through fifth grade attended eight all-school town hall meetings focused on their ideal schools. Working with adults who had a variety of jobs, over the following six months a schoolwide constitution was created. Adults and students received training, were guided through the process and worked together to build the democratic environment of their school. (McGarry & Stoicovy, 2014)

Story 31: Recommending Improvements

Student advisory boards have no governing authority but serve an official advisory capacity within a school or education agency, offering regular feedback and advice on student issues. In Arlington, Virginia, the Arlington Public School District School Board actively seeks input from students through the Student Advisory Board. The Student Advisory Board consists of high school students who provide a student voice on matters of importance to the School Board. They study important issues and make relevant recommendations to the School Board.

Story 32: Life in Schools

Headmasters or principals sometimes form a Principal's Advisory Board by asking 6 to 10 students to help process the issues in their position. A local high school in Connecticut launched a Principal's Advisory Group in February 2000. It started out with 12 participating students, and in just three years, this decision-making group has grown to include more than 186 students and 13 sub-committees. This is a non-elected student body that will look at all aspects of life at their school. They will make suggestions and recommendations to the principal and Student Congress. Students address a variety of issues, including teacher hiring, the yearly master schedule, and planning key events at the school.

Considerations for Students as Decision-Makers

Answering the question of how students can be effectively involved in district and state decision-making is one that has been grappled with by educators, administrators, and policy-makers across the country for decades. Over the last decade, as part of my work through SoundOut, I have provided technical assistance and training to districts nationwide that are interested in systematically engaging students in education decision-making. I have researched more than 40 years of involving students on school boards (Place, 1973; Kleeman, 1972; Towler, 1975), and I continue to follow national trends carefully. Indeed, the practice of involving students in school decision-making is spreading, and even though it's not widespread yet, there have been important strides made. One of my recent books, *The Future of School Boards: Involving Students as Education Policy-Makers,* studies this practice in-depth, identifying where it happens, what laws permit it, and more. (Fletcher, 2014)

On the Ladder of Student Involvement, involving students in decision-making practices covers many rungs. The lowest bar is simply and occasionally asking students what they think about school board policy-making issues. This can be a formal process mandated through policy, conducted through online surveys or in-person student forums. Another practice is to require regular student attendance at school board meetings. Generally viewed as non-meaningful forms of involvement, neither of these practices require students have an active role in the process of decision-making beyond that of "informant." Table 9 highlights a variety of approaches to using the Ladder effectively.

Chapter 49. Students as Education Advocates

Student advocacy has a long history going back to at least the 1930s, when a youth-led group called the American Youth Congress presented a list of grievances to the US Congress including public education. Through the Civil Rights movement of the 1950s to the free expression movement of the 1960s to the resurgence in student voice in the 2000s, student education advocacy is alive in the US today.

There are many faces to this effort that aren't as predictable as many adults assume. Rather than fighting against a specific expulsion of one of their friends, students today are working to change the discipline policy that expelled him in the first place. Instead of badgering a teacher or mentally checking-out of class, students today are redesigning curricula and classroom topics. Students have powerful ideas, knowledge and' opinions about topics like the achievement gap, charter schools, privatization, rural education, violence and safety, and year-around schools. They're rallying outside state capitals, speaking in school board meetings, and demanding change specifically from students' perspectives. There are dozens of cases of students advocating for policy change, procedural modifications, and cultural transformation within education.

I have discovered that advocacy activities already exist throughout education that engage students in school improvement. However, these are not inherently meaningful, and students are frequently discouraged from sharing their authentic perspectives about learning, teaching, or leadership in schools. Instead, they are manipulated and used as decorations throughout this advocacy. Research has shown that all students have the capability to learn about building, maintaining, and sustaining school improvement activities (Fletcher, 2008). I have also found that Meaningful Student Involvement presents a logical avenue to engage students as educational advocates (Fletcher, 2005a; 2005b).

Moving students from being passive recipients of teaching to active drivers of learning is the goal of more educators today than ever before. What happens when students cross the bridge from self-motivated activities that are inherently okay to leading efforts that aren't okay with teachers or administrators? Meaningful Student Involvement may push those boundaries by exploring new roles for students by infusing them as advocates for their own learning as well as the future of education, affecting their friends, their siblings, and generations of young people beyond them. It is important for adults to check their assumptions about your own ability to allow students to experience Meaningful Student Involvement through education advocacy.

Meaningful Student Involvement engages students as education advocates to work within the education system and throughout the community to change schools. Many students participate in committees, on special panels, and in functions that help raise awareness or interest in education issues.

Across the country there is a growing movement being led by students who are working with adults from their communities and schools to contribute to school improvement by calling for social, economic, racial, and environmental justice in schools. These student-led activist organizations use sophisticated analysis, appropriate action, and creative partnerships to challenge the education systems to become responsive to student voice.

Places in schools that can engage students as education advocates include:

- **Classrooms**: Student interests and identities are engaged throughout the process of curriculum decisions.
- **Administration**: Non-traditionally engaged students are encouraged to participate throughout the school environment with deliberate steps towards meaningful involvement.
- **Culture**: Creating safe spaces and promoting adults' reception of self- and group-advocacy are fostered throughout the learning environment by school leadership on all levels.

The failure of many traditional attempts by schools to engage students as partners in education leadership or democratic education lies in the mixed messages of many communities' agendas for public education. When educators have asked students to represent their peers, they often seek out the most academically gifted or popular, thereby narrowing the validity and ability of students to be valid democratic representatives. When schools offer courses to teach leadership, they can be steeped in traditional leadership models and teaching styles that alienates many students and limits important connections. Ironically, these classes are often offered at the expense of creating courses that could teach students about their own culture and heritage, which effectively negates the potential influence student leaders can have on everyday community life. Meaningful Student Involvement embraces every student as their own self, but also as the son or daughter of a family; as a member of a larger community; and as a partner in transforming schools. Understanding power, an essential component of Meaningful Student Involvement, begins in discovering and acknowledging who students are, and what education means.

Students can be powerful advocates for student involvement, as well as for other changes that students want in policy or governance. It makes a big difference for a student to say what students think; adults tend to listen to student advocates in a different way than we listen to each other. Student advocates can attend School Committee meetings and make presentations or proposals about their ideas.

Dr. Martin Luther King, Jr. once presented us with the challenge of advocacy by saying,

> "An individual has not started living until he can rise above the narrow confines of his individualistic concerns to the broader concerns of all humanity."

Meaningful Student Involvement in education advocacy happens when students are engaged as advocates for the schools they learn in; for the education system the next generation will inherit; and for the needs of the larger community surrounding the school. Students can be engaged in many ways: as members of committees, demonstrators in protests, on special panels, and in functions that help raise awareness or interest in education issues.

Stories of Students as Advocates

The roles delineated in previous chapters of this book are essentially different forms of students advocating for education. However, the following examples stand apart as uniquely specific models of students as education advocates.

Story 33: Students Rethinking Schools

In New Orleans, Louisiana, a nonprofit called Rethink has been working with students since 2008 to encourage them to dream big about the changes they want in their schools and take action to make those dreams a reality. Rethink believes students are experts on their school experiences, and actively engages them as advocates and actors throughout learning, teaching and leadership in the city's schools. All Rethink programs build off of a fundamental Rethink philosophy, culture and curriculum. At the foundation of all Rethink activities is an intentional Rethink culture that is based on the core philosophy of "power among" not "power over." This is practiced daily through the Rethink Circle. Based on Native American and African meeting protocols and customs, the Rethink Circle invites all members, no matter their age or status, to conduct daily business by sitting face-to-face in a circle of chairs, and offering their thoughts in turn. Through this simple, yet profound process, Rethinkers learn respect, equality and the twin arts of deep listening, and articulate communication. Rethink's programs include a summer leadership institute, rethink clubs at local middle schools, and the Rethink Organizing Collective for high school students. (Rethink., n.d.)

Story 35: Checking Out the Library

A fifth-grade teacher in Salt Lake City, Utah, tells the story of her students in her elementary classroom. These young advocates have helped their elementary school reconstruct its library by researching, brainstorming, fundraising, giving speeches, lobbying, writing proposals and receiving local, state and federal support. Their efforts led to brand-new facilities and classes, flexible scheduling for increased library use, and a comprehensive technology system including a computer center and computers in every classroom.

Story 36: Safer Schools in the Midwest

In Wichita, Kansas, a group of middle and high school students once worked through a local youth service agency to create safer, more effective schools for students in their community. Through a variety of campaigns, students with the Hope Street Youth Organizing program had worked to find alternatives to suspensions, end zero-tolerance policies, and implement Black history education. They also partnered with their local district to create a new teacher-training model and student satisfaction survey.

Story 37: Taking Action for Equality

South Central Youth Empowered Through Action is an organization located in Los Angeles, California. By hosting chapters on high school campuses across South LA, SCYEA aims to amplify the voices of students in education decision-making. They recently pressured the local school district to repair and build new schools with a $2.4 billion school bond, and to add $153 million dollars for additional school repairs previously overlooked in their community.

Story 38: Advise on Student Engagement

A collaborative group of students and non-profits in Boston have formed the Student Engagement Advisory Council. The groups, including Youth on Board, the Mayor's Youth Council, Boston Plan for Excellence, Center for Collaborative Education, Center for Teen Empowerment and Project HipHop, work with the Boston Public Schools to impact citywide policy and increase student engagement. (Youth On Board, n.d.)

Story 39: Human Relations Club

At Hamden High School near New Haven, Connecticut, is home to a Human Relations Club that is led by students. Through this extracurricular program, students advocate for their school to address issues of racism, sexism, prejudice and stereotyping. This program has many different activities, including an annual prejudice reduction conference, a service learning program, a cultural awareness program, and other activities. The most popular activity is an annual program where high school students go to middle and elementary schools to teach students about bullying, including bullying prevention, reporting and intervention. Successes of the club include having great numbers of students participation; high percentages of increased student empathy and understanding about racism, stereotyping and prejudice; and increased student body-wide perceptions of their capability to resolve issues important to them. Research attributes the success of the club, which is more than 20 years old, to the fact that it is student-led. One researcher wrote, "the more students are involved, the more knowledgeable and confident they become in addressing other human relations issues." (Willison, 1997)[20]

Story 40: Saving Schools Money

In 2002, the Maranacook School District in Maine was considering accepting a grant that would place a school resource officer at their schools. Students discussed this issue at length, brought it to the attention of the student senate, and in turn, the student school board representatives brought it to the attention of the school board. The student school board representatives worked with the other student senate members, who brought in feedback collected during the homeroom period, to make their case for why a school resource officer should not be brought to the campus. Because of the overwhelming number of students who expressed that having an armed policeman on campus would make being on campus an uncomfortable experience, the grant was declined fifteen to one by the school board. (Maine Department of Education and Campaign for the Civic Mission of Schools, 2006)

Considerations for Students as Advocates

A report on student activism for education equity stated, "Whatever the risks, there is no shortage of reasons for teachers and others to support young peoples' education advocacy work." (Tolman, 2003) It may be uncomfortable when students begin to speak when *not* spoken to, but their voices are too powerful, and their words too true, to be silenced for long. This book underlines the necessity of not only listening to students, not only engaging students, but actually giving students the platform to create, inform, and advocate for positive school transformation. Meaningful Student Involvement is not a complete process without this important focus on advocacy.

---

[20] Learn more about the Hamden HS Human Relations Club at sites.google.com/site/humanrelationsclubeducation/

ROLES FOR STUDENTS AS PARTNERS

Type of Action	Curriculum	Administration	Climate
Student as researchers	Examine student interest in subject, engagement in class, efficacy of methodology	Analyze student involvement, policies engaging partners, Activities of improvement activities	Compare perspectives of student voice, effects of training, attitudes towards achievement
Students as planners	Design curriculum, learning projects, classroom layout, personal learning goals	Develop new policy recommendations, staff monitoring plan, school improvement process	Create classroom behavior standards, student/teacher partnership activities
Students as teachers	Use student/adult teaching teams, student-centered methods, multiple intelligences	Provide professional development re: student voice, student-led training for teachers	Model student-driven learning throughout education, student voice in all school activities
Students as evaluators	Assess self, peers, teachers, curricula, classes	Critically explore policies and Activities absent of student voice	Contrast student/teacher relationships, respect throughout school
Students as decision-makers	Engage in classroom management, resource allocation, and consensus	Develop positions on all committees, reception mechanisms for adult leaders, committees for students only	Authorize students to mediate, create spaces for student interactions, facilitate student forums
Students as advocates	Embrace student interests and identities in curriculum planning	Encourage broad representation by nontraditional students	Provide "safe spaces" and reception for self- and group-advocacy

Table 14. Understanding Roles for Students as Partners. Figure 13 illustrates this; Table 16 elaborates on this.

Chapter 50. Engaging the Disengaged

As explored early in this book (Tables 3 and 5, and Chapter 12), any conversation about student engagement must address student disengagement. Student disengagement is not limited to any single type of learner in any particular situation. Instead, the most conforming, performing and adult-pleasing students may be deeply disengaged. Similarly, the most disruptive, antagonistic and rule-breaking learners may be most yearning for engagement. I derive some knowledge about this from my own experience in school.

As a high school student, I struggled through core subjects and excelling at non-core topics. Rather than relying on getting good grades or being accepted into social cliques in order to have fun, I frequently made my own entertainment instead. In addition to the typical pranks and social outlandishness that made many teachers cringe, I was regularly found "doing my own thing" and leading my peers in ways that made teachers uncomfortable. The most overt way I did this was through N.E.A.T.

Earth Day celebrated its fifteenth anniversary when I was in tenth grade. Reeling from the barrage of pro-environmental media coverage surrounding me, one day I went to my science teacher and asked how I could join the environmental club at my school. She quickly informed me it was only for honors students, and since my grades were too poor and I was not in her honors science classes I could not join. Determined to do something to help the neighborhood where I lived (which was later declared a Superfund environmental cleanup site by federal Environment Protection Agency), I worked with my friends to launch our own club. The honors students at our school were bused in to participate in the school's magnet science and math programs, and we soon discovered their environmental club projects were focused on the parts of the city where they lived and not the neighborhood where our school was and where we lived. Working with a group of friends, we decided our club would address local problems. We came up with a catchy name—North Environmental Action Team, or N.E.A.T.—and wrote a three-page manifesto, and then solicited all our favorite teachers to see if they'd sponsor us. When none responded, we asked every other teacher in the building. When none of them responded, we asked everyone again, and specifically the science teacher, who huffed a resolute no.

So, we decided to start our club unofficially. Never gaining an official adult sponsor, N.E.A.T. operated sporadically over the next three years. Our consciousness-raising antics were designed to upset the adults in our building who we thought failed to support us, and we generally succeeding. After creating an Earth Day card that year of recycled cardboard for the school principal, we collected more than 500 signatures from students in the building, or one quarter of the school population. The next year we regularly dumpster dived for pop cans and set them in front of the school with a placard that said, "We Love Mother Earth. Signed, N.E.A.T." Our final year a few of our members, including myself, were suspended from school for graffiting earth-friendly messages on the outside of the building for Earth Day.

All this racket embodies what I now call, inconvenient student voice.[21] These are the voices of students in school who, like myself, urgently struggle to be acknowledged. Whether or not adults like or appreciate what is said, inconvenient student voice *does* get acknowledged. The student markering on the bathroom stall, that crowd outside the class complaining about how bad that teacher is, the girl who drops out because she hated school, and the boys throwing bottles at the track because they are mad at athletes are all examples of inconvenient student voice. The student who says the wrong thing at a meeting, the student representative who brings ten friends instead of one, and the 17-year-old who insists on dropping out of school despite being told "No!" a million times, each of these are examples of inconvenient student voice.

I shared a lot of it myself when I was young, as many of the most dedicated educators have— because we all want to be acknowledged. The real inconvenience of my experience as a student was that I didn't believe I needed to be heard. Instead, I just wanted to get the words, art, and action out of me, no matter what. Sure, somebody spent time painting over school property after I tagged it, and taxpayer dollars were spent cleaning up the messes I made after I made them. Like many students, I was not thinking about it—instead, I was taking action and just doing it.

Committing to Meaningful Student Involvement throughout education means working with inconvenient student voice to discover, create, explore, and examine new ways to engage disengaged learners, and new ways to make inconvenient student voice constructive, if not always appreciated or deemed appropriate by everyone involved. (Fletcher, 2012) Research conducted by Mitra (2004) and others supports my experience, too, showing that educators can engage the disengaged through Meaningful Student Involvement.

---

[21] The remainder of this section was originally published as Fletcher, A. (Oct 2012) "Convenient or inconvenient student voice?" in *Connect*, No. 197. p 18.

Chapter 51. Whole School Programs

Towards the beginning of this book, I introduced the Spheres of Meaning. This framework visualizes the relationship between individual classroom or program activities, different types meaningful involvement, and the main avenues of education transformation. Whole school programs embody this framework.

While it is beyond the ability of most individual teachers, there is a vital necessity to engaging all students as partners throughout an individual school. Figure 13 illustrates what these partners can do. This requires teacher-to-teacher collaborations, principal leadership and parental support. It also generally means that professional development opportunities are offered for all teachers and adults working throughout a school building, as well as the designation of funds specifically to support Meaningful Student Involvement. Students should be trained, materials should be secured and strategic plans should be developed that intentionally, actively and substantively foster Student/Adult Partnerships in every area needed.

It is important to understand that schools do not have to start big, and educators do not have to reach every student as soon as they start to foster meaningful involvement in a whole school. Anyone can start small and grow forth, steadily increasing the ability of educators and enriching the capacity of students as partners. The important part is the consistent striving towards whole school education transformation, and the commitment of everyone along the way.

Story 41: The Ecology of a School

As cited earlier in this book, students in State College, Pennsylvania, participated in a schoolwide constitution creation process at Park Forest Elementary School. Working with adults as partners, fifth grade students facilitated a student convention to gather data about students' desires for their learning environment. A separate committee of students created a graphic illustration of the rights and responsibilities nominated by every classroom in the building. After drafting the governing rules for their entire school, a group of student leaders drafted a final version.

Instead of simply ending the process there, though, students held a second convention and shared their draft. After clarifying whether each student understood and agreed to what the draft said, another version was drafted. That went to each classroom anew, and the entirety of the student body voted to ratify the constitution.

The principal of the school fostered this second round of approvals in order to make sure that all students agreed to what was said. More importantly though, she did this to give every student the experience of being meaningfully involved in making decisions that affect their entire school, rather than just choices that affected them alone. (McGarry & Stoicovy, 2014) This closed the accountability loop that so often targets students without embracing adults' accountability to students. It also built a schoolwide investment and ownership through Meaningful Student Involvement. This school continues to grow its efforts to infuse meaningfulness throughout every leaner's experience with a variety of activities, including regular town hall meetings, advisory opportunities for the school's principal and other intentionally designed activities.[22]

Schoolwide initiatives focused on Meaningful Student Involvement are important because for many reasons. Primary among them is the reality that they can establish, support and sustain a collective understanding of students as partners by engaging a variety of capacities focused on change. This is an important practice, as it elevates the expectations of learners and students alike. It also builds the larger community when students move beyond their initial experiences and towards their lives beyond wherever they began to be meaningfully involved.

---

[22] Learn about Park Forest Elementary School at scasd.org/Page/4332

Chapter 52. Whole School Action

Every individual action, location, population and outcome identified throughout this book can legitimately be addressed as Meaningful Student Involvement. This approach, however, has cascading effects on both individuals and institutions (see Table 13 for examples). I contend that the more individual opportunities for meaningful involvement in a specific class, around a school building, throughout a district, within a state, or across a nation, the more meaningful education will be for every single student involved. This includes different ages, socio-economic statuses, cultural backgrounds, racial differences, and soon on.

When taken as a whole, though, individual actions within and throughout a school supersede isolated incidents and ripple far beyond the people involved. Meaningful Student Involvement simply works better when it happens more. As shown in the earlier chapter on benefits, the more people who are directly engaged in Student/Adult Partnerships the more the entirety of a school or district can be affected. There are a number of schools where this is happening today.

Several earlier examples mentioned in this book could be included here, including Park Forest Elementary School in State College, Pennsylvania; Eagle Rock School in Estes Park, Colorado; and Federal Hocking High School in Stuart, Ohio. Each of them deeply infuse Meaningful Student Involvement throughout learning, teaching and leadership in their buildings. Instead, here are three additional examples that reflect the frameworks of Meaningful Student Involvement, including the Nova Project High School in Seattle, Washington; Mission Hill School in Boston, Massachusetts; and Alternatives in Action High School in Oakland, California. All of these are public schools, and all of them foster Student/Adult Partnerships.

Story 42: The NOVA Project

In 1970, a group of students and their parents lobbied the Seattle School District to open an alternative high school that operated differently from the rest of the district. They specifically asked for a school without curriculum that centered on student interests, where teachers and students would share decision-making and activities could diverge from expectations without impeding regulations from the school board. After a multi-year fight, The Nova Project opened. Since then, the school has stayed small and focused.

Today, the mission of Nova is,

> "to be a democratically governed learning community of broadly educated, diverse, creative and independent thinkers who work collaboratively and demonstrate a high degree of individual and social responsibility." (Seattle Public Schools, 2011)

Students and adults continue to share decision-making, and Nova students have an equal voice with adults in the school in a number of areas, including curriculum, teacher hiring, the school budget, and more. Each student determines their own learning schedule, and is required to take a role in governing the school. Students at Nova learn through project-based approaches to teaching. Seminar-style courses, multi-level classes and independent study are hallmarks of the school, which targets under-resourced, under-achieving students as well as self-driven learners.

The school does not grade students, instead relying on a system of self-assessment. Students meet monthly with learning coordinators who track their progress. Students focus learning time on non-core topics primarily related to social justice. There is a weekly commitment to social activism that is supported in a variety of ways by adults throughout the school community. Students at Nova are regularly credited throughout Seattle for their community contributions and their rates of acceptance to higher education. (Nova High School, 2014)[23]

Story 43: Mission Hill School

In Boston, Massachusetts, the Mission Hill School was founded in 1997 as a pre-Kindergarten through grade 8 public school with approximately 200 racially and economically diverse students. Education thought leader Deborah Meier cofounded the school with parents, community leaders and others to provide a model to encourage other schools to innovate. Students throughout the city are chosen to attend Mission Hill based on a lottery and careful district selection.

Mission Hill features many elements of Meaningful Student Involvement. Students are considered partners throughout learning, teaching and leadership in the school, and have opportunities to co-lead the school's curricula and culture, and help identify learning outcomes. With schoolwide learning themes, students have a lot of opportunities to share their perspectives on learning and education through planning, co-teaching, evaluation and decision-making. There are also educational advocacy opportunities woven into every students' learning experience. To prove their learning, students develop and share class portfolios to share with others. Students are taught democratic habits of mind, and the school seeks to create community in order to nurture democracy. Table 18 shows why this matters. Using anti-racist and culturally relevant curriculum, the school is credited for reaching all students effectively. The school has been featured widely in media and throughout education circles for its academic success, commitment to continual innovation, and commitment to Dewey-influenced progressive education.

Story 44: Alternatives in Action High School

Students in Oakland, California, have the option of attending the nation's first-ever student-created high school. Alternatives in Action High School was originally founded as The Bay Area School of Enterprise in February 2001, when a group of ten students worked with adults to design, write, and submit a petition for a charter school to the Alameda Unified School District Board of Trustees. After a unanimous vote of approval, the school opened in September 2001. The school's Charter was subsequently renewed again by unanimous vote of the Alameda Unified School Board in February of 2006 and February 2011.

Today, the school is fully accredited by the Western Association of Schools and Colleges. The school serves a student body featuring ninety percent students of color coming from diverse economic, English language and learner backgrounds. They have created more than fifty social action projects. One hundred percent of the school's graduates are eligible for college, and ninety two percent of students are the first in their family to go on to college. (Alternatives in Action High School, n.d.)

---

[23] Learn about Nova School, aka The NOVA Project, at novahs.seattleschools.org/

Chapter 53. Large Scale Programs

While some of the most authentic and successful studies on student voice, student engagement and Student/Adult Partnerships have happened in local schools, there are a growing number of programs focused on Meaningful Student Involvement happening at the state, provincial, national, and international levels. I have had the privilege of working with several of these programs, and am a fan of many more. Following are some of them. There are several pathways for authentic student voice in Table 1 of this book.

Story 45: Speak Out

As mentioned earlier, more than 300 schools across the Canadian province of Alberta have participated in the Alberta Education Speak Out program. Originally launched as a way to foster student voice, today students and adults work together across the province to improve learning and teaching throughout schools. At Speak Out Forums in individual schools, students talk about what successful learning at looks like and how educators can facilitate it. Decision-makers on school boards, with the provincial ministry of education, and others receive reports from the forums that represent student voice. Every year, students and adults attend the Speak Out Conference, working together to establish opportunities for students to impact the education system. Speak Out also hosts the Minister of Education's Student Advisory Council. These 24 students, ages 14-19, meet with the Minister of Education several times a year and provide a new and fresh perspective on learning, teaching and leadership in schools.[24]

Story 46: Project 540

A nationwide program called Project 540 worked with 100,000 students in 14 states to engage students in advocating for school improvement. The number 540 referred to a 540-degree turn, or a revolution and a half, which represented the program's problem solving goals. Students helped schools come full circle by identifying issues that mattered to them and mapped out resources they could use to improve their schools. Next, they took their schools another half-turn by developing recommendations for change, which they presented to school officials as action plans. The program lasted for five years and was sponsored by several national organizations. (Fletcher, 2001; Germond, et al, 2006)

Story 47: SABLE

Despite being allowed otherwise in those seven states, only California and Maryland actually have full-voting members on their state boards of education. Both of those states have highly influential student organizations that openly lobby for student voice. The California Association of Student Councils, founded in 1947, proudly proclaims that all their programs are student-led. One of their most powerful activities is the , or SABLE. Each February SABLE convenes in the state capital to set education priorities and share them with key decision-makers. They have a direct audience with the Senate Education Committee, and their influence helped form a position for a full-voting student member of the California State Board of Education, whose position was created in 1969. They gained full voting rights in 1983, including closed sessions. The Maryland Association of Student Councils has similar impact in their state, with a student member serving in a regularly elected position annually. (Fletcher, 2005b)

Story 48: Generation YES

Many schools are increasingly relying on students to provide training to teachers in a variety of areas, including technology and service learning. In a program called Generation YES located in Olympia, Washington, students across the United States are receiving credit for helping teachers learn how to use complicated hardware and software in their classrooms. An alternative school in Washington State recently had students conduct an in-service for teachers across their district on service learning. (Fletcher, 2005b)

Story 49: Up for Learning

High schools in Vermont have been striving towards Meaningful Student Involvement for almost a decade. As mentioned earlier in this book, Dr. Helen Beattie founded Youth and Adults Transforming Schools Together, or YATST, to promote schoolwide transformation by engaging students as partners. Working with the frameworks for Meaningful Student Involvement and other tools, Helen partnered with dozens of schools through the Vermont Principals Association before launching Up for Learning, a new organization solely dedicated to Student/Adult Partnerships. (Cervone, 2012) Today, their model is spread entirely across Vermont, and they host several annual events to train students and adults on their work. Their annual conference has been attended by national and local experts, and many students have gone from the program to become teachers and fill other roles affecting schools. Up for Learning is going national, and has strong plans for changing the nation's education system permanently.[25] (Beattie, 2012)

Story 50: Breakthrough Collaborative

The Breakthrough Collaborative, a national program based in San Francisco, is a highly successful after-school program for students of color, believes so strongly in students teaching that their tagline is "Students Teaching Students." The organization shares the following anecdote:

> "During one of the first summers, several high school students who were acting as teaching assistants took over the classroom for a math teacher who had fallen ill. When the teacher returned, she observed that her students were working harder for the older students than they had for her. By coincidence, this 'experimental' teaching model sparked the interest of the younger students who loved having the high school students as their teachers and mentors. Suddenly, seventh and eighth grade students who never believed it was cool to be smart were reciting Shakespeare, learning the Pythagorean Theorem and studying the laws of physics. [Breakthrough] was a booming success." (Breakthrough Collaborative, n.d.)

Story 51: Anne Arundel County Anne Arundel County Schools

On example of Meaningful Student Involvement in district decision-making comes from Maryland. For the past 25 years a high school senior has participated as a voting member of the district level board of education in Anne Arundel County. These members vote on all issues, including the district budget. Also in this district, every advisory, curriculum, study committee, and special task force includes students, working on everything from grading policies to alternative learning. Students are members of every local School Improvement Team in the district, with as many as five students on a ten-member team.

Story 52: SpeakUp

For almost a decade, students in Ontario have been engaged in SpeakUp, the Ministry of Education's student voice program. The program features avenues for student involvement, with the first being the Minister's Student Advisory Council, or MSAC. MSAC has sixty students in grades seven to twelve from across the province who meet with the Minister of Education to share their ideas and perspectives. The second way is through student forums that are held in regions across the province. These forums give students opportunities to share their ideas on topics that matter to them, including curriculum and student leadership. The third way is through student-led SpeakUp projects. In these, students are helping students engage both academically and socially by leading projects that they design and implement with the support of their learning Minister's Student Advisory Council community. Thousands of students in grades seven through twelve have actively led or participated in thousands of projects in hundreds of schools. (SpeakUP, n.d.)

---

[24] Learn about Alberta Education's SpeakOUT program at speakout.alberta.ca

[25] Find about Up For Learning at upforlearning.com

Chapter 54. Healthy, Safe and Supportive Learning Environments

I have seen many conditions surrounding Meaningful Student Involvement. Sometimes well-meaning and sometimes merely systematic reactions, these conditions have always seemed vital to recognize. One of the most important conditions for large-scale implementation of Meaningful Student Involvement is establishing and maintaining a healthy, safe and supportive learning environment. Examining the projects I have witnessed and facilitated over the years, I have seen a series of elements emerge within these environments. Following are some elements that make these schools healthy, safe and supportive.

Elements of Healthy, Safe and Supportive Learning Environments

1) **Ensure meaningfulness.** Programs that stay focused on the frameworks for Meaningful Student Involvement introduced in this book are programs that sustain well. When there is a great deal of turnover and transition among educators without a return to understanding the frameworks, programs can devolve and become something other than meaningful. Without learning the consistency of the frameworks, students can become distrustful of the pathways introduced throughout this book and actually begin to undermine student involvement on their own. The best way to prevent all of this is to ensure meaningfulness, which happens through deliberation, ongoing capacity building and policy-making focused on structures, cultures and attitudes supporting Meaningful Student Involvement.

2) **Support Meaningful Student Involvement financially.** Bringing adults throughout a school community together to plan action can be complex and require a lot of support. Broadening that table to include district stakeholders, parents and students themselves can become daunting. Secure financial support for planning and implementing Meaningful Student Involvement. Structure finances to allow stakeholders to create a shared understanding of Meaningful Student Involvement and choose which actions to pursue. Also encourage a variety of approaches, from the individual classroom through district- and state-wide action, that focus on engaging every student through Student/Adult Partnerships.

3) **Build diversity into Student/Adult Partnerships.** Uniting students and adults from across a community's population and multiple subjects or grade levels within schools can be a prerequisite for Meaningful Student Involvement. This supports the development of common understandings and broad agendas for action that can engage historically disengaged students as well as traditional student leaders. Measureable outcomes should include evidence that these partnerships actually work, and not just in name only. Some are stated in Table 12 of this book.

4) **Create common data measurements.** Schools that are committed to Meaningful Student Involvement should have common data measurement tools that allow students and adults to understand what progress is and how learning has happened. Principals can support this process by facilitating students and adults working together to create measurement tools based on a school's current data, and agreed upon by both students and adults.

5) **Mutual accountability for students and adults.** Student/Adult Partnerships should always encourage mutual accountability between students and adults. This supports the meaningfulness of student involvement by maintaining collective progress for everyone involved. When students have a sense of adults' goals and can support those, they actually own, invest and support their own goals more effectively as well. Ideally, students and adults set outcomes that are shared within Student/Adult Partnerships and hold each other accountable for achieving that shared set of outcomes, instead of individual learning, teaching or leadership outcomes.

6) **Blended involvement opportunities.** Classrooms may bring together different subjects, tools, or learning opportunities from many teachers to address the many facets of a complex problem being addressed through Meaningful Student Involvement. While this can lead to leading to many, slightly different outcomes that vary from student to student, allowing integrated classrooms cuts down on competing priorities and unnecessary replication. This same approach can happen throughout opportunities, as multiple locations and issues can be addressed together to increase the impact and outcomes of Meaningful Student Involvement.

7) **Customize to local conditions.** Meaningful Student Involvement uses data and local knowledge to better establish the relevance and impact of engaging students as partners throughout education. Many well-meaning programs try to dictate that schools use a specific program or service, regardless of the school's context. It is better when districts and states dictate the frameworks for Meaningful Student Involvement without specifying that schools use a specific type of program, curricula, or service provider.

8) **Documented meaningfulness.** Students and adults involved in opportunities for Meaningful Student Involvement should regularly meet and otherwise communicate frequently in order to document constant learning and alignment to their goals. To support this documentation, school leaders can require regular reports of student involvement, including classroom curricula, meeting agendas and minutes, newsletters, or other forms of communication between students and adults.

9) **Adjust for challenges.** When working together, students and adults can see that data, school context and other stakeholders' concerns have new information that requires a change of course. Meaningful Student Involvement should allow for adjustments to the original plan. Flexible planning strategies allow for changes in plans as long as they maintain focus on the overall goal for action.

Nothing should exist for the sake of existing, and meaningfulness is one of those things. If opportunities are not focused on education, community and democracy, they are not focused appropriately. If students do not know why they are there and if adults cannot agree on the need for transformation, they are not focused appropriately. Most importantly for sustaining Meaningful Student Involvement is the need to maintain vision in action. This chapter showed why that is; the next chapter shows how.

Chapter 55. Summarizing Action

These aren't the only types of activities happening in schools today that are meaningful. Given the earlier tools in this guide, the possibilities are unlimited. However, these examples allude to a process of what I refer to as "engagement typification", where the roles of students are repositioned throughout the education system to allow Meaningful Student Involvement to become the standard treatment for all students, rather than something that is exceptional.

Consistently positioning students as in special positions does not allow adults, including educators, administrators, or parents, to integrate students throughout the regular operations of the educational system. While seeing their peers as school board members is enticing to a number of students, most school boards don't allow students to see themselves as regular and full members of the leadership and ownership of education, or as trustees for their own well-being. That is what differentiates Meaningful Student Involvement from other attempts at student engagement and student voice: By actively, consistently, and substantively positioning students as full owners of what they learn, Meaningful Student Involvement guarantees positive, powerful outcomes.

All of these approaches are tried and true, and assure that student involvement is not just another tokenistic or simplistic process; rather, it is a powerful, effective avenue to assuring learning through school-focused action. Greater goals can occur, too. One of the most important considerations in Meaningful Student Involvement can be the actual implementation of the process.

It is important to remember that if an opportunity has Student/Adult Partnerships at the core, they are meaningfully involving students. If the five elements of the Cycle of Engagement are present—including listening, validating, authorizing, action and reflecting—and are being met repeatedly, an opportunity is meaningfully involving students. If the key characteristics described earlier are present throughout an opportunity, students are being involved. The Ladder of Student Involvement can show how different opportunities can reflect the most meaningful forms of student involvement, as well as the least meaningful. Table 9 explores some of those forms in action. When adult perspectives of students are honestly acknowledged and accordingly addressed, involvement can be meaningful. The Spheres of Meaning should be interlocked and are dependent on each other, and the learning process is essential to implementing effective opportunities.

Important Points About Taking Action

In the late 2000s, the Consulting Pupils about Teaching and Learning project in the UK identified several key points about the people involved in student voice activities, and why they are involved. (Rudduck, Arnot, Fielding, McIntyre, & et al, 2003) Following I have adapted those points to make them relevant to Meaningful Student Involvement.

- **Engage Quiet Students, Too.** Adults often concentrate only on traditional student leaders who are specifically noticeable or articulate. Unfortunately, this consistently disenfranchises other students who are not that way. Focus on engaging disengaged students and quiet students, as well as nontraditional student leaders, as illustrated in Figure 22.

- **Do not Limit Action.** Avoid fostering elitism among students. Do not just engage one group of students and empower them as much as possible. Instead, spread out capacity building opportunities and elevate entire student populations all at once.
- **Keep It Real.** Focus on maintaining authenticity in Student/Adult Partnerships. Students do not value student voice activity after student voice activity without ever seeing outcomes.
- **Be Accountable.** Sharing data and offering feedback to students is essential for mutual accountability. Students need to know what is happening as a result of what they have done, what is possible and what is not possible given diverse perspectives, external pressures and the realities of schools today.
- **Be Open.** Trust and openness is a pre-condition of Meaningful Student Involvement. This requires seeing students as legitimate partners with adults. Reassure students that their ideas, wisdom, knowledge and actions are welcome and not simply accommodated, and let them know it is okay to disturb existing orthodoxy.

Part VII. Learning through Meaningful Student Involvement

Chapter 56. Introduction

Over the last one hundred years, schools have gone through repeating waves of reform. Generally occurring in cycles, each responds to the popular concerns of the era. In the 1950s, schools were focused on creating engaged citizens who could respond to the so-called "Red Scare". Standardized testing in the 1980s was a response to growing pressure from corporations, which led to the growth of a self-oriented mentality. When No Child Left Behind (NCLB) was introduced, that influence came to play again. However, they expanded slightly with the introduction of subtle language encouraging community involvement.

The language from federal education laws was interpreted in many ways throughout the 2000s, usually focused on involving parents, businesses, and even other government agencies in school improvement efforts. However, the obvious partner has consistently been left behind: Students themselves. But simply throwing students into the mix is not enough. Rather than rely on television news or hearsay from their peers, students need to be taught about learning, the education system, and school improvement. When they are being involved in school improvement efforts specifically, students should learn that education is designed to meet determined goals. They should discover that schools improve because people set out to improve them and work for change. And they identify how Meaningful Student Involvement should have a place throughout education.

If an adult parked a car on the side of a busy highway, handed the keys to a car to a 14-year-old and told them to teach themselves to learn how to drive, that adult would appropriately be held irresponsible. However, we do that every day with young people, especially when we engage them in school improvement work. This chapter assumes students have a type of authority on education no matter what grade they are in. Meaningful Student Involvement can act like Toto from *The Wizard of Oz* as it pulls back the curtain by encouraging students to identify and examine the assumptions and ideas that support current and future designs for learning.

Research has identified several commonalities that help define how educators and adults throughout the education system can facilitate learning through Meaningful Student Involvement.

- Classroom learning is not bound to one single text, topic, guide, or specific sequence. However, curricular expectations are respected.
- Activities build on information across disciplines and across content areas, both in schools and throughout the education system.
- The environment and the learning experiences are characterized by student engagement and responsive novelty.
- Time is flexible; learning experiences are not restricted to fixed increments.
- The methods are not unstructured. Instead, the structure flows through phases of learning generated by the students' investigations and actions addressing an issue within the education system. (Krogh & Morehouse, 2014)

Chapter 57. Grade Specific Approaches

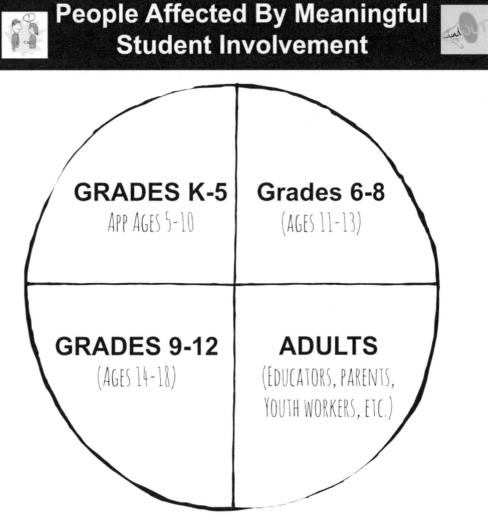

Figure 15. Grade Specific Approaches

Student voice is always a force for changing the climate of a learning environment, good or otherwise. Students have back and forth exchanges throughout the course of a school day, checking in about each others' emotions and ideas, experiences and knowledge about school, learning, teaching, classrooms, curricula, behaviors, attitudes, and more. Imagine this across a schoolwide population ranging from 250 to 2,500 students, and it becomes relatively easy to see how student voice informs school climate. Student voice also never stays the same, and it should never be static. As bell hooks wrote, "The engaged voice must never be fixed and absolute but always changing, always evolving in dialogue with a world beyond itself." (hooks, 1994) Unfortunately, it is the tendency of adults to fix student voice into one position. That alone makes it vital for educators to embrace Meaningful Student Involvement from the youngest ages to let students inform their pedagogy, school climate and culture, academic performance and achievement, and school improvement.

These opportunities also offer the potential to create and sustain collaborative learning communities where students, teachers, administrators, school staff and community advocates can continuously learn from each other. Acknowledging that this does not necessarily happen naturally in many classrooms, several skill building topics are proposed. Topics are meant to serve as complementary building blocks that will enhance students' and educators' ability to experience Meaningful Student Involvement in a variety of settings.

Meaningful Student Involvement demands more than time from educators, more than money from administrators, and more than instantaneous results from students. Instead, Meaningful Student Involvement calls for efforts to improve the organization of schooling and the effectiveness of instruction to actively engage and authorize students to transform their learning communities. The attitudes of students, educators, parents and community members must also transform. All members of the learning community must see students as valid contributors to school improvement.

Many people benefit from Meaningful Student Involvement. The following chapter connects a variety of examples of Meaningful Student Involvement with the skills needed, and the possible learning connections with a variety of participants. This allows students and educators to identify their common purposes, and to create the space that both students and educators need to share knowledge, experiences and perspectives as both learners and teachers. In order to illustrate how meaningful involvement can happen throughout schools, each table presents a different grade level. This chapter also addresses adults specifically, illustrating how integral allies are to Meaningful Student Involvement. The suggested activities and topics described for all participant groups offer opportunities for reciprocal learning through leadership: that is, adults role-modeling for students, students role-modeling for other students, and students and adults learning from each other.

Chapter 58. Exploring Grades K-5

Meaningful Student Involvement in elementary schools is experiential, tangible, and focused. Action is generally based in the classroom, where students work in small groups and gradually build their skills. (Thiessen, 2007) Meaningful Student Involvement requires specific skill building that can lead to important learning connections for young people. Following are generalized examples of activities where students have been meaningfully involved in elementary schools, and what they have learned.

Elementary School Students

As shown in Figure 15, engagement elementary school students is a key target of Meaningful Student Involvement. Engaging students as partners in the elementary level can begin in kindergarten, gradually increasing in scope, purpose, intent, and outcomes throughout the fifth and sixth grades. Introducing students to education planning by installing them as members on school improvement committee is an excellent activity. Students can learn cooperative leadership and project planning skills. School improvement can introduce them to the depth of issues in education, and contribute to developing their communications, reading, and writing skills.

Through meaningful involvement in teaching, elementary students learn to co-design, deliver, and evaluate lesson plans. Their knowledge of learning styles, teaching skills, and evaluation methods can increase. Skills in writing, communication, and the specific subject area they are teaching can increase too.

There are several ways elementary students can participate in classroom evaluation. Student evaluation of themselves and their teachers teaches self-awareness and critical thinking skills, and reinforces their communication skills. Meaningful Student Involvement in evaluation through student-led parent teacher conferences is an increasingly popular way to engage students as partners in education. They learn to present their own learning through small group facilitation. This increases their communications skills, including writing, speaking, and reading.

In elementary school, engaging students as partners in decision-making can take the form of student-led classroom governance. This happens as students learning about creating consensus, teambuilding, and applied citizenship. They learn relational skills and communication through application, and understand how they are part of something larger than themselves. When these students are meaningfully involved in education advocacy, such as supporting the school library, they can learn active listening, problem solving, and communication skills.

Students in elementary schools can also experience Meaningful Student Involvement through school organizing. For instance, a student-led signature-collecting campaigns promoting their interests can help elementary students learn about creating petitions, as well as understanding the school system and democratic process. Their writing and relational skills increase while they have an applied experience in social studies.

Chapter 59. Exploring Grades 6-8

Meaningful Student Involvement in middle schools is experiential and project-based, emphasizing teamwork and results for all students. These actions encourage students to take increasing levels of responsibility for improving their schools. They can also lay an essential foundation for successful high school and higher education experiences. (Zlotkowski, 2002) The following activities detail where students have been meaningfully involved in middle schools, including specific skill building and learning connections. Additionally, activities in middle schools span a variety of core curriculum, extracurricular activities, assessments and other activities, transforming adults' perspectives of student roles in schools. (Bryant, 2007; Knowles & Brown, 2000)

Middle School Students

Engaging middle school students are a main point illustrated in Figure 15. Meaningful Student Involvement for middle school students might begin with being engaged in education planning. For instance, full membership on school committees can facilitate student learning about school leadership, and teach them about issues in education. Their communication skills and applied citizenship skills can increase too. Engaging students as partners in education research can begin with teaching them research methods and show them the array of issues in education. They learn to assess data and design action projects, along the way learning skills in writing, data-focused math, communications, and specific issue areas that arise.

Meaningfully involving middle school students in teaching can mean student/adult co-teaching. Students can learn about classroom planning, facilitation, and self- and group evaluation skills. Their skills in writing and other forms of communication can be reinforced too. To engage students as partners in evaluation educators can use student-created school assessments in their classes. This can improve group decision-making and evaluation skills, as well as critical thinking, communications, and knowledge around specific subject areas.

Decision-making is an obvious area for a lot of meaningful involvement for middle school students. Whole school student forums led by students can teach facilitation and event planning skills. While they learn to identify issues in education for a variety of students, student partners can also improve their communication skills and their appreciation for diversity in action. Middle school students can learn about advocacy through school-focused service learning, which combines classroom learning goals with meaningful community service focused on education. Students can learn project planning skills and how to identify issues in education, as well as skills in critical reflection, communications, and group leadership. When middle school students lead community organizing they can do almost anything, including designing their own school improvement agenda. Doing this can teach them about issues in education, group processes, and collaboration. They can also learn concrete skills in communication and applied citizenship.

Chapter 60. Exploring Grades 9-12

Meaningful Student Involvement in high schools is experiential, intensive and offers direct connections between the school and the larger community. Many gains in youth development occur through conscientious, thoughtful student voice activities, specifically when Student/Adult Partnerships are formed. (Mitra, 2004) Action may happen in longer duration than in elementary or middle school years. Students lead action and have full responsibility and authority in many activities with adults acting as coaches that guide students in a mostly self-directed process of inquiry and discovery. Table 5 shares activities where students have been meaningfully involved in high schools, including specific skill building and important learning connections. High school students are often engaged in the activities from Tables 3 and 4, also.

High School Students

As Figure 15 alludes to, high school students are meaningfully involved in advocacy they can learn a variety of skills. For instance, advocating for a student-created district budget can help them learn about issues in education, group decision-making, and diversity awareness. It can reinforce skills such as writing, math, communications, and applied citizenship. Engaging students as partners in teaching by having them teach classroom courses can teach students about a variety of issues, including classroom planning, and reinforce subject knowledge about the they are topic they are teaching. The opportunity can also teach or reinforce their facilitation and presentation skills, evaluation skills, and overall communications skills.

Engaging high school students in education decision-making through full membership on school improvement committees is one way they can be meaningfully involved. This can teach them practical community building and about issues in education. The skills they can develop include conflict resolution, writing, statistical math, and the specific issue areas they are involved in addressing through school improvement. High school students can be engaged in facilitating training for teachers. This reinforces issue knowledge about whatever topic they are addressing, including diversity, youth issues, and community needs. Their skills in facilitation, communications, and writing can be developed further too.

With the range of decision-making opportunities for high school students to be meaningfully involved in, positions on teacher and principal hiring teams almost appear obvious. They can learn about group dynamics and issues in education, as well as practical considerations around hiring and firing. They also learn skills in collaboration and communication. When high school students are involved in advocacy, student-led forums and action planning can be a practical way to learn about issues in education and cultural dynamics among their peers. Their skills in facilitation, event planning, and communications can become more important than ever.

Student-led organizing provides opportunities for students to learn invaluable skills without parallel. For instance, high school students organizing an education conference for their peers and the larger community can help them learn about issues in education, event planning, issues in democratic governance and applied citizenship. They also learn concrete skills focused on communication.

Chapter 61. Learning for Adults

Meaningful Student Involvement requires educators, administrators, and other school staff to be introduced and sustained in their effort to engage students as partners in school change. Active engagement for all learners of all ages is a goal of many educators; however, the ability to incorporate Meaningful Student Involvement is a learned disposition and skill.

As Figure 15 shows, Meaningful Student Involvement supports adults as they learn to engage the knowledge, perspectives, and experience of students in diverse education settings. Meaningful Student Involvement is about culture change as much as structure change. A challenge of that is that schools aren't isolated—they do not exist in a vacuum. No matter how educators treat a student inside one classroom, for one period, students still leave the classroom and school to return to communities where they are routinely excluded from decision-making and actions that affect them, and segregated from the adults around them.

One of the essential roles to beginning Meaningful Student Involvement is that of the change agent to get started. The champion has to be an adult who can work with students as partners. That is because the role of the adult is inherently longer lasting than the role of any single student.

Thinking about where to start varies according to the role adults play within a school. Every adult in every school can have healthy, meaningful interactions with students. Janitors, media specialists, assistant principals, and coaches can forge meaningfulness by acting with respect, making meaningful investments in students, and committing to communicate clearly with students.

For teachers, curriculum is a great place to start. Building meaningfulness into a curricular approach so it embodies Meaningful Student Involvement allows teachers to reflect students' daily personal lives and connects learning to real-world outcomes. Rather than assuming students have never experienced meaningfulness, teachers can help them plumb their school experience through critical reflection and meaningful connections.

Building administrators, school counselors, administrative staff, and other school support positions face a different picture. These professionals can strive to infusing the Cycle of Engagement from Part Three into every interaction they have with students. Building the Cycle into the routine of every adult in schools can change building culture. In turn, this contributes to transforming education. The most important thing any adult in schools can do is to envision students as partners, and then act that way.

There are a variety of ways adults can learn about Meaningful Student Involvement in action. Engaging students in planning by infusing students into classroom, club, and school planning is one avenue. Adults can learn about Student/Adult Partnerships, and how to listen to student feedback. When they are involved in researching schools with students, adults can help facilitate participatory action research focusing on classroom and school improvement. Through this they can learn about the Participatory Action Research process, and how students can lead assessment. Meaningful Student Involvement in teaching can help teachers learn to build students' ability to self-teach and facilitate peer education. They can learn peer education techniques, and how to provide coaching to learners rather than traditional teaching.

Teachers facilitating authentic student-designed evaluation processes for themselves, peers, and adults in school learn evaluation methods and how to listen to student feedback. By meaningfully involving students in decision-making, adults can partner up with student groups to ensure consistent student positions on school improvement committees. This can help reinforce adults' ability to facilitate large groups and plan large events outside the classroom. Adults in schools can learn advocacy and coalition building skills through Meaningful Student Involvement. Each of these activities can reinforce what Student/Adult Partnerships are and how they functionally operate.

Chapter 62. Roles for Teachers

Given the tensions that exist throughout education today, it seems increasingly outlandish to ask teachers to do one more thing. Fortunately, Meaningful Student Involvement does not ask that. Instead, it asks teachers to acknowledge the resources already present and to utilize them in proactive, engaging ways. In a similar way that students are human resources for transformation and not problems to be fixed, teachers are vital partners for democracy. Table 18 shows why this matters.

As the single most important adult role in the education system today, it is vital to support teachers deliberately and effectively. Meaningful Student Involvement does this by engaging "the role of educators as civic intellectuals" who can facilitate student learning focused on "what it means to understand the purpose and meaning of education as a site of individual and collective empowerment." (Giroux, 2013)

This happens when educators are invested in learning not as directors or enforcers; not only as facilitators, coaches and guides-on-the-sides; but also as co-learners with students. Side-by-side, teachers can appropriately and accordingly infuse the experience of every learner in every grade with impact, depth, perspective, and ultimately, the meaningfulness at the heart of the frameworks for Meaningful Student Involvement.

By integrating Meaningful Student Involvement in the classroom, teachers can engage students in substantive partnerships that transform learning and teaching. In the classroom, educators can actively shift students from being the passive recipients of adult-driven teaching towards becoming active partners throughout the education system. See Table 22 for examples of what it looks like when that goes wrong.

Beyond the classroom, teachers can foster roles for all adults as allies to students, actively nurturing Student/Adult Partnerships and transforming education as a practice and as a system. In this way, the role for teachers in Meaningful Student Involvement echoes Theodore Sizer's goal when he created the Essential Schools Coalition by enshrining his premise of "teacher as coach, student as worker" and moving it one step further towards teacher as facilitator, student as ally. (Sizer, 2004)

More than 30 years ago, Henry Giroux exposed traditional classrooms by making their visible and invisible exchanges of power obvious. He demonstrated clearly the hidden and overt forms of domination affecting learners, showing how hierarchical relationships, top-to-bottom communication practices, rigid time schedules, rigid behavior expectations for students, and inflexible forms of evaluation entrench non-meaningful learning, teaching and leadership throughout education. All of these attributes reinforce roles for students as recipients and defeat their potential as partners in their own learning (Giroux, 1981). Table 15 shows what Meaningful Student Involvement offers, and how that differs from the attributes highlighted here.

Learning Strategies and Classroom Structures

Albert Einstein famously noted, "No problem can be solved from the same thinking that created it." Engaging students as partners in learning positions them as knowledge creators by placing them in roles to transform education. Here are descriptions of several strategies and structures that can embed Meaningful Student Involvement deeply within the classroom and throughout student learning. They all reflect Einstein's dictum, along with Dewey's belief that teachers,

> "Give pupils something to do, not something to learn; and the doing is of such a nature as to demand thinking, or the intentional noting of connections; learning naturally results." (Dewey, 1948)

These strategies and structures actively engage students in several ways. They are hands-on, interactive and generative by nature, encouraging students to critique, construct and produce knowledge through Meaningful Student Involvement. In some, students teach each other; in others, they create new knowledge with adults as co-learners. When done with Student/Adult Partnerships at their core, students are co-creating knowledge that is place-based, problem-oriented, project-driven and goal oriented. Within each of these strategies and structures are individual and group activities; the exploration of diverse perspectives; constructivist techniques for building on prior knowledge; brainstorming and problematizing; Socratic dialogue; problem-solving processes, and team teaching. None of them perfectly embodies Meaningful Student Involvement, and all of them should be adapted, critically examined and reconsidered every time they are employed.

In 2013, the Green River Regional Educational Cooperative in Kentucky won a United States Department of Education grant to reimagine learning for modern needs[26]. Focused on creating "kid-friendly" schools, the grant embodies many aspects of Meaningful Student Involvement. Identifying several teaching strategies and classroom structures, I have expanded on some of their findings in the following list that identifies strategies and structures that can foster Meaningful Student Involvement in learning and teaching. These approaches make student voice central to learning and elevate the teacher-student relationship towards Student/Adult Partnerships.

There is an important note to make before reading this chapter: No single teaching method or activity is the be-all and end-all for Meaningful Student Involvement. Not one approach holds this promise for every single student in every single classroom throughout every single school across every education system all around the world. Instead, Meaningful Student Involvement has to be invented and re-invented for every location, every opportunity and every student who is targeted for engagement.

Strategies and Structures for Meaningful Student Involvement

The following strategies and structures are provided here as a reference point for educators who want one. This not meant to be an exhaustive or all-inclusive list; instead, it's a starting point. Moving from these static descriptions towards the dynamic, ongoing and consistent space of active practice and critical reflection is vital. This is also not to limit any educator or school leader; these are not the be-all-end-all of strategies and structures for Meaningful Student Involvement. Instead, this list is meant to be a doorway that alludes to possibilities. Regardless of how you choose to do it, I encourage every determined educator to take action. As the motto of The Freechild Project says, "Only through actions do words take power."[27]

1. Differentiated Instruction

Tailoring teaching according to the individual learning needs and aspirations. This can include self-led learning time, integrated technology usage, modified curriculum and assessments, or modified teaching approaches. Differentiated instruction fosters Meaningful Student Involvement when it infuses student authority and student voice throughout learning and teaching.

2. Student/Adult Partnerships

Partnerships happen between students and adults in education when each person involved can share their earnest, appropriate thoughts and make substantive decisions, and when the contribution of both students and adults are recognized and valued by both students and adults. A student/adult partnership is one in which adults work in equitable partnership with students on issues facing students, their schools and the entirety of the education system.

3. Student-Led Learning

Students teaching regular lessons in their classes, serving as full teaching partners with teachers, and teaching students in lower grade levels can all embody Meaningful Student Involvement. (Richmond, 2014) As important or more so, though, is the practice of students teaching teachers and other adults by facilitating professional development, training workshops, and other activities from their perspectives. Not only does this fulfill the dictum that, "To teach is to learn twice," it actually moves teachers into a more responsive position by allowing them to see the world beyond student voice by learning what students deeply understand and want them to know. (McLaren, 2003) Student-led learning can foster Meaningful Student Involvement[28].

4. Serving Learning

Embedding classroom learning in meaningful service to other people, service learning can foster Meaningful Student Involvement when it is focused on transforming education. Working with adults as partners, students must identify challenges, research the issues, identify and create strategies, facilitate action, and infuse reflection throughout activities. (Fletcher, 2004)

5. Participatory Action Research

Engaging students as researchers who examine teaching, learning, leadership, or anything to do with education is called participatory action research, or PAR. Student researchers actively work to transform education during and after their research, and reflect throughout the process. Meaningful Student Involvement happens when PAR emphasizes co-learning among students and between students and adults, and embeds action with stated learning goals focused on students experiencing and transforming schools in new ways.[29] See Table 17 for examples of what issues students research.

6. Blended Learning

Blended learning combines different ways of teaching and learning in lesson plans to teach students more effectively. It enables and empowers educators to adapt and transform their lessons to reach students more powerfully. It embodies Meaningful Student Involvement because it is great for the practice of teaching; it increases students' access to knowledge; promotes social interactions between learners; develops personal agency in students; uses classroom resources more effective; and is highly adaptable. (Osguthorpe & Graham, 2003)

7. Student Created Curriculum

Students are creating, teaching and facilitating, evaluating and promoting curriculum, textbooks and other classroom learning. Expecting students to be co-creators of the classes they learn in, student-created curriculum increases in student engagement, student agency and critical thinking provide privileged learning and teaching experiences for students and educators (Nelson & Fredrick, 1994).[30] Reading, analyzing, and learning required standards can give students a basis for deepened learning and understanding, while partnerships with teachers ensure quality outcomes.

8. Learning Communities

One of my former mentors, Giselle Martin-Kniep of Communities for Learning, wrote that learning communities must infuse learners as well as teachers, administrators, parents and other adults, because "students have firsthand experiences that affect their learning and their thinking." (Martin-Kniep, 2008) By engaging students as partners throughout education teachers can foster learning communities between adults and students, throughout their classrooms and throughout entire schools and districts. Learning communities center participants in caring deeply about learning; feeling free to take risks; challenging each other and raising the expectations of everyone; respecting and valuing perspectives other than their own by seeking and valuing every member's input; intentionally seeking to do the work better, and; aggressively and continually building capacity of each member to work smarter. (Martin-Kniep, Developing learning communities through teacher expertise, 2004) By using these attributes as the basis of learning communities with students and adults, schools can foster Meaningful Student Involvement as well.

9. Inquiry-Based Learning

By asking students to discover knowledge on their own with guidance from their teachers, inquiry-based learning can be deeply integral to Meaningful Student Involvement, both in the classroom and throughout the education system. Working from the assumptions that every teacher of every subject can share equal responsibility for teaching and evaluating skills, educators can infuse inquiry-based learning in schools today by creating performance rubrics focused on student competencies, and by making skills-oriented growth 60% of their grade. Any classroom can be on the path to supporting inquiry-based learning, in turn nurturing Meaningful Student Involvement for every learner. (Markham, 2013)

10. Anytime, Anywhere Learning

With the assumption that through access to knowledgeable teachers and constant access to technology, Anytime Anywhere Learning gives schools permission to infuse technology with learning, and vice versa. This leads to fully capable students who can drive learning and teaching. By emphasizing school improvement, this approach can also lead to Meaningful Student Involvement.[31]

11. Formative Assessment

This is a process-driven test happening in the middle of learning and teaching that explores how students are performing. Through formal and informal procedures, it provides teachers with information during the learning process in order to modify teaching and learning activities to improve student attainment.[32] It typically involves qualitative feedback (rather than scores) for both student and teacher that focuses on the details of content and performance Research studies have shown that formative assessment practices that meaningfully involve students can help all learners. The results are most dramatic with struggling or disengaged students. (Chappuis & Chappuis, 2002)

12. Whole Child Approach

Schools that seek to meet the basic student needs of safety, belonging, autonomy and competence, they are more likely to become engaged in school; act in accord with school goals and values; develop social skills and understanding; contribute to the school and community; and achieve academically. Schools and communities must work together to ensure that student needs are met on all levels, including fundamental levels of health, safety, and belonging. (Dalton, Churchman, & Tasco, 2008)

13. Student-Driven Classroom Evaluation

With increasing interest in student evaluations of teachers, focus is being lost regarding the potential effects of students evaluating the entirety of the learning experience and education system. Engaging students in evaluating classes and schools; teacher performance and efficacy; and self-performance and learning can be the keys to truly transforming learning, teaching and leadership. When done in concert with educators' self-evaluation and peer evaluations among educators, there is a perfect space formed. This can include student-led parent-teacher conferences, student assessments of classrooms and curricula, as well as other approaches.[33]

14. Project-Based Learning

Organizing educators and other adults into teams with students as partners focused on learning outcomes for everyone positions project-based learning as a key avenue towards Meaningful Student Involvement. These teams, made of varying ages, abilities, genders and interests, collaboratively decide how the teams function to achieve student learning.

15. Student-Centered Learning

Given choices in how and what they learn, students can thrive from a direct connection between their own interests and classroom-based learning. Student-centered learning embodies Meaningful Student Involvement by ensuring required content is mastered through Student/Adult Partnerships.[34]

There are many other structures and approaches too; the simple reality is that they meet the aims of Meaningful Student Involvement in Table 11 of this book. That is a simple reality with a challenging truth: even the best structures and approaches can fall apart if they are not true to the outcomes stated her

---

[26] Learn about Green Valley's "Kid Friendly" Race to the Top grant at www2.ed.gov/programs/racetothetop-district/2012/finalists/applications/green-river.pdf
[27] I co-founded The Freechild Project with the belief that too many people were talking about youth changing the world, and not enough were doing it. Learn more in Fletcher, A. (2014) *The Practice of Youth Engagement. Olympia, WA: CommonAction.*
[28] Learn about student-led learning in schools at soundout.org/teaching.html
[29] Learn about Participatory Action Research and Meaningful Student Involvement at soundout.org/PAR.html
[30] For examples from a classroom at bit.ly/kDQyXO
[31] Learn about Anytime, Anywhere Learning at aalf.org
[32] Learn about formative assessment at en.wikipedia.org/wiki/Formative_assessment

[33] Learn about students as evaluators at soundout.org/evaluating.html
[34] Learn about student-centered learning at ewa.org/student-centered-learning

Chapter 61: Acknowledging Meaningful Student Involvement

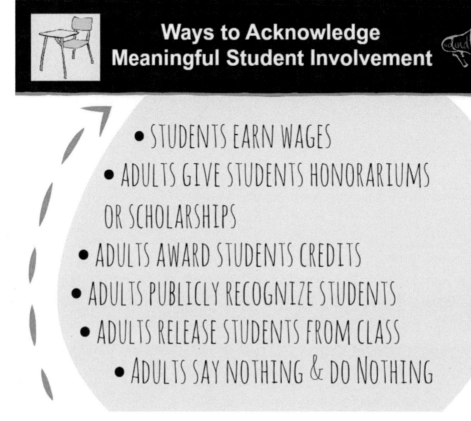

Figure 16. Ways to Acknowledge Meaningful Student Involvement

The question of giving students appropriate credit for their contributions constantly arises among adult allies to students in schools. Adults who are authentically interested in Meaningful Student Involvement are usually interested in this issue.

Research shows that acknowledging the contributions of students requires educators to walk a fine line. In her powerful book *Fires in the Bathroom: Advice for Teachers from High School students*, Kathleen Cushman identifies students who report that, "I know the other person's gonna hate me when I get praise and someone else does not." However, on the same page, another student reports, "It feels nice when a teacher singles me out for praise because it lets everyone knows I am smart." (Cushman K. , 2003) Here, I address that balancing act and suggest new approaches to acknowledging Meaningful Student Involvement. See Table 20 for more details.

There are literally dozens of ways to recognize students in schools, and schools have used all of them: certificates, letters, ceremonies, and so forth. However, when I talk with adults about it, there is a growing consensus that these steps just aren't right. The students who need to be engaged as partners in schools and who educators want to engage desperately aren't motivated by the norm. They come from backgrounds that demand adults either recognize the entire life they live and not just schools, or ignore them altogether.

With those factors in mind, a group of students and adults working with me created the illustration in Figure 16, illustrating different ways to acknowledge Meaningful Student Involvement. Following are some explanations of different ways that are featured.

Ways to Acknowledge Meaningful Student Involvement

Here are some explanations of different points on the spectrum I present in the graphic at the beginning of this chapter entitled, "Figure 16: Ways to Acknowledge Meaningful Student Involvement."

- **Students Earn Wages.** This allows adults to acknowledge the extenuating circumstances that many young people face and encourages diverse participation. It can also create equity among socio-economic classes and parity between young people and adults.
- **Adults Give Students Honorariums or Scholarships.** Students are acknowledged for sharing student voice with a flat amount that may not address all the hours they spent on a project, but still sees what they've done.
- **Adults Award Students Credits.** The learning that students partake in during their involvement is acknowledged for its validity to classroom objectives. This can help make students aware of the so-called "real-world" applications of education-focused action. Can be partial credit or credit hours or other forms of classroom validation.
- **Adults Publicly Recognize Students.** Student involvement is acknowledged in the court of public opinion by making other students, building staff, community supporters, and the general public aware of individual and group student activities. This can create a genesis of support beyond one specific group.
- **Adults Release Students from Class.** Teachers acknowledge the necessity of using classroom learning time to promote whole-school student involvement. For students who cannot afford the luxury of being involved in school activities afterschool or on the weekends, classroom hours offer the most accessible means for participation.
- **Adults Say Nothing and Do Nothing.** Student involvement is seen purely as an extra-curricular activity, meaning that it is outside the realm of regular educative activities. While opportunities for involvement are procured for students, they are not supported or sustained through any type of systemic acknowledgement of the validity of young peoples' participation.

Researcher and professor Allison Cook-Sather has observed that,

> "Because of who they are, what they know, and how they are positioned, students must be recognized as having knowledge essential to the development of sound educational policies and practices."

I inferred that Cook-Sather is suggesting student recognition comes in some ethereal way, and she may not have been suggesting paying, giving credits, or otherwise substantiating student voice. However, I'm taking her point in general, and suggesting that engaging students as partners throughout education is the first step; the next step is acknowledging the contributions they make. Appropriate acknowledgement is a vital part of sustaining Meaningful Student Involvement. Figure 16 highlights some ways; I share more in Table 20 of this book.

Considerations

Meaningful Student Involvement requires a great deal of investment from the students and adults involved. This is especially true when working with traditionally non-involved students. The extra consideration given to practically, purposefully, and meaningfully involving these students can offer strong outcomes.

The activities outlined so far offer a variety of exciting lessons and connections to important learning standards. However, there are very tangible barriers that both students and educators face in schools. Figures 18 and 20 consider what those barriers are, and further on there is a chapter with possible ways to overcome them.

ADAM FLETCHER

WAYS TO ACKNOWLEDGE STUDENTS

There are successful and unsuccessful ways to acknowledge Meaningful Student Involvement. Following are some tips I have compiled from many discussions with students and adults in schools on how to publicly acknowledge student involvement.

Typically Unsuccessful Ways to Acknowledge Students

- Basing acknowledgement on what adults value rather than what students value.
- Assuming certain types of acknowledgement are good for everyone without regard for individuality.
- Inconsistently administering acknowledgement among students.
- Holding external events with no connection to the school or individual student.
- Assuming that a group's mission is sufficient justification to become involved with no recognition or celebration of student work.
- Offering excessive recognition and celebration that seems like overkill, or even tokenism.

Typically Successful Strategies to Acknowledge Students

- Basing acknowledgement or appreciating students as individuals by addressing individual needs.
- Assigning responsibility according to proven ability in individual jobs or tasks.
- Recognizing longevity and special contributions on a frequent basis.
- Acknowledging teams of students or the entire group.

Table 20. Acknowledging Students. See "Figure 16: Ways to Acknowledge Meaningful Student Involvement" for more.

Chapter 63. Welcoming The Future, Today

The one thing that all of these approaches and considerations have in common is that rather than waiting for the future to arrive in its own time, they actively embracing the future, today. Typical approaches of talking about college, careers, and the workplace can be anathema for students of all ages. Whether due to the developmental irrelevance of time, socioeconomic factors, or conditioned apathy, many students view The Future with apparent indifference, seemingly finding it irrelevant to their present. The dilemmas with this reality are myriad, primarily because today schools are inherently future-oriented. The essential challenge seems to be, "How can The Future be materially relevant for people for whom The Future is developmentally irrelevant?"

As adults, we impose solutions to this challenge according to our own perspectives: Technology integration, project-based learning, service learning and all of the strategies listed in this chapter all have their own choruses of educators and advocates booming about their relevance in future-teaching. STEM-centric educators pull for their focuses as being the most significant for students. Some educators still believe testing and other forms of standardization are the only way to teach The Future. However, as we know from the continuous pendulum swing of educational trends, each of these do little to jostle the seeming indifference of students toward The Future.

Repeatedly I have heard students describe how they arrive to an obtuse, confusing notion of what the purpose of schools is every time they enter the building. Rather than address their confusion, well-meaning adults routinely employ the means of schooling without identifying the ends; worst still, teachers, administrators, and political leaders seem to mix the means and the ends. Students receive testing and curriculum, classroom management and extracurricular activities without ever exploring why these things should matter to them.

Rather than impose meaning on students, adults in schools make meaning with students. Research in developmental psychology has shown us clearly that young people of all ages have the capacity to develop sophisticated understandings of the educational undertakings they participate in. Unfortunately, policy and practice in schools today have not kept up with that research.

One of the biggest lessons I have learned about teaching students about The Future is the key to defining why careers, college, and the workplace should matter to students: because students themselves decide it does. Letting learners name their motivation every single time they join a class, do a project, or complete a test and determine how their learning styles need to be met, which teachers can help them learn most effectively, helps them strengthen their conception and understanding of The Future. A growing number of educators are working to embrace this challenge, and in doing this, schools are building meaning into learning and instilling a lifelong love of education into every student.

This is welcoming The Future, today, and it is what learners, educators and other adults can discover through Meaningful Student Involvement.

Chapter 64. Building Ownership

When it comes to ensuring the successful adoption, implementation and sustainability of Meaningful Student Involvement in classrooms, throughout schools and across education systems, it is vital to intentionally build ownership. The Consulting Pupils about Teaching and Learning project in the United Kingdom identified some principles focused on student voice and professional development. (Rudduck, Arnot, Fielding, McIntyre, & et al, 2003) I have adapted those here to focus on building systemic ownership for Meaningful Student Involvement.

In a project reflecting the frameworks of Meaningful Student Involvement, a 12th grade student in California affirmed this saying,

> "Now I'm very confident in myself. I know that I can make changes. Sometimes I used to think that our lives were kind of pointless. And now, it's like, you can make real changes. Now it's the school, and maybe in my career and my adult life I could actually do something, with a lot of determination and a lot of will." (Savrock, 2014)

Building Ownership With Students

Students should actively see Meaningful Student Involvement happening, whether or not they are directly involved. That means Student/Adult Partnerships should modeled, and positive behavior should be demonstrated specifically by adults that demonstrates openness to learning, teaching and leading education with students as partners. Learning about learning, learning about the education system, learning about student voice, learning about Meaningful Student Involvement, and learning about school transformation is vital for building student authority, and authority builds ownership (McCombs & Whisler, 1997). Students should receive classroom credit for participating as partners with adults throughout the education system. They should be encouraged to organize events where students can interface authentically with educators, whether they are trainings, student-adult forums, webchats, or other activities. Students should have opportunities to constantly evaluate the activities they participate in, and to see their evaluations reflected in practice. Building ownership with students should be viewed as a dynamic, responsive process that is embedded throughout all parts of schools.

Building Ownership Among Adults

The first way to build ownership in Meaningful Student Involvement is to focus on adults throughout the education system. Reassure teachers, building administrators, district leaders, school board members and others that engaging students as partners both legitimate and desirable. Build up support among adults by presenting evidence of the positive outcomes of Meaningful Student Involvement shared throughout this book. Some are clearly stated in Table 12 of this book. There should be ways that adults can watch other adults in similar roles as they engage in Student/Adult Partnerships. These "job-a-likes" should focus specifically on Meaningful Student Involvement. Adults should also have plenty of opportunities to learn about innovation and success, and safe spaces to explore barriers, challenges and apparent failures. Adults should also receive a variety of presentations focused on the real data from their location within education that demonstrates the ongoing value and sustainability of Meaningful Student Involvement. Intentionally foster reflective practice among educators through circles and other debriefing opportunities built into the day. Also, providing professional development opportunities focused on practically infusing Student/Adult Partnerships throughout every position across the education system. The imperative behind building ownership among adults is readily apparent to anyone who understands the education system; those who do not can learn it quickly by taking action.

Building Ownership Throughout Schools

Moving into the general school population, it is important to be sensitive to the anxiety experienced by students and adults who have never considered student voice, let alone Student/Adult Partnerships and Meaningful Student Involvement. It is important to encourage and support champions of Meaningful Student Involvement by providing incentives, training and professional development, and the resources needed to succeed. School leaders should work to ensure that education policies and initiatives are in harmony with the aims of Meaningful Student Involvement elaborated in Table 11 of this book. Student/Adult Partnerships should happen through all kinds of ways in all sorts of locations so that everyone in the education system has opportunities to become meaningfully involved. Individual classrooms should link with other classrooms that practice Meaningful Student Involvement. Schools, districts and state education agencies should do the same. Fostering schoolwide ownership for Meaningful Student Involvement is essential for transformation beyond simply placating and saturating schools. Instead, it is about infusing deep values change, cultural evolution and new group norms in every avenue possible. (Bragg & Fielding, 2003)

ESSENTIAL QUESTIONS FOR MEANINGFUL STUDENT INVOLVEMENT

Why will students be meaningfully involved?
- Have students identified if they want to be meaningfully involved? If so, why do students want to be meaningfully involved? If not, why not?
- Have adults identified why they want to meaningfully involve students? If so, why do adults want students to be meaningfully involved? If not, why not?
- Is Meaningful Student Involvement seen as a learning tool?

Who will be meaningfully involved?
- Is the activity for traditionally or nontraditionally involved students? If it is for nontraditionally involved students, how will their involvement be ensured? How will it be sustained?
- Is there equal representation from across the school/class/group of students targeted?

What will students be meaningfully involved in?
- Have clear goals or a distinct purpose been identified for students to be meaningfully involved in?
- Are there parameters for students, do they have complete autonomy, or are the roles for students clearly defined ahead of their involvement?
- Is there a distinct plan for educating, reflecting and assessing student involvement?

When will students be meaningfully involved?
- Is the activity in-class, during class time, during the school day, directly after school, in the evening, on the weekends, or during a break?
- What accommodations have been made in order to acknowledge the specific nuances of student schedules, i.e. homework, transportation, lost seat time, etc.?
- How often will meaningful involvement occur within the student's educational career? During one day? Throughout a week? In a quarter or semester? Throughout one school year? Beyond?

Table 21. Essential Questions II. For Essential Questions I, see Table 4.

Part VIII. Teaching Students about School

Chapter 65. Introduction

Students have a right and need to understand the complex and complete structure of the education system they are in. Starting from the youngest ages, teach all learners about learning as a process and an outcome. As they go through school, students should experience a transparent system that shows them who, what, when, where, how and why throughout the process. Everything starting with the classroom curriculum can only ever be a hollow framework devoid of meaning if students do not understand what they are involved in (Booker & MacDonald, 1999). By some point in their school experience, every student should know their primary learning style and optimal learning environment. In order to experience their meaningfulness, students need to learn the policies and assumptions behind the school rules that are drilled into them.

Previously, this handbook showed how to approach teaching students about schools. Beginning with examining the purpose of learning, it expands on a variety of perspectives until it explores how and what grade levels should examine. It then examines different areas students and adults can learn about through Meaningful Student Involvement.

Chapter 66. The Purpose of Learning

After 13 years of school, many students graduate despite being functionally illiterate about learning and the system of education they participate in. Teachers and schools simply do not teach them about schooling. What is the purpose of not knowing the purpose?

Instead, adults generally let students figure it out for themselves. We allow students to come to their own unexamined, under-facilitated and sometimes weakly informed opinions about learning and schooling. This can lead from students who are too anxious to leave school to voters who are not enthusiastic to support public education.

Before embarking on any project focused on Meaningful Student Involvement, it is essential to have a basic understanding of the focus of action, whether an individual classroom, and entire schools, or the entirety of the education system. The Meaningful Student Involvement Learning Cycle shared earlier explores the basic areas all participants should understand.

Students have been accountable to adults throughout education since schools were originally formed. As schools inevitably go the route technology is leading society, they will have to become more transparent in order to ensure ongoing support from the public. In that transparency, everyone throughout society will feel more accountability from schools. To ensure that accountability is best utilized, schools should make every position in schools and throughout education accountable to students directly, right now. If students learn this mutual responsibility while they are in school, they will be better supporters and advocates when they are out of school.

Upon graduation, every student should be able to expand on the nature of their own learning and the purpose of schools from their own perspectives, and describe a course of lifelong learning they intend to pursue. Everyone within the education system, no matter what role they play, needs to be literate about schooling if they want to change schools. Without this understanding, student involvement cannot be meaningful and schools will not be truly transformed. We must teach students about school.

Chapter 67. Examining Our Own Understanding

How much do you know about school? About the education system? Do you know who makes decisions, why they make them, who benefits and who struggles because of them? Do you understand why schools operate the way they do? Have you kept abreast of the school improvement efforts currently underway in your school, district and state?

Acknowledging the limits of our own knowledge—and being honest with students—can establish a more level playing field that nurture Student/Adult Partnerships. Adults in schools aren't used to telling students when they do not know something. This is especially true when it comes to the hallowed institutions we work for. Some claim the education system is obfuscated intentionally, while others point at all the opportunities there exists for involvement. However, rarely is this pointed out to every student.

Transparency with every student allows adults to experience Meaningful Student Involvement beyond the limits of our experiences. Some adults actually challenge students to learn beyond what adults know by exploring the underpinnings and inner-functions of the education system. By becoming intimately aware of what they know and what they do not, adults can ensure students reach past their expectations.

Students do not inherently know how to be meaningfully involved in their schools. Likewise, most educators struggle to figure out how to meaningfully involve students. While engaging students as partners is not a new concept, it has never been a widespread phenomenon in public schools. All parties involved—from students to teachers, janitors to counselors, administrators to elected officials—can stand to benefit by learning about this concept.

Meaningful Student Involvement requires focused action that allows all participants to learn the potential of their individual and collective roles. For students, developmentally appropriate learning is needed to increase their capacity for empowered participation. For teachers, administrators and school staff, learning is focused on developing the school system's ability to involve students as well as individual teachers' ability to meaningfully involve students in different kinds of classroom learning opportunities. Providing constructivist approaches to professional development for educators and other adults who work in the education system also ensures the sustainability of engaging students as partners.

Building on Flutter and Rudduck's initial portrayal of student voice affecting the architecture of school reform (2006), I referred to activities that fully embody Meaningful Student Involvement as the "architecture for ownership." (Fletcher, 2008) Strong learning is both the foundation and the roof of the building. Without intentional learning opportunities designed to increase their capacity as partners, students who are involved are often seen by adults as, at best, under-informed, naive posers, and at worst a misrepresentation of themselves and their peers. Following the analogy, without a roof over their heads they cannot experience the safe and supportive learning environments schools are meant to be. Christensen (1997) also offered a strong argument for viewing these efforts through the lenses of architecture. He suggested that guiding ideas were the foundational element of all practices in this area. In his model, attitudes and skills were secondary elements, capped by a responsive infrastructure that allowed change to happen.

Along with strong learning, other elemental components of the architecture of ownership are high and appropriate levels of student authority; opportunities for the entire student body to become involved throughout the school; interrelated strategies of involvement and school improvement; sustainable structures that nurture and support involvement, and; personal commitment by both adults and students. This architecture supports the entire structure of schooling. Just like building houses, no one builder works alone: throughout schools, students who are meaningfully involved partner with adults, including teachers, administrators, counselors and support staff.

---

* Much of this chapter was originally published as Fletcher, A. (2008) "The architecture of ownership," *Educational Leadership.* 66.3.

Chapter 68. Start to Finish, and All Points In-Between

By focusing classrooms on Meaningful Student Involvement from the beginning of students' experiences in schools, educators can fully engage students as partners. This can happen by teaching every student about their predominant learning style when they're young. At a young age, students can also learn about the process of education and the overall system of schooling. In this way, learners can at least have a common understanding of the individual and collective experiences they share.

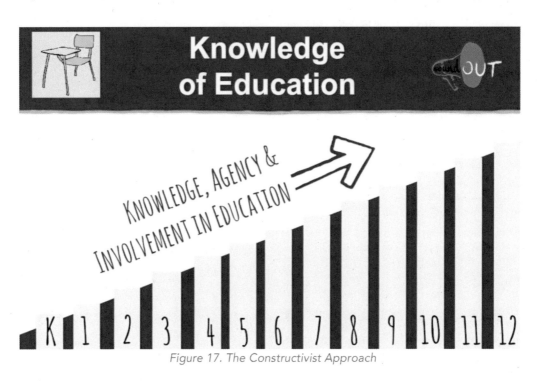

Figure 17. The Constructivist Approach

Beginning in kindergarten and extending through all grade levels until graduation, students can and should learn about schooling, learning and the education system itself in a constructivist approach, as illustrated in Figure 17. Every student begins school with an assumption set into their minds at home or from the ecology around them. That ecology includes all the parts of their lives and especially their understandings of school, and includes their family environment, their physical surroundings, their social lives, and their cultural heritage. (Fletcher, 2014) Educators and other adults can use these understandings as places to teach from by educating young students about the form, function and styles of teaching, learning and leadership throughout schools starting in the youngest grades.

From kindergarten onwards, it because vital for educators to build upon succeeding understandings held by each student. Assessing each students' range of understanding regarding schools and building upon those differences can help solidify a classroom's identity, build teamwork among classes and launch successful and vibrant Student/Adult Partnerships.

The necessity of doing this with all students, rather than an elite group, is important to comprehend. Every student should have functioning, essential opportunities to learn about learning, learning about teaching, learning about leadership and learn about schools. Only through these understandings can we elevate the overall function of schools beyond producing consumers and towards re-establishing democracy in every successive generation. That is the goal of Meaningful Student Involvement.

Validate Existing Knowledge

It is important for students to acknowledge what they already know about schools, and for educators to validate that understanding—remembering that validation from the Cycle of Engagement examined earlier in this book. Similarly to adults, students also come to school with political ideas about education. (Freire, 1970) Once students share their ideas, a facilitator can introduce the Descartes' notion of "degrees of possibility," (Bonnen & Flage, 2002) which essentially contextualizes student understanding of schools into the larger framework of learning and the education system as well. This can happen by showing students the degrees of knowledge about schools they currently have, whether ten, twenty, sixty percent or any other number, and then showing that the rest of the education circle has 360 degrees in it. If a student group understands they know about twenty-five percent of the education system, they have 335 more degrees of knowledge to understand. Helping students understand that can foster academic humility and curiosity, as the world of learning, teaching and leadership in schools grows larger and larger.

These can be both explicit and implicit, obvious and subverted. It is important to help students acknowledge their political knowledge in order to validate that it exists and build upon it accordingly. Students will continue to check what they learn against their political understandings whether or not educators acknowledge their beliefs. Meaningful Student Involvement surfaces that reality, and challenges educators to further their own understanding and those of students themselves with students as partners.

Chapter 69. Expand Understanding of Education

Expanding students' understanding of learning, teaching and leading throughout the education system is essential for authorizing Student/Adult Partnerships. Cook-Sather has explored this in-depth, starting with her important article entitled, "Authorizing Students' Perspectives: Toward trust, dialogue, and change in education". In it she wrote,

> "At the root of the terms that underlie the following discussion – authorize, authority, author and authoritative - is power: The ability to take one's place in whatever discourse is essential to action and the right to have one's part matter." (Cook-Sather, 2002)

Working with students requires engaging those terms in action. As explored in Part Three, the Cycle of Engagement hinges on authorization. A vital component is this understanding that power comes from increased ability, and increased ability comes from expanded understanding.

There are many topics that can increase students' knowledge of the purpose, function, process and outcomes of education. Teaching students about the education system requires basic knowledge about the different components of learning, teaching and leadership throughout schools. Following are some areas where students can expand understanding.

Expanding Understanding of Curriculum and Instruction

Whether it is the lessons taught in classes, the specific course of learning students follow, or the entire program of learning and teaching throughout a student's educational career, understanding curriculum is in the middle of Meaningful Student Involvement. Students should understand what it is, what it does, why it is used and who it serves. (Ngussa & Makewa, 2014) Students should have a working knowledge of the parts of a curriculum, including the learning materials, teaching methods and educational environment where the curriculum is delivered.

Examining single topic approaches to learning, integrated learning, blended learning and flipped classrooms are all keys to understanding curriculum. Students should learn the difference between moving between classrooms for different subjects, multi-age classrooms and looping grades. An exploration of organized and planned learning is key to students learning about curriculum, as well as recognizing the difference between classes and extracurricular activities like sports, clubs and student government.

Instruction focuses on teachers facilitating opportunities for students to build knowledge through problem solving. Students gather, interpret and relate that knowledge according to what they already know. Because of this process, teaching focuses on organizing, structuring and using knowledge in order to most effectively foster student learning. This happens through curriculum

Finally, students should understand the difference between the process of learning and the outcomes of teaching. The process of learning can involve all of the different elements listed in this section on curriculum so far. However, the outcomes of teaching are explored below in the section on assessment.

Expanding Understanding of Leadership

School leadership focuses on every aspect of education, from school culture to system structure, from building culture to individual attitudes. The rigid structures of hierarchy throughout education are beginning to relax as more schools see school leadership less as a managerial task and more as a community-building approach. Increasingly, principals are guide schoolwide collaboration, considering communitywide data focused on improving learning and teaching for all students. Teacher leaders facilitate connections between their peers in order to promote more effective curricula and teaching methods. The roles of student leadership is transforming, too. (Kaba, 2000; Joselowsky, 2007; Brasof, 2011 & 2015)

Working together across different perspectives, attitudes, cultures, beliefs, ideologies and outcomes, school leaders on all levels strive to do several things, including support the culture of schools, ensure school safety, plan with data, align curriculum, improve instruction, manage resources, engage communities, and closing the achievement gap among students. (Kipp, Quinn, Lancaster, et al, 2014) School leadership can also work on an informal level by building conscious and unconscious efforts to grow, change, transform and reflect on schools and the education system. As partners in school leadership, students can be meaningfully involved throughout the process.

Rather than just placing students into traditional student leadership roles, Student/Adult Partnerships recognize roles for students as key stakeholders throughout the education system. Table 15 in this book showed what these roles can look like. Acknowledging the increased ownership and ability they have through technology and other tools, Meaningful Student Involvement provides schools with opportunities to engage students in substantive ways that promote real leadership for them as individuals, and as student bodies.

Participants in the Washington Association of Student Leaders (WASL)[35] have been partnering with adult school leaders, including principals and superintendents, for more than 50 years. The Washington State Legislature mandated in 1951 that students be in control of specific funds to promote student leadership in schools in schools across the state. WASL has provided training and programs for schools to use this funding effectively for more than 20 years. The impact of their activities has led to inclusion in a new process devised to improve school leadership across the state, and more. (Kipp, Quinn, Lancaster, & et al, 2014; Fortin, 2014)

Students should understand different levels of leadership throughout the education system. Whether they are examining the role of the federal, state, or local government, or the roles of advocates and education boosters, students have been the absent partners throughout the entirety of the education reform movement. With a grasp on classroom management, school climate, school boards and more, students can truly become meaningfully involved.

Expanding Understanding of Building Design

School design covers virtually every part of education, from policy-making through construction, from curriculum planning to public relationships. The people involved, the resources used, the finances included, and the outcomes expected can all be part of the design of education. The ways that different components throughout the education system are designed are as varied as the components themselves though; having students meaningfully involved in them requires learning about the diversity throughout them. (Milne, 2006; Beattie, 2012)

The physical plant of schools must be designed, from siting the school building to determining hallway widths to identifying the number and styles of seating throughout the rooms and so forth. In a similar way, curriculum must be designed to meet the goals it has in mind, too. For every part of the design of schools there are socio-economic and political undertones, sometimes talked about but often not. Students need to have basic understanding each part of a design process in order to be meaningfully involved in it.

Formal school improvement as mandated by federal and state/provincial laws varies across the United States and Canada. Oftentimes, the design element of school improvement is grounded in data collection, agragation and dissemination. Through Meaningful Student Involvement, students can serve several roles in this planning and design process. They can be sources of data, idea generators, data gatherers, solution confirmers and agents of change who implement action. (Kushman & Shanessey, 1997)

In 2010, students in a STEM (Science, Technology, Engineering, Math) program at Omaha North High School in Nebraska[36] led a design process focused on a new building for their studies. The students created detailed plans based off charettes with their peers and advised by experts, and presented the plans to the district school board. However, faced with a low budget, the district could not afford to construct the building the students designed. Working with adult school leaders, the students presented their designs more than a dozen times, until a wealthy benefactor who was inspired by their commitment and enthusiasm stepped forward to provide significant funding for the project. (Sherwood Foundation, 2014) Today, the same school is considering building a student-designed football stadium in the school's inner city neighborhood. (Duffy, 2014)

The breadth of school design is a key to understanding the education system.

Expanding Understanding of Assessment

Students using pre-assessments by creating their own self-assessing rubric and self-assessing their performance can be very meaningful. However, infused with the characteristics of Meaningful Student Involvement presented earlier in this book, students experiences can be further enhanced by engaging them in teacher assessments, and in student-led, student-focused learning conferences where they can compare their performance to other students and set future goals. According to Berger (Berger, et al., 2014),

"Student-engaged assessment changes the primary role of assessment from evaluating and ranking students to motivating them to learn. It builds the independence, critical thinking skills, perseverance, and self-reflective understanding students need for college and careers that is required by the Common Core State Standards."

When students are engaged as partners in school assessment, they can cover any element of teaching, learning and leadership. Dovetailing with curriculum and instruction, assessment focuses on students' abilities to organize, structure and use knowledge in order to solve problems. According to Grant Wiggins, "Assessment should be deliberately designed to improve and educate student performance, not merely audit as most school tests currently do." (George Lucas Educational Foundation, 2008) Meaningful Student Involvement supports this approach by positioning students as partners in assessment through both student-led assessments of themselves and of their peers.

Student self-assessment has been shown to raise student achievement significantly. Learning happens when students "confidently set goals that are moderately challenging but realistic, and then exert the effort, energy and resources needed to accomplish those goals." Explicitly teaching students how to assess themselves not only promotes student self-confidence, but also builds and sustains learning across a variety of settings, backgrounds and goals. (Ontario Literacy and Numeracy Secretariat, 2007)

Understanding the purpose of assessment, the ways it happens and the outcomes from assessment are important to meaningfully involving students. (Harvard Family Research Project, 2002) Students learn how to assess themselves, their peers and their experiences in schools by asking key questions about education: Where are we now? Where are schools trying to go? What do we need to get there? How will we know if we have accomplished what schools are out to do? More essential questions are included in Tables 4 and 21.

Berger reports that the case of learning about the Civil War, student-led assessment would go beyond creating an essay only for a teacher to review. Instead, they would create a learning demonstration product for an authentic audience. For instance, a brochure could be made public for a wider group of readers. The audience may simply be other students, teachers, parents, or community members, but Berger states that students are motivated by moving beyond just teachers. (Berger, et al., 2014)

Even if student assessments are not required in schools or cannot be used for grading purposes, it is important to devote class time to doing them. They have been shown to increase student achievement and improve student behavior, as well as increase student engagement and student motivation.

Expanding Understanding of Culture

Meaningful Student Involvement can teach students that they can advocate, nurture and sustain a school culture that promotes all students, builds Student/Adult Partnerships and infuses the frameworks throughout the education system.(Wright S. , 2013; Alvermann & Eakle, 2007) Students should be able to identify, critique and share the shared and clear mission of their school's culture. Student/Adult Partnerships can create the project to do this, including surveying teachers, parents and other students. They can then collaborate to develop a plan for designating time and resources, and facilitating professional development and student training to build capacity. Data points taken from the research done earlier can help quantify the current school culture and areas for improvement. Students can learn about school culture by talking with their peers and adults about their school's strengths and weaknesses, as well as barriers to improving the culture. They can also learn with adults how to find assistance to break down barriers and address the weaknesses, especially as illustrated in Figures 18 and 20.

School culture can mean many things, including opinions, ideas, attitudes, feelings and actions that conspire among students, between students and adults, and among adults. (Kipp, Quinn, Lancaster, & et al, 2014) The relationships between people matter, whether they are traditional perspectives of students, as described in the frameworks of Meaningful Student Involvement, or otherwise. Actions that support a vision for school culture vary can focus on communication, team-building and community building, strategic problem-solving and shared leadership. I have labeled these as convenient student voice. Actions that weaken or act as a barrier to school culture can include bullying, cheating, abusive student-adult relationships, and smothering student free speech. I have referred to these as inconvenient student voice. (Fletcher, 2012)

One of the largely missing elements in many discussions about school culture is student voice. Student voice, which was introduced early in this book as, "any expression of any learner, anywhere, anytime related to education." (Fletcher, 2014) This means that what a student says counts as student voice; what a student does is student voice, and; the meanings behind what students say and do are student voice. From this perspective, student voice is clearly the main driver behind school culture. Meaningful Student Involvement embraces this reality by melding together student voice, responsibility and interdependence, and fostering Student/Adult Partnerships throughout the education system.

Expanding Understanding of Student Support

Student support is almost any service for students outside the curriculum and instruction in schools. It can include a range of positions for adults in schools, such as counselors, librarians, school nurses, drug and alcohol counselors, school counselors, school social workers, school psychologists, and other qualified professional personnel, as well as others in similar roles. Many of these roles can include responsibilities such as student assessment, diagnosis, counseling, educational, therapeutic activities, and other necessary services as part of a comprehensive program to meet student needs.

They might lead activities such as individualized counseling, academic information and afterschool programs. Student support services may also include post-high school career and college options; exposure to cultural events; mentoring programs; and services related to emergency family care for homeless and foster students. Focused on the whole student, their activities fall into the categories of prevention, intervention, transition and follow-up services for students and their families.

Student support services may also include any academic activities outside the regular classroom, especially for students who are experiencing challenges that create barriers to learning. This focuses on academic tutoring in reading, writing, study skills, mathematics, science, and other subjects; and education or counseling services designed to improve financial and economic literacy. In addition, student support services might provide in-service training, parent education, community collaboration and carry out student service program management.

The New York City Student Voice Collaborative (SVC) program is a school district effort to reach high school students across the city and generate a wave of student-led school improvement. SVC brings together public high school students to conduct comprehensive studies of their schools, identify relevant challenges, and implement student-led school improvement programs in partnership with staff and students. SVC meetings are bi-weekly in the fall and weekly in the spring, with approximately 30 sessions for the school year. The group consists of students of all grades (9-12) and all levels of prior leadership experience. SVC members are eligible to earn high school credit for conducting field work – meeting weekly with their school partner and liaison outside of class time to develop a student-led school improvement project – in addition to attending sessions. Each participating school is represented by two students and a staff liaison who provides students with weekly support and guidance. All SVC participants are required to serve on a school-based student leadership group. Members begin their work each year in collaboration with student allies both inside and outside of their schools. (Children First Network 102, 2011)

The work of the SVC students was hosted by the Student Support Services section of the New York City Department of Education. Many educators and school leaders see programs focused on student voice and Meaningful Student Involvement as being well-situated in that area.

Expanding Understanding of Governance

Any formal rules, regulations, provisions and control in education happens through school governance. The many levels of governance can be confusing for adults and students similarly. However, it is important to consider the depth of governance and the potential for Meaningful Student Involvement throughout. (Flutter & Rudduck, 2006; Fielding, 2001)

Student/Adult Partnerships can and should happen at every level of governance, starting from the layer of student-led governments. At that level, students should have substantial opportunities to direct significant activities and partner with adults on larger decision-making. Building level governance can include a variety of policies affecting students, parents and the neighboring communities. District governance, including grant administration and assessment, can also focus on student support, curriculum, personnel and building design. The district governance is administered by professional staff, but led by publicly elected school board members who determine policies, enact legislation and enforce compliance of district programs.

On the state and provincial levels, school governance happens through a government agency that determines how districts and local buildings comply with federal and state/provincial rules. Those rules are made by a school board, a state school leader or provincial minister of education, and by the state legislature or provincial parliament. The federal government also makes rules, enforces compliance and manages funds sent to states and districts. They are the most authoritative governing force in schools, regulating the basics of how schools should operate and educate.

Each of these levels of governance should engage students as partners who constantly assess, improve, maintain, and regulate the institutions within schools. Meaningful Student Involvement moves students from simply informing school policy with student voice. Instead, it infuses active Student/Adult Partnerships with the power and purpose they need to affect learning, teaching and leadership for all students in every school, everywhere, all of the time.

Across the United States today there are two states, California and Maryland, that currently engage students as full members on state school boards. There are 18 states that do not allow students to actually serve on district or state school boards in any form. The remaining states vary in the amount of authority and impact they allow students to have. Some of these districts wrestle with some key questions, including:

- What are the rights of student school board members?
- Which decisions should students be allowed to participate in and which should they be excluded from?
- How can school boards secure effective student board members?
- Who from local schools is best positioned to be a student board member?
- Why should student board members reflect anyone other than high-performing, high-achieving students?
- When other members are elected for two- or four-year terms, why should students serve any different terms?

For districts and states that are interested in expanding board membership to include students, consideration must be given to the issues of different legal considerations, practical implementation, resources needed, and other areas. (Fletcher, 2014)

Expanding Understanding of School/Community Partnerships

When education works to bring nonprofits, faith communities, businesses, local government agencies or community groups into schools in substantive ways, they are working to foster community/school partnerships. These are deliberate efforts to bring together a variety of formal and informal organizations and institutions from a school's surrounding community into schools or the district as a whole. Meaningful Student Involvement can serve as a bridge that spans the gap between schools and communities.

School/community partnerships can infuse learning environments with a wealth of resources, including experienced adults ready to be partners with students to improve learning. These adults can become mentors, tutors, guides, friends and teachers to students, helping illustrate directly how the community cares about students. They can also bring learning materials such as tablet computers and CAD programs; musical equipment and music education supplies; and other physical resources. In turn, Meaningful Student Involvement in school/community partnerships can lead to students teaching adults, serving as mentors to business leaders, building bridges between local nonprofits and devising student-led plans for community betterment.

There are many ways to foster these partnerships. Teaching approaches such as service learning, placed-based learning and apprenticeships can tie students together in positive, empowering relationships that benefit learning, teaching and leadership throughout the surrounding community. Students can teach adults from the community all sorts of powerful lessons, while adults benefit from having substantive solutions to real community problems.

Reports are increasingly suggesting that Meaningful Student Involvement is essential for effective school/community partnerships. A range of students need to be engaged for this to be effective, especially traditionally disengaged students. Specific efforts should be made to reach out to these students, and in turn to the neighborhoods and communities they are from and identify with. In addition to community presentations, Meaningful Student Involvement coordinators can work with academic counselor to identify about students who are good candidates and the areas they are from or identify with. This should especially include students and communities whose viewpoints, backgrounds and academic experiences can balance those students who are already engaged. Following up with students and community partners is vital to encourage them to participate and sustain their partnerships. (Benard & Burgoa, 2010; Hands, 2009)

The Seattle Youth Media Camp was a partnership between Seattle Public Schools and Service Learning Seattle, along with a local company called Social Moguls and myself. Held in a historically low-achieving school called Cleveland High School, the camp was included African American, Asian American and white students. Funded by the Corporation for National and Community Service, the Youth Media Camp was a meeting of minds where a convergence of the agendas of service learning, media literacy, STEM (Science, Technology, Engineering, Math), CTE (Career and Technical Education), and film making only happened through community/school partnerships. Students learned from a variety of community partners, including a former Black Panthers leader, a community TV news anchor, a local nonprofit media organization, and others. In turn, they created a short film from the ground up, including conception, acting, directing, supporting, gaffing, laughing, critiquing, scoring, editing, and presenting. Their powerful actions created a strong footing for ongoing change and transformation at their school and throughout the community for years to come. (Fletcher, 2012)

Expanding Understanding of Parent Involvement

When parents want to make a difference in the experience of their children in schools, or when schools want to engage parents that way, parent involvement is the key for success. Parents commit to become active partners with the school and their students. This can happen in many ways. Historically, parents have been advocates for schools, calling for better funding, increased opportunities, different classwork, or other steps towards improvement. Today, schools frequently call for parent volunteers in classrooms and special activities. Importantly, parents are becoming involved in school advocacy, meeting with policymakers and elected officials to ensure their students are receiving the education they deserve.

Interests between students and parents obviously intersect. By seeking to enhance parent involvement through Meaningful Student Involvement, schools are acknowledging these connections and enhance outcomes for all stakeholders in education. This can happen in many ways, including co-involved projects, trainings for students and parents together, and positions for students and parents to serve together as appropriate throughout the education system.

An organization in Denver, Colorado, has taken on this challenge in a deep and systematic way for more than two decades. Padres and Jovenes Unidos has been struggling to transform the education system by uniting students and parents together with a variety of initiatives. Borne of the need for better school leadership, today the organization "is a multi-issue organization led by people of color who work together for educational excellence, racial justice for youth, immigrant rights and quality healthcare for all." Jovens Unidos specifically seeks to end the school-to-prison pipeline and fight for immigrant student rights. (Padres and Jovens Unidos, 2014)

Engaging students and parents together to improve schools can build families, strengthen communities and build democracy in ways that are unexpected and enlivening. Meaningful Student Involvement provides important frameworks for imagining, enacting and enhancing efforts towards this goal. Table 18 shows what that can look like.

Summary

Engaging students as partners means ensuring each student has a basic understanding of their personal and collective identities. Teachers can embed this learning across all curricular areas and reinforce it with place-based learning, global education, and more. Students who are partners with adults are made distinctly aware of their skills, abilities, and knowledge, and are increasingly able to apply those understandings throughout their daily experiences of school. Embracing student voice in this way takes a lot of different forms that are examined later in this book.

---

[35] Learn about Washington Association of Student Leaders at awsp.org/studentleadership
[36] Omaha North High School is my alma mater. Learn more at it north.ops.org

Chapter 70. Learning about Outcomes

With standardized testing becoming widespread throughout the 2000s and 2010s an entire generation of students has become accustomed to being assessed in a variety of ways. How many of these students understand why they are being tested though? Meaningful Student Involvement takes task with learning that does not position students as partners in learning, teaching and leadership.

Learning about Building Classrooms

More than ever before, there is room within classrooms for students to lead learning. With flipped classrooms, student-led lessons and student-driven parent-teacher conferences becoming more popular, it is increasingly important to contextualize what is happening for both students and adults, including teachers, parents and others.

Students leading learning is not about students getting to do whatever they want, however, whenever and wherever they want. It is not about spoiling children, making incapable citizens or under-producing workers. However, without context a lot of these activities lose their potential effect on both students and educators.

Meaningful Student Involvement positions these activities as central to building student ownership in education, community and democracy. Given that relevance, all of these activities allow students to build classrooms and co-design education so that its sustained throughout their lives. Experiencing fully realized learning in the youngest grades may be best, since students will take the habits formed throughout their learning careers and well into their adult lives, if not all their days.

When students teach, guide and direct their peers and adults while building classroom learning, they can show educators many things. They actively show the information they know about a topic. It can build students' sense of pride, sense of efficacy and feelings of accomplishment when they participate in building classrooms. If a student teaches their parents or siblings it can strengthen their courage and build their self-esteem in healthy ways.

When planned and implemented in age appropriate ways, Meaningful Student Involvement can allow educators to see specifically what students do and do not know, what they fully understand, and where they have learning gaps. Obviously, students' oral communication and presentations skills can improve, too.

Students can also help build classrooms and other learning environments by participating in what used to be called classroom management, but is increasingly recognized as good facilitation and learning leadership. Engaged as partners in the classroom, students can help build classrooms with everything from keeping the classroom tidy to seating arrangements. Beyond that, students can be engaged in "decision-making... when managing issues pertaining to safety of students and moral issues such as racial and sexual discrimination." (Lewis & Burman, 2008)

At Park Forest Elementary School in State College, Pennsylvania, students experience a great deal of opportunities to build classrooms. Students experience such depth of ownership in building the culture of their school that during a service project for a homeless shelter, they intervened when adults began exercising too much control in the project planning. The students recommended that the group find out exactly what the families at the homeless shelter needed, and then proceeded to survey the shelter. When the group found that the families wanted Easter baskets, the students then focused their efforts on making baskets for the shelter. (Dickinson, 2014) Because of the culture fostered by Meaningful Student Involvement in their school, the students felt such ownership over their experience in the classroom that they called out adults for disrupting that experience.

Learning about Transforming Schools

Rather than being the passive recipients of school transformation, students can be meaningfully involved as partners throughout action. All the roles in learning, teaching and leadership can be co-facilitated with students, while all the outcomes can be measured by student/adult partners working together. Meaningful Student Involvement is a key to learning through transformation.

All students in every school should understand and be actively engaged as partners in the transformation, reform, improvement and other change processes going on around them. They are not the ineffectual, incapable objects of change that many educators and school leaders inadvertently treat them as. Instead, every student of all ages is capable of informing, forming, driving and critiquing school transformation efforts of all kinds. The real question is whether adults want to engage them through Student/Adult Partnerships, which are required for this work, and whether adults are specifically capable of that. For more than 100 years of schooling and more than 30 years of the current education reform movement, students have been written about, targeted, studied, analyzed, debated over, challenged and sought after repeatedly as the subjects of school improvement.

This has not been an easy road to cross. The best reformers, including Kozol (1991), Fullan (1991), Kohn (1993) and Goodlad (1984) have all called for student voice. However, the resounding response has been to simply *listen* to student voice, no matter what it has to say. Spanning as far back as the 1980s to the present, education researchers like Goodlad and others, along with critical pedagogues like McLaren (McLaren, 2003) and Shor (Shor, 1996) began examining the positioning of students in schools, either as passive recipients or practical informants for adult-driven agendas. In the late 1990s, well-meaning education-oriented nonprofit organizations began seeding youth-led programs focused on students' opinions about schools. These students learned community organizing techniques and methods, and after more than 15 years of funding from large and small philanthropic foundations across the United States are still leading organizing campaigns across the country. With the renewal of the Elementary and Secondary Education Act (ESEA) in 2001, state education agencies had a mandate to hire school improvement coaches and experts across the nation. Over the next several years, a few of these individuals led the next wave of student voice activities, including myself. Today, these activities are transitioning again from focusing solely on school improvement towards classroom practice, school leadership and beyond. Meaningful Student Involvement shows how all these disparate activities are related, and moves one step beyond.

Meaningful Student Involvement in school transformation positions students as active co-creators who learn from improving education. It gives educators and school leaders the onus for creating Student/Adult Partnerships they can benefit from in their jobs, as well as students themselves. Everyone can win through Meaningful Student Involvement in ways that student voice initiatives can never aspire to. The fragmented nature of a lot of student voice work neglects the interconnected nature of these efforts; Meaningful Student Involvement weaves this diversity together into intricate tapestries that show the future of schools in a clear, un-enigmatic way.

An example of engaging students as partners in school transformation comes from the Washington State Office of Superintendent of Public Instruction, under the leadership of Greg Williamson. Working with more than 100 high schools across the state, Williamson launched Student2Student to empower students with knowledge about many of the school improvement initiatives affecting them every day. Essentially a peer mentoring program, Student2Student trained 12th grade students in a train-the-trainer model focused on what school improvement is, what specifically happens in their schools, and why students should care about it. Then, these 12th grade students trained incoming 8th and 9th grade students at their high schools and feeder middle schools. The new high school students learned about new graduation requirements and much more. School leaders quickly noticed the amount of awareness and enthusiasm among incoming 9th grade students, and supported the program as it spread further. While they were excellent teachers, participants also provided powerful proof to education decision-makers that engaging students in school improvement is key to transforming learning, teaching and leadership.

Learning about Creating New Knowledge

The final area covered in this book related to teaching students about schools is creating new knowledge. With the proliferation of education media through the Internet over the last decade, stories of students generating powerful learning and teaching among themselves have gone from interesting anomaly to average occurrence. Flipped classrooms and other approaches to student-generated learning experiences are more common than ever, and a loud minority of educators seem genuinely excited about students creating new knowledge.

Early in his writing, Freire (Freire, 1970) explained a new concept called "banking education", in which educators treat students like empty vessels waiting to be filled with the knowledge of the educator and the textbooks they employed in the classroom. Freire railed against this approach, challenging that it was disingenuous, inauthentic and oppressive to students of all stripes. Freire wrote that as an educator, "I am not impartial or objective; not a fixed observer of facts and happenings." (Freire, 1998) Yet, this is what banking education attempted to treat educators as.

Instead, Freire—and many since him—have posited that education needs to be created and recreated for every student in order to reflect the dynamic nature of humans. Freire believed that education should focus on problem-posing; that is, examining a challenge until you can name a problem, and upon naming it going about addressing it. He believed that as humans who are learning we are changing, and because of we are changing our learning should address the world as changing, too. (Freire, 1970) This is reflected excellently in many educators' commitment to creating new and exciting ways to foster student learning in their classrooms today.

It is equally important, however, to situate students as change agents in the larger discourse of society. This is about more than voting and media discourse; its about learning as a democratic right and responsibility. Schools should always aspire to such powerful goals.

Part IX. Barriers, Ethics and Practical Considerations

Chapter 70. Introduction

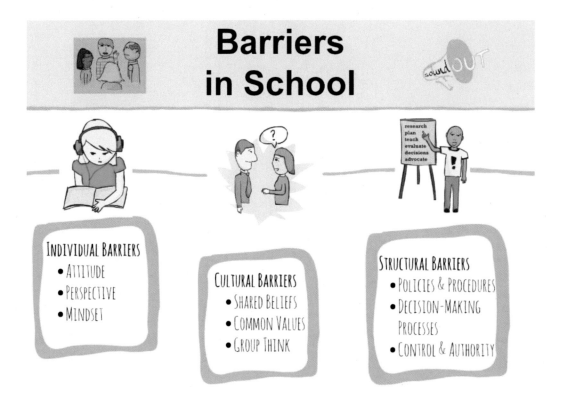

Figure 18. Barriers in School

As far back as the 1970s, people were challenging schools' lack of concern for student involvement. One report focused on student involvement in decision-making said, "Not having students on school boards is like having only foreign citizens representing us in Congress."(Kleeman, 1972) This same sentiment resonates throughout the education system today, as adults are as entrenched as they have ever been in controlling schools. This is a barrier to moving forward.

Many people who work in schools find that there are significant barriers to Meaningful Student Involvement, especially as illustrated in Figure 18. While these barriers can often seem like insurmountable hurdles, it is important to see them as challenges that encourage students, adults, and schools to grow and flourish in new and exciting ways. Alfie Kohn has identified three types of barriers to student participation in decision-making in schools. (Kohn, 1993) Following, I adapt and explore them.

Chapter 71. Education Structure

Structure in school is any formalized activity within education. There are "4 Ps" in the structure of schools: positions, policies, practices, and process. It may be tempting to neglect the importance of developing structures that embrace student voice, as it may seem daunting or impossible to change those "4 Ps". However, the education system is inherently steeped in process; that is what makes it a tool of democracy. Process is imposed by policies, enforced by practices, and secured by positions. That is why in order to maintain and strengthen democracy and education, Meaningful Student Involvement must be integrated throughout education.

The structure of schools is anything formal within education. The structure of schools includes classes, supplies, curriculum, and activities in the school. The guidelines, rules, and regulations governing schools are part of the structure, as are the times, schedules, homework, lunchtime, and playground time. Cafeteria food, vending machines, and the building environment are part of the structure too.

The formal roles everyone has within the school are structural, including teachers, principals, headmasters or principals, para-educators, aides, secretaries, librarians or media specialists, janitors, school psychologists, student counselors, speech/language pathologists, cafeteria workers, and other school support staff. The formal roles of students in schools are also structural, including the title of student, class president, club leader, honor society member, varsity football captain, student council treasurer, drama club member, school newspaper staff, etc. All of these roles, whether actively involved, passively excluded, or intentionally silenced can actually be barriers to Meaningful Student Involvement, as well. (Bhavnani, 1990)

All extra-curricular activities and assemblies are part of the structure, along with the colors, mascot, and school spirit activities. School funding, including voting-approved levies and education grant money, are structural, as is the administration of the educational system and the local, district, state, and federal laws governing education.

The structure of schools also affects students, aside from the actions of adults in schools. Traditionally, student involvement is an extra-curricular activity that happens before or after school. Activities have focused on athletics or interest-based clubs or have been token opportunities for student decision-making, such as planning dances. Another structural issue has to do with awarding credit and other forms of recognition: Adults generally are not paid to support student involvement, and students are reluctant to spend a lot of time on activities for which they receive little or no credit or money.

Structure as a Barrier and Solutions

The structural barriers in schools that limit Meaningful Student Involvement are no less than every norm, regulation and process that keeps students powerless throughout education, from their individual classrooms to highest political offices in the land. (Giroux, 1981) When asked what prevents them from meaningfully involving students, many adults specifically mention having too many things to do; classroom or school size and layout; a lack of support from the school administration; under-motivated teachers or program staff; and an absence of sustained interest. (Lewis & Burman, 2008) When asked what prevents them from being engaged, many students— specifically students of color and low-income students—suggested that culturally offensive or irrelevant structural practices in schools were to blame. (Nieto, 1994)

One structural barrier may be the hierarchy affecting educators. Despite their enthusiasm for Meaningful Student Involvement, a building principal that denies their request to do an activity in their school can quash any well-intentioned educator. One solution may be to discuss Meaningful Student Involvement with other educators online and identify who is successful at it to share that with a building leader. Another may be to seek information and materials that will encourage Meaningful Student Involvement in your school. A last potential solution may be to develop networks among peers to develop interest and support with other adults. Another challenge may be that there is little encouragement, incentives, or recognition of Meaningful Student Involvement currently existent in the school. A solution may be to develop lesson plans to integrate Meaningful Student Involvement into classes, allowing students to earn credit.

A national study from 2012 found that activities embodying Meaningful Student Involvement could be done successfully by reallocating existing school resources. (Usher & Kober, 2012) This includes teachers as resources; school curricula, assessments, technology, and learning materials; and other essential resources. Another study (Miller, Gross, & Ouijdani, 2012) recommends several potential solutions to structure as a barrier, which are adapted here:

- Encourage school leaders to think about tradeoffs. When schools begin investing heavily financially in Meaningful Student Involvement, they should reduce spending in non-meaningful activities to keep school budgets in balance.
- Fund all schools in the district equitably, and then enforce a hard budget constraint.
- Provide schools with resource flexibility that allows them to invest in their model as they see fit, while making the necessary cuts to balance their budgets.
- Teach principals how to successfully attract resources from the community and give positive recognition to principals who are successful at doing so.

Chapter 72. School Culture

Culture is a less concrete, more inherent factor to engaging student voice throughout education. Many researchers say the culture of a school is its personality: Just like individual people, schools can be kind and accepting, rude and disrespectful, wise and guiding, and any other set of characteristics. Even more so, schools can be, and usually are, any combination of those characteristics. In this way, culture actually dictates structure; it is also obvious in the attitudes, actions, interactions, and relationships of individuals throughout education. To do this work, educators, administrators and adults throughout the education not only need to open up physical spaces but also the minds of their peers so they cannot only listen to student voice, but embrace the presence and power of Meaningful Student Involvement. (Cook-Sather, 2006; Elias, 2010; Chopra, 2014)

Kohn notes that school culture "may create a climate in which teachers do to children what is done to them." He goes on,

> "Classroom teachers frequently protest that they would love to open up the decision-making process but for the fact that a significant number of decisions are not theirs to give away or even to make themselves." (Kohn, 1993)

Without substantive opportunities to contribute to whole school improvement efforts, teachers may feel stymied in their attempts to promote Meaningful Student Involvement. This is part of the school culture.

School culture is made by individuals in the building, including adults and students. The following chapter addresses each separately.

Part of the culture of schools is reflected in the ways adults relate to students, including how they get students involved. One of the frameworks of Meaningful Student Involvement examined earlier in this book was the Ladder of Student Involvement. Several of the top rungs were detailed earlier to show the highest aspects. However, following are some of the bottom rungs of the Ladder. They are detailed here because they generally reflect school culture and show us exactly how school culture can be a barrier to Meaningful Student Involvement.

Tokenizing Students

School culture might often promote tokenism. As soon as adults determine that students should be involved in something throughout education, whether classrooms, committees or clubs, they may be tokenizing students. Funneling, narrowing, focusing, or otherwise trimming the breadth, depth, or purpose of student involvement inherently poses the risk that student involvement does not genuinely reflect the attitudes, opinions, ideas, actions, knowledge, or beliefs of students. This can happen anytime adults ask students to become involved in specific ways or address a specific topic in education, including bullying, academic achievement, school transformation, or dancing on the roof. Any of this can be qualified as tokenizing students.

Tokenism happens because adults expect students to become involved the ways adults want them to, in the issues adults want them to, with the outcomes adults want. This can displace the authentic concerns, opinions, wisdom, ideas and knowledge students have about education, replacing it with conveniently chosen, adult-guided thinking or actions. It may not respect students for what they think or do, instead insisting that students only become involved in education in ways adults want, and speak or act only on what adults want to hear about.

Decorating With Students

School culture can reflect roles for students as decorations. When adults make choices about schools and then use student surveys, speeches, ideals, and actions to shore up their choices, they are decorating with students. Posing students around adults at speaker's daises, having student panels at education conferences, and putting students in suits to share their thoughts in front of school boards are some of the ways that adults use students as decorations.

This is misuse because it invalidates anything meaningful about student involvement. Instead, it only allows students to be props for adult beliefs, reinforcing the adage that "Children are to be seen and not heard." This old-world thinking could not be more antithetical to Meaningful Student Involvement. Today, students can make their authentic voices known in dozens of ways across through technology and in real time. Adults never had that access when we were young. Yet we still treat them as if they do not. That disjuncture does not serve anyone, and is severely damaging our schools. You can find several pathways to authentic student voice in Table 1 of this book.

Manipulating Students

The last way school culture is a barrier to Meaningful Student Involvement is through manipulation. Adults force students to become involved. Faced with losing academic credit, losing acceptance of their peers, or losing the favor of adults in their lives, learners are sometimes forced by adults to share student voice. That pinching of students' genuine interest in becoming involved is insidious, no matter how well-meaning it is. Making sure that students fit adults' expectations for involvement shows students that the authentic ways they reveal their thoughts, beliefs, ideals, and wisdom aren't the "right" ways to be heard. This can encourage them to change their minds in order to fit the molds presented in order to get the grade or be accepted.

Manipulation is plain wrong. It teaches students that involvement should not happen without direct reward or punishment. It demeans their basic humanity by robbing students of their innate opinions, inherent knowledge, powerful actions, and secure wisdom that as adults we can only benefit from. Instead, it positions them as consumers of schooling, as people who are incapable or undesiring of having their voices heard simply because they have a right and the ability to have their voices heard. Schools have the responsibility of being incubators of democratic society, and manipulating student involvement actively undermines that responsibility while taking away the rights of learners. See Table 22 for some examples of what that can look like.

These are some of the ways culture can be a barrier to Meaningful Student Involvement. However, there is another important factor that can inadvertently or intentionally block meaningfulness.

Chapter 73. Students as Barriers

After years of being treated as less-than-humans, or told, "it's better to be seen and not heard," it's no wonder why students may be reluctant to be meaningfully involved in schools. Kohn notes that there are three primary types of student resistance. The first is simply refusing: "That's your job to decide," students may protest. The second is testing: offering outrageous suggestions or responses to see if the teacher is serious about the invitation to participate. The third is parroting: repeating what adults have said or guessing what this adult probably wants to hear. A fifth-grader asked to suggest a guideline for class conduct may recite, "We should keep our hands and feet to ourselves." Added up together and taken individually, these can be substantial barriers to Meaningful Student Involvement. (Kohn, 1993)

This barrier can happen when students feel that they are being pushed to be involved. Rather than "meeting the challenge," they offer resistance as outlined above, and Meaningful Student Involvement cannot happen. This can be addressed by integrating Meaningful Student Involvement into regular school activities. It gives students the opportunity to experience learning without additional commitment, and can ease a student into a new experience of meaningfulness in their educational experience.

It can also happen when students are highly conditioned to accept adult authority and dominance. There are spoken and unspoken ways of behaving, speaking and interacting among students that are reinforced by the structure and culture of schools. Oftentimes, control, domination, exploitation and subordination ensure students behave the ways other students find acceptable. (Alcoff, 1992)

When students are inhibited by other students or adults who are involved in discussions, it can seem like a barrier to Meaningful Student Involvement. This can be addressed by the facilitators who intentionally create a safe space for an open discussion. This must begin with a frank conversation about stereotypes that adults and students have of each other, and addressing those stereotypes deliberately. Throughout the discussion continue to have check-ins that allow students and adults to share their honest thoughts with one another.

Other ways that students themselves are barriers come through in traditional studies about student leadership in schools and other avenues. One study (Boccia, 1997) found:

- Students are busy and their days and years in school are limited no matter what their age, so time to develop and practice leadership is short.
- Students have no knowledge base about many school issues and have no real training to take leadership roles even if the knowledge were provided.
- Students can be cynical about leadership activities, calling those who are involved "narcs", "brown-nosers", or other derogatory names.

There is truth to these typical challenges; however, as schools continue to evolve and the cultures of both general society and specific schools continue to evolve, all of these can be countered as being outdated. If they apply to a current environment though, it is important to address them.

Chapter 74. Adults as Barriers

People themselves can act as barriers to Meaningful Student Involvement . Personal attitudes, past experiences, and negative perspectives can all serve as roadblocks. Adults do things *for*— not *with*—students. Kohn offers that perspectives of control and a "lack of gumption" may hold many educators back. "Parting with power is not easy, if only because the results are less predictable than in a situation where we have control," Kohn explains (1993). Students also recognize that some educators, attempting to appear to be "empowering," actually offer too little structure in classrooms. Students have also said that adults in schools simply do not want to hear them and actively work to suppress their voices. (Alcoff, 1992)

Ironically, a lot of efforts to engage student voice have undermined student engagement in schools, especially in the school improvement process. As founding researchers in today's student voice movement, Fielding and Rudduck have shared countless lessons related to the phenomenon of adults undermining student voice. They wrote that there are three ways adults disengage student voice in schools [Author's note: bolded words are my addition]:

- **Ignore:** Students do not talk about things adults think are important, and so adults ignore what is said by students;
- **Reframe:** Adults reframe student voice in ways and with words that students themselves think are restrictive, alienating or patronizing;
- **Obfuscate:** Schools rarely if ever do things that reflect what student voices shared, at least in ways that change the quality of student experiences in schools. (Fielding & Rudduck, 2002)

Another study (Boccia, 1997) found that adults in schools:

- **Resist:** Generally resist involving students in professional matters, especially curriculum and policy.
- **Diminish:** See student voice as being a flash-in-the-pan approach to improving schools because students are in a specific school for too limited amounts of time to be invested in something that will not change until after they are gone.
- **Separate:** Want to keep students' lives in schools and out of schools separate, and discourage students from mixing the two areas.

Each of these realities actively disengage students and are a barrier to Meaningful Student Involvement.

Adults can feel threatened when they feel students aren't doing what should be done. Meaningful Student Involvement can allow a great deal of leeway for students to drive their experience of learning and teaching. It might also threaten teachers when they have to hear the unfettered ideas, opinions, knowledge, and experiences of students.

Whenever Meaningful Student Involvement happens either by choice or imposition, adults should learn new roles, language and behaviors. The experience of engaging students as partners in learning throughout education can be a severe break from adults' experiences and expectations of schools. It can help for adults to read about Meaningful Student Involvement and being trained in Student/Adult Partnerships.

Another barrier can occur when adults can assume that they easily understand the attitudes and challenges of students today. They assume their experiences as students are familiar enough because of their similarities in age, race, gender, socio-economic backgrounds, or otherwise (Slee, 1994). This eliminates the ability of students to genuinely relate to adults.

Working with adults who overtly resist Meaningful Student Involvement may be the more important thing advocates can do. Their concerns can be addressed by positioning students to offer workshops for adults on their cultures, heritages, and backgrounds. Students can also create "tip sheets" and other tools for teachers. Other adults can act as allies or critical friends to help prepare and nurture these adults' growth and challenge their resistance. If they have been mandated to become involved because of a school leader's orders, these adults can receive more guidance from their peers rather than their supervisors. If Reeves is right though, "Deep and sustainable change... requires changes in behavior among those who do not welcome the change." (2009)

Ultimately, I have discovered that we can change all the rules we want, but until the hearts and minds of adults leading the system at any level—teachers, cafeteria managers, building principals, district administrators, or boards of education—are changed, policies and rules do not really matter. Adults are the single most enormous barrier to Meaningful Student Involvement.

Most adults within the education system are inherently threatened by the capacity of students to lead their own learning. Ironically, integrating Meaningful Student Involvement throughout the school can lead to some of the best results in transforming adults from barriers to allies. There is no place throughout the education system that students cannot have deep and effective levels of impact that adults cannot have without them. Everything throughout the education system can be better because of Meaningful Student Involvement.

Chapter 75. Arguments Against Meaningful Student Involvement

Many adults throughout education have arguments against Meaningful Student Involvement. Whether they work directly with students every day, like teachers and school support staff, or if they do not interact with students on a regular basis, like building leaders and district staff, many people do not want to see Student/Adult Partnerships in effect. The following arguments are some of the barriers they cite.

- **Age:** Students under 18 years old, or 15, or 12, or 6 years old, are not capable of making decisions for the right reasons, either because of a seeming lack of life experience, underdeveloped mental abilities, or simply because of their age.
- **Ability:** Students are incompetent and because of that they will make decisions for the wrong reasons, such as arguing for more opportunity for play, for less importance placed on grades, for better cafeteria food, etc.
- **Undeserving:** Students must learn to take responsibility before they can begin to have any voice in matters that affect them, let alone guide and direct decisions that affect other students and adults throughout the education system.
- **Disrespect:** If given the opportunity, students would be ornery, rude, mean, contemptuous and otherwise disrespectful towards adults.
- **Maintenance:** Adult power should be maintained, or student behavior will spin out of control and classroom management will be impossible.
- **Integrity:** The professional integrity of educators and school leaders would be compromised by Meaningful Student Involvement because adults know better than students at almost all times in almost all ways.
- **Tradition:** Adults should never, ever be accountable to students because that undermines the relationships young people and adults have outside of schools as well as within.
- **Devaluation:** The education experience will be less effective if students have full agency and operate in complete partnerships with adults throughout the education system.
- **Ruination:** By fostering Student/Adult Partnerships, adults effectively burden students and damage their experience of childhood. The belief is generally that when
- **Innocence:** When students are kept from making substantive decisions about their educational experiences and school leadership, they can maintain their innocence and curiosity.
- **Interpretation:** When student voice is shared with adults, adults must interpret student words, culture and actions by making sense of them because students do not know what they are talking about. Then adults do whatever they want to with student voice, because they are the best judges.
- **Protection:** Students should be protected from making decisions at a young age, whatever their age is.

Some students will repeat these arguments as well as adults do. The following is an experience I had where adult arguments undermined Meaningful Student Involvement in a deep way.

Chapter 76. When Student Voice Backfires

In early 2013, I was talking with some program administrators from a state education agency about Meaningful Student Involvement when one of them brought up doing "fishbowl"-style activities with students and adults. I remembered some hard lessons I had learned about student voice while working a local school in the Pacific Northwest. Following is an account of a time when student voice backfired.

Yammering and going on about how great they felt, the room came to a hush as I began talking. Gathered around me was a group of ten students who were excited about changing their school, and I could not have been happier.

Two days earlier, I had asked the school's principal for a small group of nontraditional student leaders to join me as co-facilitators and data evaluators for a student forum at their school. Working with their small, rural school district's lead school improvement facilitator (SIF), the SIF and I secured the principal and district superintendent's verbal commitments to incorporating student perspectives on what needed to change in their school into their formal school improvement plan. Mandated by the No Child Left Behind Act, data collection routinely captured the opinions of adults throughout the school community, and rarely the students. Our project was focused on them.

This was the eleventh school I had worked with through the SoundOut School Improvement Planning Pilot Project. Partnering with a state education agency, several districts, and a university, with fiscal support from a local foundation, I felt we were ready to address the issues facing incorporating Meaningful Student Involvement in school improvement in a substantive way. Formal school improvement planning is complicated, and is based on various data to frame the challenges faced within individual schools. Once the challenge is identified, it is addressed through action, and changes are monitored. Meaningful Student Involvement infuses Student/Adult Partnerships throughout school improvement planning, and the entirety of the education system in turn.

After working out the kinks in a few schools, I thought I had struck on a relatively easy formula for these Forums. Beginning early in the morning on the first day, I led a teacher's meeting. During this session I talked to the almost every teacher for the middle and high school students I had be working with. I shared my early Frameworks for Meaningful Student Involvement with them, walked them through the process, and took questions. Sharing some initial hesitations, as a group the teachers gave verbal approval for the process ahead.

In the next two hours I facilitated intensive readiness training for the student facilitator/evaluators. Learning about student voice and school improvement, we then reviewed the process ahead. In two days, we had spent 90 minutes with each grade level in their small school leading a SoundOut Student Voice Forum. In each session, we had brief the participants about school improvement, and then ask them to answer four simple questions:

- What do you love about learning?
- What would you change about learning?
- What do you love about your school?
- What would you change about your school?

They answered these in small groups using markers and flip chart paper divided into quadrants. Students were encouraged to be frank, honest, and meaningful in what they wrote. There were just few guidelines presented, including one that came from my early morning session with teachers: Focus on characteristics, not characters. I didn't want to know the teacher's specific names that students were complaining about; I wanted to know what behaviors the teacher had that were worth complaining about. That also went for specific classrooms, topics, and other identifying features- especially in a small school! The sessions weren't intended to threaten or target anyone; instead, they were meant to identify the practical concerns of students.

Gathering up nine hours of facilitated responses, the student facilitator/evaluators and I retreated to a room at noon on day two. Spending two and a half hours leading data aggregation with these students, we discovered a variety of hopes and dreams, frustrations and failures at their school. I encouraged the student facilitator/evaluators to identify the trending data, and from that to develop a quick report-out for their peers. They identified the top five answers to each of the questions for each grade level, and shared the overall topic concerns for the whole school. Remember that every student in grades 7-12 participated in the Forums.

Beginning by leading the students in a quick, interactive activity, I turned the floor over to the student facilitator/evaluators. They walked through the data, written freshly on flip chart paper for the audience, which included every single student in the school, all the teachers, and the school support staff. After a half hour, they were finished. The audience clapped, some students stood and whooped, and the students were released for the day.

Reconvening the teachers with their principal, I began by handing out in-depth copies of the data sets we had collected. Almost immediately, teachers were disapproving. One teacher said kids should not be heard, and another teacher asked something to the effect of, "Since students didn't have anything meaningful to add to my class, so why should I listen to what students have to say about my school?" And so on. The principal stepped in to defend the process for a moment when the district superintendent piped up. Flatly, he said that he would been misled by the SIF, and that he was disappointed by the process and the outcomes, and doubted they'd use the data presented. "We cannot trust students with this responsibility."

It was not long after that I received the most heartbreaking email I have ever received. Risking his own mental and emotional safety, a student from the facilitator/evaluator team sent me an email to report of the treatment him and his peers received from the teachers in the week after I had left. He said that several teachers had said derisive things to their classes, and that more than one had been specifically punished by a teacher for their participation in the facilitator/evaluator team. Reporting back to the superintendent, I received the reply that teachers made their own determinations of how to treat their students, and that while the teachers were disappointed by what was shared with them in my report, nobody had specifically retaliated against students. "That's what you get for giving students a voice!" he said, and that was the end of our conversation.

It has been a decade since I launched the SoundOut School Improvement Pilot Project. Since the Forum I described above I have worked in hundreds of other schools across the US and Canada. I have worked with student/adult partnership teams, provided thousands of hours of professional development to educators, and consulted dozens of programs doing spectacular work for student voice. However, I have never led another SoundOut Student Voice Forum.

Examining the assumptions behind the Forums that led to the breakdown I described here, I have identified a few sticking points. First, I realize that I should have worked harder to assure the district's investment in the process of engaging students in school improvement. Rather than simply relying on the school improvement facilitator, which was a state-funded position to support this failing district, I should have handled relations with the district and the building directly. I should have worked harder to protest students' anonymity in order to ensure their safety.

Ultimately, I could have gotten deeper investment from parents. One of the greatest levers that exists in public schools is the lever of democratic control: Public schools are responsible to be responsive to voters. If public schools do not look the way voters do not want them to look, voters are responsible for their condition, and for changing them.

In the meantime, I have stayed strong and continued to work. Working more deliberately to secure adults' interest and ability to engage students as partners, I have also strived to engage parents as partners in student voice work. The levers of policy change, procedural transformation, and the transformation of classroom, building-wide, and administrative practices throughout education have been worked for too. These are hard lessons I have had in student voice. I hope you can learn from them—and maybe teach me a thing or two, too!

Chapter 77. Student Voice as a Trojan Horse

Figure 19. Student Voice as a Trojan Horse

Sometimes, adults use student voice as a Trojan horse.[37]

Everyone should benefit from Meaningful Student Involvement. However, when student involvement is less than meaningful, student voice is routinely manipulated, tokenized, or otherwise d used by adults for their own means. Students often know when their words, actions, ideas, or wisdom is being used by adults.

I call the ways adults use Meaningful Student Involvement, student voice, and student engagement "Trojan Horse Strategies." That's because adults give students a carrot by appearing to listen to their voices. Then, either intentionally or coincidentally, these same adults or others turn around and blatantly use student voice and student engagement to forward their political agendas without concern for what students are genuinely seeking.

The worst part of the Trojan Horse Strategies is they are being used a lot more in the name of student voice and student engagement. Too many schools, governments, and organizations are manipulating student voice to fit into their adult-driven, anti-authentic approaches to promoting specific education reform agendas. This is when meaningfulness cannot happen. Following is an exploration of what some Trojan Horse Strategies look like.

Trojan Horse Strategies

Adults as Parasites

By using the phrases Meaningful Student Involvement, student voice, and student engagement, adults throughout the education system imply they are listening to the unfettered opinions, ideas, experiences, and wisdom of students. This includes educators, administrators, leaders, and advocates. However, their approach is similar to that of many companies that market to young people: Listening for profit. That's what many educators, leaders, and advocates hope to receive from student voice and student engagement programs: Profit. By continually uplifting the education reform agendas of adults and couching them in student voice and student engagement, many people literally maintain or develop funding for their schools, or their versions of school transformation. They continue to maintain or develop funding opportunities for their schools by using student voice and student engagement. If that sounds greedy and parasitic, that's because it is.

Adults Maintaining Authority

Most student voice and student engagement programs use non-transparent responses to students. They do not show who was involved in making decisions, how decisions were arrived at, nor are they able to hold adults accountable for their decisions. This merely perpetuates the way schools work right now, which is to do to and for students, rather than to work with students. Meaningful Student Involvement clearly distinguishes the difference. Meaningful Student Involvement is contingent on student-adult partnerships throughout the education system. The approach advocated for by most student voice and student engagement programs is adult-dictated, adult-agenda oriented, and ultimately will only benefit adults. These student voice and student engagement programs reinforce adult authority, which is antithetical to Meaningful Student Involvement.

The Student Voice Vacuum

Ultimately, the approach of using student voice and student engagement to reinforce adults' preconceptions is the same for students as yelling into an empty well. Students speak into a vacuum where they do not know the outcomes of their contributions to educators, leaders, and advocates, and there is little or no accountability. Adults listen only when student voice and student engagement are needed, and engage students only when adults see it as necessary. Otherwise, there is little or no substantive student presence. The goal of all student engagement activities anywhere in schools should be to build the capacity of students to cause change within the education systems and communities to which they belong. Many student voice and student engagement programs actually negate students' abilities to cause that change by capturing student voice and student engagement and putting it into the hands of adults. This disengages, taking away the little authority that authentic student voice and student engagement should have. I explore pathways to authentic student voice in Table 1. It alienates students from the process of whole school transformation, and ultimately serves to extinguish any level of interest students may have in the first place.

Adults as Puppeteers

Currently, many well-meaning adults in schools inadvertently manipulate students to reinforce their own self-centered concerns about schools. Telling students what they should be concerned about, using their influence to leverage student behavior, or otherwise controlling students is a Trojan Horse Strategy. This is inherently disingenuous because students need more than to be treated as empty vessels waiting to be filled with teachers' knowledge.

As adults, we can do better than all of these. Being parasitical, maintaining unchecked authority, acting like a vacuum, and playing puppets are all examples of moral corruption, whether or not we intend them to be. Ethical responsibility binds every educator and adults in education to align their head, hearts and hands. So long as anybody in schools talks about schools being for students, we are obligated to challenge, defeat and do more than perpetuate these Trojan Horse strategies. We absolutely must. If we do not, we are actively spinning schools towards the inevitable oblivion disengaged students will lead us towards.

---

[37] This section was originally published as Fletcher, A. (Apr 2012) "Student voice and student engagement as Trojan horses" in *Connect*, No. 194/195. p 24.

Chapter 78. How To Respond to Arguments

Reviewing responses to Meaningful Student Involvement from blogs and across the Internet, I have collected a series of real statements from people who identified themselves as teachers. Following are some of these quotes, and my thoughts about these popular challenges to Meaningful Student Involvement.

Saying They Aren't Ready

Teacher: "We expect our students to graduate high school and make good decisions when they turn eighteen, but up until then, children should not have the opportunity to make many decisions that affect their school or learning."

Response: When done from a constructivist perspective, engaging students as partners in schools can encourage students to apply learning in powerful ways from kindergarten through graduation. These powerful ways, including student-led evaluations of themselves, their peers, their classes and their teachers, can allow students to identify, construct, apply, critique, and reform their own perspectives - rather than having teachers feel like they need to continuously shove it down students' throats.

Looking Down From On High

Teacher: "As long as students do not dictate every area of their education, I do not see why having them involved somewhere in their school will be a bad thing."

Response: This perspective is what is called *nobless oblige*—from the kindness of their hearts, the nobility of old France was *obliged* to help the poor because that was the right thing to do (not just because the nobles were rich off their labor!) The quote above shows the same perspective - From the kindness of their hearts, teachers are obliged to engage the students from the kindness of their hearts - and not just because students are the whole reason they have jobs in the first place! Unfortunately, this type of thinking pervades many teachers' minds, and while not terrible, it is misguided, and allows many teachers to resign from their student voice efforts when they do not go as planned without feeling bad.

Choosing the Right Ones

Teacher: "...many of the students that choose to have this voice are the students that already have a voice."

Response: I thought this entire post was right on the mark - especially from the view of a mom with teenaged children. Awesome. Right at the end of her post she offers a little more insight that I think could be reflected on so much more: *My oldest (17) is the opposite. He pretends that he does not care. Truly, I struggle daily with him and having him believe that he has a say and his say matters. The only thing he says is 'let me drop out of school, if I have a say and it matters'. How do we reach these kinds of kids? They are the ones that NEED a voice.* Well Mom, it sounds like your kid is sharing their voice, and you just do not want to hear what he's saying. I *do* believe that his words mean something, but I am not convinced they can be taken at face value: Within the phrase "Let me drop out of school" there is a lot of meaning that can, and should, be explored with the student. Explore that together, give your child a sense of authority and responsibility, and expand from there.

Teacher as the Judge and Jury

Teacher: "I think that letting the students have more say in their education is a good idea as long as they as a group agree on the topics and that the school has the last say."

Response: This last phrase concerns me the most, because like so many young teachers, this student believes that there must be ONE student voice. That effectively reinforces the current structures that exist to engage student voice in schools by squelching the diversity of perspectives that students have. There is no room for dissention when everybody must agree on the same line.

Chapter 79. Undermining Meaningful Student Involvement

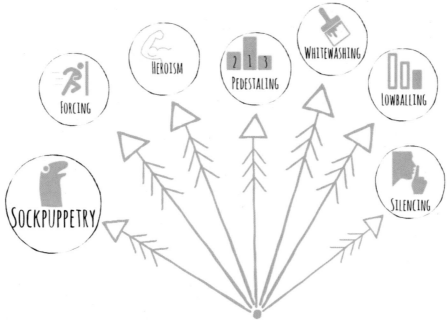

Figure 20. Undermining Meaningfulness

Wrangled into the adult-driven education system by force, students are almost always neglected in educational leadership. When they are asked to become involved, they are usually last and their voices are generally tokenized. Understanding how this happens is a key to knowing how to address barriers to Meaningful Student Involvement.

As Mitra wrote,

> "Partnering with students to identify school problems and possible solutions reminds teachers and administrators that students possess unique knowledge and perspectives about their schools that adults cannot fully replicate. Students can raise tough issues that administrators and teachers might not highlight—including examining structural and cultural injustices within schools rather than blaming failing students for not succeeding in schools." (Savrock, 2014)

Ways to Undermine Meaningfulness

Adults and students may be defeat Meaningful Student Involvement coincidentally or on purpose. In many peoples' mindsets, student voice is a tool to manipulate, twist and turn however is needed. To address that, we have to understand ways that student voice can actually subvert and otherwise undermine Meaningful Student Involvement. Following are several ways that can happen.

1. Forcing

When adults try to force something to be meaningful, it undermines their best intentions. Students do not depend on adult approval to share student voice; instead, they inadvertently and explicitly share it in dozens of ways throughout the school day. Similarly, adults cannot force something to be meaningful for students—they are the ultimate judges. Introduce Meaningful Student Involvement to students and adults, educate them about the frameworks and options, and then allow them to make up their own minds about whether they want to be involved.

2. Silencing

One of the most insidious ways that adults undermine Meaningful Student Involvement can be very overt and very subversive, sometimes at the same times. When teachers ask students to deposit their cell phones in a box before class begins, they are silencing student voice. Demanding students dress and talk a certain way before a school board or committee is silencing student voice. Leaving the experiences of students out of classroom lesson plans or ignoring the histories of the ethnic cultures students come from are examples of silencing student voice, too. Intentionally making spaces for engaging a wide range of students in activities and creating broad opportunities to learn, teach and lead in diverse ways is meaningfulness in action.

3. Whitewashing

In the United States today, there are more than 56 million K-12 students. There is no way that any one individual, organization, hashtag, or movement can represent all of those young people. In this changing nation, it is more important than ever to honor pluralism. Pluralism is when smaller groups within a larger society maintain their unique cultural identities, and larger groups honor their identities. A characteristic of Meaningful Student Involvement is Personal Commitment, which includes honoring all voices for their diversity of experience and knowledge. There's no reason to pretend that all voices are represented by one voice, specifically if that voice does not and cannot effectively represent their peers. Allowing room for diversity and difference is positive, and enhances the meaningfulness of student involvement.

4. Showboating

The student voice movement is not the same as basketball or business, and there is no room for showboating. It is a diverse movement filled with multiple perspectives and broad actions focused on many, many issues. Showboating happens when someone exaggerates their own skills, talents, or abilities. In the student voice movement, individual young people may be tempted to self-promote and make it sound as if they are the only student voice, or their organization or program is the only student voice program of value. Instead of focusing on themselves, Meaningful Student Involvement engages all voices and teaches students and adults to honor the contributions and abilities of all students everywhere all the time in order to avoid showboating.

5. Pedestaling

Adults can be easy to amaze. Seduced by mainstream media and politicians that routinely dismiss the positive power of youth, adults often feel like they've discovered gold when students stand up for themselves and work together to create change. In some instances, they lean on these students constantly and raise them to the point of infallibility. I call this pedestaling students. It includes romanticizing, which is making someone always right and out of way of questioning. Focusing on humanity, Meaningful Student Involvement has room for disagreement and mistakes, and model consensus and collaboration. It is a continuous learning process that engages all participants- adults and students- as equitable partners without artificially or superficially elevating one voice above all others.

6. Heroism

In a room with too few representatives, an especially loud voice standing above all others can sound brave and unique, especially when they represent an under-acknowledged majority. This is especially true in the student voice movement. Just because a young person puts on a suit and discusses education reform in a way that makes adults listen to them does not make them heroic or a superhero. It makes them dressed right and well-versed. In the same way, there are organizations and programs in the student voice movement that are made heroic too. They are made out to represent students well or be the "right" whenever they talk. Among the 56 million students in schools though, adults do not lionize programs that make them uncomfortable or ideas that are too far from their acceptance. The ones that are uplifted are generally satisfactory to adults who make decisions about funding, data usage in schools, and education leadership. Organizational heroism is also a danger to the student voice movement. Meaningful Student Involvement makes room for young people who do not please or appeal to them so easily, and emphasizes teaching young people about the education system that affects them so much.

7. Lowballing

There is more out there than just what you see. Many organizations and individuals today are calling for students to be informants to adult decision-making in schools. They want student voice to be heard. They want a seat at the table for students. There's a lot more at stake for students than simply being able to talk or be represented somewhere. In reality, students comprise up to 94% of any given school building's population. They should be fully integrated into the operations of every single school, if only for their energy and to educate them about democracy. Every layer of educational bureaucracy should infuse students as well, positioning in them in powerful roles that effect not only individual students, but all students; not as recipients, but as active partners who design, implement, critically assess, and make substantive decisions about the education system as a whole. Additionally, while orgs like PSU represent a sophisticated, deep understanding of the complex underbelly of schools today, many people and programs in the student voice movement simply do not get it. Reduced to reacting, they rally students around the apparent problems in schools without recognizing the deeper issues. Reaching much further than simply acting like the flavor-of-the-day, Meaningful Student Involvement positions students as constant, deliberate, and fully engaged partners throughout all of education, all of the time.

8. Sockpuppetry

A lot of adults use students as sockpuppets, feeding them verbiage and giving them the issues adults expect them to address. Intentional or not, this usage of students is designed to deceive the people who are listening to make them think what's being said is genuine student voice. In schools, sockpuppetry is often coupled with manipulation: If students do what adults say, they'll be rewarded; if they do not follow expectations, they'll be punished in some form. Students often do not know they're being used to prop up an adult's perspective. Sometimes adults use students to provide an alternate or opposite perspective to their own. This is called strawman sockpuppetry. Having no real authority to enact anything in education without adult approval, adults may deliberately position students to say outlandish or contrary things, only to show their perspective as more valid, valuable, and important. Meaningful Student Involvement deliberately positions both traditional and nontraditional student voice (see Figure 22) to be heard in safe and supportive environments. In turn, this ensures that students speak for themselves and are treated as equitable partners with adults throughout education.

Preventing the Undermining of Meaningful Student Involvement

The key to preventing student voice from undermining Meaningful Student Involvement is to follow the pathways described throughout this handbook. However, it is equally important to move beyond these pathways by inventing and re-inventing involvement in every situation for every student all of the time. Maintaining critical vigilance for purposeful or accidental sabotage is vital, as is taking deliberate steps to address the ways described above.

Preventing undermining may require what poet Audre Lorde refers to as, "transformation of silence into language and action [as] an act of self-revelation." (Lorde, 1984) Paying attention to the dangers within student voice by engaging schools through Meaningful Student Involvement honors the legacy of past and present efforts. With more students and more adults working together to transform the education system, the very least we can do is honor their contributions. Meaningful Student Involvement moves beyond that by powerfully enshrining, codifying and infusing transformation. More importantly, meaningfully involving students gives space for students and adults to share in the deliberate and ongoing critical examination of that enshrinement and codification. Not only does this discourage education systems from stagnation and irrelevance, it makes consistent critical thinking the norm, effectively elevating the roles of both students and adults throughout schools.

ADULT-DRIVEN STUDENT VOICE

Adult-Driven Student Voice is when adults motivate, inspire, inform, encapsulate, and generally make student voice become convenient for adults. It can happen throughout education, from the classroom to the school boardroom, from hallways to the bleachers. Students can be told what to say, forced to express what they think, compelled to say things certain ways, and much more. Teachers, principals, school staff, district leaders and politicians can all be responsible for doing it. Here are five characteristics of adult-driven student voice.

- **WHO:** Students who adults want to hear from are selected to share their voices. All students are equal members of the schools they attend, both in a literal and metaphorical sense. However, adult-driven student voice selects specific students who may not jostle adults' opinions or ideas to share student voice.
- **WHAT:** Students say what adults want. They usually echoing or parroting adult beliefs, ideas, knowledge, and/or experience. If they share their own, adults largely agree with what students have said.
- **WHEN:** The calendar is determined by adults for students. Students are listened to when adults have the interest or ability to hear them, and not necessarily when students want to be heard.
- **WHERE:** Student voice happens in places adults want it to be shared. Whether on a graffiti wall in a forgotten alley downtown, in a boxing gym for teenagers, in debate class, or at a city-run forum for students to share their opinions about something, student voice happens where adults approve of.
- **WHY:** Adults solicit student voice about specific issues. Students have a variety of perspectives about all kinds of subjects. However, adult-driven youth voice allows only perspectives on issues that are important to adults or that adults pick for students. If students move outside adult-driven boundaries, they are either re-directed or expected to stop sharing their voices.

Table 22. Adult-Driven Student Voice

Chapter 80. Romancing Student Voice

There's a special place where students are placed in stark contrast to their roles in our daily lives. It is yet another way that adults undermine Meaningful Student Involvement, but does not look anything like that. It begins because typically, students are segregated from adults in schools and throughout their larger communities. They are compelled to follow rules and laws they didn't make, and shown what to do with themselves through advertising, education, family life, and community norms. Nowhere along the way are they treated as full humans, capable of contributing to the larger world around them for their benefit and the benefit of others.

Until they have the experience of adults romancing student voice. This is not a loving or sensual gesture; however, it is wholly inappropriate. It takes the form of putting students on pedestals and pretending they can do no wrong (McLeod, 2011). From there, individual students can step above their peers. They get glimpses of what adults see in education and can do similar things as adults do in schools. Their access grows beyond regular students, and they become able to see where their age group peers stand, as well as some adults. With an increased amount of education and opportunity, these students often grow still more powerful, acting as young adults throughout education who are controllers of their fates and masters of their domains.

The reasons why adults romanticize student voice vary. As Rudduck and Flutter observed,

> "Schools may well feel obliged to be seen to be 'doing it'—taking it on board without having the time to think through why they want to do it, how it fits with other initiatives within the institution's development plan and scheme of values, and what the personal and institutional risks are." (2006)

Romancing student voice can create strange upside-down kingdoms within classrooms, throughout schools and across the education system. Students learn to boss around and manipulate adults to get what they want. Viewed as never wrong, they drive conversations, control situations and seemingly move mountains compared to other students. With experiences as top performing students, athletes, musicians, scholars, performers and more, they seem mighty (Ethridge, 2015)

Looking up at them is not an especially pleasant experience for other students. Some friends may hold up the pedestal by putting their energy and attitudes on the column to ensure their friends' security. Others step back and stare up in awe, wondering how these students get that power, while still other students throw rocks from the distance and try to knock romanticized student voice off its pedestal.

Adults have distinct ideas about who should be involved and how they should behave, and we often force those preferences on students as demands. The ones who shine through the morass of meaninglessness and demonstrate their effectiveness at being adult-like are generally the ones whose voices adults romanticize. The opposite is true, too: The students who do not behave how we want them to become disengaged.

The challenge for Meaningful Student Involvement opportunities is not to foster these specific pedestals for student voice. They position students as speakers at adult conferences; put students in charge of the school boards; makes some students shine while others throttle, stuck in gear without the resources and attention they need to move forward. Well-meaning adults perpetuate this by making formal student voice opportunities just for so-called student leaders. These students often already have a lot of access to adults, and merely gain more as their pedestals are made taller.

Solving the crisis of romanticizing student voice takes commitment by every adult who works with students to stop assuming students need to be held up high above their peers. Instead, new opportunities must be created for all students to experience meaningful involvement that spotlights them for who they are, rather than simply how adults want them to be.

---

5 Attributes of an "Upside-Down Kingdom" in Schools

1. **Reversed Power:** The power structure in schools is simply reversed, giving students supreme authority in single instances or overall. Students rule without question, concern or consideration for adult knowledge, skills, abilities or experiences, or those of their peers;
2. **Rulers and Subjects:** Students who share student voice in acceptable ways are addressed as student leaders; all other students are either silenced, ignored or punished for sharing student voice;
3. **The Holy Grail:** Adults regard student voice as sacrosanct, irreproachable and uncorrectable;
4. **Flawless Execution:** Students are granted full leeway to say whatever they want without correction, questioning or recrimination, especially when appropriate.
5. **"Them":** Using the pronoun "them" is a verbal reveal that shows the speaker thinks others are beneath them, untrustworthy, or irrelevant. The underlying belief is that the "other" threatens the very well-being of schools, student voice or education overall.

Chapter 81. Bringing It All Together: A Case Examination

Teachers, you tried to listen to students or you invited students to meetings, and nothing seems to work. Since then, every time you've suggested students participate in activities you think are meaningful, they do not show up; worse yet, they smirk at you and fold their arms.

As a student, you tried to speak up in class and you even went to the meeting. You were excited by what your teacher was talking about, but when you got there you only heard a group of teachers and a vice principal talking about school rules and policies and procedures and... it was all very boring. Now every time your teacher asks for volunteers to come, it feels like her stare is burning a hole in your forehead.

Each perspective here can be correct: students are routinely bored at most significant educational leadership activities, and teachers are often underwhelmed or frustrated by students' disinterest in opportunities to change their education.

The challenges of structural and cultural barriers to Meaningful Student Involvement, illustrated in Figure 18, are real. Working to change one or the other should not be seen as the major engine for Meaningful Student Involvement. Both areas should be acknowledged, examined, addressed, challenged, and transformed in order to engage student voice.

Here is an example of how structure and culture can be barriers to Meaningful Student Involvement.

Scenario: The School Committee

Teachers in a middle school decided to invite a to student join a committee, a first for their school district. During a seventh-grade Advisory period, one teacher invited a student to volunteer to participate in a meeting that evening. At the meeting, there were 6 teachers, and the one student who missed her Junior Honor Society meeting in order to attend. After sitting through three meetings without speaking, the student stopped attending. Afterwards, the teachers swore off inviting "anymore kids" because "they do not add anything" to the meeting.

Structural Barriers in this Scenario
- Teacher preparation courses and professional development training does not prepare or reinforce teachers' ability to engage student voice.
- Student voice activities should not be limited to one school or to middle and/or high schools.
- Adding student voice was an afterthought to committee planning, occurring only the day of the meeting, rather than as a course of action with framing and reflecting activities.
- The meeting was not announced in enough time to allow student participants to prepare.
- The committee meeting time conflicted with previously planned student activities, limiting the participation of more students.
- The student was not told about expectations for their involvement.

- The student did not receive training on committee participation or the issues addressed by the committee.
- There was inequitable representation between the student and the teachers.
- The student had no structured reflection focused on her experience of being involved in the committee.

Cultural Barriers in this Scenario

- While the teachers recognized the inherent benefit of engaging student voice, they were armed with good intentions, not experience-driven practice.
- Teacher didn't have knowledge of or access to materials to help them develop their committee.
- The nature of the activity had limited appeal to diverse students, specifically non-involved students.
- Committee participation was separate and unrelated from classroom lessons, despite the opportunities for applied learning in communication, leadership, and social awareness.
- Committee participation was separate and unrelated from Junior Honor Society activities, despite the connections between serving on the committee and community service.
- The teachers made no overt concessions designed to engage the student in the meeting, instead relying on her to answer the question, "What do you think?" in the same way another teacher would.
- Lacking opportunities to reflect on her participation, the student complained to other students about the experience, further disinteresting other students from becoming involved.
- The teachers' perspectives of the student and her involvement will further alienate student voice.

Major Strategy to Address this Scenario

The major strategy for overcoming these barriers is to develop a district or schoolwide plan for Meaningful Student Involvement. This plan should include professional development, policies, and financial support for encouraging and sustaining Meaningful Student Involvement, as well as integrated approaches to developing, sustaining, and strengthening the impact of students as partner.

Steps in this scenario may include...
- An individual teacher advocate learns about Meaningful Student Involvement.
- This teacher takes it upon themselves to train peer teachers and intentionally selected nontraditional and traditional student leaders, as illustrated in Figure 22. The training focuses on all aspects of Meaningful Student Involvement.
- Students learn about issues in education by incorporating their reflections on school in a constructivist learning experience centering on the committee's work. This is shown earlier in this book in Figure 17.
- Teachers and students commit to participating as equals on committee.
- Facilitation of development and reflection activities focusing on Meaningful Student Involvement are provided throughout committee activities.
- Final committee activity is focused on critical reflection and celebration of accomplishments, including Meaningful Student Involvement.

There are plenty of other examples of the structure and culture of schools serving as barriers to Meaningful Student Involvement. However, these are surmountable tasks that every school can and should overcome. Meaningful Student Involvement is too valuable to the success of learning and leading in schools and communities to continue to be neglected, alienated, or rejected.

Chapter 82. Discriminating Against Students

To truly address the barriers against Meaningful Student Involvement illustrated in Figures 18 and 20, I feel obligated to address the issue of discrimination against students in schools. Every single teacher, parent, cafeteria worker, school psychologist, education administrator, afterschool worker, summer school teachers, playground monitor, speech and language therapist, math tutor, and school principal discriminates against students. As this chapter addresses, discrimination against students is implicit and inevitable in the very structure of schooling today.

Adultism is bias towards adults. Bias towards adults, with several examples illustrated in Figure 21, happens anytime the opinions, ideas, knowledge, beliefs, abilities, attitudes, or cultures of adults are held above those of people who aren't considered adults because they are not considered adults. Because of this, our very conception of schools is adultism at work. Anyone who works professionally in schools with students as an adult is inherently adultist. This idea is reinforced by Cervone and Cushman, who wrote,

> "It is tempting to think that if you just pay attention to students' voices, you will hear what you already know. Secretly, adults—outside schools as well as in—generally believe that they know best." (Cervone & Cushman, 2002)

Ultimately, adultism is the reason schools exist. Schools demonstrate adultism through discrimination against students. This comes across in our national, state, and local laws; educational, health, nutritional, and funding policies; family norms and social customs. Everything from cafeteria tables to laws making education compulsory to the voter-denied school funding levy passively and actively reflects adultism. Seeking to make students into our visions, adults invented the phenomenon of childhood to ensure that kids were comprehendible and controllable. Because of that, the status of students has become passive, static, and predictable.

Does that make adults wrong or bad? Not all the time and not everywhere. There are times when, as an adult, I am discriminated against. Legally, I cannot go into a hospital and operate on someone, nor can I drive an 18-wheel semi-truck. Culturally, it is inappropriate for me to use a women's changing room at a store, or attend a self-help group for narcotics. None of those examples is inherently bad or wrong. They are intended to keep myself or others safe. It's the same with much well-meaning educational adultism that is intended to keep young people or others safe. If a building is burning down, as an adult I feel it's my responsibility to grab everyone and make sure they are out of the building, regardless of age.

However, in our schools adults constantly act like the building is burning down. That's what must change. People who want to change the miserable state of affairs in schools must take action to stop education adultism now. We must challenge the ineptitude of adults and their intransigence towards the changing abilities and roles of students throughout education, and push back against age-based assumptions that have nothing to do with the capacity of learners today. Education is adultism—but it does not have to stay that way.

Back when children and youth packed factories, farm fields, mines, and service jobs around the western world in the late 19th century, many adults could not find jobs. This caused adults to rally against child labor and for public schools. A lot of adults said they wanted to end children ending up on the streets without an "occupation"– especially after newspapers reported that was the case. Schools suddenly became popular as places where young people could have productive experiences throughout the day. In the early 20th century they were made compulsory in many Western nations. Moving children from compulsory labor occupations into compulsory learning occupations without their input, ideas, or contributions in any way paved the way to the state of education today. That is why adultism is the reason schools exist today.

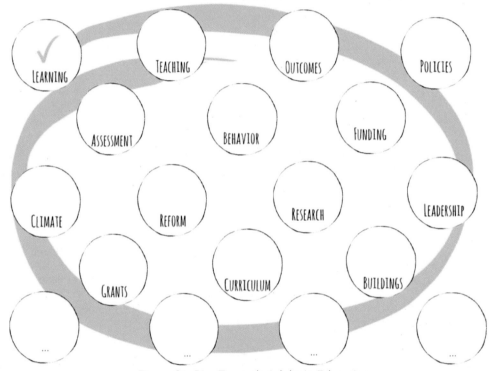

Figure 21. Bias Towards Adults in Education

The Ways Discrimination Happens in Schools

Adultism drives adult behavior throughout schools, as well as a lot of student behavior. Teaching styles frequently represent adults' values and skills rather than young peoples' perspectives and capabilities. Adults determine what is valuable for students to learn and how young people need to demonstrate their learning. They enforce inequities between students and teachers in everyday behavior, too: When teachers yell at students, they are controlling classrooms; when students yell at teachers, they are creating unsafe learning environments. Ultimately, students in schools are subjected to their parents' and their teachers' assessments of their performance in the classroom, and have no formal input into grading or graduations. Searching for adult approval to receive the most praise or achieve the best grades, students routinely appease adults with sufficient class work without actually engaging in the content being taught. They find solidarity with the adults who control their classrooms while betraying the trust of their peers as they tattle and compare each other.

Corporal punishment is legal in schools around the world today. As one of the most brutal and overt exhibitions of adultism in schools today, it is the belief that abuse has a place in educating students. Corporal punishment is any physical, psychological, emotional, or sociological punishment administered to students. In schools where students received corporal punishment, students generally have no format to appeal such punishment. They frequently do not have the ability to raise concerns over the legitimacy of the claims made against them, and they may not have the ability to raise concerns over the severity of the punishment being administered for their presumed violations. Corporal punishment may be one of the most obvious physical impacts of adultism, but it is not the only one.

In a much subtler yet obvious way, the very physical plant of the school is adultist. A hundred years ago, because of the influence of Italian educator Maria Montessori, educators began paying attention to the physical apparatuses young people were expected to learn with. Their desks got lower, the chalkboards were handheld, and drinking foundations were built at their height. These types of accommodation ended where young people were expected to stop interacting with adults. School board meeting rooms were built for adults; school counselor offices were built for adults; cafeteria food preparation areas were built for adults. Even in high schools students are generally expected to be "of average adult height" in order to operate learning instruments such as microscopes, computers, and other devices. Research suggests that within in school students comprise an average of 93% of the human population of school buildings, with adults accounting for the other seven percent. There is an awful lot of accommodation of that seven percent!

Adultism is apparent when large numbers of young people of any age are not allowed to congregate, cooperate and coordinate. Schools today are rooted in age segregation that disallows young people from socially and educationally interacting with each other. With few formal opportunities to socialize, young people may learn to distrust their peers and seek the approval of adults only. Some adults in schools lose the ability to distinguish between conspiracy and community, and they make continuous efforts to keep students from interacting with each other in schools.

Finally, and perhaps ultimately, adultism undermines the very purpose of educating students in schools. Student engagement has been shown to directly affect academic achievement. When students experience adultism, their engagement is severely affected in negative ways, no matter the environment. Classroom management, learning activities and student discipline are all affected by adultism, in all grade levels. In response to all of the bias towards adults throughout their educations (as illustrated in Figure 21), some young people completely acquiesce to adult expectations. Others completely abandon or apparently rebel against these expectations by routinely performing lowly in school through behavior or academic achievement, and through dropping out. Dropping out of school is the ultimate impact of adultism in schools.

The Student Involvement Gap

There is an inherent student involvement that is both implicit and explicit throughout schools. In every classroom throughout school across every community around the world, there are students who are involved while others are not. This may reflect conscious or unconscious discrimination; be completely chosen by students or not; and may or may not be an inherent outcome of compulsory education. Regardless of why or how it happens, it happens.

This gap is often caused by adult bias. Whether it is motivated race, gender, income, or otherwise, the gap is real for those who are stuck in it. There is adult bias for learning styles, with many teachers demanding that either students learn the way they are willing to teach, or not be taught at all. In other circumstances, adult bias focuses on student behavior, with adults relying on students complying with any seemingly arbitrary boundaries and expectations laid out by their classroom teachers and building leaders. Despite insistence to the contrary, many educators may also biased against academic ability, frustrated by their apparent inability to move underperforming or differently abled students while they are intimidated by highly gifted students. (Slee, 1994)

As shown earlier in this book in Figure 16, gap that is created by adult bias is as obvious as what happens every day in every classroom, where some students speak up while others look away, and other students are acknowledged for their contributions while others are punished for not being involved. Table 10 explores what happens when every classroom is meaningful for every student. It extends further towards the heart of Meaningful Student Involvement when we look at what student voice gets heard and which student voice gets ignored. I often address this as convenient and inconvenient student voice. (Fletcher, 2012)

Convenient Versus Inconvenient Student Voice

Convenient Student Voice entails students saying or doing things that adults are comfortable with. Student voice is convenient when adults can predict who is going to share it, what the students will express, how it will be shared, where and when it is going to happen and why students want to share it. When students talk about the non-curricular things that most directly impact them, such as cafeteria food, textbook conditions, or bathroom usage, they are generally offering convenient student voice. Convenient student voice usually comes from students who are already seen by the adults as positive role models in the school—a student leadership class, for instance, or members of the Honors Society.

Inconvenient Student Voice happens when students bring up ideas and taking actions that adults do not expect or are uncomfortable hearing. It is inconvenient because adults cannot predict it, do not expect it and frequently do not want to hear it. These topics can be those that impact teaching or governance at the school, or even be topics that some adults themselves want to discuss but fear bringing up due to the administration or other outside forces. Inconvenient student voice often comes from students who are not seen as leaders by adults, or who feel alienated by the school, and it might come at times and places that adults are not expecting.

These realities make the student involvement gap wider and more pronounced. Without direct intervention, this gap will spread and devour more students.

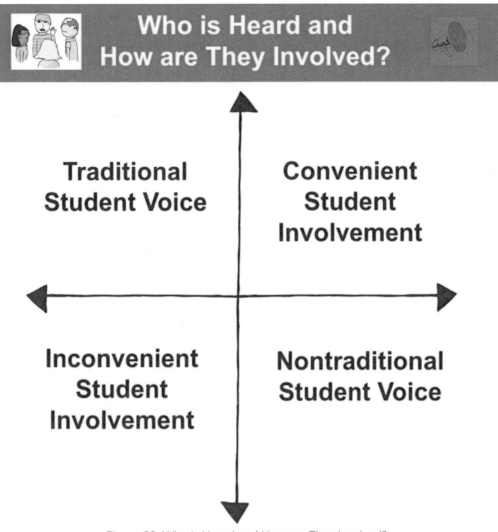

Figure 22. Who is Heard and How are They Involved?

Challenging Discrimination in Schools

In addition to those such as Montessori, who was almost uniquely oriented against adultism in schools, educators have rallied against adultism in schools without naming it as such for more than a hundred years. Massively influential, though often misunderstood, American school philosopher John Dewey constantly promoted a curriculum for schools that was footed in student realities instead of adult conveniences. He once wrote,

"Nature wants children to be children before they are men... Childhood has ways of seeing, thinking, and feeling, peculiar to itself, nothing can be more foolish than to substitute our ways for them."

This situates him squarely on the side of anti-adultist teachers. Paulo Freire justly sought authentic learning for students, too. His attitude could be summarized by his singular belief that, "the educator for liberation has to die as the unilateral educator of the educatees." This positions the student as the holder and determiner of learning, and that is anti-adultist. While some theories address students' roles indirectly, and others head-on push against the overbearing domination of adults, in schools, all are valuable as allies in this struggle.

Adultism makes schools today ineffective. The only way to begin the massive cultural and structural transformations that are required is through Meaningful Student Involvement, and engaging students as partners in learning throughout the education system.

Chapter 83. Considerations

There are dozens of very real challenges that face advocates for Meaningful Student Involvement from both adults and students. Most of those barriers fit accordingly into the above chapters; some do not.

A student named Danesia Robinson of Oakland, California, recently reflected on how students in her high school are working to change the low expectations of adults, saying,

> "Go to the district and make a change, you say, but you gotta be prepared to take the responsibility of making that change. It's not easy to make a change. You gotta stick to it. And oftentimes, as youth, we feel that we cannot do it, so we just give up. ...Facts, you need facts. You need to be educated on what [the administration is] doing, because you cannot just go up to somebody and not know what you're talking about. You gotta keep going to meetings and not let anybody run over you. You gotta be willing to study the information, you gotta be willing to survey, you gotta be willing to ask people about it. You gotta understand."

Adult allies have an important role in assisting students to become engaged as partners in school change. Christensen suggested three "guiding ideas" for adults to keep in mind:

- Adults need to truly believe students are capable of significant leadership roles in schools. Lip service will not do.
- Student leadership should have an impact on significant aspects of school life, such as climate, curriculum, instruction and governance. Planning the prom and sponsoring activities are not enough.
- Leadership needs to be viewed as an activity in which any student can participate. It is not limited to an office or position. It does not automatically arise from an election. (Christensen, 1997)

Meaningful Student Involvement demands student participation; but students are equally charged with being *willing* to change schools. Both students and adults have to work together to overcome the systemic barriers that keep everyone from moving forward with inclusive school improvement.

It is easy to assume that barriers will stop activities, especially when everyone at the table lacks commitment to Meaningful Student Involvement. However, the above illustrations of possible solutions show that through intentional facilitation and guidance, students, adults, and the structure of schools can change. The significance of Meaningful Student Involvement greatly increases when barriers are overcome. This *Handbook* explores that significance.

Chapter 84. Arguments Supporting Meaningful Student Involvement

It is important for students and adults to be able to respond to arguments against Meaningful Student Involvement. Following are some of the arguments in support.

- **Full humans:** Students are full human beings right now who have opinions, knowledge, values, needs, wisdom, beliefs, experiences and interests that can and should be accounted for throughout the education system.
- **Engagement:** Students need authentic, equitable and substantive opportunities to express their opinions, knowledge, values, needs, wisdom, beliefs, experiences and interests by engaging in active, fully equitable Student/Adult Partnerships throughout the education system.
- **Rights:** Students have the right to be involved in the systems that govern their lives, especially the education system, because they are most affected by these systems.
- **Responsibilities:** Student/Adult Partnerships foster responsible relationships between students and adults, students and authority, and students and democracy. Meaningful involvement is not giving students free reign of schools, but actively engaging students as partners with adults in order to transform learning, teaching and leadership throughout schools.
- **Uniqueness:** Students are uniquely capable of identifying challenges throughout the education system and creating innovative solutions with adults as partners. Adults may not otherwise be able to see these challenges or create these solutions without Student/Adult Partnerships.
- **Partnerships:** Meaningful Student Involvement is not about having 100% student-driven schools. As this book illustrates repeatedly, engaging students as partners in learning throughout the education system should be done through a constructivist approach by acknowledging the varying abilities, interests and actions of students. This is illustrated in Figure 17 earlier in this book. There is also no single way to foster Student/Adult Partnerships, and because of that, Meaningful Student Involvement should be recreated for each individual student, circumstance, and context being addressed.
- **Compromise:** Meaningful Student Involvement is never about "all or nothing," and compromise is inherent in throughout the frameworks.
- **Mutuality:** Fostering Student/Adult Partnerships requires mutual respect and open communication. This never makes disrespect okay, whether among peers or between students and parents, teachers, or other adults throughout the education system.
- **Capability:** All students of all ages are fully capable of becoming meaningfully involved throughout education by learning what it means to be mutually accountable in a learning community. This means students learn beyond self-interest and strengthen their understandings of and commitment to democracy and community.
- **Research-driven:** As shown in the research summary in this book, studies show that Meaningful Student Involvement can increase student engagement throughout curricular activities, extracurricular activities, informal school culture activities and the larger community surrounding schools. Research shows Meaningful Student Involvement can strengthen student motivation and belonging, as well as their senses of self-efficacy, self-agency and purpose.

- **Commitment:** Meaningful Student Involvement can build students' commitment to learning, teaching and leadership through education, democracy and community.

With these reasons and outcomes, among those listed throughout this book, every argument against Meaningful Student Involvement can be met and overcome.

Part X. Measuring Meaning

Chapter 85. Introduction

When asked how I decided what makes Meaningful Student Involvement *meaningful*, I am often reminded of John Dewey's simple dictum,

> "Give the pupils something to do, not something to learn; and the doing is of such a nature as to demand thinking; learning naturally results."

It comes to mind because thinking about education this way has never succeeded in educating the masses. At best, it implicates Dewey's own naivety about the American educational project, which has become the predominant schooling model around the world.

That quote comes to mind because it unfortunately seems to name the expectations many educators today have for student involvement: Simply do it and let the dice fall where they may. Paulo Freire argued against this writing,

> "Critical reflection on practice is a requirement of the relationship between theory and practice. Otherwise theory becomes simply 'blah, blah, blah,' and practice, pure activism."

We must have measures against which to measure the meaningfulness of student involvement. The *Ladder of Student Involvement*, introduced early in this book, is one such tool for measurement. Following are some additional considerations.

The challenge of measuring *meaning* is that the idea is inherently subjective. Everyone has different ideas of what matters to them and what defines meaningfulness. The role of education should be to help students define for themselves what matters and what is meaningful. That is essential for their entire lives, no matter what age they are. The dictum that says, "Don't teach students what to teach, teach them how to think," might also apply to Meaningful Student Involvement as: Don't teach students what meaningfulness is; teach them how to find meaning for themselves.

Teaching students how to find meaning can mean many things, happen in a variety of ways and conclude in countless outcomes. That means that Meaningful Student Involvement should focus on process, not product.

The following measures of Meaningful Student Involvement should look across the spectrum, including the people who are involved, the activities that happen, and the outcomes that emerge from the entire process. Rather than fixate on one single aspect, the remainder of this section highlights different ways, avenues, people and outcomes that can happen. Digging deeply throughout the different aspects, it also highlights the various components, including the motivation of people; student readiness; and adult readiness. It examines the culture, action, barriers and evaluation of activities. Finally, the rest of this section includes the outcomes of relationships, rigor and relevance from Meaningful Student Involvement.

Chapter 86. Measures of Meaningful Student Involvement

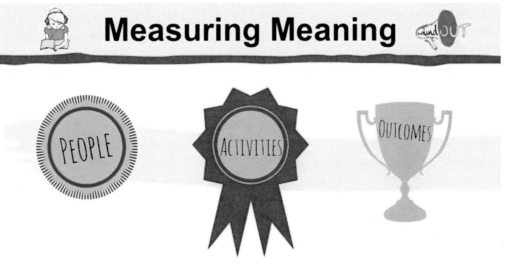

Figure 23. Measures of Meaningful Student Involvement

There are specific measures that should be evident when we measure the meaningfulness of student involvement. However, these measures are not quantitative metrics dependent on highly entwined outcomes that can be attributed to interventions, strategies, and approaches throughout the education system. Instead, the measures used here are larger systematic developments, qualitative processes, and procedural developments designed to acknowledge specific actions as well as generalized outcomes. Following are some of those measures and what they look like.

Chapter 87. Measuring People

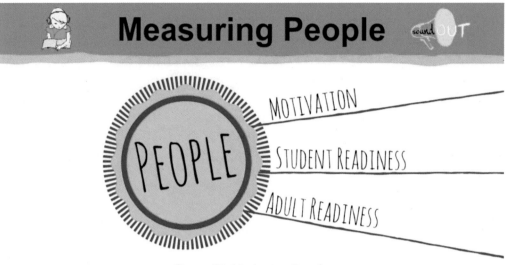

Figure 24. Measuring People

When measuring people for whether they are experiencing Meaningful Student Involvement, there are many different factors to consider. This section explores three factors: Motivation, Student Readiness and Adult Readiness. These three were chosen because of their direct impact on Meaningful Student Involvement. If people are not motivated, activities will not be meaningful. If people are not ready, they are not going to be able to sustain meaningfulness.

A) Motivation

When we think about the outcomes of Meaningful Student Involvement, it's important to identify the original motivation for action. Perhaps the first step is the most important, that the purpose of student involvement is clearly defined. It can be important to identify who declared that purpose, and whether their intention was known to everyone involved. Meaningful Student Involvement should matter in the classroom, throughout the school, and across your district.

The process of fostering Meaningful Student Involvement at your school affects how it is received. Different people who can foster the engagement of students as partners include students from the individual school who requested it, elected officials such as the school board or mayor, teachers, school leaders such as superintendents, principals, or other administrators. Identifying whether Meaningful Student Involvement was a district/state/federal policy directive can be important, and considering whether it was a response to internal or external challenges facing students in schools.

Motivation for Meaningful Student Involvement may include the expected or delivered outcomes of the action for students; teachers, principals, or other adults; building culture; the larger community, or; the entire education system. It might also include the history of student involvement in the individual school or district, positive or negative.

The final motivation to measure is whether Meaningful Student Involvement is part of a larger strategy, policy, or campaign focused on school improvement. Formalization is frequently one of the main political and professional motivations behind school change of all kinds.

B) Student Readiness

Ensuring Student Readiness for Meaningful Student Involvement is essential. This can include enhancing the capacity of students to be involved through building skills and sharing knowledge. It can also be through strategic positioning and sustainable Student/Adult Partnerships.

The first component of student readiness for Meaningful Student Involvement could be to determine whether students were involved in negotiating, advocating, or deciding there was a need for engaging students as partners in their school. It is not a requirement that they were; however, if they were, there may be more student readiness. The next step should reflect how students are be made aware of educators' intentions for their involvement. Measuring student readiness should show that students deliberately reflect on their learning through involvement, schools, the education system, school improvement, and student voice as a whole.

Meaningful Student Involvement should reflect what steps have been taken to ensure that the level of involvement is appropriate to the knowledge and ability of the students involved. The developmental needs of students should be taken into account, and skill building learning opportunities focused on the task at hand, i.e. preparing agendas and taking minutes, formal decision-making, problem-solving, action planning, evaluation, task completion, budgeting, self-management, curriculum design, research, community organizing, etc. should be available throughout the course of involvement. Advanced leadership skills should be intentionally taught to students, including how to create teams, depersonalize conflict, and how to learn from the process as well as outcomes. Students should be prepared for routines involved in the activities they are involved in.

Knowledge-acquisition opportunities should link learning with the task at hand, such as school improvement, supportive learning environments, equity and diversity awareness, standards-based learning, etc. should be available too. Students should learn about the politics and personalities involved, the bureaucratic structures and policy constraints of the education system, and the reasons why students (and other groups) have been excluded from decisions. Also, informal conversations should happen to explain potential underlying reasons for personal conflict at meetings.

In addition to students' leadership development, basic self-image and confidence of students should be built according to students' experience, ability, and exposure. Activities should also deliberately provide opportunities for varying levels of engagement from students as well.

C) Adult Readiness

Students who schools work for often become adults who work for schools. The discrepancy between their experiences in academic success, social popularity, and student leadership do not prepare them to meaningful involve students. Ensuring adult readiness for Meaningful Student

Involvement means taking time in order to critically reflect on our experiences as students and look at how we've behaved towards students as adults in schools.

Adults should be aware of what motivates students to be involved, and what students' experiences of being involved have been. Adults should become fully informed about the issues, policies, programs, services, and/or activities that affect students. Becoming clear on what the need for student involvement is, adults should know who created or advocated for Meaningful Student Involvement—students, adults, or both. Adults should feel fully informed about Meaningful Student Involvement, student voice, and the possibilities and limitations of students' roles in the activity at hand. Adults should be aware of how many adults are involved in ensuring student involvement in the activity. They should also be aware of how often adults advocate on behalf of students as partners to other adults in the system to persuade them to listen to students by listening to them, returning emails or phone calls, etc. On the flip side, they should be aware of which adults are not in favor of Meaningful Student Involvement, and how they resist, refuse, or deny student voice.

When it comes to promoting Meaningful Student Involvement, adults should consider whether adults promote the activities in a way that is fun or pleasant; gives positive recognition to Meaningful Student Involvement; and demonstrates adult trust in students. Promoting activities should not marginalize students to a limited role or set of issues in the school, and should show that adults allow students to make mistakes in the course of being involved. All activities should genuinely provide time to listen to students as part of the activities.

When considering readiness, adults should be prepared through training to provide emotional support for Meaningful Student Involvement by paying attention to students' feelings, demonstrating appropriate levels of caring about their personal issues, helping students with their challenges and problems related to Meaningful Student Involvement, and discussing sensitive topics with students.

Meaningful Student Involvement should create space for adults to offer support for students through suggestions, feedback, critical questions, and other responses to student voice. Students should have a range of options to stimulate their ideas while adults are capable of helping students organize their activities and co-facilitate when appropriate. Adults should be provided timely information, and be presented information in real, concrete terms.

Chapter 88. Measuring Activities

Figure 25. Measuring Activities

Considering that action is key to Meaningful Student Involvement, it because vital to measure what is happening. This section explores four factors affecting activities: Culture, Action, Barriers and Evaluation. Culture allows for the basic assumptions of the people involved to come through authentically, helping determine a classroom, school or district's investment in meaningful involvement. Examining action can show what meaningfulness looks like and how it can be expanded or deepened. An earnest look at the barriers effecting meaningfulness can help determine whether and how students are involved. Looking at the evaluation of Meaningful Student Involvement is a meta-cognitive activity that can embody what meaningfulness looks like.

D) Culture

When assessing Meaningful Student Involvement it's important to consider the effects on school culture. Engaging students as partners in school change should including creating the culture to support Meaningful Student Involvement for all students in all schools, all the time.

This culture should be reflected in a variety of ways. All students should feel safe to be meaningfully involved, which truly focuses on whether their involvement is equitable or not. Students should be identifying in their own language and without coaching from adults how they are meaningfully involved, how they're respected, and how they're responded to by adults.

Involving students meaningfully should transform the attitudes and systems that underlay the culture of individual classrooms, whole school buildings and eventually, the entirety of the education system. This looks like Student/Adult Partnerships that are mutually supportive and accountable for both students and adults, whether in the classroom, board room, hallways, or legislatures. Meaningful Student Involvement changes can be apparent in school when students and adults address personal challenges and organizational barriers together, leading to healthier, more school democratic cultures where everyone can be engaged as partners. Table 18 illustrates some reasons why this matters.

Other ways school culture reflects Meaningful Student Involvement include, but are not limited to, educators maintaining a substantial focus on student involvement even when students appear to be disinterested; gradual or radical shifts in student-adult relationships to reflect higher perceptions of students and the elements of Student/Adult Partnerships introduced earlier in this book; and visually observable aspects, including relaxed conversations among students and adults about education and school improvement; verbal and written reflection shared among students and adults; and rituals reflecting Meaningful Student Involvement, including committee participation, Non-Violent Communication between students and adults; and student orientation programs led by students and adults.

When schools continually demonstrate meaningful involvement in research, planning, teaching, evaluation, decision-making and advocacy, their culture demonstrates what we are looking for. There will be regular and ongoing expectations for all members of the school community to hold meaningful involvement tantamount for all learners, as well as a commitment by building leadership to professional development and training opportunities that foster Student/Adult Partnerships. Additionally, the culture of education reflects Meaningful Student Involvement when discriminatory language against students is not tolerated; clear expectations and policies reflect a commitment to Student/Adult Partnerships, and a total commitment to the Cycle of Engagement is apparent throughout learning, teaching and leadership.

E) Action

Action is the crux of Meaningful Student Involvement. All action should start by students working with adults to determine what constitutes *meaningful* student involvement. Conscientious steps should be taken to ensure that student involvement is meaningful according to that initial work. Students should understand the intentions of the process, decision, or outcomes of Meaningful Student Involvement in general, as well as the specific activity at hand, and they should know who made the decisions about Meaningful Student Involvement and why they were made initially.

Throughout the course of action the process and are the results of Meaningful Student Involvement should be recorded. That recording should be reported in writing and distributed to both students and adults. The process should include a variety of steps, including having students work with adults to identify school issues, challenges, or problems, allowing students to identify their own possible solutions or goals in their school, and engaging students in working with adults to identify possible solutions or goals in their school.

Students should feel fully informed about issues that matter to them, and learn about issues that matter to the whole school they're in, the larger community, where they live, and the entire nation. Project ideas and activities should be co-initiated by students and adults, as well.

There is a large role for students in formal school improvement. They can be involved in identifying the problems, challenges, or needs to be addressed by school improvement, as well as formulating the problem and analyzing the situation. They can co-create school improvement policy, participate in adopting school improvement policy, and be meaningfully involved in approving programs, services, and activities to implement school improvement. Students can be meaningfully involved in teaching adults about school improvement, monitoring school improvement, and evaluating the impact of school improvement. Rather than act in isolation, students should be meaningfully involved with adults and other community members in school improvement as well. (Counts, 1978)

The best action for Meaningful Student Involvement should always end in reflection. Afterwards, students who are involved should receive a written or verbal report on the outcomes of Meaningful Student Involvement.

F) Barriers

An essential measure for Meaningful Student Involvement is to deliberately acknowledge and conscientiously address the barriers to engaging students as partners throughout education. The first step in addressing barriers to Meaningful Student Involvement is to acknowledge they exist, and to name them as best as possible. While Figures 18 and 20 illustrate those names in general, evaluation must identify them specifically.

False and negative assumptions about students' abilities to participate should be deliberately addressed by students and/or adults throughout all activities. All adults in the school should be clear about the class or school's intent to foster Meaningful Student Involvement. An informal assessment should be made of whether adults throughout the learning environment, and a determination should be made whether adults provide good examples of Meaningful Student Involvement. Students' experience and inexperience addressed with Meaningful Student Involvement should be determined as well.

Barriers can be addressed when students and adults identify and address negative experiences students and adults have had with student involvement, and steps should be taken to reduce the resistance from adults and students. In some circumstances, this can mean adding an equal or greater number of students to boards, committees and other decision-making activities throughout the education system that previously only engaged a few students. However, more than likely it means creating new avenues for student voice in places where only adults made decisions before. This can happen by creating student roles for every student in decision-making affecting individual students; it can also happen by creating roles for students in activities where adults made decisions for large groups of students.

When adults throughout education actively educate students about the education system, including focusing on specific functions and outcomes, Meaningful Student Involvement can happen and the barrier of obfuscation can be overcome. A climate should be fostered in every opportunity for student voice where students feel comfortable engaging in learning, whether through question-asking, interacting, or otherwise engaging in the topic at hand. Deliberate steps should be made to foster this climate, including acknowledgment of student schedules, learning styles, developmental abilities, and other relevant actions. If activities happen outside school and school time, planning should consider whether the location and times of meetings are convenient to students; determining if the times and dates of meetings are convenient for students; choosing locations that are accessible to students and public transportation; and other initiatives or changes going on in classes, local schools, districts, or state programs that will complement the goals and processes of Meaningful Student Involvement.

A major barrier to Meaningful Student Involvement can be student credibility. If representative participation is required in an activity, steps should be taken to ensure student representatives are chosen so that they are credible among the students they are supposed to represent. Given the diversity of every school, this should include accounting for all sorts of student cultures, attitudes, beliefs and ideas. Adults should check and double check when they think a student is credible by working with students as partners to ensure credibility. Sometimes, it is appropriate to select a high achieving, popular student to represent their peers in a student involvement activity. However, there are other times when it is not meaningful for students or adults to have that same student representing students who may be low performing or acting in ways that are not appropriate for school.

Many adults are addressing student voice as giving students a say in what, when, where, how and why they learn. This is a misunderstanding of student voice and actually serves as a barrier to Meaningful Student Involvement. It positions adults as the arbitrators of student voice, placing the responsibility for students' expressions about education on the shoulders of educators. In reality, students are constantly expressing themselves; the question is whether or not adults are willing to listen and act upon what students have to say. Listening to students' needs, interests and concerns has had a big impact on school life and classroom practice; engaging students as partners in learning throughout the educational process and the entirety of the education system has an even larger impact. Overcoming the barriers presented by students, adults and schools is a key to moving in that direction.

G) Evaluation

Assessing outcomes should always be a part of Meaningful Student Involvement opportunities. Every opportunity focused on Meaningful Student Involvement should opportunities for formal and informal feedback from students. The events, opportunities, and numbers of students measured with regard to all the factors affected by the opportunity, as well as the levels, motivations, and impacts of students and adults who are involved or affected (see Figure 13 for an illustration of what this looks like). The quantitative effects of Meaningful Student Involvement can be measured, monitored, and reported, including grades, attendance records, dropout rates, the number of student participants in a given activity, and other effects of Meaningful Student Involvement (see Table 13 for examples).

Meaningful Student Involvement affects many people. Students other than those who are directly involved can provide substantial input when given the opportunity to be involved as independent evaluators in assessing action. Formal assessments of Meaningful Student Involvement completed by students and adults, and the summative impacts of Meaningful Student Involvement should be identified (see Figure 11 for an illustration). The varying short- and long-term impacts may include short and long-term effects and impacts. The effects of Meaningful Student Involvement on classrooms may include the creation of new curriculum or programs, widespread engagement of student-led evaluation and all types of meaningful involvement, and more. Table 13 examines some of these effects; Table 16 shares the types. All of these should be assessed for their presence, purpose and power.

Meaningful Student Involvement can impact school administration through the development of administrative support and structures. Professional development for school staff focused on Meaningful Student Involvement, including teachers and others, can be made mandatory or more made more available. Materials on engaging students as partners can be made widely available, too. One of the most effective measures of meaningfulness may be the amount of more appropriate, student-friendly policies, rules, or guidelines adapted in order to promote, ensure, and sustain Meaningful Student Involvement. Another structural development is the creation of more and more meaningful opportunities for all students to become involved. More accessible or convenient opportunities for students are part of that approach.

Developing this infrastructure requires new approaches to engaging students as partners. This can happen through the intentional recruitment and preparation of nontraditional and new student leaders, as illustrated in Figure 22. It can also happen with the intentional development of new social norms among the student body, between students and adults, and throughout the entirety of the school community. Meaningful Student Involvement should be assessed for those new approaches to relationships among students, between students and adults, and ultimately, between students, adults, and the education system as a whole.

The desires, dreams, and possibilities students envision for school should be acknowledged, documented and assessed throughout the opportunities, especially those of students who are not traditionally engaged in conversations about school improvement. Reports focused on Meaningful Student Involvement should be created with multiple audiences in mind, including politicians, policy-makers and other officials, as well as educators, administrators and students themselves. Additionally, significant time should be spent reflecting on who is involved in opportunities. This means students and adults should work together to examine which students participate; why they were involved; what percentage of students in a school were involved, and so forth.

Engaging students themselves in reflecting on the nature of current student involvement in your school, as well as plans or implementations focused on Meaningful Student Involvement. These reflections should also be shared with everyone possible throughout the education system. Their reflections can include benefits and limitations of Meaningful Student Involvement in school planning, education research, formal teaching and capacity development, learning evaluation, systemic decision-making, and education advocacy. Exploring which opportunities students are meaningfully involved in and why those opportunities happen is essential to evaluating and assessing Meaningful Student Involvement. Students should facilitate capacity building activities for students and adults to increase their ability to become meaningfully involved.

Assessments should be conducted by adults, too. They should have opportunities to continuously increase their capacity to meaningfully involve students, and identify limitations and possibilities of Meaningful Student Involvement throughout education. There should also be opportunities for everyone, including students and adults, to assess what the levels of commitment to Meaningful Student Involvement are from various parties throughout the education system. This means that all sorts of students, administrators, teachers, support staff, parents, and other community members should be asked whether they are committed to Student/Adult Partnerships and Meaningful Student Involvement.

Looking across your current location in education, a specific evaluation should determine what opportunities for focused student voice, substantive student engagement, and Meaningful Student Involvement currently exist. Examining your policies, you should determine whether your classroom, individual school, local district, or state education agency has policies that can ensure or deter sustainable opportunities that meaningfully involve students throughout education. That same examination should determine whether your school or organization can compensate for the budget considerations affecting Meaningful Student Involvement.

Ultimately, you should determine how far away your location is from one hundred percent Meaningful Student Involvement. Identify how many students experience meaningful opportunities and how frequently they experience them. When you have determined this percentage, you will know exactly how far you have to go.

There are many ways you can evaluate whether Meaningful Student Involvement exists and is recognizable. Simply allowing students to be involved is one way. Another way to determine existence is to examine classroom learning and determine what extent Meaningful Student Involvement is present in teaching activities. Acknowledging the classroom learning that happens through Meaningful Student Involvement should happen through students receiving credit. Other ways to identify meaningful involvement is by determining whether fiscal rewards, including stipends, scholarships, or salaries, are given to students who are involved, as well.

The quality of student involvement helps determine the meaningfulness. Sometimes, that quality is ensured through policy-making. When appropriate, schools should provide equitable or equal opportunities for students and adults to serve by establishing and enforcing substantive and appropriate terms of office, voting rights, or positions. Contingency plans should be developed to replace students whose terms, service, or job end early, and a conflict of interest policy for appropriate occasions. Policies that formally allow and encourage students to be involved in multiple activities without penalizing them are often necessary, as well as policies that give students appropriate access to adult allies who are involved including teachers, parents and support staff. Students who are involved should be allowed uninhibited access to information sources that allow them to be meaningfully involved, whether through the Internet, adults who are involved in decision-making, records, etc. Schools should also provide opportunities for students to continuously increase their capacity to be meaningfully involved through capacity building activities of all sorts.

One of the key measurements for Meaningful Student Involvement is that every student in every school has opportunities to systematically, intentionally learn about the structures, purposes, actions and outcomes of education. School should be assessed for whether they afford opportunities for students to expand their involvement in subsequent grade levels. Their learning about this should happen in a constructivist fashion, as illustrated in Figure 17 earlier in this book. This would acknowledge what students already know regardless of their grade level and expand upon it through teaching, action, reflection and critical examination.

Students should be allowed and encouraged to address schoolwide issues, not only those that affect students. The language and concepts used in Meaningful Student Involvement opportunities should be adjusted or explained to students in order to create plainly accessible ideas for everyone involved. Students should also have opportunities to learn about different aspects of the activities they are involved in, whatever it may be focused on. If students are partnering with adults to create a classroom curriculum focused on local history, they should have opportunities to learn about curriculum design and delivery, as well as local history. This is true for any aspect of planning, research, teaching, evaluating, decision-making, or advocacy.

When they are involved in ways that seek to be meaningful, it is important for students and adults to examine how their involvement happens. They should consider whether their activities **isolate** students by creating separate student involvement opportunities that are away from adults, without the context of learning, the education system, or school improvement.

Another pattern that may occur is to **involve** students, where they are deliberately partners with adults throughout schools in specific opportunities. Occasionally, schools might **integrate** students by deliberately partnering students with adults throughout learning, the education system, and school improvement. Perhaps the pinnacle involvement happens when the education system works to **infuse** students, which means that Student/Adult Partnerships are inseparably entwined with the success of education systems and cannot be extracted without causing irreparable damage.

Similarly, Meaningful Student Involvement should be measured for its sustainability. This means determining whether an approach is **isolated** as a one-time activity with low numbers of participants, singular focus of activity and few outcomes. It may be **sporadic**, with occasional opportunities, limited numbers and a limited scope of activity. Approaches could be **sustained**, with high infusion and every student in a school involved, with an unlimited scope of activity (Wood, 2005). Meaningful Student Involvement can also be determined to be **essential**, with the complete infusion of Student/Adult Partnerships throughout learning, relationships, procedures, policy and the culture of a school or education system.

A large measurement within Meaningful Student Involvement is the extent to which every student gets to experience Student/Adult Partnerships. While there is a starting point for all action, it is important for schools, agencies, or education programs to have a strategic plan for expanding Meaningful Student Involvement. Ultimately, every student in every school can experience meaningfulness, whether in their individual classroom experience or collective school wide experience, whether in special and specific district or state education agency opportunities, or in broad student organizing for education improvement. All of this should be assessed in order to determine the efficacy of approaches.

The amount of authority between students and adults should be measured. In almost every circumstance throughout schools, students are held accountable by adults. They are held accountable for their academic achievement, classroom performance, attendance, behavior, attitudes and increasingly, opportunities outside of school. However, adults are not held similarly accountable to students. In Meaningful Student Involvement, mutual accountability is essential for partnerships. Similarly, students should experience appropriately and equitably distributed amounts of authority. Considering the specific conditions for Meaningful Student Involvement when determining how much authority students has is important; however, that should not be the determining factor for whether students should have authority. Instead, every situation should be seen objectively for its potential, purpose, and outcomes. Authority— the ability to author one's story—is something that should be encultrated and codified throughout education for every participant whether students or adults. That authority should be present throughout learning, teaching and leadership as exemplified by Meaningful Student Involvement in education planning, research, teaching, evaluation, decision-making, and advocacy.

Parents should learn about Meaningful Student Involvement too. Their role in supporting, encouraging, sustaining and expanding Student/Adult Partnerships should not be under-acknowledged. In addition to teaching parents, they should also have opportunities to become engaged partners as well.

Opportunities should be assessed for whether they obligate or otherwise compel students and adults to be meaningfully involved. This helps determine amounts of authenticity and generosity, as well as the amounts of time required to build ownership and investment by the participants in Meaningful Student Involvement. These obligations can happen through mandate by education leaders, grant requirements, or agreements between students and adults. They can happen through teacher mandate over students. When policy is set in place, rules are made, or other formalized, codified decisions are written, they can be compulsory as well.

Meaningful Student Involvement necessitates continuous capacity building for students and adults. This may happen through knowledge-sharing and skill building, as well as other means. It may mean providing opportunities for students and adults to co-learn about skills such as communication, time management, project planning, meeting facilitation, budget management, and other skills. It could also mean that all partners learn about school improvement; equity and diversity in education; curricular approaches; leadership issues in education, and other issues. These continuous capacity building opportunities could also focus on topics that are core to Meaningful Student Involvement, including student/adult relationship building; inquiry-based learning; service learning; project planning; curriculum development; teaching skills; evaluation techniques; decision-making methods; and advocacy skills.

Chapter 89. Measuring Outcomes

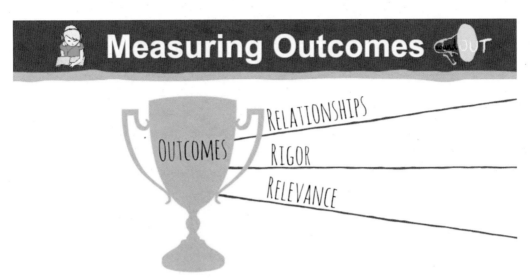

Figure 26. Measuring Outcomes

Throughout the 2000s, a lot of work was done to promote the importance of Rigor, Relevance and Relationships as the "new three Rs" in schools. They form the basis of measuring the outcomes of Meaningful Student Involvement.

H) Relationships

Relationships are the most vital factor in determining the meaningfulness of student involvement. Adults who are chosen by students to provide safe, supportive relationships with them are called adult allies. Students can seek guidance from adult allies on informal and formal bases. Adult allies encourage students to work in solidarity with other students and adults when possible, and when that's not possible they help strategize appropriate relationships. When students and adults have consciously chosen to work for equity and equality together, they form a type of relationship called a student/adult partnership. Student/Adult Partnerships can be present throughout the education system and are an innate component of Meaningful Student Involvement. These relationships include systematic, horizontal student-to-student mentorships and consultations, and gives students room to seek guidance from their peers all the time, as well as adults when appropriate.

In Meaningful Student Involvement, relationships give students opportunities to determine clearly stated goals, a plan of action, and time limits or deadlines. Students should start with short-term goals and activities in order to ensure their relationships with other students and adults, too. Students should not be expected to make representations on behalf of the whole student body. There are careful considerations for activities, including to ensure that other areas of a students' life do not suffer from their involvement, including their health, family, schoolwork, friends, or community activities. If students are selected to be involved by adults, consideration is also made to how that happens, and whether there's a suitable alternative.

Students are adults should be aware of the peer-to-peer relationships among students. It's important to encourage non-hierarchical relationships among students that are focused on equality and commonality. Furthering separating and segregating students within the student body in the name of meaningful involvement does nothing for students. Instead, encouraging cross-boundary student-to-student relationships enforces the collaborative, team-building orientation of Meaningful Student Involvement. Students who are involved should deliberately capture other students' opinions, and report back to their peers when appropriate.

l) Rigor

Rigor is a key element in ensuring that student involvement is meaningful. Measuring rigor in Meaningful Student Involvement focuses primarily on robustness and authenticity.

One element of rigor in Meaningful Student Involvement is present in having different types of students motivated and encouraged to be meaningfully involved throughout education. This is illustrated in Figure 22. Outreach should focus on historically disengaged students, differently-abled students, low achieving students, students from different youth sub-cultures, low-income students, and students from any minority populations within a school or community.

Meaningful Student Involvement should include an active recruitment program that's integrated into the course of the regular school day. Currently involved students should be encouraged to nurture their successors, while all the students should be given opportunities to learn the knowledge and skills critical to their successful involvement. Meaningful Student Involvement needs to be visible in activities, programs, services and policy-making throughout individual schools and districts, as well as state education agencies and education-oriented nonprofits. Actively involved students should have student mentors who coach them when necessary

Rigorous activities focused on Meaningful Student Involvement should have resources dedicated specifically to engage students as partners, including training and travel budgets, technology, and office space. Students should be actively encouraged to speak at meetings, and active measures within the school should promote a positive image of students among adults.

In all activities, addressing student issues should happen primarily from a positive, present, and powerful perspective. It is important for students to critically examine and critique student involvement, schools, and the larger society. However, that should not happen at the expense of maintaining their positive, present, and powerful perspectives. Participants in all activities should be prepared for turnover among the students and adults involved in Meaningful Student Involvement as well. Traditional processes should be made more flexible to accommodate engaging students as partners, including timelines and deadlines. The most rigorous Meaningful Student Involvement activities build upon existing student involvement opportunities.

Assigning school staff the responsibility is a challenging, yet essential, component to ensuring rigor. School assignments should include pay, re-balancing work loads, and otherwise compensating school staff for their work. Adults throughout the school community can volunteer to support Meaningful Student Involvement, as can students.

J) Relevance

Ensuring the relevance of Meaningful Student Involvement happens when students are integrated as partners throughout the education system, and when activities stay genuinely focused on student voice.

Relevance can be ensured when deliberate steps are taken to ensure the issues addressed by Meaningful Student Involvement are relevant to students. Capacities that are explicitly developed among student and adults should be connected to schooling and the world beyond the activity students are engaged in. Acknowledging and/or assessing student learning from Meaningful Student Involvement should happen throughout the activity, and clear classroom learning connections should be drawn whenever appropriate. Ultimately, the relevance of Meaningful Student Involvement can be determined through the assessment and acknowledgement of student and adults learning, both about engaging students as partners throughout education, and about classroom based learning, when appropriate.

Steps should be taken to ensure that recognition is relevant to students, as well as to make sure Meaningful Student Involvement is fun for both students and adults. Students should have opportunities to form friendships beyond activities. Meaningful Student Involvement can enhance the goals and mission of your school, and activities should reflect those connections.

Conclusion

The effect of Meaningful Student Involvement on student learning is key to assessing opportunities. So is examining the effects of Meaningful Student Involvement on relationships among students, between students and adults, and on the culture of schools.

Programs, classrooms, schools, districts, agencies and other places promoting Meaningful Student Involvement should create specific policies to sustain Meaningful Student Involvement. Additionally, every formal and informal procedure within educational environments should be reformed to embrace and encourage Meaningful Student Involvement. This could include curricular approaches, student development processes, adult professional development; formal school improvement planning; and other avenues.

Each of these evaluative measures and assessments are important for examining the depth, breadth, and power of Meaningful Student Involvement.

Chapter 90. Sustaining Meaningful Student Involvement

Schools have been slow to build a conception of student voice. After more than a century, we have been even slower to recognize the ability and capacity of students to be meaningfully involved in their own learning, teaching and leadership. Finally though, after all these years, here and there we are realizing that students themselves are the essential core of *every single part* of the education system. Rather than simply being our focus, adults throughout schools are finally seeing that students are the co-drivers and experts of their experiences who can and should have vital and vibrant roles throughout the course of education, in every department of every school, district, state and federal agency, and throughout the sectors outside the system that serve students, too (Mitra, 2009). As our awareness raises, we see that schools are only as effective as the least engaged student within them, and that there must be radical, deliberate steps taken to transform the entirety of the educative experience for all students, everywhere, all of the time.

However, we are realizing there is a creative tension within schools, too. Far from becoming the overlords of schools, we see that students need to become equitable partners with adults who have substantial impact in everything where they are involved. Classroom learning about the core curriculum; extracurriculars focused on their favorite topics; systemic policymaking infusing passion and purpose into the daily life of schools; and every other activity within the education system are all specifically missing the hearts, minds and hands of students. We can now see the future of schools depends on whether students can become willing to attend on their own volition, from kindergarten through graduation, and that rather than try to combat the force of freewill, schools should become attuned to students today through Meaningful Student Involvement.

When we draw these lessons deeply within ourselves, we want to ensure their successful implementation. More importantly though, is the feeling of being compelled towards making sure they keep happening long after we are gone. This opens the door of understanding how to sustain roles for students as partners throughout education. Table 15 in this book showed what some of these roles can look like.

Understanding Sustainability

Considering the space between student engagement and student voice, school improvement and the daily operations of the entirety of the education system, students and adults can see that Meaningful Student Involvement is going to become an inescapable element in the future of schools. When we consider that future, though, nothing seems inevitable. Understanding sustainability is key to ensuring Meaningful Student Involvement today and into the future of schools.

Sustainability includes the lasting experience and impact of Meaningful Student Involvement on individual students and adults; classrooms and schools at large; and the education system as a whole. Sustainability is the driving force behind implementing Meaningful Student Involvement in one classroom today, as well as what implements, maintains, critiques and reinvents the approach for every student in every school throughout every nation for every student far into the future.

The study of a multi-year project in the United Kingdom led to the recognition of several steps that promote sustained student voice approaches. Findings included:

- Working together (e.g. in pairs, groups and teams) with others (e.g. students, adults) is central to the process of learning.
- We help each other to develop views and understanding by sharing our own ideas and experiences.
- We have all got something to learn from each other (students from students / students from teachers / teachers from students / teachers from teachers)
- Action is the practical expression of real values rather than good intentions.
- Commitment to working together needs to be sustained and sustainable.
- Working together must be partnered with a deep respect for and awareness of our responsibility for other living things and our natural environment. (Carnie & Fielding, 2007)

Component One: Learning

The first component of sustainability is learning. Students and adults should be engaged as partners through learning about all aspects of Meaningful Student Involvement. These include learning about learning, learning about schools, learning about the education system, and learning about the work it takes to engage students as partners (McCombs & Whisler, 1997). Students can be meaningfully involved in helping other students learn about Meaningful Student Involvement. Additionally, students should work on issues that they clearly identify as important. However, they should also consider what issues that their school and communities value, as well. This helps determine the sustainability of Meaningful Student Involvement by ensuring the authenticity of student voice.

Component Two: Interest

There needs to be an active process for students and adults to recruit new students when others leave. Students and adults should be satisfied with each other's involvement, and that satisfaction should be measured throughout the process. Deliberate steps should be taken to overcome student disengagement if it is present or becomes apparent in activities. Overcoming fluctuating involvement of students is important, as is overcoming adult disengagement and the fluctuating involvement of adults.

Component Three: Policy

A written policy, law, or rule supporting the engagement of students throughout education is one of the primary tools sustaining Meaningful Student Involvement. In additional to formal tools, informal mechanisms are used, also. The principal or superintendent should introduce Meaningful Student Involvement to teachers and other school leaders. Social events that are organized to increase positive interactions between students and adults improve sustainability, too. Holding joint workshops with students and adults and putting a plan in place to infuse students throughout the education system, as well as the core activities of the class or school assists, too. Additional steps can help students fit into previously adult-exclusive committees or programs also.

Component Four: Communication

Sustainability measures should determine whether Meaningful Student Involvement affects students outside of the activity and in the larger school body. The larger student body should also be made aware of Meaningful Student Involvement activities, especially if they are *not* participants in them.

Component Five: Organization

A vehicle for engaging students as partners should be created in order to sustain action. This can be a committee, position, club, or class focused on Meaningful Student Involvement. Measuring activities should identify whether student action is created and sustained through policy, positions, or sharing of funds. New or more policies, positions, and/or ongoing funding should be identified to support student programs, policies, services or activities. There should be opportunities for education-improvement focused activities to be self-managed programs by students for students, as well as student-managed programs by students for students and adults both.

Component Six: Measurement

Measuring sustainability should show that there is Meaningful Student Involvement throughout the process of school improvement, including school planning, educational evaluation, classroom teaching, systemic decision-making, and education advocacy. The compositions of adult committees and boards should be changed to meaningfully involve students as well. This can happen by requiring students becoming engaged as partners in as many decisions as possible. Student advisory structures are not sustainable, as they rely on specific students being available for certain activities at predetermined times. Instead of principal advisory committees or superintendent councils, every student in every school should be actively engaged in advising school policy, practice and outcomes. Students should become meaningfully involved how and where learning happens, who is involved in making decisions happen, and why it matters. Consultative practices in schools should be expanded on, too, by infusing students throughout their operations.

Conclusion

Sustainability in Meaningful Student Involvement should focus on making sure all students and adults throughout the education system are actively involved in creating new social norms among students, and between students and adults. This can happen through student voice workshops, Meaningful Student Involvement strategies, or student engagement programs that are delivered to parents, educators, administrators, communities members, and others. Additionally, specific spaces should be created that foster Student/Adult Partnerships. These might be workspaces, offices, meeting rooms or otherwise, and should take in account the different learning and engagement needs of both students and adults.

However, all of these components aside, it might be most essential to remember what the personal side of Meaningful Student Involvement. Early in this book, I expanded on the Characteristics of Meaningful Student Involvement, including Personal Commitment. When a student or an adult has taken deliberate steps to establish and secure their own ongoing dedication to Meaningful Student Involvement, they are far more sustainable than those who have not.

Douglas Reeves wrote about this eloquently saying, "Sustainable change, after all, depends not upon compliance with external mandates or blind adherence to regulation, but rather upon the pursuit of the greater good." If that introduction to the idea were not enough, Reeves go on to explain,

"Behavior precedes belief – that is, most people must engage in a behavior before they accept that it is beneficial; then they see the results, and then they believe that it is the right thing to do.... implementation precedes buy-in; it does not follow it." (Reeves, 2009)

Ensuring personal commitment to Meaningful Student Involvement and working through these components are keys to sustaining transformation, and ultimately can be used to measure meaningfulness everywhere, all of the time.

Chapter 91. Questioning Meaningful Student Involvement

At the center of Meaningful Student Involvement, there are some core questions that must be answered. Students and adults should consider why, how, who, what, when and where opportunities happen.

Questions

Following are some core questions that can be used to evaluate, assess and otherwise measure Meaningful Student Involvement. They cover five important themes that consistently matter:

- **Framing**, which addresses how and why Meaningful Student Involvement is set up in a classroom, school or other environment;
- **Substance**, which deals with whether activities are whole and real;
- **Readiness**,
- **Measurement,**
- **Sustaining,** which looks at whether and how Meaningful Student Involvement lasts over time.

As you answer these questions for your classroom, school, district program, state agency or community activities, remember that Meaningful Student Involvement is a systems growth process that isn't reliant on a sequential process. Instead, it's a broader education transformation that takes time, can move backwards in order to go forward, and relies on deliberate and intention action for success. See Table 24 for more questions.

Framing

1. Why do you want to integrate Meaningful Student Involvement in your school?

2. What do you want to see happen because of Meaningful Student Involvement?

3. What challenges do you foresee for Meaningful Student Involvement?

4. Identify the type of opportunity for Meaningful Student Involvement you are going to plan for: Curriculum design, classroom management, building administration, extra-curricular, school improvement, district administration, regional administration, state administration, or other?

5. Identify the type of Meaningful Student Involvement activity: Planning, research, teaching, evaluation, decision-making, advocacy, or other?

6. What is the name of the activity? Write a short description of it.

Substance

7. Describe how the following steps of the Cycle of Engagement will occur: Listening? Validating? Authorizing? Mobilizing? Reflecting?

8. What level of authority will students have? Will they have *no authority* by being assigned to be involved but not allowed to make contributions? Will they have *low authority*, where adults lead and students contribute? Will they have medium authority, leading action with adults contributing? Or will they have high authority, leading with adults and contributing as equitable partners?

9. Describe student authority.

10. Identify which students will be meaningfully involved, and briefly describe how that specific group will be involved according to their: Grade level, academic achievement level, leadership level, learning styles diversity, racial diversity, ethnic diversity, cultural diversity, gender diversity, sexual orientation diversity, class type, club type, special group type, or otherwise?

11. Describe the participants.

12. Identify when Meaningful Student Involvement will occur, and provide details: In class; during school but outside of class; before or after school; on weekends; or otherwise.

13. Describe the timing, and why Meaningful Student Involvement will occur at that time.

14. Where will Meaningful Student Involvement occur? In a classroom; an office; a different student space; a different adult space; a community setting; an administrative office; or other?

15. Describe the space where the activity will occur.

16. Describe how students have contributed to creating or otherwise influencing the activity setting.

Readiness

17. How does the whole school become aware of Meaningful Student Involvement?

18. How are students prepared for Meaningful Student Involvement?

19. Do students participate in educational skill-building activities designed to increase their personal and collective capacity to be meaningfully involved?

20. What skills are increased: Social relationships within peer groups; written communication; oral communication; public speaking; listening to peers; managing change; conflict management; diversity awareness; emotional intelligence; intergenerational understanding, or; otherwise?

21. What knowledge areas are increased: Learning process; the education system; school improvement; voice; roles for students as partners in education; intergenerational equity in schools, or; otherwise?

22. How are adults in the school prepared for Meaningful Student Involvement?

23. Do adults participate in educational skill-building activities designed to increase their personal and collective capacity to be meaningfully involved?

24. Which skills are increased: Listening to student voice; treating students as partners; understanding adultism; conflict management; diversity awareness; managing change; intergenerational understanding, or; otherwise?

25. What knowledge areas are increased: Learning diversity; the education system; school improvement; student voice; roles for students as partners in education; intergenerational equity in schools; integrating student voice in curriculum; infusing student voice in building leadership, or; otherwise?

Measuring

26. Identify which stakeholders will be impacted by Meaningful Student Involvement: Student and adult participants; student body of the whole school; school staff throughout the whole school; all members of the school community; and families; younger or older students; education administration staff; members; educational support organizations, or; otherwise?

27. Specifically, how will you know Meaningful Student Involvement will affect the group(s) you selected?

28. What impact areas will be measured: Student participant learning; student body learning; student participant attitudes; student body attitudes; school staff learning; school staff attitudes; school climate; learning community; multiple stakeholder involvement, or; otherwise?

29. Specifically, how will the activity impact the outcome area(s) you selected?

30. What are the learning outcomes for the activity?

31. How will you assess learning outcomes resulting from Meaningful Student Involvement?

32. How will Meaningful Student Involvement improve your whole school?

33. How will you know Meaningful Student Involvement affected your whole school?

34. Is Meaningful Student Involvement part of your school's formal school improvement plan? If so, how, and if not, why not?

35. How will the effect of Meaningful Student Involvement on your school improvement goals be assessed?

Sustaining

36. How will student and adult reflections on the activity be utilized beyond this one

37. activity?

38. How will the activity be acknowledged to: Student participants? The student body? School staff: Parents? Others?

39. How will this activity or its outcomes be sustained beyond this plan?

Considerations

Democracy is inherently about inclusion. Because of the necessity of inclusion, schools can be blatantly antithetical to the democratic levers of control over schools. Many critical theorists, including Giroux (1993), hooks (1994), Freire (2005) and others, believe this reality operates in conjunction with the increasing surveillance society we live in, commodified culture we adopt and demonized diversity we are fed to show that public schools are adrift in purpose, or worse still, awash in a vast effort to disenfranchise citizens and de-democratize society. He is not wrong.

Many schools generally operate with rules selected by principals hired by superintendents appointed by school boards elected by citizens. Despite acting as if they are out of the purview of the masses, focused, peaceful, and powerful advocacy by students, educators, and parents will ultimately lead to stronger controls, and ultimately, more Meaningful Student Involvement.

FRAMEWORK FOR ASSESSMENT

Adapted With Permission From Fielding, M. (2001)

If you are looking for specific questions to assess Meaningful Student Involvement, look no further. English student voice researcher Michael Fielding created the following framework based on his decades of research, and I've used it effectively with many schools and districts across the United States and Canada. There are five themes to the questions.

Theme 1: Equitable Student/Adult Partnerships
- Who is involved?
- Why are they involved?
- How are they involved?
- Which students are *allowed* to be involved?
- What language, behavior and activities are encouraged and/or allowed?
- Who decides the answer to these questions?

Theme 2: Skills and Attitudes
- Are the skills of Meaningful Student Involvement encouraged and supported through training or other appropriate means?
- Are these skills understood, developed and practiced within the context of other democratic values and dispositions?
- Are these skills themselves changed or informed by those values and dispositions?

Theme 3: Systems and Spaces
- How often does dialogue and engagement between students and educators currently happen your school or agency? Who decides?
- How do the systems highlighting the value and necessity of Meaningful Student Involvement mesh with or relate to other activities, especially those involving adults?
- What action is taken for Meaningful Student Involvement?

Theme 4: Organizational Culture
- Do the cultural norms and values of the organization proclaim the importance of Meaningful Student Involvement within the context of school improvement?
- Do the practices, traditions and routine daily encounters demonstrate values supportive of Meaningful Student Involvement?

Theme 5: The Future
- Does your school or agency need new structures for Meaningful Student Involvement?
- Does your school or agency need new ways of relating to each other as students and/or educators?

Table 23. Framework for Assessment.

Part XI. The Public Student

Chapter 92. Introduction

In 2013, there was a lot of prattle in the mainstream media and online after Ta-Nehisi Coates wrote, "Melissa Harris-Perry is America's foremost public intellectual." (Coates, 2014) There was predictable disagreement from many directions, not the least of which being what constitutes an intellectual, and what constitutes a public intellectual. In the outcome of that conversation, Henry Giroux launched the Public Intellectual Project at McMaster University for many reasons, not the least of which being to promote a common understanding of what the title means.[1]

In Part Two of this book, I defined Meaningful Student Involvement as the systematic approach to engaging students as partners in learning throughout every facet of education for the purpose of strengthening their commitment to education, community and democracy. In Part Ten, I want to propose a vision expanding from that definition by elaborating on what may be the most important role of any person in schools, throughout the education system and across the entirety of our society today, the role of the Public Student.

The Public Student is any learner whose position is explicitly vital to the future of education, community and democracy. This Section explores their roles in-depth.

---

[1] Learn about The Public Intellectual Project at McMaster University led by Henry Giroux see publicintellectualsproject.mcmaster.ca

ADAM FLETCHER

Chapter 93. Essential Lessons about Meaningful Student Involvement

There are many important things that students and adults can learn from Meaningful Student Involvement. Through student activism for school reform and increasing amounts of student voice in the public realm, we can learn that students expect schools to be more public, transparent and critical institutions for students and adults alike. (Williams, 2012) If they cannot do that, students will not continue to support them into the future, which not only affects our schools, but the entire democratic nature of our society. Following are some other essential lessons about Meaningful Student Involvement (Germond, et al, 2006; Chopra, 2014; Yang, 2010; Dotta & Ristow, 2011; Dahal, 2014; Chemutai & Chumba, 2014).

1) Every school should meaningfully involve every student in every classroom.

Learning ability, grade level, interest tracking... none of these should be seen or addressed as barriers to Meaningful Student Involvement. Instead, these are point to build upon and learn from. Meaningful Student Involvement is an active, intentional process whereupon young people become purposefully compelled as learners. It is essential that no school should ever non-meaningfully involve any learner, ever.

2) Meaningful involvement does not end at the schoolhouse door.

Students must be meaningfully involved within their families and throughout their communities. This goes far beyond classroom assignments and community service. Partnering with learners in democratic governance, providing powerful opportunities for cultural expression, and creating meaningful experiences of freedom of speech throughout their community can open the doors for all students. Meaningful involvement should happen at home, in play, and through positive relationships with adults throughout our communities.

3) Every adult in every student's life should feel responsible for Meaningful Student Involvement in learning.

Only through the constant encouragement and focus of parents, teachers, youth workers, principals, religious leaders, counselors, and other supportive adults will students feel there is a real investment in their education that extends beyond their own interests. Every student should feel that educational success is their responsibility; likewise, every adult should feel that student engagement is theirs.

4) Give a student a lesson and they'll think for an hour; teach them how to learn and they will learn a lifetime.

Learning to learn is a task that many educators aspire to impart. Every student must have a constructivist understanding of the nature of learning, the purpose of schooling, the course of the education system, and the arch of lifelong learning. From kindergarten through graduation educators have more than the opportunity to teach students about learning; they have an obligation.

5) Meaningful Student Involvement is a living, breathing goal that must continuously evolve.

Will Rogers once said, "Even if you're on the right track you'll get run over if you do not move." We live in a world of transition and change; students change with the times, and often with the days. Do the same old thing and we'll get the same old outcomes we've always had. As society constantly changes, so do our students. Many educators have told me that students have changed more in the last five years than schools have in the last twenty-five. This makes opportunities for real learning through Student/Adult Partnerships.

Chapter 94. Growing Momentum

Every school in the country is focused on the question of how to improve student achievement in every content area and in every grade level. Each day, in schools with all types of individual challenges, educators use the diverse tools of school improvement to help make progress for students. While these tools often cite involvement as a key component of school improvement, that idea has rarely included students. For the sake of the future of education, it is time for students to be more than heard, and it is time for schools to take action. It is time for students to be partners in school change, and it is time for Meaningful Student Involvement.

The work of Meaningful Student Involvement is not easy or instantaneously rewarding. It demands that the system of schooling change, and that the attitudes of students, educators, parents and community members change. However, in a time when the success of individual students is being leveraged against funding for schools, it is essential to go beyond students planning school dances and leading mock elections. Those activities may actually have negative effects on students.

Despite the various types of Meaningful Student Involvement outlined in this book (see Table 16 for a summary), there is no finite model for engaging every student that can be adopted by all schools. What will be appropriate for one school might not succeed in another. Meaningful Student Involvement is part of a transformative cycle that should be continually re-examined, redeveloped and reconceived within each learning community as it evolves over time with new participants.

The potential outcomes are too great to ignore the possibilities. This Handbook characterizes Meaningful Student Involvement and its usefulness as a strategic process for improving the quality and quantity of student engagement. By making knowledge relevant to students' lives and providing supportive learning environments in which all participants can grow, Meaningful Student Involvement provides innumerable positive outcomes for all members of the education community. Most importantly, Meaningful Student Involvement shows that schooling can be a powerful, positive and motivating force when it respects and values the contributions of each and every student.

Chapter 95. The Role of The Public Student

Ultimately, Meaningful Student Involvement comes down to this: Schools must aspire to be more than just dispersing knowledge to the willing. Reducing education to a commodified exchange is one of the lowest common denominators in human existence. It makes educators and students powerless to affect change in their learning, let alone the world. Everyone involved becomes incapable of acting in democratic relationships.

Engaging students as partners throughout the education system intends to address the discrepancies facing the larger roles of young people throughout society. Disenfranchised from social purpose beyond schooling, adults allies of students in schools should strive to reinforce the notion of young peoples' public personhood and existence beyond the crass economic subjugation that motivated the identification of "youthhood" originally. We should all strive to heighten the role of the Public Student. This modern learner is the engine of democracy, fueling all other social, cultural, spiritual, educational, and economic developments throughout society.

In their most democratic sense, the public student would experience Giroux's hope for schools when he suggested that by educators engaging critically with education, curriculum,

> "should embody a public philosophy dedicated to returning schools to their primary task... creating a public sphere of citizens who are able to exercise power over their own lives and especially over the conditions of knowledge production and acquisition." (1990)

These citizens can come from this conception of The Public Student.

Without the specific role of student, democracy would simply fail. Today's neoliberal education policy would reduce the role of student to that of consumer and product as well, and oftentimes denies their roles as producer and engine. This occurs not only in classrooms, but also in school offices, school boardrooms, and education administration offices.

That said, in a society that systematically segregates young people from adults, it is important to acknowledge the unique role that only children and youth occupy, which is that of K-12 student. In our modern social construct, that has been the only place in society specifically designed for children and youth, and the role of student is the only formal role for them. Unfortunately, as schools stand today that place and role are being claimed by economic imperialists who believe schools only need to serve the capitalist hegemony, rather than the larger democratic good.

Students are innately attuned to this discrepancy of purpose. Over several decades they have come to see their role in school as that of prisoner. This is reinforced by succeeding generations of parents, teachers, administrators, voters, and politicians. Meaningful Student Involvement reframes the place of schooling in society so that its seen as the right that it is, as the powerhouse of democracy, and as the hope for the future that it is and should be.

Acknowledging the distinct identity of students is vital to integrating them throughout the education system that serves them, which is the purpose of my work in schools. That identity is one as the Public Student.

Meaningful Student Involvement transcends schools. In a time when the health of our nation's democracy is at stake, everyone must reconsider their individual role in society. Research and experience illustrates that people who have been meaningfully involved when they are young are most likely to be informed citizens who are engaged throughout their communities. As partners in school change, students are virtually ensured this positive, powerful, and productive future. The complex leadership skills and applied learning that all students can experience through Meaningful Student Involvement serve as vital components in any education system and society that calls for a more engaging, sustainable and just democracy.

Chapter 96. The Fully Realized Learner

In the middle of Meaningful Student Involvement is a picture of empowered students who are fully capable of transforming schools and the entirety of the education system through Student/Adult Partnerships. This is an important concept. Equally as important, though, is the role of the fully realized learner.

Student involvement can go even further than meaningfulness. When adults continuously sustain Student/Adult Partnerships in a classroom and throughout a school building, more happens, including student progression and evolution. As more people throughout the education system increasingly harbor realistic yet growing ambitions for students, it becomes vital for educators to harness those ambitions in order to successfully facilitate new roles for *all* students. Fully realized learners enable Meaningful Student Involvement to be highly successful, and rather than threatening schools, they should be treated as assets to the education system, inspiring others along the way.

In an era of increasingly unfettered technological access, the number of students who are actively choosing to transform their own educational experiences is growing every day. More than ever, students are getting on the Internet and zooming towards any information whenever they want it. Using devices and apps, they are collaborating and debating and pontificating and sharing with their peers in a co-driven experience focused on mutual benefit. Supported by parents who are intensely desiring a better life for their kids, many students today are literally reaching for the stars and beyond. They are calling all of society to be better, do better and become more than what we have ever imagined.

That reality is for the betterment of all of us. Despite the implications for democracy, these fully realized learners are going beyond any boundaries that were established in the eons before they were born. They are seeing past the limitations, plainly ignoring, and fully addressing the barriers previous generations stumbled towards and sometimes over. Students today are not doing this without fault, and they make mistakes. There is no romanticization here. There is, however, pure admiration of the evolving capacities of succeeding generations of students.

Beyond of these evolving capacities, we are witnessing the emergence of purely student-driven, student-led activities throughout education today (Weiss & Huget, 2015). Generally speaking, they are not happening within the confines of the education system. However, students are still learning, teaching and leading change throughout education with their actions.

For instance, there are an increasing number of student-driven, student-led student voice advocacy groups around the world today. These are groups of students who are clearly informed by research and literature, but rather than citing it and building projects responsive to research findings, they are creating new pathways to change that do not involve laboring over philosophy and instead focus on action.

The Student-Philosopher

There are students who are working on their own to improve schools. One example is from Nikhil Goyal, a student-philosopher who wrote a book about school change when he was still in high school. His book, *One Size Does Not Fit All*, was published in 2012 and offer his prescription for school improvement. As a high school student, Goyal interviewed Howard Gardner, Seth Godin, Noam Chomsky, Diane Ravitch, and others, summarizing and expanding on their perceptions with his own call to reimagine school. Goyal is a fully realized learner who is leading his peers and adults throughout society in new conversations about education reform.[38]

Student-philosophers are important examples of The Public Student, as they shine a spotlight on the roles of students throughout the education system by passionately, actively moving them from being the passive recipients of adult-driven schools towards become passionately engaged and culturally relevant critical allies of the system. In his book, Goyal does not simply lob bombs into the foyer of the school building. Instead, he conscientiously dismantles the building brick by brick, and then systematically rebuilds it according to his own vision for learning, teaching and leadership. Surely, this demonstrates intellectual depth and courage on his part, since he was still in high school when he did it. More importantly, though, Goyal opened portal for other students to do the same. His specific case cannot be said to quite constitute an example of Meaningful Student Involvement because he deliberately operated outside the confines of Student/Adult Partnerships, and completely outside of the formal structure of the education system. However, it does make him a prime candidate as a Public Student, which in turn makes the role he is fulfilling central to Meaningful Student Involvement.

The challenge of the student-philosopher is related to the heart of Meaningful Student Involvement as well. Devoid the accountability necessitated by democratic interaction, the student-philosopher may feel free to lambast people who are accountable to democratic controls in ways that they, student-philosophers, are not. However, this is also the nature of democratic discourse, and something every student should have explicit and substantive exposure to and opportunities to participate in.

Student-Led High Schools

As shared earlier in this book, there are stories emerging across the United States and Canada regarding students leading their high schools through Student/Adult Partnerships. One of the stories was about Alternatives in Action High School, a charter founded in Oakland, California, by students. Another is the Independent Project at Monument Mountain Regional High School in Great Barrington, Massachusetts. Regarded as a "school within a school", the project was intended to,

> "create a school that allows young people to be completely invested and to move every kind of human being through the same gate."

Student-driven learning fills this space, which is focused on science, history, math, and reading and writing. They work on individual endeavors and group projects, and address serious social issues throughout their learning. Students work intensively with adult mentors in Student/Adult Partnerships, and self-actualize their investment and ownership in their own learning. (Monument Mountain Regional High School, 2014) Although the school operates in sync with an adult-led mainstream high school, the story of the Independent Project is exceptional because it is a student-driven effort focused on improving education for all students, and not merely those who started it. This highlights one of the many ways the Public Student affects the lives of other students, in turn making their role central to Meaningful Student Involvement.

The challenge of student-led high schools is that, if not facilitated appropriately, they may assume student interest and ability in places where there is none. If this occurs and the attempt at Meaningful Student Involvement does not produce the results adults want to see or are comfortable with, this approach may actually enable adults to justly abandon all forms of student involvement. They tried it, it did not work and they move onto something else.

Online Learning

As more students emerge from the haze of adult-led learning, there is a growing urgency for responsive, empowering learning opportunities that meet the needs of learners where they are, instead of insisting they go to where adults want them to be. Since the advent of computers, many technologists have sought to put learning and teaching directly in the hands of young people specifically. Today, that is becoming reality more and more. First emphasized for recreation purposes, Internet-enabled devices are now being marketed explicitly for their learning possibilities and connectivity. Students are being encouraged by websites, nonprofits, and private businesses to engage in their own learning as leaders by exploring their interests, abilities and passions, and to use technology to learn far more than any school or teacher could possibly teacher them. In a time when everyone is more connected than ever before, it is no wonder why marketers are selling new devices to students. More importantly, they are appealing to young people on the premise of learning. Meaningful Student Involvement aligns on this form of the fully realized learner because both challenge the apparent irrelevance of schooling by situating students as the drivers of learning, teaching and leadership.

Meaningful Student Involvement can be challenged by online learning in a variety of ways. If this approach happens without community building and a commitment to the larger education system, the form of student empowerment and engagement that happens through online learning may serve to encourage self-centeredness and ultimately, narcissism. This can be rectified through Meaningful Student Involvement though, as students deliberately engage in the world beyond the Internet as well as learning through the Internet.

Student-Led Education Activism

Across Canada, the United States and around the world student activists are calling for substantive and meaningful policy changes in ways unseen before. They are using sophisticated campaign-building techniques, leading community organizing efforts, and driving education leadership to rethink the absence of student voice throughout school decision-making apparatuses on every level of school and in each layer of the education system. These student-led efforts focus on everything highlighted throughout this book and more, sometimes partnering with adults and other times leaving adults out of the equation entirely. This approach aligns well with Meaningful Student Involvement because of its high place on the Ladder of Student Involvement and the significant ways students address the public mechanisms of the public school system.

In the United States, one example of student-led education activism comes from an organization I greatly admire called the Seattle Young Peoples Project, or SYPP. For more than fifteen years, SYPP has operated several student-led projects targeting the Seattle school district, focusing on social justice and youth empowerment the entire time. One program called Youth Undoing Institutional Racism has worked on several anti-racism campaigns, including getting military recruiters out of schools and rehiring union bus drivers laid off during fiscal cutbacks. As mentioned earlier in this book, these students were responsible for having Zinn's important book, *A People's History of the United States*, approved by the school district for use in high school history classes. They also defeated a local high school alumni association in court, who challenged the school district's removal of a racist school mascot at the behest of Youth Undoing Institutional Racism's campaign against it.

One potential challenge of this approach to Meaningful Student Involvement is that it happens outside the parameters of formal learning and teaching in schools. Meaningful Student Involvement is not activism for the sake of action. Instead, it ensures that there is a purpose beyond this immediate moment. Engaging students in schools in the work of critiquing, improving, sustaining improvements and critiquing schools again is absolutely vital to the purpose of securing democracy and social justice for all students in every school all of the time. Meaningful Student Involvement should always reflect that, and if student-led work of any kind does not reflect that, it is not meaningful. That said, without the active engagement and ongoing allyship of adults within schools, this type of work is impossible and student-led education activism of any kind becomes vital in order to ensure that Meaningful Student Involvement can happen. Many of the specific approaches advocated throughout this book are absolutely indebted to the student-led education activism movement.

---

[38] Learn about Goyal at nikhilgoyal.me

Chapter 97. The Project

The Public Student acts with their K-12 peers and adults as partners to become academics, learners, activists, artists, cultural workers and community members who communicate ideas, engage in dialogue, and support the education system. They challenge the growing crisis of shared public values by engaging critically and conscientiously in Meaningful Student Involvement. The project of Meaningful Student Involvement is greatly enhanced by the acknowledgment of The Public Student. This young person, consciously and deliberately engaged in the world around them, does not have the boundaries of social class, race, economics, educational ability or gender that all frequently dominate student leadership in schools today. This young person does not suffer the innate fear and oppression faced by so many disengaged students throughout the history of education. This young person is not shackled by consumerist demands of shallow marketplace whims while they struggle from middle school in order to get into a top tier college.

Instead, the young person engaged in this project is The Public Student, fully accountable to themselves, their peers, the adults they partner with and the communities they belong to. They are inspired and motivated through internal fortitude and resilience, prepared to face the challenges of democratic action and determined to engage as active social justice advocates. They stand for themselves, their families, their communities and their cultures as they build democracy, spark and sustain hope, and build education for everyone, everywhere, all of the time. They are Public Students.

Within their roles as primary and secondary school learners, Public Students develop a deep understanding that education systems must be vital spaces with cultures and practices that help students become critical thinkers and engaged community members, especially those historically disengaged students those who face challenging economic and social realities today.

In partnership, students and adults work together to acknowledge and actualize the reality that schools must be deeply committed to engaging students in Meaningful Student Involvement to challenge serious problems in the education system, and throughout the society that surrounds schools.[39]

As said by The Public Intellectual Project,

> "The future of public education and genuine democracy is intertwined. If democracy is going to have a future, let alone a global one, it depends on everyone's capacity to access critical education, develop a sense of agency, form collective networks, and generate a new public culture that can resist the domination of market-driven neoliberal forces." (The Public Intellectual Project, n.d.)

The Public Student is vital to the future of Meaningful Student Involvement, and not merely because s/he embodies the ideals of education today. Rather, the Public Student holds the aspirations of community in their veins and expresses them through their learning. They hold the experiment of democracy in their souls and live them through their actions. There is no greater purpose in education than this, for now and all times.

[39] This chapter was largely adapted with permission from The Public Intellectual Project at publicintellectualsproject.mcmaster.ca/about/

Research Sources

In Table 14, "Effects of Meaningful Student Involvement," I based my findings off the following publications. These were selected for their depth, outcomes and significance in relationship to the literature surrounding Meaningful Student Involvement.

Overall

Brennan, M. (1996) Schools as public institutions: Students and citizenship. *Youth Studies Australia*, 151 24-27.

Beattie, H. (2012). Amplifying student voice: The missing link in school transformation. *Management in Education*, 26(3), 158-160.

Beaudoin, N. (2005). Elevating student voice: How to enhance participation, citizenship, and leadership. Larchmont, NY: Eye On Education.

Bragg, S., & Fielding, M. (2003). *Pupil Participation: Building a Whole School Commitment*. Cambridge: Pearson Publishing.

Brasov, M. (2009). Living democracy: How Constitution High School molds better citizens. *Social Education*, 73(5), 207-211.

Brasof, M. (2015). Student Voice and School Governance: Distributing Leadership to Youth and Adults. Routledge.

Checkoway, B., & Richards-Schuster, K. (2006). Youth participation for educational reform in low-income communities of color. In S. A. Ginwright, P. Noguera, & J. Cammarota, *Beyond Resistance! Youth activism and community change: New democratic possibilities for practice and policy for America's youth.* (pp. 319-332). Routledge.

Chopra, C. H. (2014). New Pathways for Partnerships: An Exploration of How Partnering With Students Affects Teachers and Schooling. (Unpublished doctoral dissertation). University of Washington.

Erlich, J., & Erlich, S. (1971). *Student Power, Participation and Revolution.* Association Press.

Fielding, M. (2001). Students as radical agents of change. *Journal of Educational Change*, 123-127.

Fletcher, A. (2014). *The Guide to Student Voice.* Olympia, Washington: CommonAction.

Flutter, J., & Rudduck, J. (2006). "Student Voice and the architecture of change: Mapping the territory." Retrieved November 2, 2014, from educ.cam.ac.uk/research/projects/researchdevelopment/07_06rudduck1.doc

Freire, P. (1973). *Education for Critical Consciousness.* Bloomsbury Publishing.

Freire, P., & Freire, A. (1997). *Pedagogy of the Heart.* New York: Continuum.

Giroux, H. A. (1981). *Ideology, Culture and the Process of Schooling.* The Falmer Press.

Klein, R. (2003) *We Want Our Say: Children As Active Participants In Their Education.* Sterling, VA: Trentham.

Kurth-Schai, R. (1988). The roles of youth in society: A reconceptualization. *The Educational Forum*, 52(2).

Kushman, J.W., & Shanessy, J. (1997). *Look Who's Talking Now: Student Views of Learning in Restructuring Schools.* Portland: Northwest Regional Educational Laboratory.

McDermott, J.C. (1998). *Beyond the Silence: Listening for Democracy.* Portsmouth, NH: Heinemann.

Mitra, D. L. (2008). Student voice in school reform: Building youth-adult partnerships that strengthen schools and empower youth. SUNY Press.

Oldfather, P. (1995). Learning from student voices. *Theory to Practice*, 43(2), 84–87.

Rubin, B., & Silva, E. (Eds.). (2003). *Critical voices in school reform: Students living through change.* New York City: RoutledgeFalmer.

Rudduck, J. & Flutter, J. (2004) *How to improve your school: Giving pupils a voice.* New York:

Continuum.

Rudduck, J. (2007). Student voice, student engagement, and school reform. In D. Thiessen, & A. Cook-Sather, *International Handbook of Student Experience in Elementary and Secondary Schools* (pp. 587-610). Netherlands: Springer.

Westheimer, J., & Kahne, J. (1998). Education for action: preparing youth for participatory democracy. In W. Ayers, & e. al, *Teaching for Social Justice*. New York City: New Press.

Learning and Teaching

Boma, L., & et al. (1997). "The Impact of Teaching Strategies on Intrinsic Motivation." ERIC.

Anthony, G., Ohtani, M., & Clarke, D. (2013). *Student voice in mathematics classrooms around the world*. Sense Publishers.

Britzman, D. (1992). "'Who has the floor?' Curriculum teaching and the English student teacher's struggle for voice." *Curriculum Inquiry*, 19(2), pp. 143-162.

Bryant, J. a. (2007, September). "Power, Voice, and Empowerment: Classroom Committees in a Middle Level Language Arts Curriculum." *Voices from the Middle*, 16(1).

Chappuis, J., & Chappuis, S. (2002). *Understanding school assessment: A parent and community guide to helping students learn*. Assessment Training Institute.

Cushman, K. (2003). Fires in the bathroom: Advice for teachers from high school students. New York City, NY: The New Press.

Dean, L. & Murdock, S. (1992) Effect of voluntary service on adolescent attitudes toward learning. *Journal of Volunteer Administration* 104: 5-10.

Mockler, N., & Groundwater-Smith, S. (2015). Methods for Engaging Student Voice. In *Engaging with Student Voice in Research, Education and Community* (pp. 109-125). Switzerland: Springer International Publishing.

Nelson, J. R., & Fredrick, L. (1994). (1994). Can children design curriculum? Educational Leadership, 51, 71-75.

Richmond, E. (2014, October). What Happens When Students Control Their Own Education? Retrieved from KQED: theatlantic.com/education/archive/2014/10/what-happens-when-students-control-their-own-education/381828/

Rudduck, J., Arnot, D., Fielding, M., McIntyre, D., & et al. (2003). Consulting pupils about teaching and learning. Retrieved October 17, 2014, from Economic and Social Research Council at tlrp.org/pub/documents/no5_ruddock.pdf

Schwartz, K. (2014, October 29). Students Tell All: What it's like to be trusted partners in learning. . Retrieved October 30, 2014, from KQED Mindshift: blogs.kqed.org/mindshift/2014/10/students-tell-all-what-its-like-to-be-trusted-partners-in-learning/

Smyth, J. (2007). Toward the pedagogically engaged school: Listening to student voice as a positive response to disengagement and 'dropping out'? In D. Thiessen, & A. Cook-Sather, International handbook of student experience in elementary and secondary school. Springer Netherlands.

Turley, S. (1994). "The Way Teachers Teach Is, Like, Totally Whacked": The Student Voice on Classroom Practice. ERIC.

Tyler, K., & Boelter, C. (2008). Linking Black middle school students' perceptions of teachers' expectations to academic engagement and efficacy. The Negro Education Review, 59(1-2).

Wilson, B., & Corbett, D. (2007). Students' perspectives on good teaching: Implications for adult reform behavior. In A. C.-S. Thiessen, *International Handbook Of Student Experience In Elementary And Secondary School* (pp. 283-311). Springer Netherlands.

Relationships

Alvermann, D. E., & Eakle, A. J. (2007). Dissolving learning boundaries: The doing, re-doing, and undoing of school. In D. Theissen, & A. Cook-Sather, *International Handbook of Student Experience in Elementary and Secondary School* (pp. 143-166). Springer Netherlands.

Booth, D. (2013). I've Got Something to Say: How student voices inform our teaching. Pembroke Publishers Limited.

Cervone, B., & Cushman, K. (2002). Moving youth participation into the classroom: Students as allies. New Directions for Youth Development, 96, 83-100.

Cook-Sather, A., Bovill, C., & Felten, P. (2014). Engaging Students as Partners in Learning and Teaching: A Guide for Faculty. John Wiley & Sons.

Cushman, K. (2003) Fires in the bathroom: Advice for teachers from high school students. New York: The New Press.

Delpit, L. (1988) *The silenced dialogue: Power and pedagogy in educating other people's children.* Harvard Education Review, 58: 280-298.

McLaren, P. (1989) Life in schools: *An introduction to critical pedagogy in the foundations of education.* New York: Longman.

Mitra, D. L. (2004). The significance of students: Can increasing "student voice" in schools lead to gains in youth development? Teachers College Record, 106(4), 651-688.

Mitra, D. L. (2006). Student Voice Or Empowerment? Examining The Role Of School-Based Youth-Adult Partnerships As An Avenue Toward Focusing On Social Justice. *IEJLL: International Electronic Journal for Leadership in Learning*, 10(22).

Towler, D. L. (1975). Student Representatives Serving with Boards of Education. American Association of School Administrators. Retrieved from files.eric.ed.gov/fulltext/ED109824.pdf

Wilson, B. and Corbett, H. D. (2001). *Listening to urban kids: School reform and the teachers they want.* Albany, NY: State University of New York Press.

Leadership

Borden, R. (2004). Taking school design to students. Retrieved October 16, 2014, from National Clearinghouse for Educational Facilities: files.eric.ed.gov/fulltext/ED485990.pdf

Brasof, M. (2011). Student input improves behavior, fosters leadership. Phi Delta Kappan, 93(2), 20-24.

Comfort, R. E., Giorgi, J., & Moody, S. (1997). In a different voice: A student agenda for high school reform. The High School Journal, 179-183.

Cook-Sather, A. (2006). Sound, presence, and power: 'Student voice' in educational research and reform. *Curriculum Inquiry*, 36(4), 359-390.

Corbett, D., & Wilson, B. (1995). Make a difference with, not for, students: A plea to researchers and reformers. Educational Researcher, 24(5), 12-17.

Critchley, S. (2003) The nature and extent of student involvement in educational policymaking in Canadian school systems. *Educational Management & Administration.* 311: 97-106.

Cushman, K., & al., e. (2005). Sent to the principal: Students talk about making high schools better. Next Generation Press.

Fletcher, A. (2014) School Boards of the Future: Student Involvement in Education Policy-Making. Olympia, WA: CommonAction.

Joselowsky, F. (2007). Youth engagement, high school reform, and improved learning outcomes: Building systemic approaches for youth engagement. *NASSP Bulletin*, 91(3), 257-276.

Kleeman, R. P. (1972). *Student rights and responsibilities: Courts force schools to change.* National School Public Relations Association.

Kohn, A. (1993, September). Choices for Children: Why and How to Let Students Decide. Phi Delta Kappan, 75, 18-21.

Kordalewski, J. (1999) Incorporating student voice into teaching practice. ED440049. Retrieved 3/14/11 from ericfacility.net/ericdigests/ed440049.html.

Marques, E. (1999) Youth involvement in policy-making: Lessons from Ontario school boards, Policy

Brief 5. Ottawa, ON: Institute on Governance. Retrieved 11/11/11 from iog.ca/publications/policybrief5.pdf

Place, R. A. (1973, October). Do You Need (or Want) Students on the School Board? California School Boards, 9. Retrieved from files.eric.ed.gov/fulltext/ED078500.pdf

Culture

CDC. (2009). Fostering School Connectedness: Improving Student Health and Academic Achievement. Atlanta.

Cook-Sather, A. (2002). Authorizing students' perspectives: Toward trust, dialogue, and change in education. Educational Researcher, 31(4), 3-14. Retrieved October 28, 2014, from repository.brynmawr.edu/cgi/viewcontent.cgi?article=1017&context=edu_pubs

Cook-Sather, A. (2007). Resisting the impositional potential of student voice work: Lessons for liberatory educational research from poststructuralist feminist critiques of critical pedagogy. Discourse: Studies in the Cultural Politics of Education, 28, 389-403.

Delpit, L. (1988). The silenced dialogue: Power and pedagogy in educating other people's children. Harvard Education Review, 58, 280-298.

Douglas, W. (2003). Student engagement at school: A sense of belonging and participation (Results from PISA 2000). Organisation for Economic Co-operation and Development.

Fine, M., & Weis, L. (2003). Silenced voices and extraordinary conversations: Re-imagining schools. New York City: Teachers College Press.

Fielding, M. (2001). Beyond the rhetoric of student voice: New departures or new constraints in the transformation of 21st century schooling? Forum for Promoting 3-19 Comprehensive Education, 43(2), 100-109.

Fielding, M. (2001) Students as radical agents of change. Journal of Educational Change 23: 123-131.

Freire, P. (1998) Pedagogy of Freedom: Hope, democracy and civic courage. Lanham, MD: Rowman & Littlefield Publishers Inc.

Galloway, M., Pope, D., & Osberg, J. (2007). Stressed-out students-SOS: Youth perspectives on changing school climates. In D. Theissen, & A. Cook-Sather, International handbook of student experience in elementary and secondary school (pp. 611-634). Springer Netherlands.

Holcomb, E. (2006). Students Are Stakeholders, Too! Including Every Voice in Authentic High School Reform. Corwin Press.

Holdsworth, R. (2000a). Taking young people seriously means giving them serious things to do. In J. Mason, & M. Wilkinson, Taking Children Seriously. Bankston: University of Western Sydney.

Holdsworth, R. (2000b). Schools that create real roles of value for young people. Prospects, 115(3), 349-362.

Libbey, H. (2004). Measuring student relationships to school: Attachment, bonding, connectedness, and engagement. Journal of School Health, 74(4), 274-283.

McLaren, P. (2003). Life in Schools: An Introduction of Critical Pedagogy in the Foundations of Education. Boston: Allyn and Bacon.

Zeldin, S., Kusgen-McDaniel, A., Topitzes, D. and Calvert, M. (2000) Youth In Decision-Making: A Study On The Impacts Of Youth On Adults And Organizations. Retrieved 3/14/11 from theinnovationcenter.org/pdfs/Youth_in_Decision_Making_Report.pdf

Works Cited

Alcoff, L. (1992). "The problem of speaking for others," *Cultural Critique*, 20, 5–32.

Alternatives in Action High School. (n.d.). *About Us*. Retrieved November 1, 2014, from Alternatives in Action: alternativesinaction.org/highschool/highschool.html

Alvermann, D. E., & Eakle, A. J. (2007). "Dissolving learning boundaries: The doing, re-doing, and undoing of school," In D. Theissen, & A. Cook-Sather, *International Handbook of Student Experience in Elementary and Secondary School* (pp. 143-166). Springer Netherlands.

Anthony, G., Ohtani, M., & Clarke, D. (2013). *Student Voice in Mathematics Classrooms Around the World*. Sense Publishers.

Armstrong, T. (2009) *Multiple Intelligences In The Classroom. 3rd ed.* Alexandria, VA: Association for Supervision and Curriculum Development.

Arnstein, S. R. (1969). "A Ladder of Citizen Participation," *Journal of the American Institute of Planners*, 35 (4), 216-224.

Banks, J. (1998). "Approaches to multicultural curricular reform," in E. Lee, D. Menkart, & M. Okazawa-Rey, *Beyond Heroes and Holidays: A Practical Guide to K-12 Antiracist, Multicultural Education and Staff Development*. Washington, DC.

Barton, R. (2008). "A clear signal," *Northwest Education*, 3, pp. 30-36.

Beane, J., & Apple, M. (1995). *Democratic Schools*. Arlington, VA: ASCD.

Beattie, H. (2012). "Amplifying student voice: The missing link in school transformation," *Management in Education*, 26 (3), 158-160.

Beaudoin, N. (2005). *Elevating Student Voice: How to Enhance Participation, Citizenship, and Leadership*. Larchmont, NY: Eye On Education.

Benard, B., & Burgoa, C. (2010). *Guide to a Student-Family-School-Community Partnership: Using a student and data driven process to improve school environments and promote student success.* WestEd.

Berardi, L. L., & Gerschick, T. (2002). *University Faculty Members' Perceptions of Student Engagement: An Interview Study*. [Doctoral Dissertation]. Illinois State University.

Berg, M. (2007, June 22). Director, Youth Action Research Project. (A. Fletcher, Interviewer)

Berger, R., & et al. (2014). *Leaders of Their Own Learning: Transforming Schools Through Student-engaged Assessment*. John Wiley & Sons.

Bhavnani, K. K. (1990). "What's Power Got to do With Itt? Empowerment and social research," in I. Parker, & J. Shotter, *Deconstructing Social Psychology*. London: Routledge.

Boccia, J. (1997). "Introduction," in J. Boccia, *Students Taking the Lead: The Challenges and Rewards of Empowering Youth in Schools (New Directions for School Leadership)*. San Francisco: Jossey-Bass Inc.

Boma, L. & et al. (1997). "The impact of teaching strategies on intrinsic motivation," ERIC.

Bonnen, C. & Flage, D. (2002). *Descartes and Method: A search for a method in Meditations.* Routledge.

Booker, R. & MacDonald, D. (1999) "Did we hear you?: issues of student voice in a curriculum innovation," *Curriculum Studies* 31(1), 83-97.

Booth, D. (2013). *I've Got Something to Say: How student voices inform our teaching*. Pembroke Publishers Limited.

Borden, R. (2004). *Taking School Design to Students*. Retrieved October 16, 2014, from National Clearinghouse for Educational Facilities at files.eric.ed.gov/fulltext/ED485990.pdf

Bragg, S. (2007). *Consulting Young People: A Review of the Literature*. London: Creative Partnerships.

Bragg, S., & Fielding, M. (2003). *Pupil Participation: Building a Whole School Commitment*. Cambridge: Pearson Publishing.

Brasof, M. (2009). "Living democracy: How Constitution High School molds better citizens," *Social Education, 73* (5), 207-211.

Brasof, M. (2011). "Student input improves behavior, fosters leadership," *Phi Delta Kappan, 93* (2), 20-24.

Brasof, M. (2015). *Student Voice and School Governance: Distributing Leadership to Youth and Adults.* Routledge.

Breakthrough Collaborative. (n.d.). *About Us.* Retrieved November 2, 2014, from breakthroughcollaborative.org

Brennan, M. (1996). "Schools as public institutions: Students and citizenship," *Youth Studies Australia,* 24-27.

Brewster, C., & Fager, J. (2000). *Increasing Student Engagement and Motivation: From time-on-task to homework.* Portland, Oregon: Northwest Regional Educational Laboratory.

Britzman, D. (1992). 'Who has the floor? Curriculum teaching and the English student teacher's struggle for voice," *Curriculum Inquiry , 19* (2), pp. 143-162.

Bryant, J. a. (2007). "Power, voice, and empowerment: classroom committees in a middle level language arts curriculum," *Voices from the Middle , 16* (1).

Carnie, F. and Fielding, M. (2007) "Valorising, Supporting and Sustaining Student Voice in a Local Authority over 5 years: Reflections from the field." Paper presented at the British Educational Research Association Annual Conference, Institute of Education, University of London, 5-8 September 2007. Retrieved September 4, 2012 from leeds.ac.uk/educol/documents/167729.htm

CDC. (2009). *Fostering School Connectedness: Improving Student Health and Academic Achievement.* Atlanta.

Cervone, B. (2012). *Youth and Adults Transforming School Together.* Retrieved 1 2014, November, from What Kids Can Do at whatkidscando.org/featurestories/2011/02_transforming_school/

Cervone, B., & Cushman, K. (2002). "Moving youth participation into the classroom: Students as allies," *New Directions for Youth Development , 96,* 83-100.

Chapman, E. (2003). "Alternative approaches to assessing student engagement rates," *Practical assessment, research and evaluation , 13* (8).

Chappuis, J., & Chappuis, S. (2002). *Understanding School Assessment: A parent and community guide to helping students learn.* Assessment Training Institute.

Checkoway, B., & Richards-Schuster, K. (2006). "Youth participation for educational reform in low-income communities of color," in S. A. Ginwright, P. Noguera, & J. Cammarota, *Beyond Resistance! Youth Activism and Community Change: New Democratic Possibilities for Practice and Policy for America's Youth* (pp. 319-332). Routledge.

Cheminais, R. (2013). *Engaging Pupil Voice to Ensure that Every Child Matters: A Practical Guide.* Routledge.

Chemutai, L., & Chumba, S. (2014). "Student councils participation in decision making in public secondary schools in Kericho West Sub County, Kenya," *International Journal of Advanced Research , 2* (6), 850-858.

Children First Network 102. (2011). *Student-Led School Improvement: Work, Findings, and Next Steps: Student Voice Collaborative.* New York City: New York City Department of Education.

Chopra, C. H. (2014). *New Pathways for Partnerships: An Exploration of How Partnering With Students Affects Teachers and Schooling* (Doctoral dissertation). University of Washington.

Christensen, C. (1997). "The view from the principal's desk," in J. Boccia (Ed.), *Students Taking the Lead: The Challenges and Rewards of Empowering Youth in Schools* (pp. 107-120). San Francisco: Jossey-Bass Inc.

Coates, T.-N. (2014, January 8). *What It Means to Be a Public Intellectual.* Retrieved November 1, 2014, from The Atlantic at theatlantic.com/politics/archive/2014/01/what-it-means-to-be-a-public-intellectual/282907/

Comfort, R. E., Giorgi, J., & Moody, S. (1997). "In a different voice: A student agenda for high school reform," *The High School Journal* , 179-183.

Conner, J., & Rosen, S. (2013). "How students are leading us: Youth organizing and the fight for public education in Philadelphia," *PennGSE Perspectives on Urban Education* , *10* (1).

Conzemius, A., & O'Neill, J. (2001). *Building Shared Responsibility For Student Learning*. ASCD.

Cook-Sather, A. (2002). "Authorizing students' perspectives: Toward trust, dialogue, and change in education," *Educational researcher, 31* (4), 3-14.

Cook-Sather, A. (2001). "Negotiating Worlds and Words: Writing About Students' Experiences of School," in J. Shultz, & A. Cook-Sather, *In Our Own Words: Students' perspectives on school.* Lanham, Maryland: Rowman & Littlefield.

Cook-Sather, A. (2002). "Re(in)forming the conversations: Student position, power, and voice in teacher education," *Radical Teacher* , *64*, 21-28.

Cook-Sather, A. (2007). "Resisting the impositional potential of student voice work: Lessons for liberatory educational research from poststructuralist feminist critiques of critical pedagogy," *Discourse: Studies in the cultural politics of education* , *28*, 389-403.

Cook-Sather, A. (2006). "Sound, presence, and power: 'Student voice' in educational research and reform," *Curriculum Inquiry* , *36* (4), 359–390.

Cook-Sather, A., Bovill, C., & Felten, P. (2014). *Engaging Students as Partners in Learning and Teaching: A Guide for Faculty.* John Wiley & Sons.

Corbett, D., & Wilson, B. (1995). "Make a difference with, not for, students: A plea to researchers and reformers," *Educational Researcher* , *24* (5), 12-17.

Counts, G. S. (1978). *Dare the School Build a New Social Order?* Champagne, Illinois: Southern Illinois University.

Cushman, K. (2003). *Fires in the Bathroom: Advice for Teachers from High School Students.* New York City, NY: The New Press.

Cushman, K. (2010). *Fires in the Mind: What Kids can Tell Us about Motivation and Mastery.* John Wiley & Sons.

Cushman, K., & al., e. (2005). *Sent to the Principal: Students Talk about Making High Schools Better.* Next Generation Press.

Dahal, B. P. (2014, January). *Child Participation in Schools of Nepal: Role and contributions of child clubs.* Kathmandu University.

Dalton, L., Churchman, R., & Tasco, A. (2008). *Getting Students Involved in Creating a Healthy School.* ASCD.

Washington Professional Educators Standards Board. (2009) "Defining student voice," Washington ProTeach Portfolio. Retrieved October 12, 2014, from waproteach.org/rsc/pdf/WAProTeachStudentVoice.pdf

Delpit, L. (1988). "The silenced dialogue: Power and pedagogy in educating other people's children," *Harvard Education Review* , *58*, 280-298.

Dewey, J. (1948). *Democracy and Education: An Introduction to the Philosophy of Education.* New York City: The MacMillan Company.

Dewey, J. (1938). *Experience and Education.* New York City: Collier Books.

Dickinson, M. (2014, December 9). "Do as I say, not as I do?" Retrieved from Startempathy.org: startempathy.org/blog/2014/12/do-i-say-not-i-do

Dickler, M. C. (2007). "The Morse Quartet: Student speech and the first amendment," *Loy. Law Review 53* , 355.

Douglas, W. (2003). *Student engagement at school: A sense of belonging and participation* (Results from PISA 2000). Organisation for Economic Co-operation and Development .

Duffy, E. (2014, July 26). "North High eyes a stadium of its own," Retrieved from *Omaha World-Herald* at omaha.com/eedition/iowa/articles/north-high-eyes-a-stadium-of-its-own/article_66678798-197b-5c06-b01b-5f28f4417c38.html

Dweck, C. (1999). *Self-Theories: Their role in Motivation, Personality, and Development.* Philadelphia: Psychology Press.

Dweck, C. (2006). *Mindset: The New Psychology of* Success. Random House LLC.

Dweck, C. (2010). "Even geniuses work hard," *Educational Leadership* , 1, pp. 16-20.

Dzur, A. (2013, November 8). "Trench Democracy in Schools: an Interview with Principal Donnan Stoicovy," Retrieved November 1, 2014, from *Boston Review* at bostonreview.net/blog-us/albert-w-dzur-trench-democracy-schools-interview-principal-donnan-stoicovy

Elias, M. J. (2014, November 1). "School climate that promotes student voice," *Principal Leadership 1*, pp. 22-27.

Erlich, J., & Erlich, S. (1971). *Student Power, Participation and Revolution.* Association Press.

Ethridge, B. (2015) *"Early School Leavers in Belize: Perspectives on School Experiences, the Purpose of School and Why They Left."* Dissertation at Boise State University.

Farmer-Dougan, V., & McKinney, K. (2001). *Examining student engagement at Illinois State University: An exploratory investigation.* Center for Teaching, Learning & Technology at Illinois State University.

Fielding, M. (2001). "Beyond the rhetoric of student voice: New departures or new constraints in the transformation of 21st century schooling?" *Forum* , *43* (2), 100-109.

Fielding, M. (2001). "Students as radical agents of change," *Journal of Educational Change* , 123-127.

Fielding, M. (2004) "Transformative approaches to student voice; Theoretical underpinnings, recalcitrant realities," *British Educational Research Journal, 30*(2), 295-311.

Fielding, M. (2010). "The radical potential of student voice: Creating spaces for restless encounters," *International Journal of Emotional Education* , 2 (1).

Fielding, M., & Bragg, S. (2003). *Students as Researchers: Making a Difference.* Cambridge: Pearson Publishing.

Fielding, M., & Rudduck, J. (2002). "The transformative potential of student voice: confronting the power issues," *Annual Conference of the British Educational Research Association.* University of Exeter, England.

Fine, M., & Weis, L. (2003). *Silenced Voices and Extraordinary Conversations: Re-Imagining Schools.* New York City: Teachers College Press.

Fletcher, A. (2001). *Meaningful Student Involvement Idea Guide.* Washington State Office of Superintedent of Public Instruction.

Fletcher, A. (2003). *Meaningful Student Involvement Guide to Inclusive School Change.* Olympia: SoundOut.

Fletcher, A. (2003b). *Meaningful Student Involvement Research Guide.* Retrieved from SoundOut: soundout.org/MSIResearch.pdf

Fletcher, A. (2004a). "Total infusion: District scores 100% on student involvement in decision-making," Retrieved September 15, 2012, from SoundOut: soundout.org/features/annearundel.html

Fletcher, A. (2004b). "Meaningful student involvement: Reciprocity in schools through service-learning," *The Bridge: The Journal of the University Promise Alliance at the University of Minnesota* , 37-58.

Fletcher, A. (2004c). "Students speak out: How one school opens the doors to meaningful student involvement," Retrieved 29 2014, October, from SoundOut: soundout.org/features/SAS.htmlFletcher, A. (2008, November). "Giving Students Ownership of Learning: The Architecture of Ownership". *Educational Leadership* .

Fletcher, A. (2005a). *Meaningful Student Involvement Guide to Students as Partners in School Change.* (2 ed., p. 28). Olympia, WA: SoundOut.

Fletcher, A. (2005b). *Stories of Meaningful Student Involvement.* Olympia, Washington: SoundOut.

Fletcher, A. (2012). *Student Voice and Bullying.* Olympia, Washington: CommonAction.

Fletcher, A. (2012, July 29). "Seattle youth media camp," Retrieved from CommonAction: commonaction.blogspot.com/2012/07/seattle-youth-media-camp.html

Fletcher, A. (2014). *A Short Introduction to Holistic Youth Development.* Olympia: CommonAction.

Fletcher, A. (2014). *School Boards of the Future: Students as Education Policy-Makers.* Olympia, Washington: CommonAction.

Fletcher, A. (2014). *The Guide to Student Voice, 2nd Edition.* Olympia, Washington: CommonAction Books.

Fletcher, A. (2015). *SoundOut Meaningful Student Involvement Workshop Guide.* Olympia, Washington: CommonAction.

Flutter, J., & Rudduck, J. (2006). *Student Voice and the architecture of change: Mapping the territory.* Retrieved December 28, 2011 from

Fortin, S. (2014, December 10). Interview with author.

Forum for Youth Investment. (2002). *Holding schools accountable: Students organizing for educational change.* Baltimore.

Fredricks, J., & al, e. (2011). *Measuring student engagement in upper elementary through high school: A description of 21 instruments" Issues & Answers Report.* Washington, D.C.: United States Department of Education, Institute of Education Sciences, National Center for Education Evaluation and Regional Assistance, Regional Educational Laboratory Southeast.

Fredricks, J., Blumenfeld, P., & Paris, A. (2004). School engagement: Potential of the concept, state of the evidence. *Review of Educational Research ,* 74 (1), 59-109.

(1998). In P. Freire, *Teachers as Cultural Workers.* (pp. 85-89). Boulder, CO: Westview Press.

Freire, P. (1970). *Pedagogy of the Oppressed.* (M. B. Ramos, Trans.) New York: Continuum.

Freire, P. (1973). *Education for Critical Consciousness.* Bloomsbury Publishing.

Freire, P. (1998). *Pedagogy of Freedom: Hope, democracy and civic courage.* Lanham, Maryland: Rowman.

Freire, P. (2004). *Pedagogy of Hope: Reliving the Pedagogy of the Oppressed.* New York City: Bloomsbury Publishing.

Freire, P. (2005) *Pedagogy of Indignation.* Herndon, VA: Paradigm Publishers.

Fullan, M. (1991). *The New Meaning Of Educational Change.* New York, NY : Teachers College Press.

Galloway, M., Pope, D., & Osberg, J. (2007). Stressed-out students-SOS: Youth perspectives on changing school climates. In D. Theissen, & A. Cook-Sather, *International handbook of student experience in elementary and secondary school* (pp. 611-634). Springer Netherlands.

Gandhi, M. (1931). Young India, Bombay, India. In R. a. Prabhu, *The Mind of Mahatma Gandhi: Encyclopedia of Gandhi's thoughts.* Ahmedabad, India: Navjeevan Trust.

George Lucas Educational Foundation. (2008, July 18). *What are some types of assessment?* Retrieved from Edutopia at edutopia.org/assessment-guide-description

Germond, T., Love, E. Moran, L., Moses, S. & Raill, S. (2006) *Lessons learned on the road to student engagement.* Providence, RI: Campus Compact.

Giroux, H. A. (1981). *Ideology, Culture and the Process of Schooling.* The Falmer Press.

Giroux, H. A., & McLaren, P. (1982). *Teacher education and the politics of engagement: The case for democratic schooling. Harvard Educational Review ,* 56 (3), 213-239.

Giroux, H. A. (1989). *Schooling for democracy: Critical pedagogy in the modern age.* London: Routledge.

Giroux, H. A. (1990) *Curriculum Discourse as Postmodernist Critical Practice.* (Victoria: Deakin University Press).

Giroux, H. A. (2013a). *America's Education Deficit and the War on Youth: Reform Beyond Electoral Politics.* New York City: NYU Press.

ADAM FLETCHER

Giroux, H. A. (2013b). Can Democratic Education Survive in a Neoliberal Society? In C. Reitz, *Crisis and Commonwealth: Marcuse, Marx, McLare.* Lexington Books.

Giroux, H. A. (2014). "Higher Education and the New Brutalism". *Truthout.* Retrieved October 28, 2014 from truth-out.org/news/item/27082-henry-a-giroux-higher-education-and-the-new-brutalism

Glossary of Education Reform. (2013, September 29). Retrieved November 2, 2014, from edglossary.org/education-system/

Goodlad, J. (1984). *A Place Called School.* New York City: McGraw Hill.

Grace, M. (1999). "When students create the curriculum," *Educational Leadership*, 57 (5), 71-74.

Haggar, R. (2013, June 26). *Functions of Formal Education Systems.* Retrieved November 1, 2014, at earlhamsociologypages.co.uk/essayfunctions.html

Hands, C. (2009). "Student Voice in the Process of Developing School-Community Partnerships Project Completion: August 2009 Report submitted to San Diego Unified School District. San Diego, California: San Diego Unified School District.

Harper, D. (1996). "*Students as change agents,*" Edutopia, December 1, 1996. Retrieved September 15, 2012, from Edutopia: edutopia.org/students-change-agents

Harper, D. (2000). Students as Change Agents: The Generation Y Model.

Hart, R. (1997). Children's Participation: The theory and practice of involving young citizens in community development and environmental care. United Kingdom: Earthscan.

Harvard Family Research Project. (2002). Youth Involvement in Evaluation and Research: Issues and opportunities in out-of-school time evaluation. . Boston: Harvard Family Research Project.

Hayden, T. (1962). *Port Huron Statement of the Students for a Democratic Society.* Retrieved October 24, 2014, from coursesa.matrix.msu.edu/~hst306/documents/huron.html

Haynes, C. (2014, November 13). *First Amendment: In land of the free, why are schools afraid of freedom?* Retrieved November 20, 2014, from GazetteXtra: gazettextra.com/20141113/first_amendment_in_land_of_the_free_why_are_schools_afraid_of_freedom

Holcomb, E. (2006). Students Are Stakeholders, Too!: Including Every Voice in Authentic High School Reform. Corwin Press.

Holdsworth, R. (2000a). Taking young people seriously means giving them serious things to do. In J. Mason, & M. Wilkinson, *Taking Children Seriously.* Bankston: University of Western Sydney.

Holdsworth, R. (2000b). Schools that create real roles of value for young people. *Prospects*, 115 (3), 349-362.

hooks, b. (1994). *Teaching to Transgress: Education as the Practice of Freedom.* New York City: Taylor & Francis.

Hurtado, S. (1999). "Reaffirming educators judgment: educational value of diversity," *Liberal Education* (Spring), 28.

Innovation Center. (2005). *Reflect and improve: A toolkit for engaging youth and adults as partners.* Takoma Park, Maryland: The Innovation Center for Youth and Community Development.

Jackson, D. (2005). Why Pupil Voice? Facilitating Pupil Involvement in Learning Networks. NCSL.

Jacob, O. (2012, October 15). Speak Up Intern. (A. Fletcher, Interviewer)

Joselowsky, F. (2007). "Youth engagement, high school reform, and improved learning outcomes: Building systemic approaches for youth engagement," *NASSP Bulletin*, 91 (3), 257-276.

Jovenes Unidos. (2004). *North High School Report: The Voices of Over 700 Students.* Denver: Jovenes Unidos and Padres Unidos.

Kaba, M. (2000). "They Listen to Me... but They Don't Act on It": Contradictory Consciousness and Student Participation in Decision-Making. *The High School Journal* , 21-34.

Kenny, G., Kenny, D., & Dumont, R. (2005). . *Mission and Place: Strengthening Learning and Community Through Campus Design.* Rowman & Littlefield Publishers.

Kipp, G., Quinn, P., Lancaster, S., & et al. (2014). *The AWSP Leadership Framework User's Guide.* Olympia, Washington: Association of Washington School Principals.

Kirk, R. (2014). A leadership experiment in student voice: A new kind of summer school. *OPC Register* , 16 (1), 28-32.

Kitchen, J. (2010). *"Beck and Burroughs most effective on board; community backs election law change.".* Retrieved September 15, 2012, from Examiner.com at examiner.com/article/beck-and-burroughs-most-effective-on-board-community-backs-election-law-change

Kleeman, R. P. (1972). *Student rights and responsibilities: Courts force schools to change.* National School Public Relations Association.

Klein, R. (2003). *We Want Our Say: Children As Active Participants In Their Education.* Stylus Publishing, LLC.

Knowles, T. & Brown, D. (2000). *What Every Middle School Teacher Should Know.* Portsmouth, NH: Heinemann.

Kohn, A. (2006). *Beyond Discipline: From compliance to community.* ASCD.

Kohn, A. (1993). "Choices for Children: Why and How to Let Students Decide," *Phi Delta Kappan* , 75, 18-21.

Kohn, A. (2007). *The Homework Myth: Why Our Kids Get Too Much Of A Bad Thing.* Da Capo Press.

Kozol, J. (1991). *Savage Inequities.* New York City: Crown Publishers.

Krogh, S., & Morehouse, P. (2014). *The Early Childhood Curriculum: Inquiry Learning Through Integration.* Routledge.

Kurth-Schai, R. (1988). "The roles of youth in society: A reconceptualization," *The Educational Forum* , 52 (2).

Kushman, J. W., & Shanessy, J. (1997). *Look Who's Talking Now: Student Views of Learning in Restructuring Schools.* Portland: Northwest Regional Educational Laboratory.

Lewis, R., & Burman, E. (2008). Providing for student voice in classroom management: teachers' views. *International Journal of Inclusive Education* , 12 (2), 151-167.

Libbey, H. (2004). Measuring student relationships to school: Attachment, bonding, connectedness, and engagement. *Journal of School Health* , 74 (4), 274-283.

Loflin, J. (2006). *A History of Democratic Education in American Public Education.* International Democratic Education Conference.

Lorde, A. (1984). *Sister Outsider: Essays and Speeches.* Crossing Press.

McCombs, B. L., & Pope, J. E. (1994). *Motivating hard to reach students.* American Psychological Association.

McCombs, B. L., & Whisler, J. S. (1997). *The learner-centered classroom and school: Strategies for increasing student motivation and achievement.* San Francisco: Jossey-Bass. Retrieved 9/11/17 from indiana.edu/~syschang/decatur/2007_fall/documents/2-2_mccombs_ch1.pdf

McDermott, J. C. (1998). *Beyond the silence: Listening for Democracy.* Portsmouth, NH: Heinemann.

McGarry, L., & Stoicovy, D. (2014). Writing a school constitution: Representative democracy in action. *Social Studies and the Young Learner* , 27 (1), 5-7.

McLaren, P. (2003). Life in Schools: An Introduction of Critical Pedagogy in the Foundations of Education. Boston: Allyn and Bacon.

McLeod, J. (2011) "Student voice and the politics of listening in higher education," *Critical Studies in Education* 52, 2, 179-189.

Maine Department of Education and Campaign for the Civic Mission of Schools. (2006). *Community Toolkit.* Retrieved November 1, 2014, from Maine Department of Education: maine.gov/education/mecitizenshiped/communities/student_reps.rtf

Markham, T. (2013, September 11). *Reinventing School From the Ground Up For Inquiry Learning.* Retrieved October 28, 2014, from KQED Mindshift: blogs.kqed.org/mindshift/2013/09/reinventing-school-new-learning-environment-ecosystems-for-inquiry-learning/

Martin-Kniep, G. (2005). *Becoming a Better Teacher: Eight innovations that work.* Alexandria, VA: Association for Supervision and Curriculum Development.

Martin-Kniep, G. (2008). *Communities That Learn, Lead, And Last: Building And Sustaining Educational Expertise.* John Wiley & Sons.

Martin-Kniep, G. (2004). *Developing Learning Communities Through Teacher Expertise.* Thousand Oaks, CA: Corwin Press.

Martin-Kniep, G., & Picone-Zocchia, J. (2009). *Changing The Way You Teach, Improving The Way Students Learn.* Arlington, VA: ASCD.

Miller, L., Gross, B., & Ouijdani, M. (2012). *Getting Down to Dollars and Cents: What do school districts spend to deliver student-centered learning?* Seattle: Center on Reinventing Public Education at the University of Washington .

Milne, A. J. (2006). "Designing blended learning space to the student experience," *Learning Spaces, 11* (1).

Mitra, D. L. (2003). "Student voice in school reform: Reframing student-teacher relationships," *McGill Journal of Education , 38* (2), 289-304.

Mitra, D. L. (2004). "The significance of students: Can increasing "student voice" in schools lead to gains in youth development?" *Teachers College Record , 106* (4), 651-688.

Mitra, D. L. (2006). "Youth as a bridge between home and school comparing student voice and parent involvement as strategies for change," *Education and Urban Society , 38* (4), 455-480.

Mitra, D. L. (2006). "Student Voice or Empowerment? Examining the role of school-based youth-adult partnerships as an avenue toward focusing on social justice," *IEJLL: International Electronic Journal for Leadership in Learning , 10* (22).

Mitra, D. L. (2008). *Student Voice In School Reform: Building Youth-Adult Partnerships That Strengthen Schools And Empower Youth.* SUNY Press.

Mitra, D. L. (2009). "Collaborating with students: Building youth-adult partnerships in schools," *American Journal of Education, 15* (3), 407-436.

Mitra, D., & Serriere, S. (2012). "Student voice in elementary-school reform: Examining youth development in fifth graders," *American Educational Research Journal , 49*, 743-774.

Mitra, D., Frick, W., & Crawford, E. (2011). "The ethical dimensions of student voice activities in the United States," In W. Kidd, & G. Czerniawski, *The student voice handbook: Bridging the academic/practitioner divide.* Emerald Group Publishing.

Mockler, N., & Groundwater-Smith, S. (2015). "Methods for Engaging Student Voice," In *Engaging with student voice in research, Education and Community* (pp. 109-125). Switzerland: Springer International Publishing.

Monument Mountain Regional High School. (2014). *2014-2015 Program of Studies.* Retrieved November 1, 2014, from mmrhs.bhrsd.org/wp-content/uploads/sites/4/2014/09/2015-Program-of-Studies.pdf

Morgan, B., & Porter, A. (2011). "Student researchers exploring teaching and learning: Processes and issues," In W. Kidd, & G. Gerry Czerniawski, *The student voice handbook: Bridging the academic/practitioner divide.* Emerald Group Publishing.

Morgan, J. (2011). "Students training teachers," In W. Kidd, & G. Czerniawski, *The student voice handbook: Bridging the academic/practitioner divide.* Emerald Group Publishing.

Mt. Pleasant High School. (n.d.). *Senior Teacher Academy.* Retrieved November 1, 2014, from Mt. Pleasant High School: mtpleasanths.org/apps/classes/show_class.jsp?classREC_ID=577870

Natriello, G. (1984). "Problems in the evaluation of students and student disengagement from secondary schools," *Journal of Research and Development in Education ,* 17 (4), 14-24.

Nelson, J. R., & Fredrick, L. (1994). (1994). "Can children design curriculum?" *Educational Leadership ,* 51, 71-75.

Newmann, F. (1992). *Student Engagement and Achievement in American Secondary Schools.* New York City: Teachers College Press.

Newmann, F., Wehlage, G., & Lamborn, S. (1992). "The significance and sources of student engagement," In F. Newmann, *Student Engagement and Achievement in American Secondary Schools.* Teachers College Press: Teachers College Press.

Ngussa, B. M., & Makewa, L. N. (2014). "Student voice in curriculum change: a theoretical reasoning," *International Journal of Academic Research in Progressive Education and Development* 3 (3), 23-37.

Nieto, S. (1994). "Lessons from students on creating a chance to dream," *Harvard Educational Review ,* 64 (4), 392-427.

Nova High School. (2014, November 1). Retrieved from Seattle Public Schools: novahs.seattleschools.org

Oldfather, P. (1995). "Learning from student voices," *Theory to Practice ,* 43 (2), 84–87.

O'Neill, R. E., Horner, R. H., & Albi, R. W. (1996). *Functional Assessment And Program Development For Problem Behavior: A Practical Handbook.* Cengage Learning.

Ontario Literacy and Numeracy Secretariat. (2007, December). *Capacity Building Series: Student self-assessment.* Retrieved from Ontario Ministry of Education: edu.gov.on.ca/eng/literacynumeracy/inspire/research/studentselfassessment.pdf

Osberg, J., Pope, D., & Galloway, M. (2006). "Students matter in school reform: Leaving fingerprints and becoming leaders," *International Journal of Leadership in Education ,* 9 (4), 329-343.

Osguthorpe, R. T., & Graham, C. R. (2003). "Blended learning environments: definitions and directions," *Quarterly Review of Distance Education ,* 4 (3), 227-233.

Padres and Jovens Unidos. (2014, November 1). *About Us.* Retrieved from padresunidos.org/about

Phillipson, S. (2013). *Developing Leadership in the Asia Pacific: A Focus on the Individual.* New York: Routledge.

Place, R. A. (1973, October). "Do you need (or want) students on the school board?" *California School Boards ,* 9.

Quaglia, R., Fox, K., & Corso, M. (2003, November). "Got opportunity?" *Educational Leadership ,* 68 (3).

REAL HARD. (2003). *Student Voices Count: A Student-Led Evaluation of High Schools in Oakland.* Retrieved March 4, 2011, from Kids Count Oakland: kidsfirstoakland.org/media/docs/5247_Student_Voices_Rpt.pdf

Reeves, D. B. (2009). *Leading Change in Your School: How to conquer myths, build commitment, and get results.* ASCD.

Rethink. (n.d.). *Rethink Programs.* Retrieved November 1, 2014, from Rethink: therethinkers.org/

Richmond, E. (2014, October). *"What happens when students control their own education?"* Retrieved from KQED: theatlantic.com/education/archive/2014/10/what-happens-when-students-control-their-own-education/381828/

Rigolon, A. (2011). "A space with meaning: children's involvement in participatory design processes," *Design Principles & Practice: An International Journal ,* 5 (2).

Robinson, C., & Taylor, C. (2013). "Student voice as a contested practice: Power and participation in two student voice projects," *Improving Schools ,* 16 (1), 32-46.

Rogers, A. (2004). *Student voice: Bridges to learning.* Seattle, WA: University of Washiongton.

Rubin, B., & Silva, E. (Eds.). (2003). *Critical Voices In School Reform: Students living through change.* New York City: RoutledgeFalmer.

Rudd, T., Colligan, F., & Nalk, R. (2008). *Learner voice: A handbook from Futurelab.* Futurelab and English Secondary Student Association.

Rudduck, J. (2007). "Student voice, student engagement, and school reform," In D. Thiessen, & A. Cook-Sather, *International Handbook of Student Experience in Elementary and Secondary Schools* (pp. 587-610). Netherlands: Springer.

Rudduck, J., & Fielding, M. (2006). "Student voice and the perils of popularity," *Educational Review*, 58 (2), 219-231.

Rudduck, J., & Flutter, J. (2004). *How To Improve Your School..* Bloomsbury Publishing.

Rudduck, J., Arnot, D., Fielding, M., McIntyre, D., & et al. (2003). *Consulting pupils about teaching and learning.* Retrieved October 17, 2014, from Economic and Social Research Council at tlrp.org/pub/documents/no5_ruddock.pdf

Rudduck, J., Chaplain, R., & Wallace, S. (1996). *School Improvement: What Can Pupils Tell Us? Quality In Secondary Schools And Colleges Series.* London: David Fulton Publishers.

Savrock, J. (2014, November 1). *Student Voice Is an Integral Component of School Reform*. Retrieved from Penn State University College of Education at ed.psu.edu/news/news-items-folder/mitra-student-voice

Schlecty, P. (1994). *Increasing Student Engagement.* Missouri Leadership Academy.

Schwartz, K. (2014, October 29). "Students Tell All: What it's like to be trusted partners in learning." Retrieved October 30, 2014, from KQED Mindshift: blogs.kqed.org/mindshift/2014/10/students-tell-all-what-its-like-to-be-trusted-partners-in-learning/

Seattle Public Schools. (n.d.) "About Us," NOVA Project. Retrieved January 30, 2011, from Seattle Public Schools: novahs.seattleschools.org/about/about_nova

Serriere, S., & Mitra, D. (2012). "Student voice and youth development," In C. Day, *Handbook on Teacher and School Development.* New York: Sage.

Sharan, S., Shachar, H., & Levine, T. (1999). *The innovative school: Organization and instruction.* Greenwood Publishing Group.

Sherwood Foundation. (2014, November 1). *nelovesps.org/story/dreaming-big-for-their-school-and-community/.* Retrieved from Nebraska Loves Public Schools: nelovesps.org/story/dreaming-big-for-their-school-and-community/

Shor, I. (1996). *When Student Have Power: Negotiating authority in a critical pedagogy.* Chicago: University of Chicago Press.

Shultz, J. J., & Cook-Sather, A. (2001). *In Our Own Words: Students' Perspectives On School.* Rowman & Littlefield.

Simmons, E. J. (1968). *Introduction to Tolstoy's Writings.* Chicago: University of Chicago Press.

Sizer, T. R. (2004). *Horace's Compromise: The Dilemma Of The American High School.* Houghton Mifflin Harcourt.

Skinner, E. A., & Belmont, M. J. (1993). "Motivation in the classroom: Reciprocal effects of teacher behavior and student engagement across the school year," *Journal of educational psychology*, 85 (4), 571.

Slavin, R. (2003). *Educational Psychology: Theory And Practice.* Boston: Pearson Education.

Slee, R. (1994) "Finding a Student Voice in School Reform: student disaffection, pathologies of disruption and educational control," *International Studies in Sociology of Education, (4) 2.* Retrieved August 3, 2017 from tandfonline.com/doi/pdf/10.1080/0962021940040202

Smyth, J. (2007). "Toward the pedagogically engaged school: Listening to student voice as a positive response to disengagement and 'dropping out'?" In D. Thiessen, & A. Cook-Sather,

International Handbook Of Student Experience In Elementary And Secondary School. Springer Netherlands.

Smyth, J. (2006). "When students have power: Student engagement, student voice, and the possibilities for school reform around "dropping out" of school," *International Journal of Leadership in Education* , 9 (4), 285–298.

SooHoo, S. (1993). "Students as partners in research and restructuring schools," *The Educational Forum* , 386-393.

SoundOut. (2004). *Student Voice Tip Sheet.* Retrieved October 18, 2014, from SoundOut: soundout.org/tips.html

SpeakOUT. (n.d.). *SpeakOUT.* Retrieved November 1, 2014, from Ontario Ministry of Education: edu.gov.on.ca/eng/students/speakup/

Stefanou, C. R. (2004). "Supporting autonomy in the classroom: Ways teachers encourage student decision making and ownership," *Educational Psychologist, 39* (2), 97-110.

Strong, R., Silver, H. F., & Robinson, A. (1995). What do students want (and what really motivates them)? *Educational Leadership* .

Students as Researchers Conference. (2014, November 1). Retrieved from Ontario Ministry of Education at edu.gov.on.ca/eng/students/speakup/research.html

The New York Times. (1922, September 23). Mineola high school students strike after clash between students and teachers. *The New York Times* .

The Public Intellectual Project. (n.d.). *About Us.* Retrieved November 1, 2014, from publicintellectualsproject.mcmaster.ca/about/

Thiessen, D. (2007). Researching student experiences in elementary and secondary school: An evolving field of study. In D. Thiessen, & A. Cook-Sather, *International Handbook of Student Experience in Elementary and Secondary School* (pp. 1-76). Springer Netherlands.

Thomas Dotta, L., & Ristow, M. (2011). Participação Significativa dos Estudantes: Uma Proposta de Formação Baseada na Coparticipação de Estudantes e Professores no Ensino Superior . Universidade do Oeste do Paraná – UNIOESTE et Faculdade de Psicologia e Ciências da Educação da Universidade do Porto - FPCEUP.

Thomson, P. (2011). Coming to terms with 'voice'. In G. Czerniawski, & W. Kidd, *The student voice handbook: Bridging the academic/practitioner divide.* Bingley: Emerald Group.

Tolman, J. (2003). If Not Us, Then Who? Young People on the Frontlines of Educational Equity. Unpublished paper.

Tomlinson, C. A., & McTighe, J. (2006). *Integrating Differentiated Instruction & Understanding By Design: Connecting Content And Kids.* Alexandria, VA: Association for Supervision and Curriculum Development.

Toshalis, E., & Nakkula, M. (2012). *Motivation, engagement, and student voice.* Students Center.

Towler, D. L. (1975). *Student Representatives Serving with Boards of Education.* American Association of School Administrators.

Turley, S. (1994). "The Way Teachers Teach Is, Like, Totally Whacked": The Student Voice on Classroom Practice. *ERIC* .

Tyler, K., & Boelter, C. (2008). Linking Black middle school students' perceptions of teachers' expectations to academic engagement and efficacy. *The Negro Education Review* , 59 (1-2).

Ungerleider, J., & DiBenedetto, A. (1997). Empowering Students to Address Current Issues: The Vermont Governor's institute on public issues and youth empowerment. In J. A. Boccia (Ed.), *Students Taking the Lead: The challenges and rewards of empowering youth in schools* (pp. 59-78). San Francisco: Jossey-Bass Inc.

Usher, A., & Kober, N. (2012). *Student Motivation: An Overlooked Piece of School Reform.* Center on Education Policy.

Vavrus, J., & Fletcher, A. (2006). *Guide to Social Change Led By and With Young People.* Retrieved October 3, 2014, from The Freechild Project at commonaction.org/SocialChangeGuide.pdf

Verchick, R. R. (1991). *Engaging the Spectrum: Civic Virtue and the Protection of Student Voice in School Sponsored Forums.* Retrieved November 1, 2014, from J. Marshall L. Rev. 339 : repository.jmls.edu/cgi/viewcontent.cgi?article=1883&context=lawreview

Walker, L., & Logan, A. (2008). *Learner Engagement: A review of learner voice initiatives across the UK's education sectors.* Bristol, UK: Futurelab.

Wankel, L. A., & Blessinger, P. (2013). *Increasing Student Engagement and Retention Using Mobile Applications: Smartphones, Skype and Texting Technologies.* Emerald Group Publishing.

Weiss, J. & Huget, L. (2015) *Not Your High School Cafeteria: A Subversive Guide to Youth-Led Programming.* Ann Arbor, MI: Red Beard Press.

Westheimer, J., & Kahne, J. (1998). "Education for action: preparing youth for participatory democracy," in W. Ayers, & e. al, *Teaching for Social Justice.* New York City: New Press.

What Kids Can Do. (2003, June). "Students push for equity in school funding," Retrieved November 1, 2014 at whatkidscando.org/archives/images/general/schoolfundingFS.pdf

What Kids Can Do. (2003). *The Schools We Need: Creating Small High Schools That Work For Us.* Providence, RI.

Williams, Z. (2012, February 11). *The Saturday Interview: Stuart Hall.* Retrieved July 1, 2013, from *The Guardian* at guardian.co.uk/theguardian/2012/feb/11/saturday-interview-stuart-hall

Willison, S. (1997). "The Human Relations Club: Student leaders addressing issues of multicultural education and social action," in J. A. Boccia (Ed.), *Students Taking the Lead: The challenges and rewards of empowering youth in schools* (Vol. 4, pp. 9-24). San Francisco: Jossey-Bass Inc.

Wilson, B., & Corbett, D. (2001). Listening to Urban Kids: School Reform and the Teachers They Want. SUNY Press.

Wilson, B., & Corbett, D. (2007). "Students' perspectives on good teaching: Implications for adult reform behavior," In A. C.-S. Thiessen, *International Handbook Of Student Experience In Elementary And Secondary School* (pp. 283-311). Springer Netherlands.

Wood, G. (2005) *Time to Learn: How to Create High Schools that Serve all Students.* Portsmouth, NH: Heinemann.

Wright, D. C. (2003). "Black Pride Day, 1968: High school student activism in York, Pennsylvania," *The Journal of African American History* , 151-162.

Wright, S. (2013). "Start with Why: The power of student-driven learning,"*Powerful Learning Practice Network.* Retrieved November 1, 2014, at plpnetwork.com/2013/06/21/start-why-power-student-driven-learning/

Yair, G. (2000). "Reforming motivation: How the structure of instruction affects students' learning experiences," *British Educational Journal* , 26 (2), 191-120.

Yang, H. L. (2010). *Middle School Student Involvement in China. Thesis paper.* Montreal: McGill University Department of Integrated Studies in Education.

Youth On Board. (n.d.). "Student Engagement Advisory Council," Retrieved November 2, 2014, from youthonboard.org/student-engagement-advisory-council-seac

Zlotkowski, E. (2002). *Service-Learning and the First-Year Experience: Preparing Students for Personal Success and Civic Responsibility.* University of South Carolina. National Resource Center for The First-Year Experience and Students in Transition.

Index

Resources

SoundOut.org

Our online resource center promoting Meaningful Student Involvement. Exciting examples, powerful research studies, effective classroom tools, and dozens of other resources from around the world are featured.

The Guide to Student Voice

Packed with the information students, educators, advocates, and others need to promote student engagement in schools. Featuring a professional, easy-to-read layout, this short book is packed with useful tips, powerful activities, and great guidance for anyone interested in student voice today.

SoundOut Student Voice Curriculum

A collection of twenty-seven session plans, a facilitator's guide, a student handbook and an evaluation guide designed to teach high school students about how they can become partners in changing schools. Units include students as planners, teachers, evaluators, decision-makers and advocates for education.

School Boards of the Future: Engaging Students as Education Policy-Makers

A manual for student involvement on district and state boards of education, including student representatives and students as full-voting members. It highlights examples, tips, promotional information and resources, as well as steps to implement student involvement. It also provides state-by-state profiles across the United States.

For ordering information, bulk discounts, or to book an appearance by author Adam Fletcher, contact:

SoundOut

PO Box 6185, Olympia, WA 98507-6185
soundout.org
(360) 489-9680

Made in the USA
Monee, IL
10 January 2023

24958804R00224